Blackwell Bible Commentaries

Series Editors: John Sawyer, Christopher Rowland, Judith Kovacs

John
Mark Edwards

Revelation
Judith Kovacs & Christopher Rowland

Judges
David M. Gunn

Forthcoming:

Genesis
Gary Philips & Danna Nolan Fewell

Exodus
Scott Langston

Leviticus
Mark Elliott

1 & 2 Samuel
David M. Gunn

1 & 2 Kings
Martin O'Kane

Esther
Jo Carruthers

Job
Anthony York

Psalms
Susan Gillingham

Ecclesiastes
Eric Christianson

Isaiah
John F. A. Sawyer

Jeremiah
Mary Chilton Callaway

Lamentations
Paul Joyce

Jonah
Yvonne Sherwood

Mark
Christine Joynes

Luke
Larry Kreitzer

Romans
Paul Fiddes

Galatians
John Riches

Pastoral Epistles
Jay Turomey

1 Corinthians
Jorunn Okland

2 Corinthians
Paula Gooder

Judges

David M. Gunn

Blackwell
Publishing

© 2005 by David M. Gunn

BLACKWELL PUBLISHING
350 Main Street, Malden, MA 02148-5020, USA
108 Cowley Road, Oxford OX4 1JF, UK
550 Swanston Street, Carlton, Victoria 3053, Australia

The right of David M. Gunn to be identified as the Author of this Work has been
asserted in accordance with the UK Copyright, Designs, and Patents Act 1988.

First published 2005 by Blackwell Publishing Ltd

Library of Congress Cataloging-in-Publication Data

Gunn, D. M. (David M.)
  Judges / David M. Gunn.
    p. cm. – (Blackwell Bible commentaries)
  Includes bibliographical references and index.
  ISBN 0-631-22251-0 (hardcover : alk. paper) – ISBN 0-631-22252-9 (pbk. : alk.
paper)   1. Bible. O.T. Judges–Commentaries.   I. Title.   II. Series.
BS1305.53.G86 2005
222′.32077–dc22

                                                              2004018332

A catalogue record for this title is available from the British Library.

Set in 10 on 12½ pt Minion
by SNP Best-set Typesetter Ltd, Hong Kong
Printed and bound in the United Kingdom
by TJ International, Padstow, Cornwall

The publisher's policy is to use permanent paper from mills that operate a
sustainable forestry policy, and which has been manufactured from pulp processed
using acid-free and elementary chlorine-free practices. Furthermore, the publisher
ensures that the text paper and cover board used have met acceptable environmental
accreditation standards.

For further information on
Blackwell Publishing, visit our website:
www.blackwellpublishing.com

Contents

The Blackwell Bible Commentaries series, the first to be devoted primarily to the reception history of the Bible, is based on the premise that how people have interpreted, and been influenced by, a sacred text like the Bible is often as interesting and historically important as what it originally meant. The series emphasizes the influence of the Bible on literature, art, music, and film, its role in the evolution of religious beliefs and practices, and its impact on social and political developments. Drawing on work in a variety of disciplines, it is designed to provide a convenient and scholarly means of access to material until now hard to find, and a much-needed resource for all those interested in the influence of the Bible on Western culture.

Until quite recently this whole dimension was for the most part neglected by biblical scholars. The goal of a commentary was primarily, if not exclusively, to get behind the centuries of accumulated Christian and Jewish tradition to one single meaning, normally identified with the author's original intention. The most important and distinctive feature of the Blackwell Commentaries is that they will present readers with many different interpretations of each text, in such a way as to heighten their awareness of what a text, especially a sacred text, can mean and what it can do, what it has meant and what it has done, in the many contexts in which it operates.

The Blackwell Bible Commentaries will consider patristic, rabbinic (where relevant), and medieval exegesis, as well as insights from various types of modern criticism, acquainting readers with a wide variety of interpretative techniques. As part of the history of interpretation, questions of source, date, authorship and other historical-critical and archaeological issues will be discussed; but since these are covered extensively in existing commentaries, such references will be brief, serving to point readers in the direction of readily accessible literature where they can be followed up.

Original to this series is the consideration of the reception history of specific biblical books, arranged in commentary format. The chapter-by-chapter arrangement ensures that the biblical text is always central to the discussion. Given the wide influence of the Bible and the richly varied appropriation of each biblical book, it is a difficult question which interpretations to include. While each volume will have its own distinctive point of view, the guiding principle for the series as a whole is that readers should be given a representative sampling of material from different ages, with emphasis on interpretations that have been especially influential or historically significant. Though authors will have their preferences among the different interpretations, the material will be presented in such a way that readers can make up their own minds on the value, morality, and validity of particular interpretations.

The series encourages readers to consider how the biblical text has been interpreted down the ages, and seeks to open their eyes to different uses of the Bible in contemporary culture. The aim is a series of scholarly commentaries that draw on all the insights of modern research to illustrate the rich interpretative potential of each biblical book.

John Sawyer
Christopher Rowland
Judith Kovacs

Preface

I wrote this book because John Sawyer asked me to write on Samuel (my old stomping ground), and I said, "What about Judges?" And he said, "You're welcome," but probably in a more "English" idiom. I met John first when he was a lecturer at the University of Newcastle-upon-Tyne and I, fresh from New Zealand and Australia, was a doctoral student whom he made to feel at home. He was, I learned in due course, a scholar out of step – struck by the rich resources of traditional Jewish interpretation and the work of "pre-critical" Christian scholars alike, and concerned more with the text's "final form" than hypotheses of how it might have arrived there. At the biannual meetings of that bastion of British middle-of-the-road scholarship, The Society for Old Testament Study, I came to await with keen anticipation at a paper's end a "Sawyer" question, and to enjoy the rhetorical deflections or plain incomprehension it would meet. And now, all these years later, it would seem he has stolen the march. So my first word of thanks is to John, and to fellow editors Judith Kovacs and Christopher Rowland, for devising this project and asking me to share in it. To Rebecca Harkin, senior commissioning editor in religious studies at Blackwell Publishing, I also owe thanks for her sterling support of the larger project and this particular book. All have been mercifully patient as it has edged its way to completion.

My friend Timothy Beal, of Case Western Reserve University in Cleveland, Ohio, helped me get launched, in the late 1980s, when we wrote together an entry on Judges for John Hayes' prodigious *Dictionary of Biblical Interpretation* (Abingdon, 1999), which took a little time to appear and so reliably gave me an "in press" item for my annual report each year. Tim and I planned to write this new book together, but in the event, to my regret and the reader's loss, that hope eluded us. Nonetheless, with a keen eye for economy, he contributed initial drafts of much of the ancient and medieval material, a major task, and for this I am deeply grateful. Needless to say, he is not responsible for its "final form" – that responsibility is mine alone.

Another friend and TCU colleague, Claudia Camp, rescued me from deep despond at several critical moments (with deadlines looming) by exercising into the wee small hours her considerable editorial powers and helping shape some of the masses of material I had written up. To my own credit I did not complain about a single cut. She assures me to this day that not *that* much valuable stuff was lost. She also drafted some of the synopses, and has lent her acumen to thinking through with me issues of the book's conception and organization. I thank her for both this eminently practical help, and the many long hours it cost her, and her readiness to go on hearing Judges' anecdotes when someone else might have cried, "Hold, Enough!"

In the end, however, the book simply would not have been written without the hard spadework, the wide knowledge, and the critical judgment of my research associate, Edward McMahon. He has applied his long experience to ferreting out primary material, storing extracts, checking sources, comparing editions, and I think has even come to enjoy scouring the internet. He has drafted and redrafted the bibliographies and biography, and read and reread the whole manuscript with an eye to its betterment. He, too, has joined long discussions on the commentary's design and contributed valuable insights. In short, Ed has invested so much in this book that I can hardly thank him sufficiently. Like me, I suspect he will not quite know himself when it is truly finished.

This, then, is a book that has required a team for its making, and I have been fortunate in the collaboration I have had. Many have helped, more than I can name here, including Beverly Allen, Katie Blasingame, Adam Frieberg, Amanda Link, Bernie Scheffler, Judy Siegel – who variously extracted and input sources, photocopied, scanned pictures, logged in books and prints, tracked the budget, and kept the library happy – and Diane Klein, who did most of those things, too, and whose prowess in designing and maintaining our main database proved of crucial importance. In other acts of kindness, Marvin Hayes provided scans of his etchings, Edwina Sandys pictures of her sculptures, Marion Clark a photo of her g-g-g-grandmother, from Australia, and Michael Dugdale, from England, images of Grace Aguilar. Babette Bohn, art historian colleague at TCU, helped me greatly on some art matters, and the book would not look like it does without the friendly and professional services of Cees and Wilma Meijer-Groeneveld in the Netherlands (www.iscra.nl), and Thomas Hersch in Vermont (www.antiquarianbiblical.com) whose personal interest in the project I have much appreciated. I have benefited from the constant support of my family along the way, especially Margaret, who has borne my making of books many years; also the warm collegiality of the Department of Religion at TCU, and the backing in time and money TCU generously affords me. Alex Wright at Blackwell had the vision to embrace the series and was kind enough to want me in it. And my thanks go to the many others at Blackwell who have helped at different stages, including Laura Barry, Alison Dunnett, Lisa Eaton, Lucy Judkins, Kelvin Matthews, Sophie Gibson, Cameron Laux, and Karen Wilson – and the eagle eye of copy editor, Jean van Altena. I am indebted to all.

David Miller Gunn
September 7th, 2004

To my little sister,
Mary

"And what more shall I say?" we read in Hebrews 11 : 32, a text that has shaped Christian interpretation of Judges for centuries. "For time would fail me to tell of Gideon, Barak, Samson, Jephthah . . ." Time would also fail me to tell of Judges' reception over two millennia – for much remains unsaid despite these many pages. This commentary takes account, where possible, of popular or lay reception as well as professional or clerical, yet, though venturing widely through time and space, it is narrowly conceived. It offers a Western, post-Enlightenment perspective, and as available sources expand from the Renaissance on, it focuses increasingly on the English-speaking world. This preference is marked from the nineteenth century on, when the Industrial Revolution proliferated "popular" biblical materials, and many authors, women as well as men, entered the edification market. A narrowed scope has proved more manageable for me, and I trust may prove so for my reader. But the limitation should be borne in mind. Here is no comprehensive account of European reception, though often what transpires in England and North America since the seventeenth century has its counterpart elsewhere in Europe. Nor do I track Judges in other regions, including the colonies upon which the Bible-bearing missionaries eagerly descended. That is for another person at another time. It will be apparent, too, that the sources are predominantly Christian, though I have tried to convey main lines of Jewish interpretation in classical rabbinic writings, and at times draw on more recent Jewish sources. So I reiterate, this volume's scope is both broad and narrow.

Technology has profoundly influenced the Bible's reception. So has literacy, itself a technology. The revolutionary ancient book form called the "codex," folded sheets of papyrus or parchment sewn together on one edge, probably came into popular use when Christians in second-century Antioch found it efficient for handling Scripture and other Christian writing (Robert and Skeat, *Birth of the Codex*, 1983). Indeed, the codex may have helped to form the Christian canon, the Bible viewed as one book, to strengthen the Latin version's hold on the West in Late Antiquity, and to proliferate Christian literature generally. This book form was economical, with writing on both sides of the leaf. It also made referring to different sections easy (important for Scripture) and facilitated storing and carrying. Its flat pages made pictorial illustration practical and eventually common. Scrolls continued in secular use, but by the fourth century's end the codex was dominant. In contrast, Jewish writings of Late Antiquity, including the Mishnah and Tosefta, Palestinian and Babylonian Talmuds, and Midrashim, remained in roll form alone until about the tenth century.

Printing, which propelled the Protestant Reformation and vernacular Bibles, changed both people's access to the Bible and how they read it. Most earlier extant sources are professional, from rabbinic scholars or Church Fathers, written often for other professionals. In Christian Europe, the Bible was in Latin, read by clerics and a literate elite. In the early fifteenth century perhaps 10 percent of men in England could read, and one woman in a hundred. The arcane codes of allegory and typology – whereby an Old Testament text (about Gideon or Samson) pointed to the New (Jesus or the Church) – depended upon schooled clerics transmitting meanings less than obvious to the uninitiated. In the hands of laypeople, however, the vernacular narratives of Judges read at face value, as tales of ancient events and figures, not unlike the stories of Greece and Rome also being rediscovered. As literacy increased (along with print materials), the literal-historical way of reading offered independence from religious professionals, which suited the Protestant Reformers well – as long as laypeople became not *too* independent and recognized the need for the right *kind* of professionals (Protestant, not Catholic). When Anabaptists in mid-sixteenth-century Münster began practising polygamy in literal imitation of the patriarchs, other Protestant preachers were not slow to decide things were out of hand, and not slow either to invoke traditional typology to deal with awkward texts (see, below, David Joris on Samson's marriage to the Timnite woman).

Though neither Reformer, Martin Luther or John Calvin, wrote a commentary on Judges, the book was a court of appeal for many in the sixteenth century, on topics from celibacy and divorce to the citizen's duty to uphold the lawful magistrate. Especially after typeface technology improved in the 1620s, many political tracts and sermons were printed, particularly by the Puritans, who found in Judges issues of polity and religion pertinent to the torn fabric of their own society, civil war, and regicide. So we know what many laypeople learned about Judges, if not always what they thought about what they were reading or hearing. The same is true of the sermons of the American Revolution, where the Benjamite war is scriptural support for both sides, or the importunings of Jonathan Edwards, urging the enthusiastic and the recalcitrant towards religious revival.

The innovations of the Industrial Revolution from the late eighteenth century on likewise brought changes. One reason why landscapes and artifacts of Palestine grew popular as book illustrations, along with explanations of biblical texts based on "oriental" customs, was that the steamship made travel to the "land of the Bible" cheaper and safer. As travel increased, so did the sketches, journals, and travel books which found their way into standard biblical literature, itself reaching more and more people, across old class and income barriers, because of new technologies and economies of scale. So, too, the Industrial Revolution paved the way for museums exhibiting the ancient worlds of Assyria and Babylon, shipped west, or great exhibitions "recreating" the Holy Land in America for crowds of Bible believers (see Long, *Imagining the Holy Land*, 2003).

The evidence of the monuments and the land where time stood still (today's customs were assumed to be those of yesteryear) lent historical credibility to the Bible, now coming under critical scrutiny. Combined with Romantic ideas of landscape expressing a nation's "soul" and an enthusiasm for "science," the products of Holy Land travelers and exhibitors deeply impressed Bible readers. The Rev. Samuel Manning journeyed in 1873 "to compare the Land and the Book," and, by examining Palestine's topography, to illustrate the veracity of Scripture's histories. He found "minute agreement," such as no later legend could have fabricated (*Those Holy Fields*, 1890, 5). As another wrote, recommending his own "compact Cyclopaedia of Oriental Intelligence," with correct knowledge of Holy Land facts – "and of late a remarkable progress has been made" – biblical events become "a perfect panorama before the mind's eye." Places, produce, the husbandman laboring, caravans moving, Arab banditti attacking, the very rocks and caves, fields and gardens, rivers and mountain tops – all explain Holy Writ. Without such facts, in Adam Clarke's words, "ninety-nine out of every hundred" professing to teach must remain ignorant of the Book "which alone contains the science of salvation" (Preface to *The Teacher's Pictorial Bible*, c.1875). The age of production made sure the Orient came to the West. (See PLATE 0.1, illustrations from Kitto's *Pictorial Sunday-Book*, 1845, and *Pictorial Bible*, c.1850.)

Technological changes in the twentieth century continued to expand the consumption of cheap illustrated books on the Bible and introduced a new-comer, the Bible movie (e.g. DeMille's *Samson and Delilah*, 1949). Professional commentary on Judges did not languish either; rather, such publications multiplied as advanced education expanded, especially in the later part of the century. Now electronic publishing, particularly the proliferation of materials on the web, is already transforming the scene of biblical reception, professional and popular.

Print changed people's access to the Bible's words. It also promoted a visual Bible. While a few wealthy patrons enjoyed the art of the masters, many more people, particularly among the gentry and growing middle class, found plea-sure and education in the pictures they found in printed Bibles and biblical histories. Medieval manuscript Bibles usually illustrated at most only the initial letter of a book like Judges. But in late-fifteenth-century Cologne and Nurem-berg woodcut scenes appeared adjacent to the relevant passages, influencing the choice and design of such Bible pictures for over a century. Quickly Venetian publishers followed suit, and soon Lyons in France. Sixteenth-century Luther Bibles were finely illustrated, and by the century's end some Bibles in England contained such scenes. A high point of Bible illustration (including Bible histories and Josephus's *Jewish Antiquities*) was the late seventeenth and early eighteenth centuries in the Netherlands, where superb designs by artists (such as Jan and Caspar Luyken, Gerard Hoet, and Bernard Picart) and high-quality engraving produced inimitable pictures imitated (nonetheless) well into the next century.

In Britain during the eighteenth century pictures were often in large, anno-tated "Family Bibles," which became more affordable in the nineteenth century, supported by an expanding North American market (see Gutjahr, *An American Bible*, 1999). The United States began to set the pace. In 1846, Harper's lavish *Illuminated Bible* set a new standard, with hundreds of full scenes and countless vignettes. Stereotyping, by which original composed pages were transferred to a set of single plates, improved print runs and cut prices throughout the century, and electrotyping, used to produce Harper's Bible, enhanced the quality of such runs. Other types of illustrated books appeared, particularly those designed "for the improvement of youth," among them small thick volumes of Scripture history full of pictures, again often sold in both Britain and North America. By mid-century, Holy Land landscapes (e.g. Mount Tabor, on Judges 4–5) challenged story scenes for

PLATE 0.1   *Left:* Kitto's Oriental illustrations: (a) Gaza (Judg 16); (b) Jackals ("foxes") (Judg 15); (c) Egyptian pitchers (Judg 7); (d) Scribe counting hands (cut off) (Judg 1); (e) Women grinding in a mill (Judg 16). *Right:* Bible reading and pictures: (f) Reading the Bible to grandpa; (g) Scripture history on tiles; (h) Scripture narratives; (i) A sunny sabbath; (j) Bible pictures. (See pp. 4, 6)

space, and by the century's close these were often grainy photographs. Yet narrative illustrations persisted, including two major series (by Doré and Schnorr von Carolsfeld), reproduced throughout Europe and North America. Twentieth-century Bibles less often have pictures, and ancillary literature on the Bible usually shows contemporary scenes, archaeological sites, or ancient artifacts where a century earlier an imaginative rendition of a story or character would have appeared.

The merits of biblical depictions have long been discussed, with not everyone an unqualified enthusiast. As a Wiltshire antiquarian later wrote of Cromwell's Puritan soldiers, on the subject of church windows and interiors, they had "a great fancy for smashing everything which in their diseased and heated imaginations they conceived to bear what was called 'the mark of the beast,' that is, to savour of Rome. Like the iconoclasts of the continent they had a mad hatred of anything approaching an image" (Jefferies, *History of Swindon*, 1896, 36). William Dowsing's own record of his officially commissioned destructions in East Anglia in 1643–4 is less heated than chilling. "Westley, March 22. We brake down eight superstitious pictures . . . Dullingham, March 22. We brake down thirty superstitious pictures . . . Stetchworth. We brake divers superstitious pictures . . . Cove, April 8. We took down forty-two superstitious pictures in glass . . . Southwold, April 8. We brake down one hundred and thirty superstitious pictures" (Cressy and Ferrel (eds), *Religion and Society in Early Modern England*, 1996, 183–6).

Yet pictures have usually won in the end (see PLATE 0.1). Miss E. J. Whately, in *The Sunday at Home* (1878), affirms that "one of the great improvements of the age is the wide-spread circulation of cheap and good pictures," especially a help in Bible-teaching "among the young and ignorant." Art, like music, is a handmaid to Scripture teaching, a good picture being "far more likely to impress a looker-on than any description in words could do." Still, she warns of abuse. We all know where music can lead (the dance hall?), and pictorial commentary, which may lead to misapprehension, risks worse mischief. The fault lies in artists ignorant of Scripture, working from hearsay or borrowing from "incorrect" pictures, and in admirers more taken with beauty than truth. The fault-line, she finds, lies between Catholics and "Bible-reading" Protestants alert to such mistakes. But she criticizes all the old masters for their details, showing "ignorance of Oriental customs and dress," even if these mistakes "are generally more ludicrous than mischievous."

We may today be less sure that ancient Israelites dressed and behaved just like nineteenth-century "Orientals" and be more tolerant of earlier conventions of portraying the biblical past in "modern dress" or some variation on contemporary and classical (ancient Greece and Rome) as in the seventeenth and eighteenth centuries. But Whately does usefully point, with whatever prejudice, to an unease about images that is long-lived in Protestantism. As for Judges, she cites no examples from it among the mischief, but readers of this present book are surely warned to be on their guard.

A striking feature of late-eighteenth- and nineteenth-century books on the Bible is the appearance of women as authors. Some wrote to educate young people, like Anglican Mrs (Sarah) Trimmer in her six-volume *Sacred History* (1782–6), or Baptist Esther Hewlett in her two-volume *Scripture History for Youth* (1828). Such books provide an idea of what young people were hearing and reading (see Bottigheimer, *Bible for Children*, 1996, 38–57). Their ongoing popularity reflects rapidly rising rates of schooling and literacy. In the early 1800s about half the children in England attended school for some period; by mid-century that number was much higher, with two years' attendance on average; by the century's end virtually all attended until age 12.

Rising literacy rates also crossed class barriers. Estimated literacy in England about 1650 was above 30 percent for men and 10 percent for women (Cressy, *Literacy and the Social Order*, 1980). But a major divide existed between main towns with an educated merchant class and rural areas, and also between classes, ranging from a literate gentry to largely illiterate servants and laborers; in the middle, a majority of yeomen farmers (with rights to their land) and tradespeople could read. Many who were illiterate had access to someone who could read to them, and ministers, increasingly better educated, were a vital link in the communication chain. By 1750 literacy rates had probably doubled, and many more women, especially, were learning to read and write. In America by 1795 male literacy in the north was possibly as high as 90 percent, rather lower in the south. In England, by about 1850 some two-thirds of men and perhaps half of women could at least sign their names on a marriage register (one evidence of literacy), and by 1900 nearly all could do so (R. Williams, "The Press and Popular Culture," 1978). It is no surprise, then, that Esther Hewlett's household management manual, *Cottage Comforts* (1825), directed at working-class adults, went through 24 editions in 40 years. Meanwhile, their children increasingly had access to cheap editions of Bible stories, helped by Bible societies and Sunday Schools (Bottigheimer, 56).

Both Jewish and Christian women authors found edification in biblical stories about women. Anglo-Jewish poet and novelist Grace Aguilar wrote on Jewish religion and history for American as well as English readers, though it was her romantic novels that brought her posthumous recognition. She sharply defended her Jewish heritage against Christian prejudice and presumption, as in the Introduction to *The Women of Israel* (1845), written to "infuse the spirit of truth and patriotism, of nationality, and yet of universal love, in the hearts of the young daughters of Israel" (p. 17). Harriet Beecher Stowe, famous for *Uncle*

Tom's Cabin, on the other hand, affectionately dedicated her *Woman in Sacred History* (1873) to "all Christian women who love and reverence the Bible."

Temperance leader Clara Lucas Balfour explains that while the many admirable books of the previous 20 years on "the mental capabilities, moral qualities, and social responsibilities of woman" might seem to render super-fluous her own work, *The Women of Scripture* (1847), this was not so. Too little attention had been paid to "the scriptural estimate of woman and illustrations of her duties." So she sets out to pay sedulous attention to correct historical detail, but especially to highlight "those principles of piety, feminine excellence, moral conduct, and mental power, which the sacred heroines individually exhibited" (Preface, pp. v–vi). Such accounts of women of the Bible became a small industry, along with other popular sources for Sunday reading such as *The Sunday at Home: A Family Magazine for Sabbath Reading* (1878) published in parts by the Religious Tract Society and bound at the year's end, or the illustrated *Sunny Sabbaths, or Pleasant Pages for Happy Homes* (c.1860) which provided biblical instruction for old and young alike.

The Industrial Revolution thus transformed popular culture by making biblical materials abundantly available to laypeople and to women in particu-lar. By the time women's rights leader Elizabeth Cady Stanton penned her tren-chant criticism of Judges in *The Woman's Bible* (1898), the stories of Deborah, Jael, and Jephthah's daughter had been subject to a century of published review by women. Not that women were the only ones interested in biblical women: "eminent divines" (men, of course) were hardly slow to supply their own authoritative view – and fill the market niche.

One inconvenience of a focus on women was that it highlighted the biblical book's violence. A women hammers a tent-peg through a man's head, another drops a fatal millstone, a daughter is sacrificed by her father, a woman burnt to death, another raped, killed, and cut up, many with their children are put to the sword, and other daughters, with their fathers' consent, are subjected to abduction and forced marriage. Not a pleasant list, especially not for teach-ing children, often in the eighteenth and nineteenth centuries the province of women. One of the small joys of writing this commentary has been to watch the strategies deployed in the face of these biblical "facts." Earlier writers tend to tackle the problem head on, allowing that providence in its inscrutable wisdom may sometimes so dispose. Indeed, a death like that of Jephthah's daughter could even be cause for celebration – a view that has its adherents still today. One of the earliest children's books in the British Library, frequently reprinted in Britain and America, is James Janeway's *A Token for children: being an exact account of the conversion, holy and exemplary lives, and joyful deaths of several young children* (1709). "Thirteen model children die in its pages," notes the Library's laconic survey (www.bl.uk). Later authors are inclined to blame

the "primitive" times or, with Mrs Annie R. White, who edited *Young Folks'*
Monthly, to cut the Gordian knot. In *Easy Steps for Little Feet: From Genesis to*
Revelation (1896) she simply skips Judges entirely. At least Bishop Gilmour's
illustrated *Bible History . . . for the Use of Catholic Schools in the United States*
(1869 [1904]) devotes two pages to the book.

Perhaps my favorite is the Rev. T. Rhondda Williams, a minister of progressive views, dutifully tackling Judges with his Sunday School class in
Brighton, England (*Old Testament Stories in Modern Light*, 1911, 66–7). Having
observed that the book is full of people fighting, against Canaanites and among
themselves, he remarks:

> You may imagine, then, that this Book of Judges is not pleasant to read—much
> of it is quite ghastly. You must not go to it for any ideals of life, or to learn any-
> thing about your own duty at the present time, except as you can see that it is
> your duty not to imitate the ways of most of the people of whom you read in it.

Still, he owns it an interesting picture of old times, "and in reading it you can
be thankful that you live in better times." So he relents: "I shall tell you a few
of its stories." These include Jael, Jephthah's daughter, and a passing mention
of the death of Samson's Timnite bride. But there he draws the line.

A few decades later, while Chamberlain bargained with Hitler, Bishop
Bertram F. Simpson, who won the Military Cross amid the Great War's
slaughter, recalls that as a curate he taught Judges to a class of elementary
schoolchildren in central London. Very doubtful that "so bellicose a narrative"
was a wise curriculum choice, he found the children loved it – "not so much
for the battles, though there is a militant streak left in most childhood, but
because of the stories of the great heroes from whom the book takes its name.
Gideon, Jael and Samson have been beloved favourites in the nursery for many
generations" (*The Story of the Bible*, c.1938, I, 281).

The human "heroes" of Judges have long attracted readers. Official
patristic and medieval Christian interpretation, whether written commentary
or spoken homily, tended to bypass the heroes' human qualities in favor of the
spiritual codes their actions generated. Samson carrying off the gates of Gaza
intimated Christ unbarring the gates of Hell. (Forget the prostitute.) Yet it was
hard to avoid depicting brute strength in a picture on a church wall or window,
and a fifteenth-century ceiling boss in Norwich cathedral – not that anyone
could see it – shows a vulnerable man snoozing in a female lap. Bring Delilah
into the picture, and it was hard to avoid talking of human failings and even
tragedy. The bravest man of all, says Ambrose of Milan in the fourth century,
could succumb to the money (she was bribed!) that flowed into the woman's
lap (*Duties of the Clergy*, ii.xxvi). And in the twelfth century Peter Abelard

laments for strong Samson's ruin by a woman (*Planctus Israel super Samson*). Strong, fond, and foolish Samson. By the time Joseph Hall was writing his *Contemplations* on the Bible's "historical passages" in the early seventeenth century, it had become common to ponder not only God's disposing of events, but what in Samson himself led to his death, what kind of woman was Deborah to sustain her high office, why Gideon so needed to be reassured, or Jephthah to make his vow and his daughter to acquiesce. If there was a code to be read, it was usually a moral one, a lesson for living. Beware, for example, lest fond makes foolish.

Hall, like Shakespeare, often uses interior monologue (soliloquy) to explore motives and choices, and in so dramatizing his characters he establishes their subjectivity. Says Samson, thinking on marriage to the Timnite woman, "It is not mine eye only, but the counsel of God that leads me to this choice. The way to quarrel with the Philistines is to match with them." Better yet is Jael's long soliloquy on confronting Sisera: "What if I strike him? And yet, who am I that I should dare to think of such an act?" Or Hall himself narrates the inner process, as when Samson faces his own death: "His renewed faith tells him, that he was destined to plague the Philistines; and reason tells him, that his blindness puts him out of the hope of such another opportunity." By such devices Hall often conveys to his reader choices the commentator confronts. Some decades on, Puritan preacher Thomas Lye (1682) deploys similar rhetoric to press his own choice – his topic is indulgent parents – by pouring scorn on the father of the Levite's wife in Judges 19. The erring woman thinks to flee "to her own dear father's house"; but does he received her? "Methinks I hear him in a just indignation thus accosting her: 'Why, how now, impudence? what makest thou here?'" Which is, of course, just what the father does *not* say.

A century later, Anglican vicar and novelist Laurence Sterne has perfected and complicated the style. He starts with the woman leaving: "—Then shame and grief go with her, and where-ever she seeks a shelter, may the hand of justice shut the door against her.—Not so; for she went unto her father's house in Beth-lehem-Judah, and was with him four whole months.—Blessed interval for meditation upon the fickleness and vanity of this world and its pleasures!" Soon, however, the preacher begs leave to stop "and give the story of the Levite and his Concubine a second hearing: like all others much of it depends upon the telling; and as the Scripture has left us no kind of comment upon it, 'tis a story on which the heart cannot be at a loss for what to say, or the imagination for what to suppose—the danger is, humanity may say too much" (*The Sermons of Mr Yorick*, iii, 1766).

Taking Sterne as his linchpin, Stephen Prickett has argued that the rise of the novel in eighteenth-century England influenced readers to treat biblical narrative with the same attention to the motives and feelings of characters as they would any secular novel, with the proviso that Scripture recounted the ways of human characters and God not as fiction or conjecture but reality (*Origins of Narrative*, 1996, 107–31). His case for an intimate connection is well made, but we see here how much earlier such reading had its roots, at least as far back as Joseph Hall – who, incidentally, was much read in the eighteenth century and well into the next.

The popular interest in biblical characters shows up in books of sermons, like William Enfield's *Biographical Sermons* (1777), or Thomas Robinson's often reprinted and pirated *Scripture Characters* (1790). Robinson originally designed the latter, he tells us, as sermons for a "plain Congregation" (St Mary's, Leicester) – and "presumes not to solicit the attention of critical readers, who are pleased with novelty of sentiment, literary remarks, or the embellishments of style and language." For such persons he does not write, but "for the serious inquirer after sacred truth." He finds many advantages in the study of sacred biography. It better demonstrates God's moral government and represents human nature in practice than does doctrinal speculation. It shows the benefits enjoyed by God's true servants and promotes self-knowledge. "By looking at the excellencies of others, we are convinced of our own duty, and our sad declensions from it, much more forcibly than by the mere reading of precepts and directions." And (in the spirit of Sterne), while we are called upon "to censure 'hypocrites and deceivers,' we are at the same time constrained to tremble for ourselves, to examine what resemblance we bear to them, and to beware of those temptations, by which they were seduced" (Preface).

It must be added that either Robinson found no excellencies in the characters of Judges or he judged the book not one of the Bible's "Principle Histories," for he skips it altogether – a not uncommon strategy among Scripture instructors. Others, however, plunged in. The author of *Sacred Biography* (1818) includes Deborah, Gideon, Jephthah, and Samson. He echoes Robinson's views of the task at hand, with an additional nod to the Enlightenment: "Biography is of all others the most useful and important branch of human knowledge; and 'the proper study of mankind is man.' . . . The lives of others are but the history of our own. In them we see what we ourselves are." Yet sacred biography has an even higher claim, since God alone truly knows human capabilities.

Scripture biographies proliferated in the 1800s, becoming one of the most common genres of biblical commentary. It could not be celebrated better than by the inimitable purveyor of nineteenth-century "self-help," Samuel Smiles. "The great lesson of Biography is to show what man can be and do at his best." Yet, as we might suspect, this is not all. "At the head of all biographies stands the Great biography, the Book of Books. And what is the Bible but a series of biographies, of great heroes and patriarchs, prophets, kings, and judges, culminating in the greatest biography of all, the Life embodied in the New Testament?" (*Character*, 1871). So once again we get from Judges to Christ, but not this time via typology.

The enthusiasm for character as the key to religion did not extend to everyone. The Rev. Isaac Williams, troubled by Jael, cautioned that "one cannot draw out Scriptural characters with that marked individuality and strong relief, which arrests the interest in secular history or fiction." And so "in most cases it is the lesson, not the character, that we can give" (Preface to *Female Characters of Holy Scripture: In a Series of Sermons*, 1860). Harriet Beecher Stowe sharply disagreed:

> We have been so long in the habit of hearing the Bible read in solemn, measured tones, in the hush of churches, that we are apt to forget that these men and women were really flesh and blood, of the same human nature with ourselves. . . . In this respect, the modern fashion of treating the personages of sacred story with the same freedom of inquiry as the characters of any other history has its advantages. It takes them out of a false, unnatural light, where they lose all hold on our sympathies, and brings them before us as real human beings. Read in this way, the ancient sacred history is the purest naturalism, under the benevolent guidance of the watchful Father of Nations. (*Woman in Sacred History*, 1873, Introduction)

Stowe was trying to deal with an issue that kept intruding into sacred biography: namely, what to do with apparently deficient characters, of which Judges has arguably more than its fair share. The difficulty is compounded by Hebrews 11, listing Gideon, Barak, Jephthah, and Samson as exemplars of faith. The tendency of the genre, as Smiles's remarks illustrate, is to seek out "excellencies," treating characters as models for emulation. We see this again clearly in the twentieth century, in a volume on "Using and Teaching the Bible" in *The Master Library* (1923, IX, 214), sold widely in the United States as a Christian educational resource. Beyond all other beauty which the Book of Books reveals is that of character: "Here, in spite of all the limitations of the age in which they lived, are shown the most splendid characters in history," showing perfection of spirit, courage, and high purposefulness – "brilliant and outstanding men." No one from Judges is listed, and obviously not Deborah!

The popularity of Scripture biography is obviously related to the rise of fiction and of historical studies, forming a kind of scriptural halfway house. It was the Bible communicated like fiction but not fictitious, and like history but not skeptical. The religious literature of the eighteenth and nineteenth century is full of defenses against the "critics," who seemed to be making headway. The famous French philosopher Voltaire, among other Deists, radically attacked books like Judges for their cruelty, immorality, and distorted view of God. Other scholars, particularly in Germany, labored to discern the original authors, redactors, and components of biblical books, and challenged received wisdom. But this *Wissenschaft*, or "science," which by the mid-nineteenth century had become standard fare in German universities and scholarly commentaries, took until late in the century to establish itself in English, as what is now known as "historical criticism." Though dominant among British and American scholars throughout the twentieth century, and despite seeping into educational literature for "mainstream" Protestants and, later, Catholics, it had little effect on many lay readers. In Britain these were a dwindling number, anyway. In the United States, however, the century saw a well-entrenched majority of conservative, evangelical readers adhering largely to the reading conventions and "pre-critical" commentators of the eighteenth and nineteenth centuries. This remains true of the United States today.

Distinctive late in the twentieth century is the consideration given to the women of Judges by feminist critics, some of it reaching a wide audience. In part as a response to this re-engagement at least one scholar-preacher, Joseph Jeter Jr., has now ventured a whole book on Judges, offering full sermons and an imaginative wealth of resources for preaching today on "some of the most horrible literature ever written" (*Preaching Judges*, 2003). Also striking among scholars is a renewed appreciation and analysis of the book's narrative art and irony. Still, Ehud, Abimelech, and Micah have languished. Gideon has received even less attention, the Levite's wife much more. Deborah still has her admirers. Jael, Jephthah's daughter, and Delilah continue to fascinate, and Samson to puzzle.

The present volume samples scholarly discussion of the past century and draws upon popular writing influenced by historical criticism. It makes no attempt to cover the full range of popular literature on Judges.

The commentary is constructed around the biblical book's main constituent stories and characters. The first chapter deals with the entry into the land and includes the cameo stories of Adoni-bezek who lost thumbs and big toes, Achsah who asked for water, and Othniel the first "judge" (Judg 1:1–3:11); the second chapter is on Ehud's assassination of Ehud (Judg 3:12–31); the third chapter covers Deborah and Barak defeating Sisera, and Jael putting a spike through his head (Judges 4–5); the fourth chapter discusses Gideon testing God and defeating the Ammonites (Judges 6–8), and the next its sequel, Abimelech's abortive kingship (Judges 9); the sixth chapter examines Jephthah, his vow, and his daughter's sacrifice (Judges 10–12); the seventh chapter deals with Samson the Nazirite, from annunciation to self-immolation, and, of course, his Timnite bride, the prostitute of Gaza, and Delilah (Judges 13–16); the eighth chapter treats Micah, his Levite, and the rampaging Danites (Judges 17–18); and the ninth chapter closes with a story of rape writ large, the Levite's woman and the Benjamite war (Judges 19–21).

Each chapter begins with an abstract of the story (the "argument," as older commentaries called it) and a summary of the discussion. (Names are given as commonly found in English, usually Protestant, sources, with Catholic alternatives where these differ.) A reader desiring a brief overview of responses to Judges over the centuries is invited to read through these summaries. Two main sections follow: "Ancient and Medieval" and "Early Modern and Modern." The former runs from Josephus and Pseudo-Philo, includes the classical texts of rabbinic Judaism, the Christian Fathers of Late Antiquity, and sources from the Middle Ages. It concludes with the fifteenth century and the onset of printing. The latter starts with the Renaissance and the Protestant Reformation, and continues through the Enlightenment up to the present day. Given its extent, this section is often broken up into topics, often main characters – for example, in the third chapter, "Deborah," "Barak, Sisera, and Sisera's mother," "Jael" – or main talking points – in the seventh chapter, "Typology," "Edifying history," "Foxes and fire," "Captivity and death," among others. By and large each section or subsection proceeds chronologically from earlier to later sources, and often the chapter ends with a "Recent reception" subsection focusing mainly on scholarly reception over the past century. This last review will seem cursory (to say the least), given conventional commentaries, but it does attempt to give the reader interested in the state of Judges scholarship today some guidelines.

The illustrations offer a small sample of the visual art of Judges, with preference given to works originally designed for reproduction, such as print suites or Bible illustrations, and to published engravings of paintings rather than photographs of the original, since these are what most people saw before the late nineteenth century. Because of limitations of space, most of the plates are composites of pictures, many of them cropped or providing detail only and much reduced, so providing only a flavor of the real thing. The folio engravings of Gerard Hoet and Caspar Luyken, for example, are magnificent, far beyond what can be conveyed here.

The Bibliography at the end of the book is subdivided into Ancient and Medieval, Early Modern and Modern, and Graphical sources. It is followed by a complete list of illustrations. Also included in the end matter are a short glossary of terms, events, and interpretive methods perhaps unfamiliar to some readers, and a set of brief biographies (where information was available). An index of names includes both primary and secondary-source authors, and an index of main subjects concludes the book.

A few idiosyncrasies need to be mentioned. First concerns the reference system. In the main text, the date supplied for a source is the original (as best could be determined). Details in square brackets are those of the edition used, when it is reasonably certain that its content does not differ significantly from the original. In the bibliography, however, a date in square brackets is the original, and the principal date is that of the edition used. Second concerns the reference materials. There are many secondary sources discussing topics covered here. That they are not mentioned does not mean that they are unavailable. But I have chosen to focus on primary sources, and the bibliography reflects this choice. Third, where possible, life-spans are supplied when (deceased) authors and artists are first mentioned, as well as dates of their works. Likewise a few words describing the person are offered. In larger chapters, where a reader may be consulting only one section, this information is sometimes repeated. The result may appear (and be) inconsistent as well as redundant to some readers, but it is intended to be helpful to others.

The story begins, after Joshua's death, with the Israelites asking God which tribe will begin fighting the Canaanites. Judah, chosen, defeats King Adoni-bezek (Adonibezec) and cuts off his thumbs and big toes, as he had earlier treated 70 kings. Coming to Debir, or Kiriath-sepher (Cariath-sepher), Caleb offers his daughter Achsah (Axa) to the man capturing it. Othniel (Othoniel) succeeds, and also gains land given to Achsah by her father as well as the upper and lower springs she further requires of him. But despite some military success, Judah cannot drive out the inhabitants of the plain with their iron chariots. A man of Bethel (formerly Luz) betrays his city to the house of Joseph, but many Canaanites (Chanaanites) remain, either undefeated or subject to forced labor under the Israelites.

An angel announces that the Lord has left the Canaanites as adversaries because Israel failed to tear down the altars of their gods; and Israel indeed proceeds to worship these gods, to be plundered by its enemies, and then saved by judges raised up by the Lord, the first being Othniel.

The sparse account of Othniel (3:7–11) encapsulates a framework repeated, and varied, in Judges. The people turn from the Lord. He brings upon them foreign oppressors. They cry for help. He then raises up a deliverer who defeats the oppressors, and the people enjoy "rest." This pattern of reward and punishment is often viewed as the book's dominant theme, though some, especially recently, see already in chapter 1 the suggestion that life rarely comes so neatly packaged.

By the eighteenth century, discrepancies between Joshua and Judges had become a problem: why do cities captured or destroyed in the former reappear, still inhabited by Canaanites in the latter? Indeed, did Joshua not annihilate *all* the Canaanites? Such historical questions about Israel's origins and early organization continue to dog scholars.

Though these early chapters lack the engaging stories that follow, readers over the centuries have not hesitated to derive lessons about justice from Adoni-bezek or about proper behavior from Achsah, her father, and her husband.

Ancient and Medieval

Early Christian and Jewish interpreters pay Judges 1–2 little attention, focusing rather on the major figures of subsequent chapters. Rabbinic reference is usually related to a text from the Torah. In discussing the beginning of Leviticus ("And Yhwh called to Moses"), *Midrash Leviticus Rabbah* (1:1) takes the angel appearing to the Israelites at Bochim (Judg 2:1–5) as evidence that *mal'ak* ("messenger," "angel") can refer to prophets as well as members of God's heavenly host, for this *mal'ak* "came up to Bochim from Gilgal" (Judg 2:1), not "from above," to pronounce God's judgment. The rabbis agree that this "angel" was the priest Phineas (see also, on this text and Num 20:16, *Midrash Numbers Rabbah*, 16:1; Moses Maimonides, *Guide for the Perplexed*, 16).

Among commentators on the Christian life, the monk John Cassian (360–435) sees the cycle of suffering-repentance-deliverance (Judg 2:10–19) and its first two deliverers (Othniel and Ehud) as illustrating how often severe suffering will drive a person to God, "whom we scorned to follow in the days of our wealth" (*Conference of Abbot Paphnutius*, ch. 4). Much later, a thirteenth-century guide for anchoresses (*Ancrene Wisse*, v [158]), stressing confession as a devotional practice, reads allegorically the book's opening where God nominates Judah as leader after Joshua's death. Joshua means "health" and Judah "confession." Joshua is dead when the soul's health is lost through deadly sin. Canaan is the sinful self, the devil's land, reclaimed by confession, that is, by Judah who "goes before you."

Othniel, the first deliverer in Judg 3:9, plays an earlier role in 1:13 as Caleb's younger kinsman who captures Kiriath-sepher (called Debir) in order to win in marriage Caleb's daughter, Achsah. (The story is also told in Josh 15:15–17.) Kiriath-sepher means "city of the book." An ancient Jewish tradition takes this name literally: Othniel captured 1,700 legal traditions the Israelites forgot while mourning Moses' death. "Said R. Abbuha: Nevertheless Othniel the son of Kenaz restored [these forgotten teachings] as a result of his dialectics" (*B. Talmud Temurah*, 16a; Rashi on Joshua 15; cf. Ginzberg, VI, 185). Accordingly, Othniel is remembered by some as a great scholar who set up an academy for Torah study (e.g. Targum to 1 Chron 2:55). Indeed, according to rabbinic texts identifying him with Jabez (1 Chron 4:9–10), Othniel's righteousness was so great among his fellow Israelites that God did not hold him accountable for Israel's continued unfaithfulness during his reign, but granted him eternal life, allowing him to enter Paradise alive (see Ginzberg, VI, 187).

Jewish historian Josephus (c.37–c.100 CE) tells of the indolence and political lethargy of the Israelite masses. By their luxury they forfeited their hard-earned independence and prosperity, and Keniaz (not Othniel, who is Kenaz's son in the Bible) was hard-pressed to find a few Israelites who, "out of shame at their present state and a desire to change it," would help him attack the Cushan garrison. Only after seeing his initial success were more Israelites willing to join him (*Antiquities*, v.182–4 (3.3)). (Whiston translates "Othniel, the son of Kenaz" anyway; Josephus's contemporary Pseudo-Philo has Cenaz as the first judge, but tells a very different story.).

Josephus also establishes a chronological order to the book's events which has continued into the modern period. The story of the Levite and the Benjamite war (Judges 19–21) and the Danite migration (Judges 18) occur early in the period of the judges, not at the end. This arrangement was well supported in Jewish tradition and adopted by Christian commentators (for details, see below on Judges 17–18).

Early Modern and Modern

It is universally noted, writes Matthew Henry (1662–1714), that Joshua left no successor with like authority. Hence it became incumbent on the tribes themselves to consult God through an oracle, as at the book's outset: "For God himself, as he was their King, so he was the Lord of their Hosts" (*Exposition*, 1708). The "judges" of the book, says Thomas Scott (1747–1821), "were not a regular succession of governors, but occasional deliverers, of different tribes and families, employed to rescue the nation from oppressors, to reform religion, or to administer justice. They do not seem to have assumed any degree of regal magnificence, or to have exercised any expensive or burdensome authority; yet they were for the time the immediate vicegerents of JEHOVAH the King of Israel" (*Holy Bible*, 1788–92).

For Scott, the book shows, "in a most affecting manner, the consequences of attending on the worship and service of God, or of neglecting them, in respect of national prosperity or adversity." Israel's condition "does not appear so prosperous, nor the national character so religious," as might have been hoped. A little later he is less restrained, speaking of the people's "sloth, cowardice, and unbelief" which "created them almost an infinity of trouble and misery afterwards." But echoing other readers, he thinks it probable that sanctuary worship was regularly maintained by a pious remnant "amidst the repeated apostacies and multiplied idolatries of the nation in general." Often cited as evidence is the book of Ruth, set in the time of the Judges, with its exemplary characters, Naomi, Boaz, and the Moabite woman, Ruth.

A recurring issue for readers of Joshua and Judges is the apparent discrepancy between their accounts of conquest. Cities the former declared captured, destroyed, and their inhabitants wiped out, apparently need capturing all over again. (The problem is also internal to Joshua; cf. chs 10–11 and chs 16–17.) Hence the campaigns against Hebron and Debir (Judg 1:9–13) – in Josh 10:36–40 these cities are utterly destroyed – often prompt the conjecture that the old inhabitants had returned while Joshua was absent subduing other parts of the country (so Symon Patrick, *Commentary*, 1702; Henry, *Exposition*). That there were no inhabitants left, according to Joshua 10, is a further problem best left unmentioned.

Skeptical philosopher Voltaire (1694–1778) is only too happy to mention such problems. On Judg 3:8, where Cushan-rishathaim of Mesopotamia makes Israel serve him for eight years, Voltaire cites an English Deist. Thomas Woolston "dares declare frankly that either the story of Judges is false, or that of Joshua is, from one end to the other. It is not possible, he says, that the Jews could have been enslaved immediately after having destroyed the inhabitants of Canaan with an army of six hundred thousand men." Equally inconceivable is how the 600,000 men could have exterminated all the original inhabitants but then be allied with them. "This crowd of contradictions is unsustainable." In his own voice Voltaire pretends to confess that Scripture is indeed difficult to understand. Perhaps there have been copyists' transpositions, he wonders, adding that it takes only one to spread obscurity in any history. But having sewn enough doubt and implicitly equated Scripture to just any history, he ends with his typical mock allegiance to orthodoxy: "We repeat that the best thing is to rely on the approved interpreters of the Church" (*Bible enfin expliquée*, 1776 [133]).

Twentieth-century critics basically agreed with Voltaire – the stories were not easily reconciled, and Joshua's sudden conquest was historically unreliable. Instead, the "gradual settlement" of Judges 1–2 (and Joshua 16–17) represented more accurately what happened. German scholar Martin Noth developed a popular hypothesis of tribal political organization, modeled on the ancient Greek "amphictyony" whose constituent members retained independence but united around a central sanctuary to wage war (*Das System der Zwölfstämme Israels*, 1930). By the century's end, however, Noth's amphictyony was largely discarded, and few scholars thought it possible to write a history of the Judges period based on the biblical text. The stark contrast between Joshua and Judges, moreover, was reassessed by literary critics reading the former as itself presenting a complex understanding of how the Promised Land was taken (cf. L. Daniel Hawk, *Every Promise Fulfilled*, 1991).

Jerusalem's conquest in Judges 1 has its own problems. First, Adoni-bezek in verse 7 is taken by his Judahite captors to the city, where he died, whereas verse 8 tells, as if a subsequent event, that the Judahites fought against the city, took it, put it to the sword, and burned it. Second, Judg 1:21 reports that the Benjamites did not dispossess the Jebusites of Jerusalem who have lived with them there "to this day" (confirmed by Josh 15:63). In Judg 19:11–12 it is a city of Jebusites, with no Israelites. David, moreover, had to capture the city from the Jebusites to make it his capital (2 Sam 5:6–10). Responses to the problem are various and ingenious.

In the late sixteenth century, the widely used Geneva Bible put verse 8 in parentheses and translated, "Now the children of Judah *had* fought against Jerusalem, and *had* taken it" (italics added). The official King James (or Authorised) version of 1611 (KJV) dispenses with the parentheses but keeps the tense, to the same effect: the capture had happened earlier, in Joshua's time. Others disputed this solution. Although Joshua defeated Adoni-*zedek*, king of Jerusalem, and took all the other cities in the vicinity, Jerusalem itself is not mentioned as taken. Rather, they say, Adoni-bezek had probably seized the city after Adoni-zedek's death left the throne vacant. (Alternatively, Joshua took the city only to lose it on going to take other parts of the country.) After capturing Adoni-bezek, the Judahites brought him to the *siege* of Jerusalem, while it was still holding out. As for inconvenient verse 21 (the Jebusites have dwelt in Jerusalem "to this day") and David's taking the city, it is explained that although the Judahites won the city, they could not take the stronghold or castle where the Jebusites remained until David's time. It was this "fort" (KJV) that David took (cf. Patrick, *Commentary*; Henry, *Exposition*).

Yet another version has the Judahites previously taking the lower city but not the upper city where Jebusites still lived (squaring with Josh 15:63). It was to the lower city that Adoni-bezek was taken. Soon after, the Judahites seized and sacked the upper city (squaring with Judg 1:8). Subsequently, during one of the "oppressions," the Jebusites regained control and rebuilt the upper city (an incident unreported) where they remained until David retook it (Kitto, *Bible History*, 1841 [193]).

Adoni-bezek earns credit for accepting his mutilation and providing an edifying lesson. As one writer observed to General Washington, as he prayed that God would arm him against all evils, "Sir, men of great honour and worldly glory stand but in slippery places. Adonibezek, a mighty prince, was made fellow commoner with the dogs" (Stephen Case [?], *Defensive Arms Vindicated*, 1779 [716]). On a more practical note, it was often explained, convincingly, that the point of the mutilation, aside from equity, was to render the king "uncapable of War hereafter, being unable to handle Arms, by reason of the Loss of his Thumbs; or to run swiftly (which was a noble Quality in a Warrior) by the loss of his great Toes" (Patrick, *Commentary*, 1702).

For those uncomfortable about the Israelite retaliation, it was probably done by the "secret instinct and direction of God"; otherwise, it was carried out upon being informed by others of the king's tyranny and cruelty; either way, it was a just requital (Matthew Poole, *Annotations*, 1685). Certainly as far as Mrs Trimmer (1741–1810) was concerned, writing for the improvement of English youth, the matter was entirely straightforward: he was "justly condemned" (*Sacred History*, 1783 [xlvi, 202]). Esther Hewlett (1786–1851), with a similar audience, points out that the captured king acknowledged the "retributive justice" that had overtaken him. "How often has it been seen," she advises, "that with what measure we mete to others, it is measured to us again!" (*Scripture History*, 1828, 3). Young Americans read the Rev. John Howard (1795–1868) expatiating on the same theme. He adds that Adoni-bezek's punishment "is a warning to those in authority that God will judge mankind as they themselves have judged their fellow-creatures; and if this be not verified in this life . . . it will certainly be in the next" (*Illustrated Scripture History*, 1840 [126]). Or, as the author whom these educators seem to have been reading puts it, a little more strongly, "the great and mighty Men of the Earth shall be mightily tormented if they abuse the Power they are intrusted with, for the glory of GOD, and for the good of their Subjects" (Nicolas Fontaine, *History*, 1690 [80]; cf. Joseph Reeve's version of Fontaine's *History* for Catholic youth, 1780).

Children's Bible histories begin appearing in the eighteenth century, and Trimmer is among the pioneers. While she, Hewlett, and Howard refer to Adoni-bezek's fate, and Howard includes an illustration, the king is more often missing from such books, the more so as the nineteenth century wore on. In the twentieth century he is rarely discussed at all, let alone pictured with his bodily parts being severed.

Earlier, however, his mutilation was regularly pictured in Bibles, histories, and pictorial suites, from the first days of printed illustrated Bibles in the late fifteenth century until well into the nineteenth century. It is the only illustration from Judges in the suite of woodcuts by Hans Holbein (1497–1543), court painter to Henry VIII (*Historiarum Veteris Testamenti Icones*, 1538) (PLATE 1.1b). He derived it from a Venetian Bible of 1490. Since the story comes early in Judges 1, the picture often heads the book: typical is a 1690 Vulgate from Venice. As with Holbein's king, it seems he is about to lose all of his fingers, not just his thumbs (PLATE 1.1c). Likewise, in the famous suite of copperplate engravings (*Icones Biblicae*, 1626) by Matthäus Merian (1593–1650), used in Zetzner's Luther Bible of 1630 (the "Merian Bible"), were it not for a successfully singled-out thumb and great toe already on the chopping block, we might expect Adoni-bezek shortly to lose five more toes (PLATE 1.1d). There is no such problem, however, in the influential "Great Bible" of 1700, published by Pieter Mortier (1661–1711) in Amsterdam. Here (Jan Goeree is the designer) the instrument of choice is a chisel (PLATE 1.1e). The scene later fell into disfavor, and an American reader of Harper's celebrated *Illuminated Bible* of 1846 might have been surprised to find it at the head of Judges. These executioners also clearly know their business (PLATE 1.1a).

> Behold the punishment so just,
>   Of him who had a tyrant been.
> God's righteous judgment ever must
>   O'ertake us all, though not foreseen.
> (Howard, *Illustrated Scripture History*, 1840)

Contrasting with Adoni-bezek are Caleb and Achsah (Judg 1:11–15), a story repeated from Josh 15:15–19. It tells the familiar tale of the hero who wins the hand of the king's daughter. ("Fathers among the Israelites . . . exercised a more absolute authority, in disposing of their daughters in marriage, than is customary among us; and these generally acquiesced in the choice made for them," says Thomas Scott (*Holy Bible*, 1788–92).) Told in few words, the narrative demands of its reader mental leaps, while difficulties in the Hebrew text have also occasioned head-scratching.

Othniel's family affiliation is ambiguous: literally "son of Kenaz brother of Caleb who was younger than he." Some have thought him to be Caleb's nephew, others his brother. The ancient Greek versions are split on the matter, but in the Vulgate he is Caleb's brother, and so into the modern period. Symon Patrick (1626–1707) notes that if Othniel were Caleb's brother, that would make him Achsah's uncle, and the marriage improper. He insists that Caleb is consistently

PLATE 1.1 Adoni-bezek's fate: (a) *Harper's Illuminated Bible*, 1846; (b) Holbein, 1538; (c) Latin Bible, 1690; (d) Merian, 1626; (e) Goeree, 1700. (See p. 23)

called the son of Jephunneh (e.g. Josh 15:13) so Othniel, son of Kenaz, cannot be his brother. Rather, "brother" should be taken more broadly as meaning "kin" (*Commentary*, 1702, on Josh 15:17; similarly Poole, *Annotations*, 1685). Along similar lines, it has recently been suggested that Othniel is described as a Kenizzite by clan and a kinsman ("brother") of Caleb (Robert G. Boling, *Judges*, 1975).

The narrator tells us that Achsah came, but not from where. Had she been sent away for the campaign's duration, or was she arriving at her husband's home from her father's house? More significantly, did *she* press *him* to ask her father for a field (so the Hebrew text), or was it the other way round (as in the Greek versions and the Latin Vulgate)? Patrick, again with propriety in mind, wonders whether this means that she moved her husband "to give her Leave to ask it of her Father." He then would have given her permission, perhaps thinking it "more proper" for her to ask than he himself (*Commentary*). Accordingly she did, says Matthew Henry, "submitting to her Husband's Judgment, tho' contrary to her own" (*Exposition*). The reverse argument is that having his wife press or "nag" him (the verb is usually pejorative) reflected badly on the image of the first "savior judge" and so was probably a "tendentious" change from an original where the husband nagged the wife (so Boling, *Judges*) – which behavior apparently did the hero's image no damage.

A woodcut in John Kitto's *Pictorial Sunday-Book* (1845) illustrates the scene by borrowing from Nicolas Poussin's *Arcadian Shepherds* (Paris, Louvre), painted c.1650 and very popular in the eighteenth and nineteenth centuries. Poussin's shepherd traces with his finger a tomb inscription (*Et in Arcadia ego*, "Even in Arcadia, [there] am I"). Kitto's woodcut replaces the tomb with a spring, and Othniel points now to Achsah or perhaps to the water. Either way, life has replaced death as the central symbol. The viewer is left wondering whether Othniel is pressing Achsah to ask for this water or congratulating her for having won it (PLATE 1.2a).

Whichever text is read, Achsah does the asking. She asks for a present, a "real, tangible" blessing (George F. Moore, *Judges*, 1895). Another debate concerns what first happens when she arrives on the ass. The Hebrew word translated "lighted from off" (KJV) or "alighted from" (RSV) occurs only here (= Josh 15:18) and in Judg 4:21, and its meaning has been discussed, particularly since the ancient Greek and Latin has her sighing and crying out from her ass. Alternative proposals, however, have tended to be found wanting, some more than others: the proposal to render "she broke wind" as in the New English Bible "has not found wide acceptance" (Boling, *Judges*).

Caleb greets her with "What wilt thou?" (KJV), as though he already knows she wants something. Or his question might be translated, "What's wrong?"

PLATE 1.2   Achsah: (a) Kitto's *Pictorial Sunday-Book*, 1845; (b) Singleton, c.1800. (See pp. 25, 27)

(Boling), as though her demeanor was amiss. "You have given me a south land" (KJV) or "Negeb land," she says to her father, a "dry country," that is: "Give me also springs of water." Clearly the reader lacks information: Caleb has already given her land, but it does not satisfy her. She is asking for more. If she has dry land, she needs springs of water. Or as one writer paraphrases: "Thou has already given me a pleasant Estate in the South Part of the Country; but it is hot and dry; and likely to prove barren; give me, I pray thee, this Parcel of Land, which is well watered" (Laurence Clarke, *Compleat History*, 1737). The story ends simply: without further word, Caleb gives her not one source of water but two, the "upper springs" and the "lower springs."

Henry supposes these to be two fields, named from their springs, though he is partial also to the thought of one field, watered from the heavens above and the earth below, alluding to blessings of soul and body (*Exposition*, on Joshua 15). He much approves of Achsah. She dutifully consulted her husband, and she managed the undertaking "wonderful well" and "with a great deal of Art." We learn thereby that not only should husbands and wives "mutually advise, and joyntly agree about that which is for the common Good of their Family," but "much more should they concur in asking of their Heavenly Father the best Blessings, those of the upper Springs."

Othniel too wins approbation. It would seem he had a soft spot (a "kindness") for Achsah before Caleb's offer which prompted his bold undertaking. "Love to his Countrey, an Ambition of Honour, and a desire to find Favour with the Princes of his People, would not have engaged him in the great Action, but his Affection for Achsah did . . . and so inspir'd him with this generous Fire. Thus is *Love strong as Death* . . ." (Henry, *Exposition*).

A little cooler is Thomas Gaspey (fl. 1840–60) in *Tallis's Illustrated Scripture History for the Improvement of Youth* (1851, 88). "The daughter, like some young ladies who have lived since her time, seems to have thought it would be right to get as much as she could from her father for her husband . . . she was so fortunate as to obtain all she asked." Children will naturally look to their parents for aid, and parents, inasmuch as they are able, will be disposed to give it. Still, children should not be too importunate, for "the most selfish are not always allowed to fare the best." Somehow we seem to have strayed a little from the story. But H. Singleton's picture (cf. PLATE 1.2b), and the accompanying verse, bring us back.

> Achsah her lord to Caleb brings,
>   Already his fair field possessing,
> To ask the boon of water springs,
>   And with them the paternal blessings.

Romantic novelist Grace Aguilar (1816–47) has no hesitation commending the story to young Jewish women, for it is, she argues, "the very first instance of chivalry which history records." Chivalry – "when marvellous deeds were done, and dangers dared, all for the smiles of women" – had the virtue of making woman "a subject of consideration, respect, and love," very different to the "slavery and degradation" the critics saw as her lot in ancient Israel. (Aguilar might well have had Voltaire in mind.) Caleb clearly knew the esteem in which Achsah was held, or would not have offered her as a reward for valor. And Caleb sought her for herself, not her property, since she had to urge him to ask her father for a field. Achsah herself was not afraid to ask her father and judged him right. Aguilar concludes: rather than confirming "our being degraded," does it not "elevate us to a perfect equality with our brother man?" (*Women of Israel*, 1845, 215–17).

Christian commentators in the early modern period and later resume the ancient rabbinic discussion of the name Kiriath-sepher, as the city of Debir was formerly called (Judg 1:11). The city, Patrick notes, was probably where the ancient archives were kept, a city of learning, as Athens was among the Greeks.

John Kitto (1804–54), self-taught scholar and widely published author, devotes one of his "family circle" readings (*Daily Bible Illustrations*, 1850 [II, 282–5]) to the "Book-City," no doubt so named from being either eminent for books or archives, or the resort of men conversant with literature. He notes that the ancient Jewish Targum calls the place Kirjath-arche – or the city of the public records of the Canaanites. In verse 49 it is called Kijath-sannah, which may refer to traditional law and learning, and is translated in the ancient Greek versions a "city of letters." In short, this city tells us that there were books in Canaan. "By the dear love we bear to books, which place within our grasp the thoughts and knowledge of all ages and of all climes, we exult in this inevitable conclusion." And whatever the quality or number of those books, "they were precious in the eyes of the Canaanites." But what, asks Kitto, became of those books? When Caleb acquired the city, did he preserve or destroy them? Whereas Henry supposed that a desire for Israel to acquaint itself with ancient Canaanite learning spurred Caleb to master the city (*Exposition*, on Josh 15:13–19), Kitto doubts that Caleb would respect books containing, to him, much that was "profane and abominable."

> Besides, the collection very probably included records and covenants respecting the ancient arrangements of estates and territories, which a conquering people could have no interest in preserving, but had a very obvious interest in destroying. So it is by no means unlikely that old Caleb threw the entire bundle of books that formed the library of Kirjath-sepher into the fire.

The books of Kiriath-sepher also interest feminist critic Danna Nolan Fewell, reflecting on Achsah and the "(e)razed" City of Writing (1995). Spelling out the city's former name as "city of books" casts the conquest in a different light for a reader who respects learning and culture. Though the predominant tone of Joshua and Judg 1:1–18 is triumphalism, by mentioning the former name the text shows "traces" of other values undermining the triumph. Fewell is also interested in how Achsah's story may be read as a whole, what meanings present themselves, and what undermines these. Her larger point is that biblical texts, like others, are inherently unstable, always subject to the choices readers make and what drives those choices.

Fewell leads her own reader through the text's ambiguities, setting out choices. Are Caleb and his clan Kenizzites, so not strictly Israelites but foreigners? In that case, instead of celebrating a conquest by Israel or Judah, does the story suggest it took foreigners to do what Israel/Judah could not? Achsah's name means "bangle" or "anklet." Asks Fewell, "Is she a person? Or is she a trinket? Is she a subject in her own right? Or is she simply an ornament in the story, a 'charming personal touch'?" Considered as "trinket," a reader might see her as but another spoil of war. "To her father, she is bait. To her future husband, she is his due reward. . . . Who needs to consider seriously a girl named Trinket?" Yet she takes initiative and insists on a gift. How, then, does she understand herself? "Is she aware that she, like the land, is to be taken and owned by a victorious soldier? Or does she see herself as the landowner, attempting to improve her property?" What is her relation to her husband, Othniel? Does she "urge" him or "nag" him? Or is it rather Othniel who is the subject of this verb? Fewell notes what we saw above, that often the decision favors Othniel's interests. "In the end," she argues, "we see how interpreters are preoccupied with how the biblical text models men."

Finally, Fewell offers alternatives. Is the text literal or figurative? Does Caleb represent God, Othniel Israel, Achsah the land? "Isn't God's promise of the land conditioned upon a successful conquest?" Or perhaps Othniel and Achsah represent an ideal Israel, undaunted by obstacles – like a few iron chariots. (Of the Israelites in verse 19 Thomas Scott writes, "their courage and faith failed them at the sight of the iron chariots . . . They forgot how Joshua had attacked and destroyed the Canaanites . . . and when they lost their confidence in God they could do nothing" (*Holy Bible*, 1788–92).) Or does Achsah tell of Israel finding itself in a land which is not exactly the promised land of milk and honey, an Israel needing to ask to be blessed with the very basic necessity of life, water? Does the story, then, subvert the divine promise? Not necessarily, says Fewell. An imperfect land "may be what provides life its challenge. It may be what provides the plot for the ongoing story. It may be the very thing that will build Israel's (and God's) character."

The third cameo story in Judges 1 tells of the man of Luz (Bethel) who showed the spies from the house of Joseph how to enter the city (Judg 1:22–6). In return they undertook to "shew mercy" to him (KJV), or deal "kindly" (RSV), "justly" (Boling), or perhaps better, "loyally" with him. After the city was taken, the captors honored their undertaking and let him and his family go free. He went to Hittite territory and built another Luz. The similarity to the story of Rahab and the spies at Jericho is frequently noted (Joshua 2, 6). But whereas Rahab and her extended family afterwards joined Israel, so "she dwelt in Israel to this day" (Josh 6:25), the man of Luz and his family separate themselves from their conquerors and re-establish their city. "He seems to have acted, not from faith to God, or love of Israel, but out of fear, and to save his life; and therefore, when set at liberty, he did not unite interests with the worshippers of Jehovah as Rahab had done" (Thomas Scott, following Henry).

Divine agency in the plot of Judges has been a source of confusion for readers, nowhere more so than in Judges 1–3. Did the Israelites, through their own failures, allow the Canaanites (the "nations") to remain in the land, as much of chapters 1–2 suggests, or were these failures caused by God, as 2:20–3:6 has it? Taken as a whole, the text seems to want to have it both ways, rather as the story of the Exodus tells both that God hardened Pharaoh's heart and that Pharaoh hardened his own heart. Readers, however, tend to opt for one or the other, as we see below with Protestant Reformers Martin Luther and John Calvin. Esther Hewlett, in the nineteenth century, is typical when she blames "the slackness of the people and the consequent want of the divine blessing among them" for their enemies' presence among them, intermarriage, and the people's slide into idolatry. Divine activity ("Now these are the nations which the Lord left, to test Israel by them," Judg 3:1) becomes for Hewlett divine passivity ("want of the divine blessing"), and we are left with human "slackness" as the fundamental cause (*Scripture History*, 1828, 15).

In his *Treatise on Good Works* (1520), Martin Luther (1483–1546) uses this passage to illustrate a principle: worse sin and vice occur in time of peace than "when war, pestilence, illness, and all manner of misfortune burden us." Moses understood this: "My beloved people has become too rich, full, and fat: therefore have they resisted their God" (Deut 32:15). Thus the Israelites, now settled in the Promised Land, needed to discipline themselves by keeping God's commandments. John Calvin (1509–64) finds in Othniel's role as deliverer a lesson of God's goodness, power, and providence: "For sometimes [God] raises up open avengers from among his servants, and arms them with his command to punish the wicked government and deliver his people, oppressed in unjust ways, from miserable calamity" (*Institutes*, 1550, iv.20.30). Like others, he fails to mention that it was, however, God who brought the oppression from which the people needed deliverance. If the oppression was unjust, then this calamity, the text might seem to say, was of God's making.

As we have seen, some approve of Adoni-bezek for accepting the divine justice of his fate. Thus, in his posthumous collection of sermons, *The Crook in the Lot* (1737), Scottish Presbyterian minister Thomas Boston (1677–1732) points to him as one who rightly sees "the doing of God" in his affliction. Boston's book continues to be widely read. Two months after the September 11, 2001, terrorist attacks on the World Trade Center and the Pentagon building in the United States, a new edition appeared, to speak directly to this trauma. The cover displays a photo of the Trade Center's twin towers, along with the subtitle, *The Sovereignty and Wisdom of God Displayed in the Afflictions of Men*. From Adoni-bezek's twin thumbs to New York's twin towers and the thousands of lives therein, apparently, God's guiding and judging hand may be seen.

> "Then God was angry with them; and He punished them by sending cruel nations to conquer them, to burn their houses, to steal their children, and drive away their cattle. . . ."
> "Served 'em right for going back on their promises," said Willie.
> "Yes, brother," answered Clara, "and we must remember if we disobey God we are sure to be punished."
> "Right again, my child," said Aunt Charlotte; "all the Old Testament history has its lessons for us now."
> (Charlotte M. Yonge, *Aunt Charlotte's Stories*, 1898, 137–8)

Another way of reading Judges 1–3 is to relate it to the larger story of which it is a part, Genesis–2 Kings. Adoni-bezek speaks of captured kings eating at his table. At the end of Kings, with nation devastated and people scattered, Jehoiachin, king of Judah, eats at the table of his captor, the king of Babylon. Israel's dispossession, insists the narrator, has been divine punishment. Given this ending, Adoni-bezek's story reads like a parable. As Israel constantly breaks its covenant with God, as in the first chapters of Judges and as the story unfurls, what would be its just requital? A thumb for a thumb, so to speak, would have brought the story to a swift conclusion. As it turns out, the larger story from Judges to Kings seems to suggest more like a thumb for 70 thumbs. God "has a way of offering two springs of water instead of one, and requiting one thumb for seventy" (David M. Gunn and Danna Nolan Fewell, *Narrative*, 1993, 158–63).

Questions of theodicy and equity, however, are not the burning ones for many readers. Rather, they wonder at how readily Israel falls into idolatry: "Who would not think idolatry an absurd and unnatural thing?" For Joseph

Hall (1574–1656) the only conclusion can be the one Luther drew. "Let him that thinks he stands, take heed lest he fall" (*Contemplations*, 1615 [ix.3, 106]).

One long-standing line of thought is bolstered by the biblical metaphor denoting worship of foreign gods – instead of Israel's own god – as adultery or prostitution (so "play the harlot," Judg 2:17). It is assumed that idolatry involved illicit sex. John Kitto explains the conquering Hebrews' recurring predicament as a consequence of their failure to exterminate fully, or at least banish, the "dangerous and corrupting" Canaanites. Intermarrying with them, they wove a web in which they became entangled. Their Canaanitish relatives invited them to festivals where "lascivious songs" honored the gods, and "fornication and unnatural lusts were indulged in *as part of the Divine service.*" Thus the rest of the world's propensity to idolatry "spread itself among the chosen like a plague" (*Bible History*, 1841 [191–2]).

In his *Personalities of the Old Testament* (1939), popularizing historical-critical scholarship, Fleming James describes the report of God denouncing the worship of local deities (Judg 2:1–5) as probably inserted by a later "Deuteronomic" editor to explain the people's suffering. But the explanation may have preserved a true recollection of the Israelites inclining to the "Canaanitish Baals"; and "this sensuous, narrowly local worship had let them sink back into sectionalism." Only loyalty to "Yahweh, the desert-God," could unite them in the military exploits needed (p. 66). "The peril of Israel," George Matheson (1842–1906) earlier observed (*Representative Men*, 1903, 159–60), "was not irreligion; it was too much religion of a bad kind." Worshiping Baal meant worshiping "sensuousness, if not sensuality"; it meant reverencing "the bodily nature of man" – the lust of the flesh and the eye – and pursuing animal pleasures and exercising strength; it meant reverencing "the oppression of the weak by the strong, the reign of violence and the empire of physical force."

Some years later, Jesuit priest John L. McKenzie (1910–91) discusses the two main "fertility" goddesses appearing in Canaanite religion: Ashtar (Astarte) and, prominent in the epic texts from Ugarit, Anath. The goddess, he claims, is the female principle deified, source of life and sexual pleasure. She is represented nude, with her sexual attributes emphasized – such clay figurines, doubtless insuring the sexual desirability and and fertility of Canaanite women, have been found in large numbers. The goddess of sex is also a goddess of violence: "The warlike Anath appears nude astride a horse and brandishing a weapon." It is thus clear why this religion was both popular and repudiated. Such a debased cult one would hesitate to call a religion. "It was more than nature worship and more than humanism; it was a candid profession of faith in sex as that alone which saves and satisfies" (*World of the Judges*, 1966, 41–2).

To Benjamin Warfield (1851–1921), conservative Princeton theologian, the focal point of the stories of Othniel and the other leaders in Judges was the coming of the "Spirit of Jehovah" upon them. God is presented as the "theocratic Spirit," as the "source of all the supernatural powers and activities which are directed to the foundation and preservation and development of the kingdom of God in the midst of the wicked world." Accordingly the Spirit endows the "theocratic organs" of these leaders – Othniel, Gideon, Jephthah, and, most remarkably, Samson – with the supernatural gifts necessary for the fulfillment of their tasks, as, for example, strength, resolution, energy, and courage in battle (*Biblical and Theological Studies*, 1895 [138–9]).

Very differently does the Rev. Thomas E. Miller (fl. 1900–30), in tune with liberal historical criticism, view the spirit coming upon Othniel (*Portraits*, 1922, 21–32). He doubts some "conscious, supernatural endowment" made him realize he was chosen: "the Spirit of God moves no doubt in a mysterious way, but He moves in human fashion and through human channels." Othniel broods and prays over the wrong inflicted by Eglon, King of Moab, until convinced that "Jehovah will not suffer a heathen foe to triumph over His people." It is then "he feels the Divine urge compelling him." This is "the answer of the human spirit to the ever-present and ever-pleading spirit of God." For Miller, like most readers, Othniel was a truly religious man, more akin to Gideon than Samson. He judged Israel before going to war, and his patriotism, courage, and sympathy for his oppressed people were rooted in his "passion for righteousness." He "grasped the truth, which even yet we are slow to learn, that righteousness alone exalteth a nation." Sin is "a clog on the wheels of progress."

Interpreters have generally found Othniel himself – unless vested with a burning passion for Achsah – a rather colorless character. His exploit against Cushan-rishathaim is told in skeletal fashion (Judg 3:7–11). Othniel is the model judge against whom all others are measured, in part because so little is said of him that there is little chance of finding flaws. He is, as the literary critics say, an entirely "flat" – "empty" even – character.

> Othniel is the embodiment of an institution; all the key words assigned to judgeship in chapter 2 [vv. 16–19] are applied to Othniel here, and his career conforms to the paradigm there. He is 'raised up' by Yahweh; he 'saves' Israel by 'judging' and going out to war. It is Yahweh who gives him victory over the enemy, a victory which ushers in an era of peace which lasts until after his death. . . . there are no complicating details. (Barry G. Webb, *Judges*, 1987, 127)

The story's setting is the familiar one in Judges. The Lord supports a foreign power against the Israelites, in this case Eglon, king of Moab, because they have done evil in his sight. Eglon captures the "city of palms" (Jericho), and the Israelites serve him for 18 years. The people cry for help to the Lord, who raises up a deliverer or savior, Ehud (Aod) the Benjamite, "a man lefthanded" (KJV; cf. GB "lame of his right hand"). Ehud makes a two-edged short sword (GB "dagger") which he girds on his right thigh, presents tribute (KJV "a present") to the king, a "very fat man," and departs. At Gilgal's "quarries" (KJV; cf. RSV "sculptured stones") he turns back, claiming to have a secret message (literally "word") for Eglon. Alone with the king in his "summer parlour" (KJV; cf. RSV "cool roof chamber") he says that he has a message from God (or "divine word") for him. Eglon rises from his chair. Taking his sword with his left hand, Ehud buries it in Eglon's belly; "the dirt comes out," and he exits, leaving the door locked. By the time the servants have discovered the murder, Ehud has escaped and rallied Israelites in the hill country of Ephraim. They seize the fords of the Jordan and slay some 10,000 Moabites. So the land "has rest" for 80 years.

Ehud's brief story is little known today. Yet it has sometimes been a focus of discussion, as on the political issue of regicide or the religious significance of the king rising from his throne, a topic gracing many a sermon. The assassination details, including the sword ensconced in the king's belly and the enigmatic phrase about the "dirt" (KJV, RSV; LATIN *stercora*, "excrement") coming out, have generated extensive discussion, as perhaps only biblical trivia can do. Both deception and killing have prompted concern: is Ehud's action morally defensible and a model for imitation?

Ancient and Medieval

Ancient Jewish historian Josephus (37–c.100 CE), his eye on his Greco-Roman audience, explains the crisis facing Israel after the death of Keniaz (Othniel in the Bible) as due to a lack of good government (in which Rome prided itself), aggravated by failure to pay homage to God and obey the laws (*Antiquities*, v.185–97 (4.1–3)). His story's hero is named Judes, "of gallant daring" and able to turn his superior strength in his left hand to his own ends. Rendering his story palatable to his audience's literary tastes, Josephus has Judes, for example, "courting and cajoling" King Eglon with presents so as to endear himself also to the king's courtiers; his subsequent access to the king thus becomes more understandable, and so the plot more acceptable. Judes smites the king in the heart, not the belly, no doubt a more heroic smiting; and there is no mention of the king being fat, or of the scatalogical detail ("the dirt came out"), suggesting perhaps a more worthy opponent. This history is decidedly in the vein of epic, not comedy.

Josephus also explains why Eglon rose from his seat to receive the Benjamite's message, a motivation with a long subsequent history. Judes told him "he had a dream to disclose to him by God's commandment," whereupon the king leapt up "for joy at news of this dream." Other early Jewish readers were impressed by this "heathen" arising to receive God's message (literally "a word of God" or "divine word"). *Ruth Rabbah* (2:9): "The Holy One, blessed be He, said to him: 'Thou didst arise from thy throne in honour of Me. By thy life, I shall raise up from thee a descendant sitting upon the throne of the Lord." The postulated descendent was Solomon, descended from Moabite Ruth, thought, with her sister Orpah, to be King Eglon's daughter.

Christian monk John Cassian (c.360–c.435) has a different interest. In the ancient versions, the Greek Septuagint and the Latin Vulgate, Ehud is ambidextrous: he "used either hand as the right hand." For Cassian, the text is figurative, understanding left as the "sinister" side. Ehud shows that we, too, can acquire spiritual power if we subordinate the "unfortunate" to the "fortunate," so that both belong to the right side, "the armor of righteousness." All people have within them two parts – two hands, so to speak – and none of the saints can do without their "left hand": by it "the perfection of virtue is shown, where a man by skilful use can turn both hands into right hands" (*Conference of Abbot Theodore*, ch. 10).

A later medieval writer, Geoffrey of Monmouth (c.1100–55) may have used Eglon's death as a model for the death of Constantine, king of the Britons, in his *History of the Kings of Britain* (completed 1136). "A certain Pict that was Constantine's vassal came unto him, and feigning that he did desire to hold secret converse with him, when all had gone apart, slew him with a knife in a springwood thicket" (vi.5; see Fowler, *Bible in Early English Literature*, 1984, 202).

Like other figures in Judges, Ehud in the Middle Ages is a "type" or forerunner of Christ. A pictorial version of such typology is found in the *Mirror of Human Salvation*, from the early fourteenth century on. The (Latin) text was in four columns, at the head of each a miniature, the first depicting a New Testament event and the others its Old Testament prefigurations. Ehud appears alongside Samson and Benaiah (2 Sam 23:20), both killing lions. The key picture is Christ conquering the devil. Eglon, then, represents the devil. He is generally depicted as seated on his throne, as in a 1455 French exemplar (Hunterian Museum Library, Glasgow (MS 60, fol. 42r)).

The artist(s) in the Bruges studio who produced the miniature clearly had no interest in, or knowledge of, the text's details. The same seems true of a German *Mirror*, printed about 1481 (Peter Drach, Speyer). Here Ehud wields not a short sword but one longer than his leg, against not a standing but a seated king (PLATE 2.1a). The typological meaning of Ehud's deed thus appears to outweigh concern for the literal text. The seated Eglon and Ehud's long sword became conventional. In a fourteenth-century stained glass window in the French church of St Etienne, Mulhouse, Ehud again brandishes a substantial sword before an Eglon who, with crossed legs, is decidedly seated. Whether the scene conveyed a typological meaning is unclear, though likely.

Literal, however, is clearly the interpretive mode of a great thirteenth-century picture book (Pierpont Morgan Library, New York), with scenes from the Creation to David (Cockerell, *Old Testament Miniatures*); yet it, too, is free with the details (fol. 12r; PLATE 2.1b–c). Ehud plunges a dagger into the king's belly with his *right* hand, and intestines tumble out. But the belly is hardly fat, and the king slumps sideways in his throne as if seated all along. The escaping

---

PLATE 2.1   Ehud slays Eglon and escapes: (a) German woodcut, 1481; (b) and (c) Medieval French picture-book; (d) Goeree, 1700; (e) Miller's *Scripture History*, 1833; (f) Bawden, 1968. (See pp. 36, 42, 47, 52)

Ehud, emerging from an upper window, blows a horn held in his right hand. If he now clutches the bloody dagger which belongs in the belly, at least he uses the correct (left) hand. Whether those who perused the manuscript were bothered by these details, we know not.

Early Modern and Modern

The Protestant Reformation saw interest in Judges surge. The book spoke to burning issues of civil authority and the relationship between religion (Church) and State, issues that tore Europe apart during the sixteenth and seventeenth centuries. It was a book about war, the overthrow of enemies, and the divine calling of leaders.

Writing to instruct "some princes and their subjects" on the war with the Turks, Martin Luther (1483–1546) urges that a few people matter, though some will scoff at him for saying so. The "good that God did through Ehud" (and Gideon, Deborah, and Samson) shows that sometimes only one person makes all the difference (*On War against the Turks*, 1529 [192–3]). On the other hand, in an appeal *To the Assembly of the Common Peasantry, May 1525*, an anonymous "radical" is clear that the oppressive princes and clerics ("you werewolves, you band of Behemoths") are no different from the Moabites of Judges (ch. 4 [108–9]). To Anabaptist David Joris (1501/2–56), the struggles in Judges were spiritual wars. He urges his readers to listen to the Spirit, not flesh and blood; to not threaten, before overcoming, the enemy; to be nothing but prudent. Only when subordinate to the Spirit should they, like Ehud (in the company of Moses, Phinehas, Jael, David, and Christ himself), be ablaze with wrath (*Wonderful Working of God*, 1535 [115]).

That Ehud acted directly against a ruler interested many. An influential account of Judges was the Latin commentary (c.1561) by Oxford professor and Reformation theologian Peter Martyr Vermigli (1499–1562). Poet and politician John Milton (1608–74) appeals to Vermigli's discussion when arguing that Ehud's action provides scriptural authority for subjects sometimes needing to depose their rulers (*Tenure of Kings and Magistrates*, 1649, 27). Milton was not arguing in the abstract: he began this defense of regicide during Charles I's trial and published it soon after the king's execution. The Greeks and Romans, he says, held it not only lawful, but "a glorious and Heroic deed" to kill without trial an infamous tyrant. And "among the Jews this custom of tyrant-killing was not unusual": Eglon's death is an example. Opponents (Royalists and Presbyterians) claimed the case did not apply to Charles, since Eglon was a foreign enemy, and Ehud had God's special warrant. Milton responds that a ruler who overturns Law is no different from "an outlandish King" and, as a tyrant, has become an enemy. As for special warrant, the text makes no such claim. Rather, Ehud was raised to be a deliverer and acted against a tyrant on just principles, as circumstances dictated (*Tenure*, [212–15]). As he put it later, God did not instruct Ehud directly; rather, the Israelites cried to God: "and we too have cried; the Lord raised up a deliverer for them, and for us too" (*Defence of the People of England*, 1651, ch. 4 [399–402]).

One lesson for moderate Calvinist Joseph Hall (1574–1656), who for a time served the royal family, was that God's justice can use one sin (Moab's ambition) to punish another (Israel's idolatry), and God has no end of instruments of judgment (*Contemplations*, 1615 [ix.3, 107–8]). But this thought prompts a qualification regarding contemporary politics. (Hall is living in tumultuous times.) "Though Eglon were an usurper, yet had Ehud been a traitor if God had not sent him. It is only in the power of him that makes kings, when they are once settled, to depose them. It is no more possible for our modern butchers of princes, to show they are employed by God, than to escape the revenge of God, in offering to do this violence, not being employed." The contrast with Milton is palpable.

Hall and others of this period connect the story to ordinary people. Hall finds, for example, that a people's security causes their corruption. "Standing waters soon grow noisome." At war the Israelites scrupulously resisted idolatry; but "at peace with their enemies, they are at variance with God." We need to be vehement in our cries of repentance, which will be heard. For, he adds in allegorical vein, we too readily live "in bondage to these spiritual Moabites, our own corruptions." As for God's purposes, there is no limit to the means he may use, including enriching those he hates. By faith, God may encourage and enable the most improbable of his holy designs by using the unlikeliest means (i.e. "a man wanting of his right hand"). Hall echoes the ancient commentators on Eglon's rising: "This man was an idolater, a tyrant; yet what outward respects doth he give to the true God?" He warns, however, against trusting outward appearances: "external ceremonies of piety" may well be found with falsehood in religion, and these must be measured carefully as either shadows of truth or "the very body of hypocrisy." He finds Eglon's manner of death fitting: "This one hard and cold morsel, which he cannot digest, pays for all those gluttonous delicates, whereof he had formerly surfeited."

Finally, in an optimistic flourish, Hall praises Ehud for his calm and collected departure. Like Ehud, the person who would undertake "great enterprises" has need of wisdom and courage: "wisdom to contrive, and courage to execute; wisdom to guide his courage, and courage to second his wisdom: both which, if they meet with a good cause, cannot but succeed."

Eglon's rising to receive the "word of God" intrigues English Puritans. The heathen king's reverence provides Thomas Manton (1620–77) with a salutary example as he urges his listeners to guard the senses during devotions ("How may we cure distractions in holy duties?" 1661 [411]). Milton, less charitably, concedes with Hall that sometimes "certain temporary virtues (or at any rate, what look like virtues) are found in the wicked" and instances, among others, Eglon (*Christian Doctrine*, c.1658–60 [ii.1.21, 646]). Elsewhere he admits this enemy king, who arose when God's name was spoken, "did not despise the divine power"; yet Eglon was still an enemy and rightfully deposed. The comparison with Charles I is decidedly not to Charles's advantage (*Defence*, 1651, ch. 4). It is in the tenor of Manton, however, that William Gurnall (1617–79) in his hugely popular *Christian in Complete Armour* (1655–62) invokes the "awful carriage" of the heathen king. He is a supreme reproach against sermon-sleepers. At the word of God, the heathen Ehud arose, but "thou clappest down on thy seat to sleep. O how darest thou put such an affront upon the great God? How oft did you fall asleep at dinner, or telling your money? And is not the word of God worth more than these?" (ii.2 [124]). (Gurnall is also alive to life's little ironies: "Yea, the king will rise to hear this message that comes from the Lord, and so gives him a greater advantage to run him into the bowels" (ii.5 [250]).

Yet neither Manton nor Gurnall can quite match the exposition by Matthew Henry (1662–1714):

> Tho' a King, tho' a Heathen king; tho' Rich and Powerful; tho' now Tyrannizing over the People of God; tho' a fat unwieldy Man, that could not easily *rise*, nor *stand long*, tho' *in private*, and what he did not under Observation; yet, when he expected to receive Orders from Heaven, he *rose out of his seat*, whether it was *low* and *easy*, or whether it *high* and *stately*, he quitted it, and *stood up* when God was about to speak to him, thereby owning God his superiour.

For Henry the lesson is the same, however. Eglon "shames the irreverence of many who are called *Christians*" (*Exposition*, 1708). Nearly two centuries later, in fewer words, evangelist F. B. Meyer (1847–1929) repeats the point: Eglon's rising "was a mark of respect, the attitude of attention. It is with similar awe that we should ever wait for the revelation of the Divine will" (*Our Daily Homily*, I, 1898, [213]).

Henry, like Hall, attributes Eglon's "extreme fatness," which renders him vulnerable, to his "Luxury and Excess" – fitting, then, that his place of death be his summer parlour, "where he us'd to indulge himself in Ease and Luxury." The moral: "those that pamper the Body, do but prepare for their own Misery." Eglon's name signifies "*a Calf*" and "he fell like a *fatted Calf*, by the knife, an acceptable Sacrifice to Divine Justice." Mention of "*the coming out* of the *Dirt or Dung*," however, makes this proud tyrant's death "the more Ignominious and Shameful." He is left "wallowing in his own Blood and Excrements." Thus, says Henry, "does God *pour contempt upon Princes*."

Finding the door locked (3:24), the king's retainers decide he must be "covering his feet" and wait. Henry takes the phrase to mean the servants "concluded he was lain down to *Sleep*, had *cover'd his feet* upon his couch, and was gone to consult his Pillow about the Message he had receiv'd, and to *dream upon it*." But the Hebrew phrase is susceptible of a quite other meaning. As Symon Patrick (1626–1707), Bishop of Ely, explains: "They concluded he was easing Nature, as this Phrase is commonly understood here, and in 1 Sam. xxiv.3. for when they were about that Business, the long Garments which they wore in those Countries were so disposed, as to cover their Feet." Simon opts for the sleeping interpretation nonetheless. It is what they "were wont to do in those Countries in the Heat of the Day; (2 Sam iv.5.) and then lying down in their Cloaths, it was necessary to cover their Feet for Decency's Sake, to keep their Garments from slipping up, and exposing those Parts which should not be seen." This suits the story better, because "the other Business being soon dispatched, would not have occasioned their waiting so long" (*Commentary*, 1702). Other eighteenth-century commentators try to keep it simple: the attendants supposed that Eglon "had a mind to retire," "was either reposing or easing himself," or, more deftly, "had a mind to be private" (Laurence Clarke, *Compleat History*, 1737; Thomas Stackhouse, *New History*, 1742; S. Smith, *Compleat History*, 1752).

Between them, Patrick and Henry help give sleeping a long life. More than a century and half later the Rev. Ingram Cobbin, in his *Commentary on the Bible for Young and Old* (1876), mentions no alternative, though his explanation conveniently avoids also any mention of the unmentionable "parts." "[The servants] thought the king was asleep. 'He covereth his feet,' they said; for, as they wore slippers, when they went to sleep on a sofa, they dropped them, and wrapped them round in the tail of their long garment."

Younger readers usually learned only that the servants thought their lord was asleep or "lying down to rest" (*Young People's Illustrated Bible History*, 1872; Elsie E. Egermeier, *Bible Story Book*, 1922). The nice alternative was the king wanting to "be alone" (Henry Davenport Northrop, *Charming Bible Stories*, 1894), though the *Bible Story Library* (1956) is careful to define "alone" as meaning "alone with that man." Safer still, in J. W. Buel's *The Beautiful Story* (1887) the servants decide his majesty wanted "to prevent interruption while considering some weighty matter brought to his attention by the late messenger." More often young readers learned nothing about Ehud or the king. The story was simply omitted altogether.

In printed Bible illustration from the end of the fifteenth century on, as in free-standing art, Ehud is found infrequently and certainly with no hint of scatalogical interest. Medieval illustrators' indifference to the story's details is apparent also in early modern depictions well into the eighteenth century, despite the attention those details were receiving from the textual commentators. Where Ehud is pictured at all, reference is sparse to his corpulence, his rising to receive the message, the disappearing dagger, and the scatalogical interpretation.

The scene is absent from many of the earliest illustrated printed Bibles, beginning with the pioneering Cologne Bible (Quentel, c.1478) and the early Luther Bibles (e.g. Zetzner's famous "Merian Bible," Strassburg, 1630). But it does appear in sixteenth-century Bibles. A Latin Bible published by Tornaesius (J. de Tournes) in Lyons in 1556 has a column-width woodcut depicting the aftermath of Eglon's death. He lies on his back on the floor front left while Ehud escapes through a door front right. The king is not noticeably fat, and a large hilt protrudes from his stomach, from which entrails spill onto the floor (cf. the Pierpont Morgan MS, above). The Renaissance architecture which frames the scene, however, does convey a sense of space and airiness appropriate perhaps for a "summer parlour."

While depiction of Ehud is also sparse in the seventeenth century, the scene is not uncommon in the superb Dutch engravings of the early eighteenth century. The "Great Bible" (*Historie*, 1700) published by Pieter Mortier (1661–1711) includes a rendition by Jan Goeree (1670–1731) in which a wall divides the picture, so that we see both inside and outside the chamber (as often in modern cinematography). The contrasting scenes express Ehud's subterfuge. Inside, Ehud plunges a dagger into the standing king's (hardly corpulent) belly, while outside, two attendants wait, one leaning against the wall, head turned as if perhaps he had heard a noise, or maybe just to glance past his companion, who is looking away, at other attendants further off. A dog sits patiently by, head also turned away, apparently undisturbed by the violence taking place through the wall (PLATE 2.1d, p. 37).

Gerard Hoet (1648–1733), in Pierre de Hondt's *Figures de la Bible* (1728), depicts instead the murder's aftermath. A crowd of courtiers throngs into the spacious room in consternation, with wild gestures and heads turning. Eglon is slumped forward on the floor, a dagger hilt protruding from his plump body to signal the deed (despite the text), and on the floor about him telltale stains. In the distance, through the balcony balustrade, we glimpse a diminutive Ehud escaping. As often in Hoet's work, a dog joins in the uproar.

Ehud's deception regularly elicits defense. John Milton examines whether it is in breach of the ninth commandment, which he expounds as forbidding falsehood injurious to one's neighbor, "one with whom we are at peace, and whose lawful society we enjoy." Clearly Eglon, as an enemy, is excluded from the law's purview, and in any case Ehud acted upon divine prompting (*Christian Doctrine*, c.1658–60 [ii.13.13, 758–64]).

Textual ambiguities also alleviate the charge. Symon Patrick observes of Ehud's announcement of a message from God that the speech was true but not in the sense Eglon understood, that Ehud "had met with some Divine apparition in the way, or been at some oracle." For Ehud does not say he has a message from Jehovah ("the Lord"), the God of Israel, but from Elohim ("God") which was also a common name for all gods ("gods")." Patrick (followed by Henry) indicates why Eglon might have readily believed Ehud bore a secret oracle. The key is verse 19: "But he himself turned again from the quarries that were by Gilgal, and said, I have a secret errand unto thee, O king" (KJV). "Quarries" may be better translated, as in the Septuagint and the Vulgate (and KJV margin), as "graven images," set up, the commentators suppose, by the Moabites. Certainly Gilgal was famous for God's presence. Perhaps, argues Henry, Ehud went as far as the images before returning in order that, "telling from what place he return'd, the king of *Moab* might be the more apt to believe he had a message from God." In the event, that message was a dagger "deliver'd, not to *his Ear*, but immediately, and literally to *his Heart*." The text says "belly," but "heart" – as in Josephus – lends itself better to Henry's explanation of the rhetoric! It may also help an English reader to know that "errand" and "message" are both translations of Hebrew *dabar*, "word" or "thing."

This reading is neatly encapsulated in Dr Northrop's *Charming Bible Stories* (1894): Ehud "went back to Gilgal, to the place where the men of Moab kept the images of their gods, as though he would have worshiped there. . . . Ehud said, I have a secret errand to thee, O king, making as though he had a message to deliver him from the gods." (By contrast, the Rev. Jesse Lyman Hurlbut's ubiquitous *Story of the Bible for Young and Old* [1904] omits the quarries/ graven images altogether and has Ehud announce to Eglon, "I have a message from the Lord to you.") More than a century later, J. Clinton McCann summarizes: "what Ehud may have seen as he crossed the Jordan were images of Chemosh, the Moabite god. Since Eglon would have known Ehud had crossed the Jordan to deliver the tribute, Eglon may even have been expecting from Ehud a favorable word from Eglon's own god, Chemosh. In any case, he is tricked" (*Judges*, 2002).

But perhaps the great Methodist preacher and writer, Adam Clarke (1762–1832), should be allowed the last word on this topic:

> *I have a message from God unto thee* is a popular text: many are fond of preaching from it. Now as no man should ever depart from the literal meaning of Scripture in his preaching, we may at once see the absurdity of taking such a text as

this; for such preachers, to be consistent, should carry a *two-edged dagger* of a *cubit length on their right thigh,* and be ready to *thrust it into the bowels of all those they address!* This is certainly the *literal meaning* of the passage, and that it has *no other meaning* is an incontrovertible truth. (*Commentary,* 1833).

Despite misgivings, Ehud has generally been received since the Reformation as an exemplar of faithful service to God. His story culminates with him blowing the trumpet on Mount Ephraim and gathering Israel to battle. Evangelist Jonathan Edwards (1703–58) finds here a scriptural model as he demands unwavering support for the New England revival in 1742. It is a most dangerous thing, he warns, to be slow and backward in honoring God in any great work, just as the refusal of soldiers in an army to follow the general into battle merits severe punishment (*Present Revival of Religion,* 1742 [348]).

Yet some of Edwards's contemporaries caustically voice another view of Ehud. "How many crimes have been committed in the name of the Lord!" exclaims French philosopher Voltaire (1694–1778), sarcastically sketching the story of this "Jewish saint." "It is his example," he concludes, "which, among Christians, has been used so often as an excuse to betray, to unseat, and to massacre so many sovereigns" (*Sermon of the Fifty,* 1749 [16]). Elsewhere he elaborates, listing assassinations over the centuries, including that of Julius Caesar "under the same pretext as Ehud, namely liberty." He targets Milton for writing an entire book justifying the "judicial assassination" of Charles I (see above): consider it, he adds, "the dictionary of assassinations." At least, with Ehud and regicide, here was one argument against the Bible which could hardly earn him hostility from the court of France! Still, he covers himself by ironically reasserting convoluted orthodox arguments: God does not explicitly order Ehud to bury his poignard in his king's belly; yet Ehud was rewarded by being made a judge; but this example is not conclusive, since a particular decision of God cannot take precedence over human laws deriving from God himself. That is, "Ehud was inspired by the Lord, and [the regicide] monk Jacques Clément, was inspired only by fanatical rage" (*Bible enfin expliquée,* 1776 [134]; in 1589 the Dominican mortally stabbed the protestant king, Henri III, while alone with him in his chamber on the pretext of delivering a letter).

The Deists were not alone in castigating Ehud for regicide. Earlier in Scotland, Sir George Mackenzie (1636–91), the Lord Advocate, won the title of "bluidy Mackenzie" for persecuting Covenanters bound by oath to establish Presbyterianism in Scotland. Mackenzie, on the contrary, held the divine right of kings to be a cornerstone of stability for Church and State. In support of Charles II, and imposing episcopacy, he upbraids his opponents: "All murders become sacrifices by the example of Phineas and Ehud; all rapines are hallowed by the Israelites borrowing the ear-rings of the Egyptians, and rebellions have a hundred forced texts of Scripture brought to patronize them" (in Moffatt, *Bible in Scots Literature*, c.1923, 154–5).

Voltaire also reserves a place for Ehud in his *Philosophical Dictionary* (1764 [267–8]) under the entry for "Fanaticism." "Fanaticism is to superstition what delirium is to fever and rage to anger. The man visited by ecstasies and visions, who takes dreams for realities and his fancies for prophecies, is an enthusiast; the man who supports his madness with murder is a fanatic. . . ." The only remedy for this malady is the philosophic spirit. Religion, "far from being healthy food for infected brains, turns to poison in them." Ehud's example is forever in the minds of such "miserable men" – along with Judith, who slew Holofernes (Judith 13:10), and Samuel, who chopped up King Agag (1 Sam 15:33). "They cannot see that these examples which were respectable in antiquity are abominable in the present; they borrow their frenzies from the very religion that condemns them."

Given such attacks, we appreciate why educator Mrs Trimmer (1741–1810) reassures her youthful readers of the propriety of Ehud's deed yet betrays some anxiety. "There is an appearance of great treachery in Ehud's proceedings in respect to the king of Moab, which nothing could justify, but his having received a command from God to destroy Eglon, in order to set Israel free; therefore, his example is not to be imitated in this particular" (*Sacred History*, 1783 [xlix, 212]). She is not only at odds with skeptical Voltaire, but even more so with Puritan Milton, who took Ehud's action to justify regicide precisely without God's direct command.

Mrs Trimmer, however, has other advice besides not to kill kings. For example, God may choose "a weak instrument in order to shew his own Almighty power." Like Joseph Hall, whom she much admired, and Matthew Henry, whose commentary she was probably using, she assumes (no doubt as a right-hander herself) that Ehud "was no expert warrior till strengthened of God." Henry notes that the Greek version calls him ambidextrous, but is certain the Hebrew, "*Shut of his Right Hand*," means left-handed, and so "*less fit* for war, because he must needs handle his Sword but awkwardly" (*Exposition*, 1708). However, to Esther Hewlett (1786–1851), also writing for youth, left-handed (because ambidextrous) was an advantage: Ehud "could use either hand equally well, and thus strike a blow at unawares" (*Scripture History*, 1828, 16). Her view, too, is widely shared.

Trimmer returns to another long-standing topic when she insists that Eglon's "exemplary punishment" shows him guilty of "presumptuous sin." In Henry's words, he was not murdered or assassinated, but put to death by the agent of divine justice "as an implacable Enemy" to God and Israel. For Trimmer, God's use of the Moabites was but a temporary expedient which, having aroused the Israelites to faith, exposed the Moabites once more to the curse against idolatry and hence God's wrath. She is, of course, trying to deal with the problem of theodicy (God's justice) in this and other stories in Judges where God summons "enemies" to oppress the Israelites and then has them slaughtered, apparently for doing their job (xlix, 213). Hewlett, who justifies Ehud's "seeming treachery" as at God's direct commission, takes a different tack when she explains that "Jehovah himself being king in Israel, Eglon had as it were usurped His throne, and justly deserved the punishment of death which Ehud was appointed to execute." She thus solves the problem of theodicy by forgetting what the problem was: Eglon seized the throne precisely by divine direction. No matter. As with Hall, Henry, Trimmer, and other faithful users of this text, the final point is clear: "but this act, and similar ones, form no precedents for imitation" (p. 17). Or, as Henry put it more passionately: "No such commissions are now given, and to pretend to them is to Blaspheme God, and make him Patronize the worst of Villanies."

For many, theodicy disappears into a question of human morality. The biblical character, chosen by God to be a "deliverer," is assumed to be a moral exemplar. The primary problem here is Ehud's "treachery." The author of *Sunny Sabbaths or Pleasant Pages for Happy Homes* (c.1860) draws on familiar arguments. Although a tyrant's assassination "was accounted meritorious by the judgment of antiquity," wholly to approve Ehud's act is "impossible." Fraud and falsehood vitiate any action, and we need not believe God commanded Ehud. "While we admire the patriot therefore, we must condemn the assassin, and lament that he compassed his design to liberate his country by dark and treacherous means." Here are elements of Milton's argument about Antiquity's approbation and lack of a direct command by God, but now put to contrary use. The author finally argues, as is common in this period and later, from cultural or historical relativity: "At the same time it would be unjust to judge his conduct by the higher intelligence and morality of Christian times. It was a barbarous age, and therefore was stained by barbarous deeds."

As often as not, the deficient ancient culture is classed as "Oriental" and said to be unchanging from ancient until modern times. John Kitto's statement is classic (*Bible History*, 1841 [197–8]): Ehud's deed was a murder, albeit of a public enemy, and its only excuse "the fact that the notions of the East have always been, and are now, far more lax on this point than those which Christian civilization has produced in Europe." All means of getting rid of such an enemy are just and proper, "and it is by Oriental notions rather than by our own that the act of Ehud must, to a certain extent, be judged." In other words, the charitable judgment of Ehud is at the "Orient's" expense.

The "Orient" comes into view, too, in nineteenth-century illustrations of the story. In contrast to the neoclassical Ehuds and Eglons of earlier periods, the figures and settings increasingly reflect what was being reported by travelers of "everyday life" in the Ottoman Empire or as far afield as India, as well as the widely celebrated findings of archaeologists in Egypt and Mesopotamia.

Ebenezer Miller's *Scripture History* (1833), another of this popular genre for young readers, presents a standing, portly Eglon replete with turban, like some Turkish pasha or Indian prince (PLATE 2.1e, p. 37). An illustration in *Cassell's Illustrated Family Bible* (c.1870) shows Ehud presenting his gifts before an enthroned Eglon who looks like an Assyrian king from one of the reliefs unearthed in Austin Layard's Nineveh excavations not long since. The palace surroundings, like many a biblical scene of the later nineteenth century, blends Assyria and Babylon with ancient Egypt (PLATE 2.2a). The Ehud of Ford Madox Brown (1821–93), stylized in the manner of the English nineteenth-century pre-Raphaelite school, is gesturing with his right hand to heaven while grasping a curved dagger strapped to his right thigh. Eglon is following the pointing finger. Perhaps he is about to rise, boosting himself behind with his left arm and grasping the chair arm with his right. A wine glass falls from a small table, and a pitcher topples, perhaps prefiguring the king's imminent fall. The flowing robes conjure up the romantic world of the Bedouin, while the background is redolent with the ancient Orient of the archaeologists. The picture was widely reproduced (PLATE 2.2b). The present-day world of the Levant (Syria and Palestine) is even more evident in the fallen Eglon of James Tissot (1836–1902), whose biblical paintings, though seldom this one, were often to be seen in books on the Bible in the early twentieth century (*Old Testament*, II, 1904). For the most part, series of biblical illustrations in the nineteenth and early twentieth centuries, including the most popular (Schnorr von Carolsfeld and Doré), lacked the episode.

Concern to interpret the Bible through new evidence of the modern and ancient Orient was in part produced by a new sense of "history." Readers from the eighteenth-century "Enlightenment" increasingly realized that the familiar stories came from unfamiliar times and places. Typical of the new "historical criticism," Thomas E. Miller (*Portraits*, 1922, 33–44) tries to avoid the problems of divine justice and human morality by taking historical relativity even further than Kitto does. Although the "compiler" of Judges writes of the Israelites crying to God who raises up a deliverer, such "primitive" language does not mean that Ehud was divinely inspired. We must distinguish between what the text says happened and what actually happened. Likewise with God's strengthening of Eglon against Israel, suggesting "God was the prime mover toward the invasion." In neither case should we attribute direct responsibility to God. Ehud perhaps believed himself under God's guidance, just as Abraham did when called to sacrifice his son Isaac. But God would certainly make no

PLATE 2.2 Ehud before Eglon: (a) Cassell's *Family Bible*, c.1870; (b) Madox Brown, c.1860. (See p. 47)

such demand of an earthly father. "And it is equally certain that God would not sanction, far less inspire, the acts of treachery and regicide associated with the name of Ehud."

Here, as often in modern biblical criticism, a "believer" reads the text in terms of a given theology of God's nature, at the same time recognizing the text to be a human production subject to the constraints of its social, cultural, and historical context. Important for Miller is not what the story says happened but some historical reality lying behind it. Typically, also, Miller verifies the story by appealing to its ancient historical context while conveying his own superior vantage point. "Did his own people justify the deed of Ehud? We need not be surprised if they did. We must remember we are dealing with a period 1200 years before the Christian era . . . and while we cannot, on moral grounds, justify the act of Ehud, neither can we apply the standards of the present day to that far-distant time. It was a rough and barbarous age." *Portraits* appeared four years after a war that saw probably the greatest slaughter then known in history.

For professional readers of Judges in the twentieth century the starting point in English was often *Judges*, by George F. Moore (1851–1931), in the International Critical Commentary (ICC) series. These volumes provided detailed and technical discussions which drew heavily on German historical-critical scholarship concerned with sources and editing ("redaction"), philology (grammar and word meanings), geography and social customs, and historical reliability. Moral and theological issues took a back seat.

Moore sees Judges as comprised of old folk materials handed down at the Gilgal sanctuary and reshaped by an author promoting the theological program of Deuteronomy, early in the sixth century. Moore's philological notes include the difficult verses 3:22 and 23, which contain two words of uncertain meaning, found only here. He argues for emending verse 22 (cf. Vulgate and Targum) to read "and the dirt [i.e. feces] came out" from the anus, "the usual consequence of such a wound in the abdomen." This is a long-standing solution. (One commentary explains that not only was "dirt" from the "usual place" a common consequence of violent death, but "besides, there were, no doubt, violent convulsions raised in his bowels by this sudden strike" (*Holy Bible*, Newcastle upon Tyne, 1788).) On the servants' reluctance of the servants to intrude ("he is relieving himself") he comments: "the sense of decency in such matters is very highly developed among Orientals, as it was in general in the civilized peoples of antiquity." He provides, too, an elaborate account of how locks are commonly constructed in the "East"; no doubt this was the very same kind of lock.

On historical reliability, Moore notes that Eglon's taking the "city of palms" or Jericho (Judg 3:13; cf. Deut 34:3) causes difficulty: Joshua totally destroys

Jericho (Josh 6:21–6), and it is only rebuilt in Ahab's reign (1 Kgs 16:34). Nor do the directions Ehud took (Judg 3:18–19, 26) fit with Jericho: from there Gilgal is not on the way to Mt Ephraim but, exactly the opposite, to the Jordan fords. Perhaps, then, Ehud's exploit was not originally in Jericho, as commonly thought, but rather east of the Jordan. Moore also finds the Jordan slaughter "not free from derangement and repetition." "Source criticism" sought linear narrative and viewed disjunction or repetition as suspect. So here the "problems" are "generally attributed to the interference of the editor, but may arise from the combination of two accounts."

Finally we come to the hero's deception. Moore notes the arguments for Ehud using an intentionally ambiguous phrase to address Eglon (cf. above), but doubts the author had this "ingenious equivocation" in mind or "would have thought it worth while to protect, by so slender a pretext, Ehud's reputation for veracity. He tells of it as a clever and successful ruse, with no more reflexion on its morality than on that of the assassination itself." In short, Moore thinks that the traditional apologists for the Bible have been wasting their time expounding on the difficulties of the "moral aspects" of Ehud's deed – "on which the narrator in Jud. 3 certainly wasted no reflections."

For the later twentieth century the Anchor Bible series replaced the ICC. In *Judges* (1975) Robert G. Boling (d. 1995) is especially interested in the social background and history of the period. Less convinced than Moore that Ehud's story is a complex composite, he notes how its "wealth of detail and obvious narrative humor" contrast stylistically with the larger story of Judges. This is because it has been incorporated from an Israelite "saga" without revision. It sets up a contrast between Ehud, a "loner," and Othniel's "administration" at the outset of the period. He also disagrees with Moore on the notorious verses 22–3, emending the text, but differently. He claims support from the Septuagint and compares an ancient Akkadian word for "hole" that "may well" refer to some architectural feature. "In any case, there is no warrant for taking the word as referring to the vent of the human body." On historical reliability, Boling cites late thirteenth- and early twelfth-century archaeological and literary sources as supporting a geographical expansion of the Israelite tribes in the early Judges period. He is less sure of Ehud's larger role. The narrator's main interest is the "single-handed diplomatic treachery" which gained Ehud victory and secured peace. That Ehud is called a "savior" of Israel and one who "judged" Moab raises an issue with which the early narrator "and his hearers" also wrestled: "What had it meant to be 'Israel' in that early period?" And he observes, "there is no mention of the Yahweh spirit in connection with Ehud."

This observation is also telling for Italian scholar J. Alberto Soggin in another standard scholarly commentary (*Judges*, 1981, in The Old Testament

Library series). He concludes that "there is no real political or theological inter-est in the ancient [original] narrative." Ehud simply represents the people in a "secular" story which is neither historical narrative nor pure legend. A "Deuteronomistic" editor introduces theological interests with the idea of Ehud as "judge" and the war as "holy war," making the story part of the regular cycle in Judges, an action whereby God again frees "his unfaithful but penitent people." Soggin, like Moore, finds the reference to Jericho ("the city of palms") historically improbable. The real question is whether Eglon's palace was east or west of the Jordan, a matter he discusses at length. As for the slaying, he notes both the difficulty in the Hebrew and the ancient witness (Vulgate and Targum) to the meaning, "So the excrement came out of the body."

Soggin sees this "scatalogical theme" as part of the narrative's "somewhat coarse" humor. The name Eglon, "little calf," is probably intended as a carica-ture (but with no cultic connotation), and Ehud is from "majesty," used essen-tially of God; hence the *dramatis personae* are a fat man with a ridiculous name and a hero, maimed but no less capable for that, with a name alluding to God. Eglon's being fat connotes perhaps his "lack of mobility, his good-natured and therefore unsuspicious character, his ridiculous aspect." Distancing himself a little from this brand of humor, he adds: "Humour, too, differs from people to people and from age to age." Like most Western commentators, however, Soggin does not consider whether "fat" might be a respected mark of opulence befitting a king, as in many societies. (The Septuagint calls him "exceedingly handsome.")

Robert Alter's book, *The Art of Biblical Narrative* (1981), proved a turning point in biblical criticism. His literary-critical "close readings," especially of Genesis and Samuel, helped shift interest from historical origins to how bibli-cal narrators told their stories and what these meant in their "final form." He had little to say about Judges, except for Ehud's tale. To the reader of Matthew Henry (see above), some comments come as no surprise. Eglon's name, sug-gesting "calf," informs the writer's imagination: "The ruler of the occupying Moabite power turns out to be a fatted calf readied for slaughter." And Alter, like Soggin, finds Eglon's fat to be both token of his "physical ponderousness, his vulnerability to Ehud's sudden blade," and emblem of "his regal stupidity." Yet Henry might have balked at Alter's further suggestion, more characteristic of a post-Freudian age, that Eglon's fat "may also hint at a kind of grotesque feminization of the Moabite leader: Ehud 'comes to' the king, an idiom also used for sexual entry, and there is something hideously sexual about the description of the dagger-thrust" (p. 39). Alter's reading, particular of the story's humor, has been often cited since.

Writing for pastors and laypeople in the Interpretation series (*Judges*, 2002), Clinton McCann calls the story "virtually slapstick comedy." He adopts a suggestion (not well founded) that Eglon's name itself connotes "fat," producing a term like today's "fat cat." So the story is a contest between Eglon, the royal "fat cat" getting rich off the Israelites, and Ehud, the "lone ranger" – from the Israelite perspective, a comedy. "It has a happy ending, the good guys win, and it is funny." McCann, following Alter, elaborates on the text's double meanings and sees Ehud's tricky speech as characteristic of a folklore trickster. He too sees poetic justice in the one who exacted tribute from Israel ending up "slaughtered as if he were Israel's sacrificial offering to God." And, like Soggin, he points his reader to the "bathroom humor": "In contemporary terms, figuratively and literally, Ehud beats the crap out of Eglon." Finally, McCann offers a theological message, familiar but with a twist. That God uses a "trickster" like Ehud as an instrument of divine "restorative justice" is "instructive – indeed, one might even call it *incarnational.*" God uses whomever is available, seldom exemplary "instruments," including Jacob and "other murderers" like Moses, David, and Paul.

Among recent Bible illustrators of the Bible, Ehud again finds little favor. As in earlier centuries, however, the story occasionally appears. For *The Oxford Illustrated Old Testament* (1968), Edward Bawden's starkly drawn figures have often a comic touch. Eglon, risen and weighty, receives a left-handed thrust to the belly while gazing heavenwards. His wide-open eye nicely suggests the surprise he got, not from above but below (PLATE 2.1f, p. 37).

Again the Israelites do evil in the sight of the Lord; this time they are sold into the hand of Jabin, king of Hazor (Asor), whose general is Sisera (Sisara). With his 900 chariots of iron Jabin oppresses Israel for 20 years. People would come for judgment to Deborah (Debbora), a prophetess and wife of Lappidoth, under her palm in the hill country of Ephraim. Deborah summons Barak (Barac) to bring 10,000 warriors to fight Sisera by the Wadi Kishon. Barak demurs unless Deborah accompanies him. She agrees but warns that the enemy general will fall into "the hand of a woman." Faced with Barak's successful onslaught, Sisera escapes on foot to the tent of Jael (Jahel), wife of Heber the Kenite (Habar the Cinite), who was at peace with Jabin. She invites him in, covers him with a rug, and gives him milk to drink; he instructs her to stand guard. Instead, when he is asleep, she takes a hammer and drives a tent-peg through his head. Barak arrives to find him dead.

Deborah and Barak then celebrate the victory in song. The poem tells of God's triumphant march, Deborah arising as a "mother in Israel," the tribes gathering (but some absent), and Sisera's army destroyed, swept away by the torrent Kishon. Absent Meroz is cursed, but Jael is praised as most blessed of women, and her deed detailed. In contrast, Sisera's mother is depicted await-ing her son's return, trusting that he is late only because he is dividing the spoils of victory.

From earliest times, readers have taken a keen interest in the gender roles of the characters. Deborah takes precedence as leader over the little-admired Barak, though that leadership is often thought to need explanation. For the rabbis she is sometimes seen as a purveyor of Torah, other times as too proud in singing of herself. Whether she is a suitable model for women is a persistent question in Christian interpretation. Some see her as an exception to the rule for properly submissive women; others elevate her strength on its own terms, or as a model of motherly virtue, or as better constrained by marriage, as in Peter Martyr Vermigli's letter to the new Queen Elizabeth I advising her to "join [herself] to some godly Barak."

If Deborah presents a problem, Jael intensifies it, sometimes adulated as a type of Christ, the Church, or Mary, sometimes demonized as the epitome of deceit and even lust. Patriotic or self-serving, whether directed by God or not, it is widely agreed that she should not be imitated. Her violation of "Eastern" hospitality is an increasing concern from the eighteenth century on, as readers grow more conscious of different social and historical settings. But also expressed, from the nineteenth century, is awareness that her action perhaps protects her or others from the rape that Sisera's mother assumes is the due right of the battle's victors.

Historical issues have bothered recent interpreters, who have debated whether Deborah's song in chapter 5 (often regarded as very early) is a more or less accurate depiction than the prose of chapter 4.

Ancient and Medieval

Although rabbinic texts frequently mention Deborah and Barak as judges together (e.g. *Midrash Ruth Rabbah*), Deborah's greater authority is widely acknowledged. *Midrash Genesis Rabbah* (40:4) says that Barak surrendered his principal position when declaring he would fight Sisera only if she accompa-nied him. Hence Judg 5:1 makes Deborah the "primary" voice: "Then sang Deborah, and Barak. . . ." Jewish historian Josephus (c.37–c.100 CE) has Deborah reply to Barak, "You surrendered to a woman a rank God gave you; I do not decline it!" (*Antiquities*, v.203–4 (5.3)). And it is she who saves the day. The Bible has Deborah's command, "Up! For this is the day . . . ," follow directly upon the listing of Sisera's forces. Josephus amplifies: dismayed at the enemy host, the Israelites and Barak decided to retreat, but Deborah stopped them and ordered them to fight.

She is called "woman," or "wife of," Lappidoth ("flames"). God raised Deborah to prominence long before Sisera, it is said, because she devoted herself to keeping the sanctuary bright with fire. She urged her husband, thought by some to be Barak, to carry candles there (hence the name Lappidoth), and she herself made the candles with extra thick wicks. So God distinguished her as a prophet and judge, causing her light to shine throughout the land (*B. Talmud Megillah*, 14a; cf. *Seder Eliahu Rabbah*, 10:48–9). If Barak was Deborah's husband, which not all are agreed, why did she have to send for him? That is, why did they live apart, she in Ephraim, he in Kedesh in Naphtali? Medieval scholar David Kimchi (c.1160–1235) answers in his commentary that Deborah followed the pattern of Moses, who separated from his wife when he became a prophet.

Devoted to sanctuary lighting, she was also, some argued, a devotee of Torah study, an ascetic for the Law. Rashi (1040–1105), famous for his commentaries, interprets her line "Lord, when you went forth out of Seir" (5:4) as referring to the giving of the Torah, by alluding to Deut 33:2, in Moses' blessing of Israel: "The Lord came from Sinai, and rose from Seir unto them." Deborah is saying, Rashi explains, that Torah "is detrimental to forsake and rewarding to cling to," for amidst awe and might it was given from Sinai and Seir; accordingly Israel was either delivered into the hands of adversaries or saved, depending on whether they forsook or pursued Torah. This explanation appears earlier in the *Targum Jonathan* to 5:4. The Targum also has Deborah say (5:9) that she was sent to praise those teachers of Israel who, despite the affliction, did not cease from studying the Law, teaching the people its words, and giving thanks before God.

Not surprisingly, Deborah is sometimes compared with Moses, both of whom celebrated in song God's deliverance of Israel from oppression (e.g. *Mekilta deRabbi Ishmael*, Shirata 1, on Exod 15:1). Indeed, according to *Midrash Song of Songs Rabbah* (4:3), the song itself had the power to wipe Israel's slate clean. Judg 4:1 reports that the Israelites *again* did evil in God's sight, but after the song, in Judg 6:1, we read simply that they did evil. Every word (or missing word) counts. "Were they now doing it for the first time? The truth is that the song had wiped out all that went before."

Yet some were also anxious about a woman in authority over Israel. *B. Talmud Megillah* (14b) says that "haughtiness does not befit women." Deborah, like Huldah, proved unduly proud. She summoned Barak when herself she should have gone to him, and Huldah spoke of the king as the "man" instead of the "king." Hence they both have "ugly" names – Deborah, meaning "hornet" (bee) and Huldah "weasel." She spoke so much of herself in her song, it is claimed, that the spirit of prophecy departed from her for a while during its composition (*B. Talmud Pesahim*, 66b; *Zohar*, 4:196). Lest Deborah be a precedent for other women being leaders, such texts are quick to assert that the exception proves the rule. Women should normally be subservient. This position was not left unchallenged, however. "In regards to her deeds, I call heaven and earth to witness that whether it be a heathen or a Jew, whether it be a man or a woman, a manservant or a maidservant, the holy spirit will suffuse each of them in keeping with the deeds he or she performs" (*Midrash Eliahu Rabbah*, 10).

The Canaanite general Sisera was playfully represented as a tyrant of Goliath proportions, making his defeat so much more remarkable. By age 30, he had conquered the world; at his voice, walls fell down; his body was vast beyond description; if he bathed in the river, enough fish were caught in his beard to feed a multitude; and 900 horses were needed to draw his chariot (Ginzberg, iv.35). He was thus to be compared with another young conqueror, Alexander the Great, and with Joshua's whole host at Jericho. But others saw him as a blasphemer of God and an enemy of Judaism, recalling Antiochus Epiphanes IV, the Seleucid tyrant responsible for the "abomination of desecration" in 167 BCE.

Sisera abused and reviled the Israelites while oppressing them (*Midrash Numbers Rabbah*, 10:2), so deserved an ignominious death at the hand of a woman, Jael. As in the case of the trickster Ehud, rabbinic tradition inclines favorably towards Jael's actions, despite their transgressing customary rules. Since Jael is blessed "above all women . . . most blessed of women in tents" (5:24), *B. Talmud Nazir* (23b) uses her murder of Sisera to argue that well-intended transgressions are as good as obedient actions with ulterior motives. Taking "women in tents" to refer to Israel's ancestral mothers, this text views Jael as blessed even as Sarah, Rebecca, Rachel, and Leah were. Such praise is all the more remarkable given Rabbi Johanan's claim, in this same discussion, that Sisera had intercourse with her seven times before she killed him. But did she derive pleasure from this? No, for "the favours of the wicked are evil to the righteous" (cf. *Midrash ha-Gadol*, 1:336 (Ginzberg, VI, 198 n. 85): she killed him when, drunk, he asked her to submit to his passion).

Some have wondered at Jael's seductive powers, elaborating on her beautiful appearance, dress, and even tent decor (Ginzberg, VI, 198 n. 85). The first-century (CE) historian known as Pseudo-Philo (*Antiquities*, 31:3) has her scattering roses on the bed prepared for Sisera, upon seeing which the general decides that if saved he will go to his mother and marry Jael. Others find her attraction elsewhere. After all, the biblical text makes no mention of her appearance: she simply speaks to Sisera, and he responds. Seeing this, *B. Talmud Megillah* (15a) suggests she inspired lust by her voice. Another tradition suggests she gave him milk from her own breast (*Rimze Haftarot*, quoting a haggadah; see Ginzberg, VI, 198 n. 85).

Early Christian interpretation produces a different Jael, valued as a type or forerunner of Christ or the Church. In the third century anti-Marcionite work "The Harmony of the Fathers," the woman's victory with a wooden weapon anticipates Christ's victory over death on the cross: "Suddenly renegade, a woman's hand—/ Jael's—with wooden weapon vanquished quite, / For token of Christ's victory (*Reply to Marcion*, iii). For Ambrose (c.339–97), bishop of Milan, Jael prefigures rather the Church (the bride of Christ). He spells out details while expounding Deborah's virtues in his *Treatise Concerning Widows* (viii). Like Jael, the Gentile Church, guided by prophecy, gains the final victory over the enemy. As with the typology of Gideon's fleece (see the chapter on Gideon), this one incorporates anti-Jewish polemic. The victory, says Ambrose, is conceded by the Jews who failed to follow up, "by the virtue of faith," the enemy they initially put to flight.

Ambrose reminds his readers that, as history, Judges 4–5 tells of war and a woman (primarily Deborah) who is a model for other women, but, as a "mystery," the story is about "the battle of faith and the victory of the Church." The Church does not overcome "the high places of spiritual wickedness" with worldly weapons but with spiritual arms. Thus Sisera's thirst being quenched with a bowl of milk means he was overcome by wisdom, for "what is health-ful for us as food is deadly and weakening to the power of the enemy."

Allegorical and typological interpretations are developed by Jerome, Isadore of Seville, and the Venerable Bede, among others. Sisera comes to represent Satan in the spiritual battle of good versus evil. And Barak's reluctance to go to war without Deborah foreshadows Israel's inability to confront and over-come Satan, thus anticipating the need for ultimate deliverance by the cross of Christ. In the medieval *Speculum Humanae Salvationis* ("Mirror of Human Salvation") we find Jael, who overcame the enemy general Sisera, prefiguring Mary, who "conquered our enemy the Devil." Associates of Jael are Judith, who decapitated the enemy general Holofernes, and Queen Tomyris, who decapi-tated King Cyrus (see Herodotus, I.201–16).

For Ambrose, the "mystery" of Judges 4–5 concerns not only theology, "the battle of faith and the Church's victory," but also practical matters, for he is using the story to enlist women as church leaders. A few other early Christian interpreters admit, albeit reluctantly, that Deborah's political and military lead-ership was divinely sanctioned: "it was the Spirit of God who used her as His agent, for she was also a prophetess, although her prophecy is so obscure that we could not demonstrate, without a long discussion, that it was uttered concerning Christ" (Augustine, *City of God*, 18.15; cf. Cyril of Jerusalem, *Catechetical Lectures*, 16.28). For Ambrose, however, Deborah's leadership was no exception to any rule in ancient Israel. He did not doubt that there were many other women of similar virtue. Indeed, she was not merely on a par with the other judges, but superior to most, for no fault was found in her career, whereas "most of the judges were causes of no small sins to the people." He thinks her story has been told so "that women should not be restrained from deeds of valour by the weakness of their sex. A widow, she governs the people; a widow, she leads armies; a widow, she chooses generals; a widow, she determines wars and orders triumphs. So, then, it is not nature which is answerable for the fault or which is liable to weakness. It is not sex, but valour which makes strong." Concludes the preacher, "You, then, who are women have no excuse because of your nature" (*Treatise Concerning Widows*, viii).

It is certainly in the spirit of Ambrose's Deborah that the artist of a thirteenth-century French miniature shows her riding to battle with Barak (St Louis Psalter, Bibliothèque Nationale, MS lat. 10525, fol. 47). Reaching from behind him, she points the way past his drawn sword. His head is turned back to her, and she looks determinedly at him. There is no question but that she is leading, albeit from behind, and teaching men war (PLATE 3.1d, p. 67).

Early Modern and Modern

Deborah

For those who would use the Bible to establish (or justify) the social order, Deborah's role as leader was an ongoing concern well into modern times. In a letter (1532) to the magistrate at the Wartburg, Reformer Martin Luther (1483–1546) urges vigilance against Anabaptists "seeking to infiltrate also in your vicinity and to infect our people with their poison." He sarcastically professes his astonishment that "in their spiritual wisdom" some of these unauthorized preachers "have not learned to adduce examples of how women have prophesied and thereby attained rule over men, land, and people," and if women, why not these men? His list starts with Deborah and includes notable biblical women from Sarah to Mary. He avoids ("for the present") explaining why Deborah and the other Old Testament women did have the right, with God's approval, to teach and to rule, presumably as exceptions that prove the rule. Instead he hastens to 1 Tim 2:12, where there is a ministry that women should be silent and not preach ("Infiltrating and Clandestine Preachers" [383, 390–1]).

We are not surprised to find Balthasar Hubmaier (1480–1528), Anabaptist theologian, viewing Deborah's example differently. He establishes the normal rule: "In this gathering, women shall be silent and at home they should learn from their husbands, so that everything might take place properly and in order. (1 Cor. 14:34; 1 Tim. 2:12; Joel 2; 1 Cor. 11)." Then he allows the exception: "But where the men are afraid and have become women, then the women should speak up and become manly, like Deborah, Hulda, Anna the prophetess, the four daughters of the evangelist Philip, and in our times [the Protestant Bavarian noblewoman] Argula" (*Theses against Eck*, 1524, § §22–3).

In his commentaries, Protestant Reformer John Calvin (1509–64) is clear on the issue. Commenting on the Exodus, Calvin qualifies Miriam's leadership as performed "towards the women," and claims her victory song (Exod 15:21) led to "her base envy with regard to Moses; for being highly praised, she thought herself equal to him in dignity." He segues immediately to Deborah: "it was an extraordinary thing, when God gave authority to a woman," so that "no one may consider this singular precedent as a common rule" (*On Micah*, 1551, 6.4). Calvin's trump card here is the one Luther played, namely 1 Tim 2:12, where Paul forbids women to teach or have authority over men (*On the First Epistle to Timothy*, 1556, 2.12). Such treatment of Deborah's story is repeated often and is still found today.

Another way to deal with Deborah's authority was to enlist her as an honorary man, so to speak. As Erasmus put it after celebrating the heroes of ancient Greece, what is more celebrated than "the memory of Judith, Deborah, and Rahab, who, since they surpassed their own sex and showed manly strength of soul, are celebrated not among women but among heroes?" (*On the Writing of Letters*, 1522 [95]).

Circumstances ring the changes on this rhetoric, which affirms women's capacity while maintaining men's privilege. In the sixteenth century a fierce debate was taking place in Europe, the "debate about women" (*la querelle des femmes*). It reached back into the previous century, as early as Christine de Pisan's *The Book of the City of Ladies* (*Livre de la cité des dames*, 1405), and would continue into the next. What was the "nature" of women as compared with men? What roles should women play in society? Should they be formally educated, own property, engage in politics? What freedoms should they enjoy?

Some women, often under pseudonyms, attempted to argue for equality with men, as did some men. Some argued for women's superiority. A defense of "the nobility and preeminence of women," by Henricus Cornelius Agrippa (1529), circulated widely in England in the sixteenth and seventeenth centuries, influencing many polemicists. Some men trenchantly insisted that women were inherently wicked and weak: notoriously popular in England was Joseph Swetman's *The arraignment of Lewd, Idle, Froward, and Unconstant Women or the vanity of them, choose you whether, With a Commendation of wise, virtuous, and honest Women, Pleasant for married Men, profitable for young Men, and hurtful to none* (1615). Others argued for them being weak but not wicked. But the most familiar refrain was akin to Luther's and Calvin's dictum: women were definitely weak, arguably wicked, and those illustrious figures of Antiquity, including Deborah and Jael, were exceptional. So were powerful political figures of their own times.

Faced with contemporary political reality, the Italian-born Protestant theologian Peter Martyr Vermigli (1499–1562) advises Queen Elizabeth, immediately upon her accession in 1558, to "play the role of holy Deborah for our times. Join to yourself some godly Barak. Bring the Israelites who are oppressed in various ways into the sincere and pure liberty of the Gospel." She should have no fear, for God will be with her, "so that like the brave woman Jael you will strike the head of Jabin with the hammer of your might and drive it into the ground from whence it came so that he may cease to be troublesome to your godly nation." Nor should she let herself be shaken because born a woman and not a man. "Where else does God's power appear more than in infirmity?" (*Life, Letters, and Sermons*, Letter 200, 175–6).

William Gurnall (1617–79) likewise feels free to praise Queen Elizabeth as "our English Deborah," as he urges his readers to bless God for the translation of the Scriptures into English, sponsored by the Queen. Like Deborah, the Queen was a bringer of liberty (*Christian in Complete Armour*, 1655–62, ii.10 [605]).

Less felicitous is the rhetoric of Scottish Reformer John Knox (c.1513–72). In 1554 he wrote on a burning political question, "Whether a Female can preside over, and rule a kingdom by divine right, and so transfer the right of sovereignty to her Husband?" His answer is that while God's biblical law "ordains the woman to be in subjection, and not to rule," nevertheless the Gospel does not abrogate hereditary rights, and if a woman is acknowledged as Queen in compliance with law and custom, then it is a "hazardous thing" for godly persons to oppose political regulations. This would be like Deborah. But if she were not to be like Deborah, but rather an ungodly and tyrannous ruler, Queen Athaliah's case (2 Kings 11) would serve as a precedent (*Questions Concerning Obedience to Lawful Magistrates*, 1554, q2). But Knox's impatience with the continuing rule of Mary Queen of Scots and Mary Tudor of England, both Catholics, led him to harden his position on the debate over women and produce a work of enduring notoriety, *The First Blast of the Trumpet against the monstruous regiment of Women* (1558). "Who can denie," he writes, "but it is repugnant to nature, that the blind be appointed to lead such as do see? That the weak, the sick and impotent persons shall nourish and keep the whole and strong?" That the "foolishe, madde and phrenetike" govern the discreet and give counsel to the sober of mind. "And such be al women, compared unto man in bearing of authoritie. For their sight in civile regiment is but blindness;

their strength, weaknes; their counsel, foolishnes; and judgment, phrensie, if it be rightlie considered." Knox's timing, however, was less than perfect. Mary Tudor died that year, to be succeeded by another woman, the Protestant Elizabeth. He was not her favorite.

A century later, by contrast, Puritan poet and politician John Milton (1608–74) followed those pressing for women's equality. Pointing to Deborah's standing as prophetess, Milton argues that every believer can be an "ordinary minister" whenever necessary and when provided with requisite gifts, and "the term *prophet* is applied not only to one who can foretell the future but to anyone endowed with exceptional piety and wisdom for the purpose of teaching" (*Christian Doctrine*, c.1658–60 [i.29.28, 570–2]).

For an earlier seventeenth-century writer (whose satires Milton attacked), the answer is mixed. Joseph Hall (1574–1656) asks himself, Who does he see raised up out of millions to be prophet and deliverer? No prince of Israel, not Barak the captain, nor Lappidoth the husband, but "Deborah, the wife of Barak," honoring woman and wedlock. As in rabbinic tradition we find praise tinged with discomfort (what was God thinking of?): "Who shall ask God any reason of his elections, but his own pleasure?" Hall sees Barak's involvement as a welcome qualification of Deborah's leadership. "Deborah was to sentence, not to strike; to command, not to execute. This [latter] act is masculine, fit for some captain of Israel. She was the head of Israel; it was meet some other should be the hand. It is an imperfect and titular government, where there is a commanding power without correction, without execution" (*Contemplations*, 1615 [ix.4, 109]).

Still, some roles were certainly to be shared between men and women. It is a universal duty, and always the way of saints, urges Puritan preacher John Wells (1623–76) to sing psalms and spiritual songs to God. This means "by all sexes." Miriam sang as well as Moses; and Deborah as well as Barak (c.1670s [77, 80]).

Deborah, with Jael, Judith, and Esther, was regularly found in a lineup of "strong women" (*femmes fortes*) drawn from the Bible, classical antiquity, and recent history, often used to demonstrate women's capabilities and provide models of moral instruction for women. Sometimes the biblical women belong in a print suite such as that published around 1600 by Philips Galle (1537–1612) from designs by Marten de Vos of Antwerp (1532–1603). It includes also Jael, Ruth, Abigail (2 Samuel 25) and the wise woman of Abel of Beth-maacah who advised disposing of Sheba's head (2 Sam 20:22). Deborah sits under an attractive date palm, a small scroll in one hand, a staff of authority in the other. Behind her is an army camp. A Latin inscription credits her with exerting power through justice and war, assiduous in her attention to Israel (PLATE 3.2a, p. 73).

Another series of 20 women circulating in the seventeenth century was composed by French Jesuit Pierre Le Moyne (1602–71). The author presented each figure through "Portraiture, Poesie, and History," a design he thought more likely than the usual "formless and dry" school philosophy to appeal to his female readers. Translated by John Paulet, marquesse of Winchester, the work appeared (with copper engravings) in 1652 as *The Gallery of Heroick Women*. Accorded first place, Deborah, "The Gallant Jewes," is introduced, under her palm, with a fanfare: "You never beheld a Tribunall like that of this Governesse. Surely their enters more splendor and pride in the Thrones of Kings, but lesse naturall Majesty and true Glory." Her character matches her station. "Surely also no woman was ever heard to speak more soveraingly, nor with an Authority accompanied with more sweetnesse and efficacy. Prophecy and Law were never expounded by a more powerful mouth." Like many Catholics, Le Moyne finds nothing to reprehend in Deborah, unlike "the diffidence of Moses and Aaron, the imprudence of Joshua, the incontinence of Samson, the fall of David, and the follies of Solomon."

Le Moyne is clear where he stands on the question, "Whether Women be capable of Government?" He states, "I know very well that there be Politicians who are against the government of Women; but I know also, that these Politicians [*sic*] are no Evangelists, and that there is no Creed as yet made of their Opinions. The example of *Debora* is a famous and Prophetical proof against their Doctrine." Echoing Ambrose, he sees a widow governing a nation, ordaining war and peace, and encouraging faint-hearted men to victory. Hers is the glorious Regency of a Widow, a description hardly unconnected to the book's dedication to the Queen Regent of France. In his "moral reflection" on Deborah, Le Moyne observes that sometimes "souls of the first magnitude may be found in the bodies of the second sex"; God's instruments receive their virtue from his hand, not from their own matter, and merit respect and obedience – "and *our Regent* . . . hath much of resemblance with the Jewish Regent," having the spirit of wisdom, gaining battles, and giving judgments. One wonders whether Le Moyne knew the story of John Knox.

The argument over women continued unabated into the eighteenth century. Arguments were met with counter-arguments. Thus Sophia's *Woman not inferior to man: or, a short and modest vindication of the natural right of the fairer sex to a perfect equality of power, dignity and esteem, with men* (1739) provoked in return A Gentleman's *Man superior to woman; or, a vindication of man's natural right of sovereign authority over the woman* (1739, 1744).

In North America, Jonathan Edwards (1703–58) places Deborah's curse against Meroz for failing to help (5:23; "a dreadful curse from Christ") upon those opposing his recent glorious work of revival (*Distinguishing Marks of a Work of the Spirit of God*, 1741 [275–6]). And why did Meroz hold back? Edwards's answer touches not only on women's roles but also on slavery.

Probably "they argued a priori; they did not like the beginning of it, it being a woman that first led the way, and had the chief conduct in the affair; nor could they believe that such despicable instruments, as a company of unarmed slaves, were ever like to effect so great a thing." So pride and unbelief combined to make them unwilling to follow Deborah to battle. By the same token, Deborah's song makes clear that divine blessing will come the way of persons who arise, honor God in such a work, and vigorously promote it. Here Jael, above all, is the exemplar (. . . *Present Revival of Religion*, 1742 [364]).

Some widely read commentaries, such as that by Thomas Scott (1747–1821), tread lightly on the issue, while insisting on Deborah's credentials (*Holy Bible*, 1788–92). Despite her extraordinary call, as a woman Deborah could not *personally* undertake a judge's military expeditions; "but she used her authority to repress iniquity, to reform religion, and to execute impartial justice." Given the feminine plural ending of "Lappidoth," Scott wonders if it is the name of a town, an occupation (lamp maker?), or an adjectival construction signifying inspired (woman of illuminations?) or illustrious (a light of Israel?). He settles on the traditional "wife of Lappidoth" as "most natural." Deborah's role was to exercise her authority for the people's good "with that disinterested assiduity which a mother shows to her beloved children," especially in supporting true religion.

Anglican educationalist Mrs Trimmer (1741–1810) likewise avoids controversy over roles, simply noting Deborah's extraordinary understanding and fortitude, and her gift of prophecy. Reflecting a common supposition, she thinks Deborah's wise admonitions, inspired by God, had probably "brought the people to repentance" (*Sacred History*, 1783 [xlix, 214]). *Sacred Biography* (1818) saw her behaving like a true prophetess, very reasonably, "not with the zeal of an enthusiast, nor in an inactive reliance on supernatural assistance; but in the use of the best adapted means" (p. 296). Yet the gender question persists. When Deborah says that God gave her dominion over the mighty (Judg 5:13, KJV) she suggests that "by endowing a woman with more than manly sagacity and resolution, and by making her the life and soul of a sinking nation" God created "a new thing in earth" in order to have the people's undivided praise (p. 302).

For Anglo-Jewish poet and novelist Grace Aguilar (1816–47), intent on rebutting derogatory accounts of her ancient forebears, Deborah's "vast superiority of mental and spiritual acquirements," acknowledged and revered by her countrymen, was "rather an *unsatisfactory* proof of the degradation of Jewish women." She was clearly a prophetess in her own right, distinct from her husband, and clearly God is no respecter of persons when judging hearts, heeding neither one sex's weakness or apparent inability nor the other's natural powers. Yet clearly, too, Deborah's status as wife was not such that her elevation was extraordinary, given her talents. Were women on a par with slaves, as some claimed, she could never have obtained the people's respect, obedience, or even attention. She would never have been entrusted with such gifts and could never have been a prophetess," for her words would only have been regarded as idle raving," or a judge, for want of training and experience. As it was, in her God "made a WOMAN His instrument to judge, to prophesy, to teach, and to redeem," while yet retaining her "woman nature."

Practically speaking, Deborah's character cannot bear upon her descendants' conduct, "for woman can no longer occupy a position of such trust and wisdom in Israel" (Aguilar advocated a reformed Judaism); but, in theory, "we may take the history of Deborah to our hearts, both *nationally* and individually." Deborah proves that the Law could not have contained "one syllable" disparaging to women. With Deborah's history in their hands, the young daughters of Israel need little other argument to convince their adversaries (Christian and Jewish) that they require no other creed nor a denial of the Oral Law "to teach them their proper position" (*Women of Israel*, 1845 [218–27]).

A year or so later, Christian temperance leader Clara Lucas Balfour (1808–78) was writing in England of Deborah's memorable elevation "to public dignity and supreme authority" in terms like Aguilar's. Balfour finds in Deborah a model of womanhood, commanding authority without, as the common error supposes, sacrificing "womanly qualities." She chooses to be known as "wife." The important point is God's ability to "magnify Himself in the weakness of his instruments"; yet Balfour, like Aguilar, stresses Deborah's intellectual superiority. She sits under the palm tree, without pomp and parade. "How simple the actual environment, how August the mental splendour!" (*Women of Scripture*, 1847 [90–1, 103]).

Balfour makes the novel case that Barak's insistence on Deborah accompanying the army (of men) also proves her "essentially feminine character." "The human mind is far more affected by contrasts than by similarities. Had Deborah been a fierce, stern, masculine woman, she would have aroused [among the men] no enthusiasm, her character would have approximated too closely to their own—she would have been a sort of second-rate man, instead of being, as she was, 'A perfect woman, nobly plann'd / To warn, to comfort, to command.' " Thus it was "the presence of a thoughtful, spiritual, intellectual woman as leader of the armed host, that awakened energy and strengthened hope" (pp. 93–4).

By the nineteenth century's end the struggle for women's emancipation had taken on a new energy in the United States, well reflected in *The Woman's Bible* (1898). Elizabeth Cady Stanton (1815–1902) wrote on Judges in Part II. Noting that Lappidoth might be a place rather than a husband's name, Cady Stanton dryly agrees that Deborah "had too much independence of character, wisdom and self-reliance to have ever filled the role of the Jewish idea of a wife"

("Judges," ii). Yet, though a woman of great ability, the divinely appointed chosen leader, one of the great judges of Israel, she is not listed in Hebrews 11 with ("hesitating and lukewarm") Barak: "Men have always been slow to confer on women the honors which they deserve." Going to battle, Deborah had the insight that in Barak's mind "he was already pluming himself on his victory over Sisera," so she told him that Sisera would be delivered into a woman's hands. What an "extra pang" such a fate would bring to a man's death, Cady Stanton declares sarcastically, though "fortunately, poor Sisera was spared the knowledge of his humiliation." She is trenchant:

> We never hear sermons pointing women to the heroic virtues of Deborah as worthy of their imitation. Nothing is said in the pulpit to rouse them from the apathy of ages, to inspire them to do and dare great things, to intellectual and spiritual achievements, in real communion with the Great Spirit of the Universe. Oh, no! The lessons doled out to women, from the canon law, the Bible, the prayer-books and the catechisms, are meekness and self-abnegation; ever with covered heads (a badge of servitude) to do some humble service for man; that they are unfit to sit as a delegate in a Methodist conference, to be ordained to preach the Gospel, or to fill the office of elder, of deacon or of trustee, or to enter the Holy of Holies in cathedrals.

No doubt Robert L. Dabney (1820–98), standing squarely in the tradition of Luther and Calvin, was the kind of divine whom Cady Stanton had in mind. "A few years ago," he reports, "the public preaching of women was universally condemned among all conservative denominations of Christians." But not now. "Now the innovation is brought face to face even with the Southern churches, and female preachers are knocking at our doors." They profess to appeal to Deborah among other prophetesses (Miriam, Huldah, Anna). "But the fatal answer is, that these holy women were inspired. Their call was exceptional and supernatural. There can be no fair reasoning from the exception to the ordinary rule." And if any should claim supernatural inspiration, well then, "If any of our preaching women will work a genuine miracle, then, and not until then, will she be entitled to stand on the ground of Deborah or Anna" ("The Public Preaching of Women," *Southern Presbyterian Review*, 1879).

Cady Stanton demands to know where were the sermons urging women to emulate Deborah. She would probably have appreciated hearing the young Rev. Reverdy C. Ransom (1861–1959), later Bishop Ransom, speak to the Ida B. Wells Woman's Club at Bethel African Methodist Episcopal Church in Chicago (June 6, 1897). Harsh living conditions have damaged the greatness of black women, Ransom contends; their condition is a result not of inherent short-comings but rather of societal abuse and neglect. But changes were taking place for both black men and black women, and women's nobleness was shining through. His text is Judg 5:24, where Deborah speaks of Jael as blessed. These were "two of the most remarkable women in biblical history." When the nation's men had become awed into submission and had lost courage, a woman's patriotism and courage inspired them to fight their foes "until victory perched upon their standards." For her part, Jael slew the "chief enemy and persecutor of her race." Thus, "we set these women before you tonight as the saviours of their race and of their nation and the deliverers of their country" ("Deborah and Jael" [75–6]).

Ransom's confidence in the power of women to inspire men, with Deborah as exemplar, finds its counterpart in England. The Rev. Stopford A. Brooke (1832–1916), sometime chaplain to Queen Victoria, preaches that Deborah's religious passion so mingled with her patriotic rage at her people's misery as to "drive her into insurrection." She sat under her palm, "but not with downcast eyes, and folded hands, and extinguished hopes." Strength of character, intellect, clear-sightedness, tact, and divinely given wisdom were Deborah's endowments. "We want in England," declares Brooke, "women who will understand and feel what love of country means, and act upon it; who will lose thought of themselves and their finery and their pleasure in a passionate effort to heal the sorrow and to destroy the dishonour, dishonesty, and vice of England; to realize that as mothers, maidens, wives, and sisters, they have but to bid the men of this country to be true, brave, loving, just, honourable, and wise, and they will become so" (*Old Testament and Modern Life*, 1896, 177).

Throughout the twentieth century writers have praised Deborah as one of the most remarkable women in the Bible (in "all history," writes one), and usually, until late in the century, they have rehearsed the refrain of woman's weakness and God's use of it to his greater glory. "Thus the faith of a weak woman became for her people both the spark that revived the dying flame of faith in Yahweh and the bond that reunited the tribes that had become discordant and enervated" (Rudolf Kittel, *Great Men and Movements*, 1925, 54). But she did continue to bother some: "Deborah was a woman with a home and a career. For the most part she honorably maintained the cares of life, but we think that public life made her just a little less feminine and a little more masculine than she, as a woman, should have been" (Robert Burns Wallace, *Introduction to the Bible as Literature*, 1929, 52).

In art Deborah is depicted under her palm tree gesturing to her audience (Barak alone or with other men) or resolutely pointing the way forward. Apart from the early modern "strong women" series, she tends to lose out in Bible illustration to the more dramatic Jael. In the later nineteenth century, however, portraits of her enjoyed renewed popularity, particularly in books about biblical women, often written by women. The portrait by Charles Landelle (1812–1908) in Harriet Beecher Stowe's *Woman in Sacred History* (1873) shows

PLATE 3.1   Deborah and Barak: (a) Landelle, 1873; (b) Wylie, 1906; (c) Wilhoite, 1940; (d) Miniature, thirteenth century; (e) Taylor, 1820. (See pp. 58, 67–8)

her standing under the tree, hand thrust forward in declamation, a scroll clutched at her side, her mouth set, and eyes piercing under dark brows. The picture's strong appeal is evident from its regular appearance (with variations) in other books over the next quarter-century or so (PLATE 3.1a).

Gustave Doré (1832–83) unusually shows Deborah at the top of steps singing her song of triumph (no obvious sign of Barak!) but retains the conventional upraised arm and gesturing finger (*Sainte Bible*, 1866; *Doré Bible Gallery*, 1879). At the turn of the century, Jennie Wylie's (fl. 1900–10) young woman points strongly across the picture. She reflects the text (Judg 4:4) by being seated. Wylie's art belongs to one of the finest periods in book illustration and stands out in its strong lines and simplicity (Sparrow, *Old Testament in Art*, 1906; PLATE 3.1b). Deborah, by Mariel Wilhoite, in Olive Beaupré Miller's (1883–1968) *Heroes of the Bible* (1940) is hardly an artistic triumph, but makes a point. She stands under the palm before Barak in traditional pose, hand upraised. But in her other hand is a distaff, a toddler tugs at her skirts, and a younger sibling sits and looks on, arms raised like his mother's. This Deborah is emphatically a mother (PLATE 3.1c). One Deborah who does not point is seated serenely in a chariot on the way to battle, Barak standing beside her (PLATE 3.1e). English artist and writer Isaac Taylor, Jr (1787–1865), in a style reminiscent of William Blake, manages to capture her fortitude in a way that also harks back to the medieval miniature. There pointing, here motionless, yet in both renditions in charge (*Boydell's Illustrations of Holy Writ*, 1820).

Barak, Sisera, and Sisera's mother

Barak has a checkered history of reception. Few accord him much praise, though he garners some. His place in Scripture biographies is small, usually ancillary to Deborah, and his entries in Bible dictionaries often just a line or two. The adulatory adjectives and attributes clustering around Deborah tend to be missing for Barak. Joseph Hall is not atypical when he dryly observes: "He is sent for, not to get the victory, but to take it; not to overcome, but to kill; to pursue, and not to beat Sisera. Who could not have done this work, whereto not much courage, no skill, belonged? yet, even for this, will God have an instrument of his own choice" (*Contemplations*, 1615 [ix.4, 109]).

A century or so later, and Thomas Scott makes much the same judgment in his annotated Bible (1788–92). Yes, Barak had faith, but he also had misgivings and "reluctancy." In not "honouring God as he ought to have done, he was deprived in part of the honour which he would otherwise have obtained." Esther Hewlett follows Scott's judgment almost to the letter, adding that Barak "hesitated to rely simply on the command of God, and seemed inclined to cling to an arm of flesh" (*Scripture History*, 1828, 20). For Mrs Trimmer, Barak's refusal came from his being "diffident of himself," for which she lays no blame (*Sacred History*, 1783 [xlix, 214]). For Clara Lucas Balfour, Barak's faith "lacked both the firmness and energy that distinguished Deborah's," and while agreeing to go, Deborah herself manages to convey that assent in language of "mingled reproof and prophecy" (*Women of Scripture*, 1847 [92]). As for Barak's success in the battle itself, the writer of *Sacred Biography* (1818) feels the need to offer the qualification that whatever praise is afforded Barak's conduct and "the intrepidity of his little army," in part at least the victory was miraculous (p. 297).

The carnal Barak is the theme of a reflection by evangelical preacher F. B. Meyer (1847–1929) on Judg 4:9 (*Our Daily Homily*, i, 1898). Unable to rise to the "splendor of the situation," Barak preferred the inspiration of Deborah's visible presence to the "invisible but certain help of Almighty God." Despite his mention as a hero of faith in Hebrews 11, "his faith lay rather in Deborah's influence with God than in his own." Thus he illustrates the "carnal Christian," unable to deal directly with God but dependent upon the medium of another's prayers and words and leadership. "Barak must have Deborah. It is faith, though greatly attenuated." Likewise, for Robert F. Horton (1855–1934), Barak was "that type of man that finds it easier to believe in a woman than in God." Still, it is "no reproach for any man to recognize this note of authority in the inspired woman" – who was, after all, speaking God's words. Divine authority, however, was apparently not quite efficacious in itself: "Besides, she wielded one of the most powerful weapons that women employ in their influence over men, the faculty of enthusiastic and admiring praise" (*Women of the Old Testament*, 1899, 124).

As regards Sisera, Joseph Hall's summing up serves as a template. Like the rabbis earlier, Hall paints him as arrogant, looking with scorn at the handful of Israelites, fearful only that "it would be no victory to cut the throats of so few." Pride, however, takes a beating, as "proud Sisera, after many curses of the heaviness of that iron carriage, is glad to quit his chariot, and betake himself to his heels" (*Contemplations*, 1615 [ix.4, 109]). Other writers follow suit. He was "intoxicated with pride and vanity, and rendered insolent by his former successes" (*Sacred Biography*, 1818). Here "we have another instance of its being the good pleasure of the Deity to humble the tyrannical and the proud":

> Soon are the mightiest laid low
> By the omnipotent's command.
> See haughty Sisera, Israel's foe,
> Dies, sleeping, by a woman's hand.
> (Gaspey, *Tallis's Illustrated Scripture History*, 1851)

> "Did old Sisera ever get whipped?" asked Willie.
> "Yes," answered Aunt Charlotte.
> (Charlotte M. Yonge, *Aunt Charlotte's Stories*, 1898)

The long tradition of reviling Sisera, however, does relent. The Jewish mystic Abraham Isaac Kook (1865–1935) finds redemption even for him. It is an "art of great enlightenment" to purge the heart of anger, to pity those mired in wickedness, to find their good aspects and minimize their guilt. For in the end "such wicked persons are also due to be mended." An ancient tradition teaches that Sisera's descendants taught Torah in Jerusalem; here "we reach the depth of compassion, which calls on us not to be caught up in the stream of hatred even of the fiercest enemy" (*Lights of Holiness*, 1950, III [236]).

Sisera's mother garners more interest than her son, though again she tends to be painted in single colors. She shows the wrong sort of hope, the Rev. Thomas Lye (1621–84) tells us in a sermon. Hope should include a "holy and confident expectation" of God's providence. "Hope looks, and looks out, as expecting God's appearing; not as Sisera's mother once did, who looked for a victorious success, and expected that her son should have returned a triumphant conqueror, richly laden with spoils and booty, whereas the wretch lay bleeding at the feet of Jael." No, "such a vain, groundless hope draws a blush into the cheek, and covers the face with confusion" (1661 [372]).

She exemplifies "an ungodly and sensual heart," declares the Rev. Thomas Scott, scandalized by the details of her hope.

> How shameful are these wishes of an aged mother for a beloved son, and his officers and soldiers; that a woman of honour and virtue, as we say, could delight her fancy with conceiving the Israelitish virgins divided among the conquerors, as their property, to be exposed to their unbridled domineer lust! And that nothing more excellent could be conceived by her trifling mind, than to see her son, and his attendants and concubines, arrayed in fine garments, wrought by the singular skill and industry of their vanquished enemies! (*Holy Bible*, 1788–92)

The irony is not lost on Scott: "Her ladies in *their great wisdom*, suggested that Sisera only waited to divide the immense spoil which had been taken; and she *as wisely* pleased her vain mind with the soothing imagination!" She is left, fittingly, "to enjoy her imaginary triumph, and meet her bitter disappointment." As Grace Aguilar writes, the scene is "infused with a species of satire, giving indescribable poignancy" (*Women of Israel*, 1845 [223]). Moreover, the author of *Sacred Biography* (1818) shrewdly observes the effects on Deborah's audience of her so "personifying" Sisera's mother and attendants. By depicting them as "prematurely enjoying the triumph of the subjection of the Israelitish damsels to their own pride, and the pleasure of their warriors," the poet "also excites the gratitude and joy of her fair countrywomen, by gently hinting at the dreadful dishonour from which they had been preserved. This too diminishes the concern which might otherwise have been felt for the cruel disappointment which the mother of Sisera endured" (pp. 303–4).

Sometimes, however, Sisera's mother finds sympathy, pathos even. Canadian William Kirby (1817–1906) writes his pride at being a son of Britain (from Yorkshire) into his poem of Canadian resistance to invasion in the War of 1812 (*Canadian Idyls*, 1880). The setting is a mansion on Lake Ontario. A lovely girl ("Canadian of an English stock") looks from the lattice and cries to her mother to listen to the sounds of battle: "O, Great God! / Who gives us fathers, brothers, for our love, / Who cannot die for them, as they for us!" So the women stood

> Pale-lipped, with eyes that just held back the tears,
> Like Sisera's mother at the lattice, far
> Gazing along the hills, crying in pain,
> "Why come no tidings? Have our men not sped?
> Our loyal men who went down to the fight . . .
> For King and country dying, if they must!
> While their true women hope, and fear, and trust,
> And deck their chambers with the freshest flowers,
> And spread the couches soft for their repose,
> Sharing their weal and woe unto the end."
> . . . Evening came, and night,
> And still they watched; those faithful women all,
> Till morn returned, when every flower and tree
> Watered the earth with dripping dew, like tears,
> As over some great sorrow that befell.

Perhaps, too, there is pathos in the Oriental scene in Mrs S. T. Martyn's *Women of the Bible* (1868; PLATE 3.2d).

Jael

Martin Luther, as a young man, follows medieval tradition. Sisera is pride, the chief of all sins; so too the ungodly man, conscience-struck, flees from the host of his sins. Jael represents the Church, the bride of Christ (who, like the Kenite, is related to Moses), which offers first the milk of gentler doctrine to calm him and then pierces his spirit with the strong word of the Gospel (*First Lectures on the Psalms*, 1513–15 [II, 129–31] on Ps 83:9). Such allegorical and typological understandings of Jael have continued for centuries, among both Catholics and Protestants.

Renewed interest in the Virgin Mary by Catholics from the late sixteenth century on brought visibility to Jael as a prefiguration of Mary. Babette Bohn shows how Italian art developed two main depictions. The first, less usual, is "a scene of manifest violence, with a dynamic Jael forcefully wielding her mallet to subdue a struggling Sisera." It displays no moral ambivalence towards the victorious and virtuous woman. An early and dramatic example from Bologna, possibly by Girolamo Siciolante (c.1521–c.1580), now in the Galleria Davia Bargellini, has Jael pinning Sisera under her knee as she positions the spike. Her right arm, grasping a small hammer, is fully extended for the blow (one hopes her aim is good). Sisera's left arm reaches up vainly in protest (PLATE 3.2c). A mid-seventeenth-century fresco (Luca Ferrari), in the Basilica of the Madonna della Ghiara in Reggio Emilia, depicts another struggling Sisera, and was clearly included because of Jael's association with Mary.

More popular in Italy, as elsewhere, is the traditional version deriving from the Middle Ages (e.g. Queen Mary's Psalter (BM MS 2.B.VII), early fourteenth century). It shows a sleeping victim, as in Judg 4:21, and an unperturbed heroine, right arm raised to hammer in the pin. As the story's human dimensions are dramatized in Baroque art, however, Jael acquires the tones of a richly attired temptress rather than an inspired agent of God, let alone a type of the Virgin. A notable exception is the beautifully restrained rendition (1620) by Italian Baroque artist Artemisia Gentileschi, more celebrated for the violence of her Judith paintings. (See further Babette Bohn, "Death, Dispassion, and the Female Hero," 2005.)

Among Protestants, too, Jael lives on in typology. In the mid-nineteenth century, the Rev. Isaac Williams (1802–65) preached on Deborah and Jael, the (Anglican) lectionary text for the day. He owns that Deborah celebrates Jael's "treacherously slaying one who had relied on her hospitality" and, to compound the problem, "exults in the sorrows" of Sisera's mother. The moral difficulties yield, however, to typological solutions. Jael prefigures Mary, so the story contains "a secret prophecy respecting Redemption and the victory over sin and death by means of a woman: it was keeping up a memorial of the promise made to Eve – of her seed bruising the serpent's head." Jael's stratagem, like Judith's, intimated that Satan "our great enemy" should be overcome unawares "by the faith of the blessed Virgin" (*Female Characters*, c.1860 [82–3]).

As Williams's starting point illustrates, Jael has a long history of ambivalent reception. While revivalist Jonathan Edwards in 1742 could proclaim her a prime exemplar of support for the Lord's work, Puritan John Gibbon (1629–1718) had a different association. In a sermon, he urges his listeners to be well skilled in "unmasking the sophistry and mystery of iniquity, in defeating the wiles and strategems of the tempter, and in detecting and frustrating the cheats and finesses of the flesh with its deceitful lusts." For sin's model is Jael. "When sin, like Jael, invites thee into her tent, with the lure and decoy of

PLATE 3.2   Deborah, Jael, and Sisera's mother: (a) and (b) de Vos, c.1600; (c) Siciolante, c.1550; (d) Martyn's *Women of the Bible*, 1868; (e) Goltzius, c.1600. (See pp. 61, 71–2, 75)

a lordly treatment, think of the nail and hammer which fastened Sisera dead to the ground" (1661 [98]).

It is the Reformation shift towards literal-historical reading that changes Jael's reception. She becomes a person subject to contemporary social conventions and moral expectations, though she is still read in terms of theological doctrines – including the belief that the Bible is Holy Writ – and the desire of readers that her story convey some moral or spiritual truth. As a cipher for Mary or the Church she is a positive figure. As a woman with a mallet and nail, and a sleeping guest, she is a problem. As the First Herald of the ruling Council of Florence said of (Donatello's sculpture of) Jael's frequent companion, Judith, in 1504, "it is not good to have a woman kill a man." She kills him, moreover, in a deceptive abuse of hospitality, as the Rev. Williams, among countless others, reminds us.

Another Puritan preacher, Richard Rogers (1550–1618), whose *Commentary on Judges* (1615) comprised 103 sermons, typifies many from the Reformation on as he argues around the problem (pp. 221–6). Jael's act is counted by some as "barbarous cruelty and trechery," and certainly readers should in no way feel at liberty to imitate the details of Jael's deed. Yet he cannot leave it at that. She acts, he insists, out of faithfulness against God's enemy – an understanding shared with traditional typology – and by God's special commission which overrides all else. Accordingly, Rogers bids his readers, as members of the Church, zealously to resist its enemies, like Deborah, Barak, and also Jael. But not exactly like Jael!

With Joseph Hall, Shakespeare's contemporary in his younger years, readers contemplate Jael as an actor on a stage, disclosing an interior monologue, like a Shakespearean soliloquy. While Sisera doubtless dreams of battle, Jael, "seeing his temples lie so fair, as if they invited the nail and hammer," entertains the execution.

> What if I strike him? And yet, who am I that I should dare to think of such an act? Is not this Sisera, the most famous captain of the world . . . ? What if my hand should swerve in the stroke? what if he should awake while I am lifting up this instrument of death? what if I should be surprised by some of his followers, while the fact is green, and yet bleeding?

In like manner she runs the gamut of possibilities. Could the murder be hidden? Could her heart allow such treachery – was there not peace between her house and him? had she not extended him hospitality? But are these not the idle fancies of civility? Is not Sisera at defiance with God, a tyrant to Israel? Is it for nothing that God has brought him into her tent? May she now repay Israel for the kindness shown her grandfather Jethro? Does God not offer her the honor of rescuing his people? "Hath God bidden me strike, and shall I hold my hand? No: Sisera, sleep now thy last, and take here this fatal reward of all thy cruelty and oppression."

Like Rogers, Hall is sure that God was in charge: "He, that put this instinct into her heart, did put also strength into her hand: he that guided Sisera to her tent, guided the nail through his temples." Thus "he, that had vaunted of his iron chariots, is slain by one nail of iron, wanting only this one point of his infelicity, that he knows not by whose hand he perished!" (*Contemplations*, 1615 [ix.4, 110]).

Consistency is not always the commentator's highest priority. William Gurnall uses Jael's offering Sisera milk to illustrate those enjoying prosperity in a wicked state but damned because of it. God gives them more than they desire, "and all to bind them faster up in a deep sleep of security, as Jael served Sisera: he shall have milk though he asked but water, that she might nail him surer to the ground – milk having a property, as some write, to incline to sleep" (*Christian in Complete Armour*, 1655–62, ii.1 [66]). Here Jael does God's work. Elsewhere, she plays the role of deceptive ensnarer. Sisera is the naive Christian taken in by the hypocrite's sanctimonious talk: "Sisera had better have gone without Jael's butter and milk, than by them to be laid asleep against she came with her nail." Likewise, far happier for many now not to have become drunk on the gifts and seeming graces of those who will but take advantage, "the more easily to fasten their nail to their heads" (ii.5 [251]).

Sustaining positive approval was Jael's place in the popular lists of "strong women" (see on Deborah). In Philips Galle's print suite (c.1600) she is commended for her opportune perforation of the unjust enemy Sisera, a deed of daring making her name famous (or notorious!). She sits daintily, one leg tucked in behind the other, brandishing a mallet in her right hand and looking down, with the ghost of a smile, at a large and viciously pointed tent-pin in her left hand. In a background scene she kneels in traditional pose beside the sleeping Sisera, pin against his temple and mallet aloft (PLATE 3.2b). For her "strong woman" portrait she is sometimes seated as here, sometimes standing or tip-toeing. But she is always unmistakable, known by her implements, which may be flourished ostentatiously as in Pierre Le Moyne's *Gallery of Heroick Women* (English edn, 1652), or amusingly tucked away, like the tent-peg in the copper engraving designed by Hendrick Goltzius (1558–1617) from a folio sequence of Old Testament "heroes and heroines" (PLATE 3.2e). Le Moyne's description of Jael invokes divine approval – "Jahel inspired by God received [Sisera]" – and is unstinting in its praise. "Certainly she could not have given a more hazardous [blow], nor of greater consequence: and the Age of our forefathers which was an Age of Miracles and of prodigious Adventures, hath never seen anything of like Courage, nor of greater Fame."

> In Jahels Brest a Hero's Soul survives,
> Which prompts her modest thoughts to brave atchives:
> Her flaming eyes declare with how much heat,
> She did an Army in one Head defeat.

"Heat," it should be added, was thought to be a characteristic of men (cf. Le Moyne on Deborah, above).

Le Moyne worries lest his proposal of Jael's example to gallant women will be rejected: they will "abhor the blood and cruelty of this Precedent." But, he urges, they may imitate her "without violating the Laws of Hospitality; without exasperating the mildness of their Sex; without inraging or staining the Graces with blood." If there are no more Canaanites or Sisera to overcome, yet "uncircumcised vices and forreign habits" abound, along with "commanding and tragical Passions." These "spiritual Tyrants" demand present-day Jaels to confront them. As for her deception or "infidelity," judge the act by its inner meaning. Not only has "the holy Ghost himself" praised Jael in the song of Deborah the prophetess, but had Jael kept her word to Sisera, she would have breached her faith and betrayed her brethren (assuming she and Heber belonged to God's people). Heber's treaty, moreover, was made under duress, and so reasonably revoked. So Jael's deed was in fact "an Heroick Act of fidelity" towards God whom she obeyed, the Law of her Ancestors which she re-established, her people whose yoke she broke, and posterity "to which she conserved both Religion and the Sanctuary, Freedom and Hope." The usual caveat follows: the act is extraordinary, to be admired and respected but not copied. A Gallant Woman in search of a pure model of fidelity, "without the least appearance of stain," should look elsewhere.

The caveat is tenacious. Much earlier, Dutch printmaker Lucas van Leyden (1494–1533) included Jael in a series of woodcuts (1516–19) ostensibly celebrating the "Power of Women." In the foreground she kneels, tent-pin poised against the sleeping general's head, mallet raised – the classic pose. In the far background, left, Sisera drinks the proffered milk, while to the right Jael points Barak, amid soldiers crowding the door, to the deed. The milk, of course, reminds the viewer directly of the problem – the deception. In a subsequent edition, a plaque set in the picture's frame describes the slaying and concludes with a reference to the misogynist view of Ecclesiasticus 25: nothing exceeds the malice of a woman. The power of women has been reframed.

Much later, in *La Bible enfin expliquée* (1776 [436]), Deist philosopher Voltaire (1694–1778) reports the view of the "critics" (as if not including himself) that Jael's action was "even more horrible" than Ehud's assassination of King Eglon. Though praised by Deborah, "today with us she would get neither reward nor praise. Times change." He wants to attack the Bible's credibility as a moral authority, and Jael simply comes in handy. A century on and she serves a different purpose. In a poem by John Leicester Warren, Lord de Tabley (1835–95), she takes on traditional connotations of both Eve and the snake as partners in the Fall. Thus she plays the role of *femme fatale* so popular in literature and visual art in the closing decades of the nineteenth century. A more misogynist reception of Jael is hard to find (in Horder, *Poets' Bible*, 1889, 315):

> She stood, the mother-snake, before her tent,
> She feigned a piteous dew in her false eyes,
> She made her low voice gentle as a bird's,
> She drew the noble weary captain in.

In the shelter of her home, her guest lies down to sleep, trusting in "the sacred old alliance with her clan," and surely safe beneath the mantle she laid for him – "He was too noble to mistrust her much."

> His fading sense felt her insidious arm
> Folding him warmly. Then he slept – she rose,
> Slid like a snake across the tent – struck twice –
> And stung him dead.

Both Voltaire and Warren are a far cry from the simple approbation accorded both Bible and woman by Scottish Canadian poet Archibald McKillop (1824–1905), the "blind bard of Megantic" ("The Bible", 1860, 69, 70):

> So, friends, let us read, and always give heed
> To Moses, and David, and Paul;
> For books without end, have been printed and penned,
> But this one excelleth them all . . .
> We must not forget the shepherd, who met
> Goliath the great, with a stone;
> Nor valorous Jael, with hammer and nail,
> Who fastened the Captain alone.

The Rev. H. C. Adams (*Judges of Israel*, 1866, 102–16) even finds virtue in the competing views. "Mrs. MASON. You consider the matter then to be one, respecting which we can arrive at no certain conclusion? MR. MASON. I do, and therein to my mind consists the chief value of this narrative." He believes the five discussants have fairly represented current opinion. "Three of you think that Jael was woman of the highest and most devoted faith, and the other two think her a traitress, and an assassin." And yet the question has been discussed for centuries. "Does not this give us a striking proof, of how small is the value of human judgments – how all-important the judgment of God?" In the Last Day, a single moment will determine the question for ever.

Ambivalence, however, more often describes how Jael is received. Thomas Scott (*Holy Bible*, 1788–92) typically conveys unease as he tries to find her blameless. Probably Jael really intended Sisera kindness when inviting him in, but then a divine impulse led her to consider him God's enemy and destroy him. Her faith overcame "all reluctancy and every feminine fear." As usual, all this was exceptional and no model for normal behavior. He approves also of her not assenting to Sisera's request to deny his being there – she would not "utter a falsehood to oblige him." But here Scott cannot contain his irritation at a matter which Jael's story brings to mind: namely, the practice of instructing servants to tell unwelcome visitors that their masters are "not at home," in other words "to *prevaricate* (to word it no more harshly)" in order to save their masters an inconvenience. This practice sets a very bad example to the servants and is "a very criminal deviation from 'simplicity and godly sincerity.'"

Whether a model for emulation or not, Jael long continued to be a popular subject for illustration. Often she stands at the tent entrance and points out the slain Sisera to Barak arriving hot foot from battle: she appears thus for the first time in a Luther Bible (Schramm, *Lutherbibel*, 1923, fig. 553), from Hans Lufft (1495–1584) of Wittenberg, and in some of the finest illustrated Bibles of subsequent centuries. These include Nicholas Visscher's beautiful Print-Bible (*prentbijbel*) of c.1650 where the earlier design by Matthäus Merian (1593–1650) is accompanied by verses in Latin, French, Dutch, German, and English: "But Sisera fled, yet Jael gave the wound, / She through his temples nail'd him to the ground" (PLATE 3.3a); also the 1700 "Great Bible" of Pieter Mortier's (1661–1711) – this composition (unsigned), including Jael's clothing, gesture and wooden mallet, finds its way into Esther Hewlett's *Scripture History* (1828) (PLATE 3.3b). The design by Gerard Hoet (1648–1733) in Pierre de Hondt's folio *Figures de la Bible* (1728) brings us inside the tent. At the opening Jael tells Barak what has happened; Sisera is foregrounded, his head prominently pegged (PLATE 3.3c).

Gustave Doré chooses a similar perspective, but his Jael, who commands the picture, draws aside the door drapes to display the corpse to a Barak reduced to a background onlooker. The pin is nothing if not discrete (*Sainte Bible*, 1866; *Doré Bible Gallery*, 1879). The other widely reprinted and copied series of the time, the classically styled woodcuts by Julius Schnorr von Carolsfeld (1794–1872), cleverly combines both traditional scenes. Jael kneels beside Sisera with an outstretched finger nearly touching his head and her other hand

PLATE 3.3   Jael kills Sisera: (a) Merian [1626] 1650; (b) Hewlett's *Scripture History*, 1828; (c) Hoet, 1728; (d) Northcote (1746–1831). (See pp. 78, 80)

raised, still clutching the hammer but now pushing back a curtain to disclose the body to Barak who steps up to a wooden doorway and peers in (*Bibel in Bildern*, 1860; *Bible in Pictures*, 1869).

Occasionally, as in *The Child's Bible* (1884), the nailed corpse is discretely avoided; instead Jael stands before the tent and beckons an approaching Barak. But mostly nailing is not a problem, no matter the audience. Indeed, one of the most popular illustrations in the nineteenth century is the design by James Northcote (1746–1831), pupil and biographer of Sir Joshua Reynolds. Northcote's Jael is a raven-haired young woman who peers over the sleeping Sisera. The long spike's wicked point is stark against a lit white drape, so too the wavy hair of a handsome young Sisera. The hammer has to be sought. Glistening black armor heightens further the contrast between the young man and the young woman. Without the hammer and spike, this is a scene from a gothic romance (PLATE 3.3d).

Perhaps the youthful figures commended themselves to publishers as a lesson to youth. Northcote's picture appears in mid-century in Tallis's *Family Devotions* and *Illustrated Scripture History* as well as in the *Scripture History* by John Howard which sold well in America. Another volume for family reading makes Jael's nailing of Sisera a centerpiece and the appropriate text (4:21) a decorative highlight (*Sunny Sabbaths or Pleasant Pages for Happy Homes*, 1860). A century later and Jael still turns up in children's Bibles, though less commonly in the act of hammering. She kneels beside Sisera and offers him a bowl of milk, smiling ever so sweetly, as in *The Children's Bible in Colour* (1964), or eyes demurely downcast, as in Hadaway and Atcheson's *The Bible for Children* (1973). She does sneek up on him, hammer in hand in Christie-Murray's *The Illustrated Children's Bible* (1976), but the lethal peg is hidden from view. (See further on Jael, Bottigheimer, *Bible for Children*, 1996, 142–51.)

To many, then, despite her "horrid and unnatural" act, Jael remained a model for faith. That a divine impulse explained her deed is widely understood in nineteenth-century literature; and in so delivering Israel from oppression, she deserved Deborah's blessing (cf. *Teacher's Pictorial Bible*, c.1870; or James S. Forsyth, *Women of the Bible*, 1896, 53–4). Also common is the concluding moral, that "the weak by the assistance of heaven, often prove the overthrow of the strong and wicked" (Kitto, *Bible History*, 1841 [128]). At worst, given the text's silence about her motives, "circumstances" could be inferred, which "the Spirit of God has not thought proper to disclose," sufficient to justify an otherwise inexplicable proceeding (*Sacred Biography*, 1818, 298).

Motives, however, were not in short supply. She may have suffered under Sisera herself, or been moved by patriotism (if an Israelite) or gratitude towards Israel, or been aware of just how "atrocious" was Sisera's character (*Calmet's Dictionary*, 6th edn, 1837; cf. James Gardner, *Christian Cyclopedia*, 1858, 552).

Convinced, like most, that Jael was ordained to execute divine judgment, Mrs Trimmer seeks in her "critical situation" the clue to her immediate motivation. Had she refused Sisera shelter, he would most probably have killed her; or he might later have prevailed against Israel and slaughtered many, whereas by "cutting him off" she would complete Barak's victory, fulfill God's will, and gain highest honor for delivering the oppressed people from the dread general (*Sacred History*, 1783 [ii.49, 215]).

A distinctive explanation starts to make its appearance. Close consideration of Jael's immediate situation also spurs the Quaker historian, John Hoyland (1750–1831) of Sheffield in Yorkshire. Jael's is a "deed of horror." But the song's conclusion accounts both "for her conduct, and for the warmth of the strains with which this act was celebrated."

> The wretched females of the vanquished people usually became a prey to the brutal lust of the victors. This was a case so common, that the mother of Sisera, and her wise ladies, are represented as so lost to female delicacy and compassion, as to exult at the idea of assigning the virgins of Israel to Sisera and his soldiers, as mere instruments of a brutal pleasure: ". . . Have they not divided the prey, to every man a damsel or two? . . ." May we not suppose both Jael and Deborah, animated with righteous indignation against the intended violaters of their sex? (*Epitome of the History of the World*, I, 1812 [477–8])

Clara Lucas Balfour takes a similar path (*Women of Scripture*, 1847 [99–102]). Deborah's song she finds replete with "feminine" characteristics of piety, gratitude, tenderness (Deborah as mother), enthusiasm, and irony; nor is Jael's vehemence any less feminine. Jael's action and Deborah's enthusiastic approval are best understood in context: the speech of Sisera's mother and her wise ladies alludes to the fate, "far worse than death," from which the Hebrew damsels had been rescued. "Humiliations of the most degrading kind" had been averted. Little wonder "this mother in Israel should praise the treacherous and cruel act of Jael, looking less at the terrific deed than its consequences." Here Balfour adduces the support of Joseph Hall's interior monologue: "If a Christian Divine in modern times could write thus of such a fearful act . . . we shall cease to wonder that a Hebrew prophetess, whose people had by that act been delivered from countless miseries and dangers, should have extolled it." Yet her unease has the final word: "Happy are we that our pure and holy Christianity appeals to our nobler feelings, and recognises pardon, love, and peace, as the divine attributes of our faith and practice."

The sense of Jael's violation of hospitality continued to loom large, especially for commentators drawing upon the "Orient." John Kitto (1804–54), who had traveled in the "Holy Land," tells us in his *Bible History* (1841 [203]) that Sisera knew a Bedouin's tent, especially the women's section, to be an inviolable sanctuary, and "infamy worse than death" awaited anyone allowing injury to befall the guest or fugitive admitted to it. He accepted shelter there because of the "peace" between his master and the "emir," Heber. But while he slept, Jael realized she could win great favor from the victors by "anticipating" his almost certain death at their hands. Kitto condemns such a motive as "grossly opposed" to those notions of honor among tent-dwellers on which Sisera relied, thus "a most treacherous and cruel murder," wholly unjustifiable, given knowledge of Oriental principles. Deborah's foretelling was not divine sanction, and her praise issued from the first excitement of victory. In *The Pictorial Sunday-Book* (1845, 171), however, Kitto makes more allowance for a political act. Jael realized that her itinerant tribe's safety depended on its standing with the most powerful host nation, and with Jabin's power ended, that meant the Israelites – who would be grievously offended to find their enemy in Heber's tent. "And found he would be." By anticipating Sisera's end, she could "avert all evil from the house of Heber" and "make the now powerful Israelites its firmest friends."

Imaginatively, in *Bible History* Kitto had considered that Barak, on seeing the slain Sisera, "might then have pondered whether, had Sisera been the victor and himself the fugitive, the same fate might not have been his own." Kitto had not considered that Jael might likewise have wondered whether, failing action, her fate might not have been similar. But in his *Cyclopaedia of Biblical Literature* (1846; "Jael") he views more closely the woman's predicament. Recognizing, like Hoyland, that the victor's despoiling of the vanquished was a common occurrence, not confined to Canaanites, he relates this fact specifically to Jael's own situation. "Molestation" and "rather rough treatment" by the Israelites is what he sees in store for her camp and what her deed averted – and there is no disputing Deborah's unqualified praise. He therefore revisits Jael's motives in this "painful transaction" and finds them "entirely prudential." Yet, in the end, he veers off into a negative judgment, "grieved to see the act vindicated as authorized by the usages of ancient warfare, of rude times, and of ferocious manners." There was peace between the house of Heber and the prince of Hazor. Jael's actions may have been "prudential," but they were not "right."

The "molestation" argument, however, is not lost on Harriet Beecher Stowe (1811–96), of *Uncle Tom's Cabin* fame. Like Kitto, she refuses to appeal to ancient warfare and "rude times" for justification of the deed. Unlike Kitto, she turns that argument on its head. Jael's deed "has been exclaimed over by modern sentimentalists as something very shocking"; yet, she notes, when recently an Austrian "tyrant" who had "outraged noble Hungarian and Italian women" was himself "lynched" by the brewers of London, "shouts of universal applause went up." A woman "cannot meet her destroyer in open, hand-to-hand conflict," so must seek other means. "Deborah saw, in the tyrant thus overthrown, the ravisher and brutal tyrant of helpless woman, and she extolled the spirit by which Jael had entrapped the ferocious beast, whom her woman's weakness could not otherwise have subdued" (*Woman in Sacred History*, 1873, 102).

On Deborah's blessing of Jael Stowe follows in the steps of Hoyland and Balfour, but looking first to the outrages that must already have happened at Sisera's hands during the years of oppression. "It is a woman driven to the last extreme of indignation at outrages practiced on her sex that thus rejoices." Hence the energy of her blessing on the woman who dared deliver. "When the tiger who has slain helpless women and children is tracked to his lair, snared, and caught, a shout of exultation goes up." By "an exquisite touch," through the words of Sisera's mother, the poetess reminds the reader of what, but for this nail of Jael, would have been "the fate of all Judaean women." And in the reckoning of this haughty princess, "a noble Judaean lady, with her gold embroideries and raiment of needle-work, is only an ornament meet for the neck of the conqueror, – a toy, to be paraded in triumph" (p. 105).

Curiously, the outspoken women's movement leader, Elizabeth Cady Stanton (*The Woman's Bible*, 1898, 20–1), is less sure of her direction. She echoes the common condemnation of Jael, whose deception and cruelty "is revolting under our code of morality" and "seems more like the work of a fiend than of a woman." The best Cady Stanton can do is acknowledge that Deborah and Barak in their hour of victory did not neglect to honor Jael for what "they considered" a heroic deed. And Jael herself – she no doubt "imagined herself" in the line of duty, specially called by the Lord.

If Cady Stanton doubts a divine impulse, F. W. Farrar (1831–1903), convinced the deed is heinous, categorically dismisses it. "Surely we require the clearest and most positive statement that Jael was instigated to such a murder by Divine suggestion" (Smith and Fuller, *Dictionary*, 1893, I.2, "Jael"). As a way of obviating Deborah's praise, he wonders whether she offers not moral commendation but a statement of fact: namely, that "the wives of the nomad Arabs [*sic*] would undoubtedly regard Jael as a public benefactress, and praise her as a popular heroine." Otherwise, her passionate exultation is no worse than "the terrible verses" of Ps 137:8–9. If, in the nineteenth century after Christ, many could bestow the title "angel of assassination" on Charlotte Corday (who killed French revolutionary Marat in his bathtub), it is hardly strange that a thousand years before Christ some would extenuate and even praise Jael.

In the end Farrar invokes the increasingly popular "rude times" argument: "we must not judge the rude impassioned Bedouin chieftainess by the moral standard of Christianity, or even of later Judaism." Or, as another writer puts it, we should conceive her not a Christian nor even a Jew, "but a nomad, warm with the passions of the desert and the vertical sun, swayed by the impulses of goodness which she had not learnt to regulate, a blind believer in the mysterious name of Yahweh." Moral criticism of her is too often "unhistorical" and denies the "relativity of all moral conduct" (Robert F. Horton, *Women of the Old Testament*, 1899, 130).

Perhaps nothing better sums up the confusion sown by Jael's story than the account by John Ruskin (1819–1900) of his attending a Bible lesson by the much loved Unitarian scholar F. D. Maurice (1805–72). Ruskin's mother had read the Bible with him constantly until he was 14, and he had grown up believing its every word was true. Maurice, however, took "an enlightened modern view." He "discoursed in passionate indignation," warning that "such dreadful deeds could only have been done in cold blood in the Dark Biblical ages"; and that "no religious and patriotic Englishwoman ought ever to think of imitating Jael by nailing a Russian's or Prussian's skull to the ground,—especially after giving him butter in a lordly dish." Ruskin sat silent. At the close he ventured to inquire why Deborah had praised Jael.

> On which Maurice, with startled and flashing eyes, burst into partly scornful, partly alarmed, denunciation of Deborah the prophetess, as a mere blazing Amazon; and of her song as a merely rhythmic storm of battle-rage, no more to be listened to with edification or faith than the Norman's sword-song at the battle of Hastings. Whereupon there remained nothing for me,—to whom the Song of Deborah was as sacred as the Magnificat,—but total collapse in sorrow and astonishment; the eyes of all the class being also bent on me in amazed reprobation of my benighted views, and unchristian sentiments. And I got away how I could, but never went back. (*Praeterita*, 1885–9, III, ch. 1)

The story's violence certainly did not deter those who would teach children about the Bible. They often took the simple route. "But when Sisera was asleep God spoke to Jael and told her that Sisera was his enemy, and that she had been chosen as God's means of justice" (*Bible Stories and Character Building*, 1911, I, 131). Some chose the even simpler route: "Then while he was covered with the mantle, Jael slew him, for she knew that he was a very wicked man" (*Great Stories of the Bible*, 1924). No explanation was necessary for the reader of the popular picture puzzle or symbol book (derived from the "hieroglyphic" books of the eighteenth century on) where all that was needed were the missing words, such as "temple" (e.g. Lindley Smyth, *Happy Sundays*, 1908) (PLATE 3.4b). And the illustrators and versifiers have simply enjoyed themselves. (e.g. E. Miller, *Scripture History*, 1833) (PLATE 3.4a).

> The villain slept. She tiptoed round
> And nailed his noggin to the ground.
> (Jeanne Steig, *Old Testament Made Easy*, 1990)

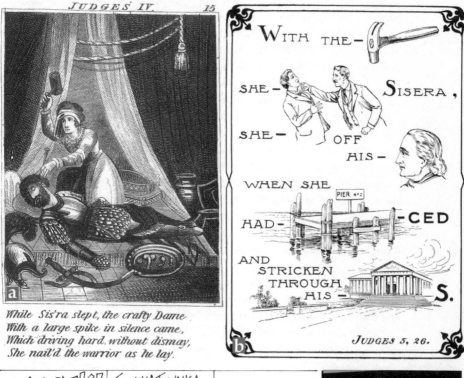

PLATE 3.4 Jael kills Sisera (continued): (a) Miller's *Scripture History*, 1833; (b) Smyth's *Happy Sundays*, 1908; (c) Gaiman and Hollings, 1987. (See pp. 84, 86)

The adult comic book creators have certainly not passed up a chance with Judges, which provides many of Knockabout Publications' *Outrageous Tales from the Old Testament* (1987), including that of Jael (Neil Gaiman, writer, and Julie Hollings, artist). For blood and gore these graphics are not to be outdone, though there are a few relatively restrained moments (PLATE 3.4c).

As so often, the details of a biblical story are grist to the interpretive mill. An issue surfacing sometimes in popular literature is whether the prose (ch. 4) and poetic (ch. 5) narratives differ significantly. With the rise of historical ("higher") criticism, especially from the nineteenth century on, differences supported claims for different sources. By the early twentieth century, the theory of two sources, and their relative dating, was firmly entrenched. The two sources "agree in the main," observes James Hastings (1852–1922), "but there are some striking disagreements." The song, upon which the prose depends, is "obviously ancient, and may well be contemporary with the events it describes; it is not only one of the finest odes in the Hebrew language, but it possesses the highest value as a historical document." Either Deborah composed it herself, or it came from a contemporary (*Greater Men and Women*, 1914, 446–7). Essentially this view has prevailed to the present day, especially under the influence of the historian and biblical archaeologist W. F. Albright and his pupils during the latter part of the twentieth century.

One of the crucial details concerned Jael's killing of Sisera. Did she kill him sleeping (so the prose narrative) or standing up, perhaps while drinking (as the poem suggests)? Thomas Scott typifies attempts to harmonize: "When Jael had driven the nail through the head of Sisera, she perhaps cut it off with his own sword, though indeed no intimation is given of it in the history; and the words may merely be a poetical repetition of the same idea by a variety of terms. – When he felt the anguish of the nail penetrating his head, perhaps he struggled to arise, but fell down again, and bowed, and died at her feet" (*Holy Bible*, 1788–92).

For those supporting the two-source theory, the claim that the song was more ancient usually settled the issue and had the advantage of lessening the Jael problem: killing a standing man was apparently preferable to killing a sleeping one. So the prose version "makes the case against Jael blacker "(J. H. Bernard, "Jael," in Hastings, *Dictionary*, 1902) by having her murder Sisera as Macbeth murdered Duncan (Hastings, *Greater Men and Women*, 451). Yet it was not hard to turn this argument around. Precisely the (claimed) effect of lessening the problem made the song suspect. German professor Rudolf Kittel (1853–1929) is certain that the later prose "legend" has kept more faithfully the deed's "entirely repulsive perfidity" (*Great Men and Movements*, 1925, 57). While Sisera was standing drinking the milk, Jael was seized with a patriotic rage, approached him from behind, and crushed his skull. "The song idealized the act and thus made it more acceptable to our natural feeling. Instead of by carefully planned assassination, Sisera was killed by suddenly roused passion." Perfidious Jael!

Recent reception

Variant sources meant variant histories. George F. Moore (1851–1931) of Andover Theological Seminary, whose historical-critical commentary (*Judges*, 1895) is still in print, is typical. Discrepancies between prose and poem stem from one narrative, about Zebulun and Naphtali warring against Jabin of Hazor, being combined with another, about a war with Sisera, king of Harosheth. These have been superficially harmonized by making Sisera Jabin's general. Moore likes the idea that Heber ("if not a later editorial addition") belongs to the original Jabin story; but since Jael is inseparable from Sisera in the plot, she must belong to the Sisera story. In making her Heber's wife, an editor harmonized them "by an artifice similar to that by which Sisera was made Jabin's general." What is more, "it might be further surmised that in the original story Jabin met at the tents of Heber a fate like that which overtook Sisera at the hand of Jael." Yet having got so far, Moore adds, "But all this is mere conjecture" (p. 109).

Jael's mode of killing he regards as "more ingenious than sure; a blow of the mallet upon the temple was a simpler and safer plan than to try to drive the blunt wooden pin through his head." He will not follow "apologists," who judge Jael's deed by absolute ethics, into the "morasses of casuistry into which an unhistorical ideal of religion and revelation leads them." The ancient standards were lower than those of "Christian morality," and the deed should be judged relative to them (pp. 126–7).

As for history, the song "agrees entirely" with its historical situation, though he allows that there is little evidence for what that situation was. Still, he detects no anachronisms, and above all, it gives "the impression of reality." Admittedly, to infer a contemporary origin or historical truth from an "impression of reality" is not strictly necessary. After all, "it is the pre-eminent gift of the poet to create this impression even when his story conflicts with our knowledge; – think of Homer, Dante, Shakespeare." But he will stick with the "impression." In any case, he doubts that Semitic poets had the capacity to create the illusion of historical reality. No, more likely this poem was inspired by the actual events than fashioned as "a supreme work of the creative imagination." A few pages on, however, and the reader can rest assured that it is indeed "a work of genius" of the "highest art." All is well, and both history and art are preserved.

Twentieth-century scholars have mined Judges for history. The characters often represent tribal groups and shed light on early tribal locations and movements. McCormick Theological Seminary professor Robert G. Boling (*Judges*, 1975) takes mention of Kenite Heber and his wife Jael to mean "an entire clan migrated and changed sides in the time of Jabin" (p. 97). Like others, he judges Deborah's song a valuable contemporary record. Yet an up-to-date reading differs from its predecessors "thanks mainly to the recovery of a plausible social setting for the Song." He believes that texts from Mari in Mesopotamia, many centuries earlier, corroborate early Israel's military muster, and supply details about land tenure and booty distribution (p. 116).

Archaeological and physical evidence are prominent. Boling notes excavation at Taanach claiming to show destruction c.1125 BCE. This the dig director "was inclined to associate" with events in the song. Megiddo (Judg 5:19) was apparently not then occupied, hence the poet's interest in the stream ("waters"). Boling cites as a "striking parallel" a swollen river story from a modern archaeological campaign. In spring, rains made travel in the muddy plain difficult for the director's supply wagon. Indeed, in 1903 no fewer than three of his horses drowned in the "swollen Qishon." (Swollen river stories are a commonplace of Kishon commentary; the Rev. Samuel Manning's friend who "crossed it dry-shod in the morning, when riding from Haifa to visit El Muhrakah, was exposed to considerable danger when endeavouring to recross it in the afternoon, and narrowly escaped being swept away" (*"Those Holy Fields,"* 1890, 172)). Familiar, too, is Boling's explanation that the song understood the stars (Judg 5:20–1) to cause a flash flood that overflowed the river's banks and mired down the heavy chariots, making them prey to Israel's foot soldiers standing "on the heights of the plain" (v. 18) (pp. 116–17). (Compare the earliest "explanation," by Josephus: a tempest drove rain and hail in the Canaanites' faces so that they could not see, their bows and slings were useless, and their hands too cold to hold their swords; whereas the Israelites had the wind at their back (*Antiquities*, v.205–6 (5.4)).)

Boling shares a view of Judges 5 as a "cultic song" sung at gatherings of the Israelite tribal federation, or "amphictyony" (a term drawn from ancient Greek parallels by German scholar Martin Noth). The otherwise decentralized tribes would join those in covenant with Yahweh to muster for a campaign or celebrate a victory. The genre of the victory hymn "is well known in examples from fifteenth to twelfth century Egypt and Assyria" (p. 117). The song is composed in more or less regular metrical patterns and strophic (verse) arrangements. Hebrew "meter" is based upon lines that break into two or three segments, often in parallel. Boling argues that some verses display patterns resembling those from late first-millennium Ugarit, in present-day Syria, "and mark the Song as archaic" (p. 106).

By the close of the twentieth century, however, scholars were less confident that they could match to the text's details a demonstrable social situation and historical event. The amphictyony hypothesis was shelved. Few were prepared to write a history of the Judges period. Archaeological evidence was being reassessed and its relation to the biblical texts challenged. Some argued that the stories were composed so many centuries after the purported events as to render them wholly unreliable as historical evidence. Even the early dating of the song of Deborah had its critics, though the "consensus" still reigned.

Modern criticism has continued to explore the precise meaning of words, often by comparing their use in other biblical passages or with lexical items in other ancient Semitic (or "cognate") languages. Where exactly did Jael plant her tent-peg? Boling argues that the rare Hebrew word *rqqh* (4:21, 22; 5:26), traditionally "temple," refers to "some portion of the head visible from the outside," since in the Song of Songs (4:3; 6:7) it lies behind the woman's veil. He looks for "some vulnerable spot such as the upper neck, behind the lower jaw," settling on "neck" (p. 98). Interestingly, Josephus's Jael drives her nail through Sisera's "mouth and jaw" (*Antiquities*, v. 208) and an ancient Greek version (LXX[A]) has "jaws." The NEB translates *rqqh* as "parted lips" in Songs (but not Judges!). There – in a descriptive sequence of eyes, hair, teeth, lips, tongue, *rqqh*, neck, breasts – a sexually charged comparison to a "split pomegranate" suggests a partly open mouth including lips and a glimpse of teeth (Fewell and Gunn, "Controlling Perspectives," 1990, 393). Given the ubiquity of "temple" in biblical commentary, literature, and art above all, this small revision is unlikely to gain much (so to speak) headway.

Other traditional concerns about the text hold sway. J. Alberto Soggin (*Judges*, 1981) is as bothered by Jael's "wretched assassination" as any in the long line of readers shocked at Jael's breach of hospitality, "sacrosanct in the ancient Near Eastern world." His best bet is that, as a Kenite, she was tied in kinship to Israel and so confronted, through no fault of her own, with a "complex conflict of loyalties." Still "the scene remains sinister" (p. 78).

The century's closing decades, not unlike a century earlier, are remarkable for the burgeoning study of biblical women. Jo Anne Hackett tries to re-construct a social world which includes their varied lives rather than write a political history of "elite power groups." In Deborah's decentralized and rural agrarian society, she argues, public and private spheres were not widely sepa-rated, so "her public life as judge need not have interfered with her domestic life." As judge she legitimized the battle against the Canaanites as a "holy war," and this public context transformed the domestic term "mother" ("mother in Israel") into a term comparable to "father" as a leader's title in the prophetic tradition (1 Sam 10:12 and 2 Kgs 2:12; cf. Boling, *Judges*, 118). While shown as not relying on men for her power, Deborah, identified by her husband, is also pictured in a traditional role. Given women's prominence in Judges and their often faring better than the men, perhaps some of these stories derive from literature "composed by and/or preserved in women's circles" ("In the Days of Jael," 1985).

From a literary-critical perspective, Deborah's story is one of the "strong countercurrents of affirmation of women" within the "patriarchal context of bibical literature." Such stories, argues J. Cheryl Exum, "undermine patriarchal assumptions and temper patriarchal biases, often challenging the very patriarchal structures that dominate the narrative landscape" ("Mother in Israel," 1985). She reminds her reader that "wife of Lappidoth" may be translated "fiery woman," approving the NEB footnote, "spirited woman," and she reads Deborah's accomplishments as including "counsel, inspiration, and leadership." That is, "a mother in Israel is one who brings liberation from oppression, provides protection, and ensures the well-being and security of her people."

Still, the text's dominant ideology is not easily undermined. Esther Fuchs, examining "deceptive women" in the Bible, finds that while deception by men is commonplace and accepted, deception by women is acceptable only "when her motives are selfless and when she attempts to promote the cause" of men. Yet women are tarnished by deception, nonetheless ("Who is Hiding the Truth?," 1985). Hence, like Soggin and many others, she sees Jael as exhibiting "courageous loyalty to the Israelites," but she also sees the repeated account of her deceptive hospitality injecting her image "with a foul taste of treachery." In other words, the ambivalent response to Jael's deed by readers over the centuries is a response to the narrative's ideological design. The national heroine is simultaneously a threatening figure to men; she conveys the message, "the safest thing for man to do is to distrust woman."

Fuchs might easily have appealed to Geoffrey Chaucer's (1343/4–1400) wife of Bath for support, for in the book which the wife's last husband used to read, continuously and avidly, Jael was joined to a myriad wicked wives:

> . . . of wyves hath he red,
> That somme han slayn hir housbondes in hir bed . . .
> And somme han drive nayles in hir brayn
> Whyle that they slepte, and thus they han hem slayn.
> (*Canterbury Tales*, ll. 765–70)

Though if the husband took the message, the wife did not – in exasperation she finally tore three pages out, right where he was reading, and for good measure, with her fist, "took him on the cheke." When the reciprocal beating was done, the Wife gained governance of house and land, and the book was burnt.

One means of casting "deceptive" female characters in a negative light is by suppressing their motivation, especially when the deception is "directly related to women's inferior status and political powerlessness" (Fuchs, 137). Jael, of course, exemplifies this condition. The murder "is sudden and surprising," and the text offers no explicit motive (Yairah Amit, "Judges 4: Its Contents and Form," 1987). Jael's side of the story is not presented. That leaves her vulnerable. Yet this has not prevented readers from searching for her motivations, as we have seen.

Readers have become ever more alert to the story's gender reversals. In Jael's case this starts with the irony of Sisera addressing Jael with a masculine form when he tells her to stand at the tent's entrance. He assumes that only men are significant ("If any man comes and asks, Is there any man here?"). And the answer she is to give, No, proves prescient. Sisera will indeed become "no man" but rather, as some have read the text, a raped and murdered woman. The language of the killing in both prose and poetry is laced with maternal and sexual overtones. Of Judg 5:27, Susan Niditch sums up ("Eroticism and Death," 1989, 50):

> Double meanings of violent death and sexuality emerge in every line. He is at her feet in a pose of defeat and humiliation; he kneels between her legs in a sexual pose [Hebrew *rgl*, foot or leg, is a euphemism for genitals]. He falls and lies, a dead warrior assassinated by a warrior better than he; he is a supplicant and a would-be lover. . . . He is despoiled/destroyed. The woman Jael becomes not the object of sexual advances . . . but herself is the aggressor, the despoiler.

So images of maternal nurturing and protection, the giving of milk and the covering with a rug, give way to seduction and a reverse rape (Fewell and Gunn, "Controlling Perspectives," 1990, 403–4). If the spoils of victory are alike for Canaanite and Israelite (see above), the "molestation" and "rough treatment" Kitto sees in store for the Kenite camp might as well mean rape for Jael, short of a dead Sisera in her tent and a hammer in her hand. Indeed, her predicament may be worse. Her husband is a Kenite, a descendant of Moses' father-in-law and most likely an itinerant smith ("Joiner Smith"). But he has "separated" from the Kenites. What would draw him north to a king whose power lies in his force of iron chariots? Are Jabin's iron chariots Heber's livelihood? "No wonder Heber was not a home that day as the chariot force was readied for battle. Nor, we may guess, would he be likely to return in a hurry." So gender and politics put Jael in jeopardy. She acts for survival (pp. 393–6).

Feminist criticism has increasingly recognized ambiguity in the way biblical stories depict gender relations, suggesting that the ideology of male domi-
nance is far from secure, but also that biblical affirmations of women as often
as not involve some compromise with patriarchy. Deborah, for example, leads
her people and brings liberation. She also celebrates Jael's killing. Readers
have had all sorts of problems with that praise. Fewer have been troubled
by Deborah's depiction of Sisera's mother, though, as we have seen, it has disturbed some.

There is irony here, but there is also more at stake. As Hoyland and Stowe
argued, our sympathy for the mother "is brought up short by the callous attitude that is attributed to her in connection with the Jewish girls whom she
imagines her son to have taken captive" (Freema Gottlieb, "Three Mothers,"
1981, 202). Another reader speaks of the "alienation that makes her speak of
other women as "wombs" to divide among the men, the thieves (violators) of
women" (Mieke Bal, *Murder and Difference*, 1988, 65). But why project such
"alienation" upon the Canaanite women? Why must the reader be hardened
against them? (Fewell and Gunn, 1990, 408). Perhaps because the song has
already spoken of Canaanite captives, including, no doubt, women and children. The Israelite army has come for its own plunder – a womb or two for
every soldier. "By forcing the Canaanite women to approve unconsciously their
own imminent rape, the singer victors can end their recital in mocking
triumph. So the singers, themselves now party to the same way of violence
against women, are justified. Deborah, woman in a man's world, is justified."

Again the Israelites do evil, God hands them over to the Midianites (Madian), who lay waste the land, and the people cry for help. A prophet sent by God reminds them of their past deliverance from Egypt and their failure to heed God's voice. The angel of the Lord comes to Gideon (Gedeon) and, over his objections, insists that he, Gideon, will deliver Israel. Gideon asks for a sign. The angel makes food into a flaming sacrifice, convincing Gideon that he has seen an angel (6:1–24). That night, at God's command, he breaks down his father's altar of Baal (whence he is called Jerub-baal) and is rescued from the people's wrath only by his father's intervention. The enemy now invade the Jezreel valley. Possessed by the Spirit of the Lord, Gideon calls out an army. He seeks another sign, and God obliges with a miraculously wet and dry fleece (6:25–40).

The army is too big, insists God, concerned that Israel will take the credit should he grant victory. He orders that those who profess themselves fearful, the majority, be sent home. Yet still too many remain, so God orders a test: those who lap up water like a dog are chosen, leaving an army of 300 men (7:1–8). At divine prompting, Gideon enters the Midianite camp, overhears the telling of a dream, and is encouraged. With trumpets and torches inside empty jars the 300 approach the enemy camp. They blow their trumpets, smash their jars, hold their torches, and shout. The Midianites, fallen into confusion, are routed. Gideon calls out the Ephraimites to seize the "waters" and the Jordan. They capture and kill Oreb and Zeeb, two Midianite princes (7:9–25).

The Ephraimites reproach Gideon for not having asked them earlier to fight against Midian, but he mollifies them (8:1–3). He pursues Zebah (Zebee) and Zalmunna (Salmana), kings of Midian, but, seeking aid, is rebuffed by the towns of Succoth and Penuel (Phanuel). Once the kings are captured, he punishes the elders of Succoth and slays the men of Penuel. Zebah and Zalmunna challenge him to slay them himself, and he obliges (8:4–21). Asked to rule over the Israelites, Gideon declines. From Midianite spoil, however, he makes a golden ephod, "and it became a snare to Gideon and his family." The land rests for 40 years (8:22–8). Abimelech is born, Gideon dies, and the people turn to the Baals and forget their God. Nor do they show kindness to Gideon's family (8:29–35).

Christian interpreters in Late Antiquity and the Middle Ages make use of Gideon's story more than any other in Judges, except perhaps the story of Samson. In both cases the texts are read allegorically to yield spiritual or doctrinal tenets of Christianity, or typologically to show how the Old Testament has prefigured the New. Gideon's fleece, infused with dew, is a type of the Virgin Mary, impregnated by the Holy Spirit. Or it is an anti-Jewish allegory of God's grace being withdrawn from Israel in favor of the Church, an interpretation countered by medieval Jewish scholars and tempered (but not wholly abandoned) among Christians by their shift after the Reformation towards reading the text more literally as the history of a doubting or cautious hero.

From the earliest Jewish commentators on, readers have consistently asked why Gideon asks for signs and what this says about him as a model leader. The signs and "tests" themselves have occasioned much (some might say inordinate) discussion of the enigmatic "lapping" test. Readers, too, have been drawn to Gideon's humble origins – seeing him as an "ordinary" man – and to his humility, part of an abiding interest in what today is called the hero's "character." Yet was Gideon justified in his violent treatment of Succoth and Penuel? And why did he make the ensnaring ephod? From the Enlightenment on, other issues emerge. Critics have examined the story's historical setting and reliability, and found in the modern "Orient" illumination of the ancient text. Throughout, readers have sought a "message." For many, it lies in Gideon's response to the men of Israel: "I will not rule over you, and my son will not rule over you; the Lord will rule over you."

Ancient and Medieval

After 40 years of peace, the Israelites again displeased God (Judg 6:1). The first-century CE historian known today as Pseudo-Philo elaborates in *Biblical Antiquities* (34.1–5). Scoffing at Israel's devotion to its law, Aod the Midianite magician effected a magic trick by means of some angels to whom he had been sacrificing: he showed the Israelites the sun's light by night. Amazed, they declared, "Behold what the gods of the Midianites can do, and we did not know it." Testing the Israelites, God let the magician's angels carry on, and the Israelites ended thoroughly deceived. So God gave them over to the Midianites, who reduced them to slavery.

Midrash Ecclesiastes Rabbah (1:4) equates Gideon's judgeship in God's eyes with that of Moses (Samson equaled Aaron, and Jephthah equaled Samuel). These associations "teach you that whoever is appointed leader of the community, though he be the lowliest of the lowly, is the equal of the most celebrated of the former celebrities." The medieval *Sefer Chasidim* (p. 129) explains that insignificant leaders who work for the sake of Heaven "are comparable in God's view to *tzaddikim*," the legendary "righteous ones" of earlier generations. Were this not so, every person could justifiably ask, "Why wasn't I born in an earlier generation when people were much smarter? Then I could have learned much more Torah" (so also Rashi, on 1 Sam 12:11 and Deut 19:17).

Still, while generally praising Gideon for his concern over Israel's suffering and his zeal for God, Jewish discussion does not overlook his errors, particularly his creating the golden ephod (Judges 8). Pseudo-Philo in fact has Gideon making idols, not an ephod (a priestly vestment), and worshiping them. He sees here a dilemma for God, which explains why the hero is not punished. When Gideon destroyed Baal's sanctuary, everyone predicted that Baal would avenge himself. Were God to chastise Gideon for making the ephod, people might say that Baal was punishing him. Better to let him die at a good old age and chastise him afterwards! (*Antiquities*, 36:4). Rashi (1040–1105), whose commentaries became standard for Jews and influenced Christians (e.g. Nicholas of Lyra [c.1270–1349] and, later, Protestant scholars), grants that Gideon's intentions were good. Rashi imagines that he used the nose rings [KJV, "earrings"] of Israel's defeated enemies "to serve as a reminder of the great victory, by showing how immense their army was that the nose rings of the nobles amounted to all this gold" (on Judg 8:24–7). Nonetheless the ephod became a "snare" and an object of idol worship. In addition to this error by Gideon, a tradition counts at least seven ways in which he transgressed the Law when he sacrificed in a place formerly dedicated to an idol (Judg 6: 25–32). But according to *Midrash Numbers Rabbah* (14:1) and Rashi (on Judg

6:25 and Ps 119:126), these faults were forgiven because his intention was righteous.

Christian interpretation of Gideon's fleece was relentlessly chauvinistic. It was bound up with Ps 72:6 (71:6), which the Vulgate (following the Greek Septuagint) read as "He shall come down like rain upon the fleece (*vellus*), and like moisture dripping upon the earth." (In the Hebrew text, the noun in Psalms (*gez*), like that in Judges (*gizzah*), is related to "shear" or "shave" (*gzz*), and while usually meaning "fleece" can also be a "reaping" or "mown field," which better suits Ps 72:6 – hence kjv "mown grass." In both places the Greek translators used *pokos* (related to "shear") which always means "fleece.") But with the Vulgate psalm read as a messianic prophecy, the cryptic "rain upon the fleece" was no problem when matched with Gideon's story. As Ambrose (c.339–97) explains, here is disclosed "the mystery of the old history where Gideon, the warrior of the mystic conflict, receives the pledge of future victory." Gideon knew that the rain was "the dew of the Divine Word" which came down first in Judaea (the fleece) whereas elsewhere (the ground) remained without "the dew of faith." But then "Joseph's flock began to deny God," and when the "the dew of the heavenly shower was poured on the whole earth," the Jews began to grow "dry and parched in their own unbelief," while the Church was watered by prophecies and the Apostles "in the salutary shower of the heavenly Scriptures" (*Concerning Widows*, iii.18–19; cf. *On the Holy Spirit*, i.1–11, and Jerome, *Letter LVIII*). This anti-Jewish allegory early became standard for Christians. Of ten substantial references to Judges (seven involving Gideon) by Ambrose's famous pupil, Augustine (354–430), five make this point. Before Christ, grace was latent in Judaism, "hidden in a cloud, as the rain in the fleece" (Sermon 81.9); since Christ, the Jewish people have become dry, "reprobate," while grace is patently visible among all the surrounding "nations" (*On Original Sin*, ch. 29).

The victorious Gideon prefigures Christ. In similar vein, the meal prepared for the angelic visitor means the Eucharist to Ambrose (*On the Holy Spirit*, i.2). The dew is variously the Divine Word (as with Ambrose and Augustine), the grace of the sacraments, or even Christ himself who comes down for the lost sheep of Israel to a chosen "Mother." As John Chrysostom (c.347–407) says of Ps 72:6, " 'He shall come down like the rain into a fleece of wool, and like the drop which distills upon the earth' because He noiselessly and gently entered into the Virgin's womb." So the miracle of the "fleece," impregnated with the divine dew, is understood as a type of Mary's virginal conception (e.g. Anthony of Padua, *Sermo in Purificatione*, 3.722b; also medieval lyric poetry – see Jeffrey, *Dictionary*, 1992, 306). Thus a prayer (c.1448) by Scottish cleric and diplomat Richard Holland (in Moffatt, *Bible in Scots Literature*, c.1923, 47–8) addresses Mary:

Thou stable throne of Solomon,
Thou worthy wand of Aaron,
Thou joyous fleece of Gideon . . .

This typology is pictured in the so-called *Biblia Pauperum* which illustrated, from about the thirteenth century on, how the Old Testament points to the New. A blockbook version – each page a single woodblock – was printed in 1460. Gideon appears twice, in the first and thirty-third illustrations. Each contains three main panels, the central scene being key. The first page depicts the Annunciation to the Virgin Mary. In the left panel Eve, an apple in each hand, faces an upright serpent. A text explains that Mary fulfills Gen 3:14 – the serpent (Satan) will crawl on its belly and the woman will crush its head – and another says the serpent will lose its power when a virgin bears without labor (thus reversing the Fall – Gen 3:16).

In the right panel kneels Gideon, beside the fleece, entreating an angel. He prayed, says the text, "for a sign of victory in the fleece being filled with a fall of dew which prefigured the glorious Virgin Mary made pregnant without violation, by the pouring out of the Holy Spirit." Below Gideon the prophet Jeremiah announces that the Lord has created a new thing upon the earth, a woman shall compass a man (Jer 31:22). The angel's words to Mary, "The Lord is with you," are also addressed to Gideon. They signal victory, Christ's victory over Satan and death, and Gideon's over the Midianites (PLATE 4.1a).

The other page's central panel shows doubting Thomas touching the wound in the side of the risen, victorious Jesus. Gideon, in the left panel, stands opposite the angel who brings the promise of victory. The text explains that the promise to Gideon indeed came to pass, and that he signifies Thomas to whom Christ came as an angel of great counsel to strengthen his faith. In the *Glossa Ordinaria*, the standard summary of interpretation from the twelfth century on, Gideon's caution before his visitor is recognized as spiritual discernment, not lack of faith: he was ascertaining that an angel of light and not darkness confronted him (PL 113.526).

Other Gideon episodes receive attention from early Christian interpreters, although none as much as the fleece story. Ambrose, for example, points to the fire arising from the rock and consuming the sacrifice as an assurance of Christ's presence in baptism; hence the person of the minister is not vital to the sacrament (*On the Mysteries*, v). Also on baptism, Ephrem the Syrian (c.306–73) refers to Gideon's men who lapped like dogs: just as they lowered their heads to the water before heading to victory, so the faithful descend into the baptismal waters to emerge triumphant in the spiritual fight (*Hymns*, 7).

PLATE 4.1 Gideon's fleece: (a) *Biblia Pauperum*, 1460; (b) Quentel's Bible, c.1478. (See pp. 97, 100)

Jewish commentators countered Christian supersessionist use of the fleece with careful contextual reading. Ps 72:6 is a metaphor not of a fleece but of a mown field – may the righteous king's decree be absorbed in the people's hearts like rain on mown grass (Rashi on Ps 72:6, referring also to "reaping" in Amos 7:1). In Judges the fleece was precisely the sign Gideon requested, a sign that God was with him as deliverer of Israel from the Midianites. Joseph Kimchi (c.1105–70) considered it absurd that a divine sign's significance would not be realized until long after the fact. Arguing against Christian interpretations of Isa. 7:14 as referring to the virgin birth of Jesus, he observes that signs come not after but before events. Gideon's signs, assurances that he would win a victory, are typical (*Book of the Covenant*, 55).

Early Modern and Modern

Allegorical, typological, literal

Protestant Reformers, Luther and Calvin, like their Christian precursors, used Gideon's story more than any other text in Judges. While Martin Luther (1483–1546) principally opposed allegory, with Gideon's fleece he follows tradition. Like Jerome, Ambrose, and Augustine a millennium earlier, he finds the Jews to be "dry" and reprobate, God's grace now flowing to the rest of the world. He claims that Old Testament passages may seem "fleshy and thick," but properly understood, emptied of the "flesh" or literal meaning, they reveal the "skin" or spiritual meaning. Thus Gideon's fleece, representing Judaism, initially received the divine dew, showing that the "Law" is properly "spiritual"; but it became "judgment instead of righteousness, hardness instead of sweetness" (*First Lectures on the Psalms*, 1513–15, on Ps 104:2). By contrast, John Calvin (1509–64) reads more literally. He takes the hero's doubts to show that "in every saint there is always to be found something reprehensible" (*Commentary on Hebrews*, 1549, on ch. 11). The miracle of the fleece is not an allegory, but rather a sign of events to come (cf. Joseph Kimchi). Signs prepare the minds of the faithful, "so that they may not doubt but that God will do what he has promised" (*Commentary on Jeremiah*, 1559, on Jer 44:29–30). Because of doubt, "Gideon was torpid, but when he saw by this miracle that victory would be given him, he boldly took the work assigned to him."

Focus on human motivations and aspirations reflected humanistic explorations in narrative literature and art already well developed when Calvin wrote. Woodcut illustrations in the new printed Bibles were mostly of story scenes. In Heinrich Quentel's pioneering Cologne Bible (c.1478), one of the only three pictures in Judges (20 in Genesis) depicts Gideon. He kneels with the fleece before God, as in the medieval *Biblia Pauperum*. Illustrations often combine scenes to round out an episode or story: here in the background Gideon's soldiers lap from a river flowing to the viewer (Judg 7:4–8) (PLATE 4.1b).

With literal reading grew the idea that the Bible should be subject to the same critical inquiry as other literature. A humanist anticipating modern scholarship's "historical criticism" was Jewish philosopher Benedict (Baruch) de Spinoza (1634–77) in the Netherlands. His *Theologico-Political Treatise* (1670) examined the Bible according to the rules of reason alone, in an argument for freedom of religious expression and debate. Without extrinsic assurance, he writes of Gideon, "prophecy cannot afford certainty." The "fact of revelation" – the appearance of an angel or of God himself – was not enough for a man of faith like Gideon, who demanded a sign in order to know that it was God talking to him (ch. 2).

Literal-historical interpretation also opened stories like Gideon's to being understood as lessons for daily living. Thus moderate Calvinist Joseph Hall (1574–1656), conscious of life's vicissitudes, observes of God chastising the Israelites by the Midianites, "It is a good sign when God chides us; his round reprehensions are ever gracious forerunners of mercy; whereas, his silent connivance at the wicked argues deep and secret displeasure: the prophet made way for the angel, reproof for deliverance, humiliation for comfort . . . Sins, not afflictions, argue God absent." Hall also speaks of Gideon's public spiritedness, noting that when God says, "The Lord is with thee," Gideon answers, "Alas, Lord, if the Lord be with us." Gideon's immediate identification of himself with his people offers a lesson: "The main care of a good heart is still for the public; neither can it enjoy itself, while the church of God is distressed" (*Contemplations*, 1615 [ix.4–5, 110–11]).

No few vicissitudes in the sixteenth and seventeenth centuries were born of religio-political strife. Interpretation of Judges is never far away. Swiss playwright Hans von Rute (d. 1558) sees Gideon as an ancient precursor of the Protestant Reformation. At the peak of Catholic persecution of radical Anabaptists, his play *Gedeon* (1540) presents the biblical hero, careful to do God's will, as an iconoclastic reformer. The cult of Baal caricatures a Catholicism obsessed with idols and altars and corrupted by priestly greed. (vv. 1136–49). Gideon's destruction of Baal's altar, enacted on stage, re-enacts Swiss iconoclasm of the previous decade (see Ehrstine, *Theater, Culture, and Community*, 2002, 171–2).

Writing to General Fairfax in 1648, Oliver Cromwell (1599–1658), commanding Parliament's New Model Army, implicitly identifies with Gideon's reformation of Israel. In hopes that England may discern God's spirit and will in current events, Cromwell declares that political events "lately come to pass" have been "the wonderful works of God; breaking the rod of the oppressor, as in the day of Midian—not with garments rolled in blood, but by the terror of the Lord; who will yet save His people and confound His enemies, as on that day" (in Stoddart, *Old Testament in Life and Literature*, 1913, 142). In turn, Milton's young protégé, Andrew Marvell (1621–78), wrote a comparison of Cromwell to Gideon, both of whom refused a crown, into his encomium, "The First Anniversary of the Government Under His Highness the Lord Protector" (1655). Gideon, having conquered "two Kings grown great," extends on the peace a "Warlike power" as he razes Penuel and suppresses Succoth's elders (Judg 8:4–23):

> No King might ever such a Force have done;
> Yet would not he be Lord, nor yet his Son.
> Thou with the same strength, and an Heart as plain,
> Didst (like thine Olive) still refuse to Reign.

(Two years later Marvell was finally awarded the post of Assistant Latin Secretary to the Council of State, for which Milton had recommended him in 1653.) The comparison of Gideon and Cromwell lingers. Scottish Free Church Presbyterian Alexander Whyte (1836–1921) compares Gideon's little army to "Colonel Cromwell's soldiers" and calls them "Gideon's three hundred Ironsides" (*Bible Characters*, 1905, 14).

Gideon is often a model of virtue, valor, and wisdom. In John Milton's *Paradise Regained* (1671; 2.430–9) he is the first example Jesus gives of such a person, and in *Samson Agonistes* (1671; 277–81) "matchless Gideon" is Israel's "great Deliverer" of his generation. Likewise, Gideon's pitchers, trumpets, and lamps are shown to Christians in the celestial Armory of the House Beautiful, in John Bunyan's *Pilgrims Progress* (1678), as examples of instruments by which the Lord's servants in former times "had done wonderful things" (Jeffrey, *Dictionary*, 306).

He parallels David as a model of trust in God for religious poet William Cowper (1731–1800). Ordered forth against the invaders' camp, "with arms of little worth, a pitcher and a lamp," Gideon with his trumpets made his coming known, "and all the host was overthrown." In this victory Cowper exclaims that he has seen the day when with a single word God has helped him say, "My trust is in the Lord," and his soul "hath quelled a thousand foes, / Fearless of all that could oppose." Of the possibility that Gideon himself might have been less than trusting, the poet betrays no hint unless it be in the last lines:

> But unbelief, self-will,
> Self-righteousness, and pride,

How often do they steal
My weapon from my side!
Yet David's Lord, and Gideon's friend,
Will help his servant to the end.
(*Olney Hymns*, 1765–73, IV: "Jehovah-Nissi")

The poem was much read. An equally enthusiastic religionist quotes it a century later in Sara Jeannette Duncan's novel, *Vernon's Aunt: being the Oriental Experiences of Miss Lavinia Moffat* (1894).

A less sanguine view is taken by English Presbyterian minister Dr Thain Davidson (1833–1904), who notes Gideon's evidently vindictive spirit (Succoth and Penuel). Still, we must see him, like Elijah, Martin Luther, and John Knox, in the light of their own times. "Rough times need rough measures; and if, occasionally, the cause of truth may be injured by the rude violence of some stern iconoclast, I suspect it more frequently suffers from the compromising weakness of half-hearted professors" ("Gideon," 1896, 52).

Typological interpretation of Gideon has continued, among Catholics and Protestants alike, to the present day. It was a live option in Scotland in the eighteenth century for the Rev. John Brown (1722–87), whose Bible commentary and *Dictionary* long found favor wherever English was read. "Was our Redeemer prefigured by Gideon?" he asks. His indirect answer cleverly links Gideon, Christ, the reader, and the evangelical preacher.

> How mean his debased condition! but express, solemn, and seasonable his call to his work, and miraculous the confirmation thereof! How important and necessary his work of our salvation! With what burning zeal he offered his sacrifice, overthrew idolatry, and restored the true love and worship of God! By a few weak and unarmed preachers sounding the gospel-trumpet, and displaying its light and fire from their earthen vessels, he still foils sin, Satan, and the world. . . . How kindly he invites us to share with him in his victories! how mildly he pacifies his unreasonable friends! and what terrible vengeance he inflicts on his despisers . . . and will on all such as deny his poor people supply in their time of need! (*Dictionary*, 1769)

Augustine's anti-Jewish allegory of the fleece also colors Christian reception in the modern period. It finds a place in a Bible history (1670) written by Jansenist priest Nicolas Fontaine (1625–1709). Originally for children, it was published for adults in English in 1690 (*History of the Old and New Testament*), and available in various versions, French and English, well into the nineteenth century – read by Protestants as well as Catholics. Drawing upon "the Fathers,"

Fontaine accords the supersessionist allegory as much weight as he does the explanation of Gideon's "humble Fear and Distrust" as proper humility for our instruction (so Ambrose). He adds, " the Grace of God is a kind of Heavenly Dew, without the continual supply of which our Souls are in the same condition, in which we see a dry and barren Ground is."

In early English editions, a full-page picture accompanies each episode's explanation. Gideon kneels in the traditional posture beside the fleece, which is connected by lines of light (or dew?) to heaven, emphasizing the divine (PLATE 4.2d). By contrast, the seventeenth-century Dutch illustrator, Jan Goeree (1670–1731), in Pieter Mortier's famous "Great Bible" (*Historie*, 1700), has eliminated direct reference to God. He shows a kneeling Gideon, not imploring a sign, but wringing out the fleece into a large and rapidly filling bowl and looking back to the ranks of soldiers (indicating the point of the test) while the sun rises above distant hills (PLATE 4.2a). The engraving reflects literal-historical reading, which continues into the next century (Goeree's design is often borrowed, as in Esther Hewlett's *Scripture History*, 1828)

The supersessionist allegory finds nineteenth-century expression in a poem, "Gideon's Fleece," by Irishwoman Cecil Francis Alexander (1818–95), renowned for "All Things Bright and Beautiful" among other hymns (in Baynes, *Illustrated Book of Sacred Poems*, 1867, 301–3). "Type, strange type, of Israel's early glory," she writes, "Heaven-besprinkled when the earth was dry." But "Mystic type, too, of her sad declining, / Who doth desolate and dewless lie." Yet Alexander's interest is less supersession than the individual Christian's readiness to receive the dew of God's grace. (Contrast Thomas Grinfield's "An emblem," where supersession is precisely the point (in Horder, *Poets' Bible*, 1889, 317)). Her reader is to dream no more of Israel's glory and grievous fall: "Hath that sacrament of shame and splendour / To thine own heart not a nearer call?" She ends with supplication:

> Christ! be with us, that these hearts within us
> Prove not graceless in the hour of grace;
> Dew of heaven! feed us with the sweetness
> Of Thy Spirit in the dewless place.

In part the allegory's long life is due to its expression via Ps 72:6 (71:6) in both the Roman Breviary, the Catholic Church's prayer book, and the Church of England's Book of Common Prayer, which from 1662 until recent times incorporated Miles Coverdale's translation of the Psalter: "He shall come down like the rain into a fleece of wool, even as the drops that water the earth."

PLATE 4.2   Gideon: (a) Goeree's fleece, 1700; (b) Cole's angel, c.1720; (c) Tissot's angel, 1904; (d) Fontaine's *History*, 1699; (e) Doré's lapping, 1866. (See pp. 103, 110–11)

The lapping test has provoked no end of explanation. The received text (Hebrew, Vulgate, and English translations) is hard to follow. In KJV, God tells Gideon to separate out "every one that lappeth of the water with his tongue, as a dog lappeth" from "every one that boweth down upon his knees to drink" (Judg 7:5). A reader might expect those lapping like a dog would put their mouths down to the water and do just that, lap up the water, whereas the kneelers would presumably scoop up the water to drink, not lap, from their cupped hands. But the next verse tells us that the 300 chosen were those "that lapped, putting their hand to their mouth" as opposed to those who knelt to drink! Scholars over the past century have usually argued that the text has gone wrong (cf. G. F. Moore, *Judges*, 1895). A copyist perhaps mistakenly transposed the phrase "with hand to mouth" in a text which originally read, " 'Everyone who laps with his tongue, the way a dog laps, set apart by himself; and everyone who goes down on his knees to drink water, with hand to mouth, set apart by himself.' The total of all who lapped with their tongues was three hundred men; all the rest of the people went down on their knees to drink water" (Boling, *Judges*, 1975).

Mostly, however, the discussion has produced little but "obscurity" (so Moore). Ancient historian Josephus (*Antiquities*, v.216 (6.3)) dodges the problem by having the majority, stalwarts, "bending" or "lying" down (*kataklithentas*) to drink (Whiston: "bent down on their knees") and the 300, cowards, fearfully raising the water to their lips with their hands. (God chose cowards so that the victory be obviously his alone.) Subsequent interpreters, attempting to harmonize the Bible and Josephus, are divided over whether the 300 are stalwarts or cowards. The water-scoopers are often said to be *standing* and scooping. Like a dog? No problem. Grotius was of a mind (so Symon Patrick, *Commentary*, 1702) that they lapped, "just as the Dogs do of the River *Nile*, as they run, for fear of the Crocodiles." Another commentator claims that among the ancients it was not uncommon "to take up the water in their hands, and lap it thence like a dog; and it is remarkable that the Hottentots, at this day, have a custom very similar." To which yet another adds, "they stoop down; but no further than to reach the water with the right hand, by which they throw it up so dexterously that their hand seldom approaches nearer to the mouth than a foot. . . . They perform it nearly as quick as the dog" (from William Jenks, *Comprehensive Commentary*, 1835). The illustration in Harper's famous *Illuminated Bible* of 1846 clearly distinguishes between a kneeling and a standing drinker, each with cupped hand to mouth. Each has clearly scooped. But who is the lapper?

Nothing daunted, Scottish professor George Adam Smith (1856–1942), in his *Historical Geography of the Holy Land* (1896), explains the test's suitability by reference to the terrain. The Israelites who bowed, "drinking headlong," would be unaware of their position vis-à-vis the enemy, whereas those who merely crouched, lapping up water with one hand, their weapons in the other and their face to the enemy, were aware of their danger and ready against surprise. The test was a test of attitude, which "both in physical and moral warfare, has proved of greater value than strength or skill" (p. 397). This interpretation, where "alertness" is the key, was popular in Smith's day and remains so. Another Scot, missionary John Inglis (d. 1914) in *Bible Illustrations from the New Hebrides* (1890, 36), finds an explanation when he sees native people stooping and throwing up the water into their mouths with their hands. "I observed that, as a general rule, it was the strong, the vigorous, and the energetic who drank water in this way; never the feeble, the lazy, or the easy-going."

The skeptics of the late seventeenth and eighteenth centuries bring a new approach to Gideon, as to other Old Testament texts. They attack Gideon as a model. They attempt even more to undermine the story's credibility. French philosopher Voltaire (1694–1778) typically pretends to defend the text while savaging it. He purports to take issue with a claim that the Gideon story must be an interpolation because it is unworthy of the majesty of God's people. With feigned impatience, Voltaire replies that what is worthy or not is not ours to decide. Gideon does only what Abraham does; and God also gives Moses a sign. Indeed, "God gives signs to almost all the Jewish prophets. Whether in a palace or a barn, does not matter." Voltaire has now closed in on his point. God, he says, always dealt with the Jews directly, "gave them signs himself; it was always a matter of himself. He always appeared as a man." Now the punch line: "But could anyone recognize him?" For Voltaire, like many other *incredules*, anthropomorphism, the biblical depiction of God in human form, was a debased understanding of the Deity.

Voltaire finds the story improbable, from its miracles to its doubting hero. Accept such stories, he has his regular interlocutor, biblical scholar Dr Calmet, saying in their defence, or reject the whole Bible. True, says Voltaire; and the reason the skeptics have a problem, he adds maliciously, is that they will never understand that those ancient times bear no relationship to our present times. His final stab: "We here pass over in silence the people of Succoth, whose backs Gideon broke with desert thorns for having refused refreshments to his troops wearied from such great carnage" (*Bible enfin expliquée*, 1776 [137–8]).

Character

The "scripture biographies" proliferating from the late eighteenth century on were part of the counterattack against the skeptics. Sound reading of Scripture built sound Christian "character" and restored religion. Robert Wilson Evans (1789–1866) observes of Gideon after meeting with the angel, "Gideon forthwith was a different man. He felt the might in which the Lord had bidden him go forth. All his slavish despondency vanished, and a lofty spirit, equal to the mighty occasion to which he was called, possessed him" (*Scripture Biography*, 1835, 59–64). As with Israel and Gideon, true religion is the key to a country's fortunes; "and from that point will start every true patriot that attempts to raise his fallen country. . . . The greatest political blessing of our own country [is] secondary to the preservation of the pure faith of the church of God." In the age of the novel, Evans explores the *inner* religious life of Gideon, as in his reflections on Gideon's transformation after the battle: "Now he experienced the deep delight of the humble thankfulness, and the utterly downcast prostration before God, which fills the bosom of him, who is conscious of having been made his instrument for good."

Interest in character development continues through the century and well into the next. Gideon's humble origin also produces a lesson about character and class. The Rev. Dr Thain Davidson writes that "obscurity of birth is no obstacle to a life of noble service . . . Never be ashamed of it, if your hands are horny with honest toil; never account it a thing to be concealed, if you were born in a thatched cottage that had but two rooms and an attic; or if your old father is a weaver, or follows the plough, or keeps the tollgate, or works in the village smithy, think it no dishonour to say with Gideon, 'My family is poor in Manasseh, and I am least in my father's house'" ("Gideon," 1896, 46–7).

Such expositions of Christian improvement by studying Bible characters naturally exhibit some concern to protect Gideon's good name. Mrs Trimmer (1741–1810) wrote to facilitate Bible study in schools and families. Rather than seeing fearful doubt in Gideon's test with the fleece, she finds prudence (cf. the medieval *Glossa Ordinaria*). Having gathered numerous soldiers, "he was desirous that they should have as satisfactory a proof as he himself had received, that he was appointed of GOD to be the deliverer of Israel." The divine response not only showed that the Lord was indeed with him, but "was a great means of strengthening his own faith, at the same time that it awakened that of others" (*Sacred History*, 1783 [lii, 229]). Although perplexed as to precisely what God intended by the lapping test, she is clear that his purpose was to destroy the Midianites "in a wonderful manner, so as to leave no one room to suppose his own skill or valour had gained the victory" (cf. Josephus). Whatever directions seemed good to God's infinite wisdom, the Israelites were bound to obey. Trimmer mostly extols Gideon's character: for example, he subdues the Ephraimites' anger by "magnifying their exploits and speaking humbly of his own" (liii, 233; so later, Kitto, *Pictorial History*, 1844, 385; and a century on, Fleming James, *Personalities*, 1939, 69).

Gideon's humility is often central in moral lessons. Is it self-denial or self-doubt? Most say the former, focusing on his refusal to be king over Israel (8:23). Scottish minister and editor James Hastings (1852–1922) considers his principled refusal "deserves to be ranked with the most illustrious examples of patriotic self-denial that history has recorded" *(Greater Men and Women*, 1914, 476–7). An American educational volume on "leaders of olden days" praises Gideon for his fearlessness, wit, and "the modesty which moved him to decline the greatest honor that Israel could offer" (Athearn, *Master Library*, 1923, I, 294). Few have put it more eloquently than an Englishman much read in America, John Kitto (1804–54). "We are called upon to admire his truly courteous and self-retreating character, and that nice and difficult tact—difficult because spontaneously *natural*—in the management of men, which is a rare and finer species of judgment, and by which he was intuitively taught to say the properest word, and do the properest deed at the most proper time" *(Pictorial History of Palestine*, 1844, I, 385). Kitto has in mind particularly Gideon's response to the disgruntled men of Ephraim (Judg 8:1–3; cf. James, *Personalities*, 1939, 73).

Others, however, find in him self-doubt, especially at his calling (6:11–18). Even so, a lesson may be learned. For Archibald Alexander, in *Feathers on the Moor* (1928), precisely Gideon's self-doubt and weak faith make the story inspiring. "Yet it is this diffident, self-distrustful soul that God lighted upon to be the saviour of his people." Doesn't God's choice of "a confessed doubter" have "a very modern sound?" Isn't it "glorious encouragement" for Gideon's brethren in a new world where old doctrines seem not to fit, questions never before dreamed of beset young people, and there seems "no room or work in the Kingdom of Christ for restless and questioning minds."

> And it is such a delusion! With this page open before us, let us tell young Gideon of to-day, with his new Science and new Psychology, and his new view of Scripture that is changing the whole face of truth for him, that Jesus Christ needs him and wants him just as he is. Here, in this ancient Scripture, is a Modernist of the Old Testament called and used and honoured of God. (pp. 62–3)

Whether self-denier, self-doubter, or both, Gideon does not escape criticism for making the ephod after victory (cf. rabbinic discussion). Mrs Trimmer, pioneer educator, believes his mistake in this regard "shews the ill effects of a bad education. He was the son of a priest of Baal; and, though converted by a *divine vision* to the *belief* of the *true* GOD, he might have neglected to inform himself of the *ceremonial part* of religion, and he probably remained satisfied with the rectitude of his intentions" *(Sacred History*, 1783 [liii, 234]). Indeed Trimmer and others are confident of his pure intentions (cf. Hewlett, *Scripture*

History, 1828, 29–31). Good intentions are not enough, she insists, and he should have studied God's laws, "especially as the *temporal* happiness and prosperity of the people of Israel depended on a punctual observance of those ordinances which GOD appointed" (p. 234; so also Kitto, *Pictorial History*, 1844, 209, and James, *Personalities*, 1939, 73).

Whereas Trimmer considers Gideon's mistake to result from poor education in the Law, James Hastings sees a deeper flaw: "like many other good men, he appears to have been unable to worship Him except in a visible form, with the usual, in fact the universal, result—the gradual but certain deterioration of the moral and spiritual instincts of those who so worship Him" (*Greater Men and Women*, 1914, 477). Presbyterian preacher Alexander Whyte puts a Pauline spin on the flaw: Gideon knew the letter of the Law but not its spirit. "All through his magnificent life of service, in Paul's words, the law of Moses, the law of God, had never entered Gideon's heart" (*Bible Characters*, 1905, 17). (Whyte imaginatively supplies the story with many details, including Pascal's idea that Gideon's mother cut the fleece into an undergarment for war.)

Gideon illustrated

Increased European and American interest in the "Orient," with steam making travel easier, shows up in nineteenth-century commentary. Edward Hughes (pl. 1850) explains to school students that the "nomadic Arabians" at the outset of Gideon's story "poured into Palestine," trampling down fields, gardens, and vineyards, plundering, and rioting, "as the Bedouin Arabs are accustomed to do at the present day, when not restrained by force" (*Scripture Geography and History*, 1853 [184]). Similarly John Kitto makes the past present (or the present past): districts bordering on the desert, where local government is not strong or Arab semi-cultivators not an obstacle, "are still subject to similar visitations." Until very recently, he reports, the very area east of the Jordan invaded by the Midianites "suffered much from the periodical sojourn and severe exactions of the Bedouin tribes" (*Pictorial History*, 1844, 382; see, a century later, Kittel, *Great Men and Movements*, 1925, 61; *Master Library*, 1923, I, 293).

A splendid pictorial rendition of the lapping episode in orientalizing fashion is by Gustave Doré (1832–83). Men are gathered by a pool at dusk (cf. 7:9, "that same night"). Gideon, mounted and helmeted, resembles seventeenth and eighteenth-century "classical" Gideons (cf. Zetzner's "Merian Bible," 1630). Most of his soldiers, however, with flowing robes and headdresses, belong unmistakably to the artist's contemporary "Orient." Against the grey of distant hills and clouded skyline are several turbaned figures mounted on camels, their long lances black against the fading light (PLATE 4.2e, p. 104) (*Sainte Bible,* 1866; cf. James P. Boyd, *Young People's Bible History,* 1893).

A tone of European cultural and moral superiority pervades much (though not all) commentary, in scholarly and popular works alike. The Midianite army's disarray before Gideon, explains classical scholar William Smith (1813–93), resulted from plans "admirably adapted to strike a panic terror into the huge and undisciplined nomad host. . . . We know from history that large and irregular Oriental armies are especially liable to sudden outbursts of uncontrollable terror" (*Dictionary,* I, 1863, "Gideon"). More sympathetic is Canadian bishop W. C. Bompas (1834–1906), who thought himself to represent the best interests of indigenous people of the Northwest. The frontier provides his parallels: "Such forays have been often made in modern times by the wild tribes of North American Indians, but the natives of the extreme North are at present inoffensive." The Midianite chieftains' names, "Raven" and "Wolf" (Oreb and Zeeb), he compares to those of "many a modern Indian," and Zalmunna ("Wandering Shade") reminds him of a Saskatchewan plain chief called Wandering Spirit – both names "implying the consignment to the shades of death of the victims of their fury" (in Cody, *An Apostle of the North,* 1908, 355).

Gideon's story in general has inspired little notable English poetry. But the scourging of Succoth's elders and the fate of Zebah and Zalmunna have had their appeal. Marvell's "Anniversary" (above) refers to the incidents. In an early poem, "Buonaparte" (1832), Alfred Tennyson (1809–92), a proud Briton, writes of Napoleon:

> He thought to quell the stubborn hearts of oak,
> Madman!—to chain with chains, and bind with bands
> That island queen who sways the floods and lands
> From Ind to Ind . . .
> . . . at Trafalgar yet once more
> We taught him: late he learned humility
> Perforce, like those whom Gideon schooled with briers.

Still, young English poet Susanna Strickland (1803–85) cannot but admire Gideon's enemy kings ("Gideon's fleece," 1831):

> Proudly then Zalmunna spoke:
> Dost thou think we dread the stroke
> Doomed to stretch us on the plain
> With the brave in battle slain?
> Leave yon tender boy to shed
> Tear-drops o'er the tombless dead:
> Like the mighty chiefs of old,

Thou art cast in sterner mould.
Rise, then, champion of the Lord,
Rise! and slay us with the sword:
Life from thee we scorn to crave,
Midian would not live a slave!
But when Judah's harp shall raise
Songs to celebrate thy praise,
Let the bards of Israel tell
How Zebah and Zalmunna fell!

Commonly illustrated since the Reformation are Gideon's encounter with the angel, the fleece test and lapping, and the rout with trumpets and lamps. Occasionally another scene appears, such as the destruction of Baal's altar – the actual deed, with crowbar (altar) and hatchets (sacred trees) as in *Cassell's Illustrated Family Bible* (c.1870), or the subsequent consternation, as designed by Gerard Hoet (1648–1733) in Pierre de Hondt's *Figures de la Bible* (1728) in the Netherlands, source of the finest engravings of the late seventeenth and eighteenth centuries.

Gideon's appearance with the angel is a favorite of illustrated Bibles and, above all, children's Bible stories. The angels are winged. They tend to be women (despite the text). They stand or hover beside the rock, touching it with a staff, and fire ascends, often in spectacular blaze. Sometimes Gideon pours broth over the meat and unleavened cakes; at other times he stands back in fear of the theophany. These angels are no match, however, for the divine visitor in a series of "above Two Hundred Historys Curiously Engrav'd by J. Cole" (c. 1720). Suspended in the air (as often at Manoah's sacrifice), this angel has a fire-starting style of incomparable panache (PLATE 4.2b, p. 104).

Highly unusual is the angel conceived by James Tissot (1836–1902), famous for his many watercolors illustrating the Bible (PLATE 4.2c, p. 104) (*Old Testament*, II, 1904). No wings or heavenly light distinguish angel from ordinary man. He sits, feet crossed, under a great oak. Within reach are altar-like rocks on which lies the meal-become-sacrifice, and he extends a sinewy arm to ignite the fire. The picture captures the narrative's irony: the reader knows that the visitor is angelic ("Now the angel of the Lord came and sat under the oak at Ophrah"), whereas Gideon does not ("Pray, sir, if the Lord is with us, why then has all this befallen us?"). Recognition dawns when the fire consumes the food and the angel vanishes ("Then Gideon perceived that he was the angel of the Lord"). Tissot's angel transforms an otherwise conventional picture.

Lapping scenes are legion. Men stand, kneel, scoop, and lie face down to the water in sundry terrains and costumes. Occasionally one or two look around, perhaps in wonderment. In Luther's Wittemberg Bible of 1534 (published by Lufft), a tall figure, spear in hand, talks and gestures to a kneeling soldier.

Perhaps Gideon is selecting the man. Or perhaps the gesture means, "I don't get it either!" (PLATE 4.3a). Master copperplate engraver Matthäus Merian (1593–1650) shows Gideon mounted and pointing, faced by a soldier, mouth agape. Does the man's open palm convey incomprehension or obedience? That Gideon is lit, the soldier shadowed, may suggest where illumination lies. In the background scene, lapping flourishes. Gideon singles out a kneeling soldier drinking from his helmet. Presumably he is *not* one of the 300. Others clearly lap, without putting their hands to their mouths, while yet others kneel and scoop, without clearly lapping (PLATE 4.3b) (*Icones Biblicae*, 1626; Zetzner's Merian Bible, 1630). The literal picture reminds us that the received text itself is, literally, a muddle.

The trumpet and lamp scene is much favored. Luther's 1524 Bible shows Gideon's three groups closing in, torches aloft, and led by trumpeters, while Midianite confusion, a bundle of bodies, fills the foreground. In the small woodcut of a 1556 Latin Bible (Lyons: Jean de Tournes), Bernard Salomon's elegantly posed soldiers hold a pitcher or two, but wonderfully wrought trumpets catch the eye. The enemy flee (PLATE 4.4a). The nineteenth century sees Julius Schnorr von Carolsfeld (1794–1872) beautifully reworking this design and finding many imitators (PLATE 4.4b) (*Bibel in Bildern*, 1860; *Bible in Pictures*, 1869). Most magnificent is the double-folio design by Gerard Hoet (PLATE 4.5) (de Hondt's *Figures*, 1728). The viewer stands with a troop of trumpeting torch-bearers striding in from front right. Below, in the darkness, is chaos in the Midianite camp. Beyond, to right and left, the lights of the other two companies gleam. Catching attention, bottom right, a young man stumbles over a rock, still clutching aloft his jar-shaded torch. Or is he is about to smash the jar on the rock? Or both? At any rate, he is out of "synch" with the team. His neighbor, blasting away in concert, glances down at him out of the corner of his eye. Hoet relates high drama where the heroes remain human.

Merian (1626) brings the viewer inside the Midianite camp among startled soldiers seeing the band of fiery, trumpet-blowing invaders in the quickly closing distance (Fontaine's *History* borrows this design). The 1899 drawing by E. A. Abbey (1851–1911) maintains the Midianite perspective, though the trumpeting light-bearers have almost overwhelmed picture and viewer. Yet, etched by the light, a woman's face aghast stands out against the dark – also a recumbent baby and an intruder's long fingers clawing at the tent awning (in Griffith, *Great Painters and Their Famous Bible Pictures*, 1925). Perspective is eliminated, and the opposing parties balanced, in the *Oxford Illustrated Old Testament* (1968). Edward Bawden (1903–89) schematizes his woodcut so that individuals merge into three neat companies of bright trumpeters, left, and in a tangle of grey fighters, right. Night makes a third, dividing column into which figures step or fall. Bawden's picture distances the viewer from the opposing

PLATE 4.3   Gideon: (a) Lufft's Bible, 1534; (b) Merian, 1626; (c) Szyk, 1949. (See pp. 112, 120)

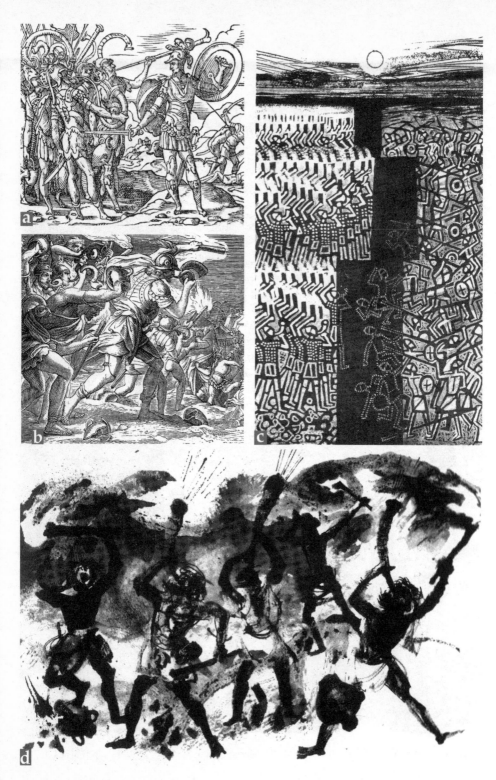

PLATE 4.4   Gideon's trumpets: (a) Salomon, 1556; (b) Schnorr, 1860; (c) Bawden, 1968; (d) Klaasse, 1959. (See pp. 112, 116)

PLATE 4.5   Gideon's trumpets: Hoet, 1728. (See p. 112)

parties, establishing initial objectivity. Eliminating individuals may convey that this is not Gideon's victory. The patterning also tames the violence (PLATE 4.4c). No violence, either, in Piet Klaasse's (1918–2001) illustration for Klink's *Bible for Children* (1967) – nor any self-immolating Midianites. Klaasse illustrates simply a joyous ruckus of prancing trumpeters (PLATE 4.4d)

Recent reception

For nineteenth-century scholars, tracing the origins and compositional history of biblical texts, became important. For example, that Gideon is also called Jerubbaal indicated two originally independent sources (known as J and E) later woven into a single narrative. American seminary professor George F. Moore (1851–1931) argues that after witnessing the divine messenger (6:11–24), Gideon would not have required another sign. The fleece test (6:36–40) therefore derives from the missing parallel account where Gideon is summoned in a dream or night vision, "as commonly in E." Likewise the surprise attack on the Midianites (7:16–22) Moore finds "redundant and confused" – carrying the concealed torch would occupy two hands, leaving none for the horns. His hypothesis: the E source supplied the trumpets, and J the jars and torches (*Judges*, 1895).

In similar scholarly vein, the Rev. T. K. Cheyne (1841–1915) of Oxford treats "Gideon" and "Jerubbaal" stories separately in the *Encyclopaedia Biblica* (1903, "Gideon"). The Rev. C. F. Burney (1868–1925), another Oxford scholar, details the contributions of sources and editors (*Judges*, 1918, xxiii): D (the Deuteronomist), D^2 (a later hand influenced by the former), E (the Elohistic narrative in the Hexateuch, Judges, and 1 Samuel), E^2 (later work by a member (or members) of the Elohistic school), J (the Jehovistic (or Yahwistic) narrative in the Hexateuch, Judges, and 1 Samuel), JE (the combined narrative of J and E – a symbol used when it is not possible, or not necessary, to distinguish the sources), R^{E2} (redactor of the school of E^2, the principal editor of Judges), R^{JE} (redactor of J and E in the Hexateuch, Judges, and 1 Samuel), R^P (redactors of the Priestly school (influenced by the Hexateuchal document P) of Judges and Kings), X (an unknown source in Judges 20, 21).

Determining the narrative's disparate origins is still a concern later in the century for Italian scholar J. Alberto Soggin (*Judges*, 1981). Gideon's destruction of the Baal altar (6:25–32) was possibly a minor local conflict. Inserted into Gideon's call narrative, the story added a matching internal struggle to the external struggle against the Midianites (cf. 6:14–16). Like Moore, Soggin finds the fleece test (6:36–40) out of place. He differs on 6:11–24 and 6:36–40 being parallels, however. Rather, the first passage relates to the messenger's identity, the second to the mission's outcome. So they reasonably follow each other.

In seeking a text's historical roots, critics have tried to describe its component literary genres. Soggin defines Gideon's call (6:11–24) as a common sanctuary legend, whereas the fleece story is an edifying anecdote like some in rabbinic Judaism: a strange request produces a miracle or acute observation. Behind the story might lie some instance of divination before battle, but as the story developed, all divinatory elements were eliminated as scandalous.

Older questions persevere in historical-critical commentary. What did the drinking manner of the 300 signify (7:4–8)? "They were the rude, fierce men," concludes Moore. Soggin joins the less sure. Confusion characterizes the test. Why lapping like a dog should be better suited to holy war than drinking kneeling, hand to mouth, is not easily established. Suffice that the merit of the victory was God's alone. Other scholars are quite sure. Having (not unreasonably) emended the text, Robert G. Boling (d. 1995) espouses "alertness" (see G. A. Smith, above): the hand-to-mouth kneelers can more easily watch their backs than the lying-down lappers. In the footsteps of Josephus, he argues that thereby God gains greater glory, having chosen "not only a smaller force, but also those less suitable to a military enterprise" (*Judges*, 1975).

Critics continued to find explanations in contemporary customs of the region. Arab life *in situ* has been a special favorite. Moore says that it is "with true Arab spirit" that Zebah and Zalmunna challenge Gideon to give their death-stroke with his own hand (8:18–21). Soggin observes that "the blood vendetta is an institution which is still accepted today in the Bedouin world and also in certain Mediterranean regions, where it sometimes leads to interminable feuds." Illustrating Judges in the compendious *Story of the Bible* (c.1938, I, 275), by British scholars for the general public, is a photograph: GIDEON'S TEST SEEN TODAY AT GILBOA'S SPRING. The small print explains that we are seeing Arab soldiers (bent, scooping with one hand) demonstrate the test's suitability, "all drinking correctly save one" (left foreground, on knees, head down, rear up). He is plainly not "alert to the danger of surprise attack." With G. A. Smith, paraphrased, in support, this settles the long debate. The camera does not lie.

Ancient Near Eastern texts have also provided many a clue. Drawing upon Babylonian texts, Burney elucidates the cult object, the "Asherah" (6:25), as probably symbolizing Yahweh's consort worshiped by Amorite inhabitants of Canaan. On the meal Gideon prepares (6:19–23), Boling refers to a Hittite "Soldier's Oath" involving "an array of such visual aids as a bowl of fermenting yeast, crackling sinews, and mutton fat dissolving on a hot pan." The angel "here turns Gideon's religiosity into an enlistment opportunity."

Boling, like many of this period, enlists archaeological data to amplify the "history" behind the text. He dates Gideon and Abimelech a half-century earlier than Deborah and Barak on the basis of (unspecified) archaeological evidence from Shechem and Taanach. He regularly identifies place names with modern archaeological sites – Succoth, for example, with Tell Deir 'Alla in the Jordan valley. Undeterred by excavation evidence against sizeable village occupation in the relevant period – the narrative specifies 77 officials and elders – Boling dates Gideon's dealings with Succoth to the early twelfth century and designates it "a rural rallying point very much distrusted by the free-wheeling judge." Thus provided with a historical time and place, how could the story itself not be historical?

Probably the classic "archaeological" account is by John Garstang (1876–1956) of Liverpool University (*Foundations of Bible History: Joshua Judges*, 1931). He too takes pains to "place" the text. His book is abundantly illustrated with small grey photos of sites (plus an Appendix on "Places and archaeology"). As for temporality, his chronology makes Boling's look loose: the Midianite oppression occurred c.1161–1154 BCE. It was not an organized raid, but a general nomadic movement impelled by draught and weak Egyptian rule. Not so, responds Boling: Midian's revival was probably due to immigration from eastern Anatolia and northern Syria, bringing with it the domesticated camel. Ruled by kings, the invaders with their superior "camel corps" were not nomads, he insists.

The persevering reader learns that twentieth-century use of archaeology and ancient texts to explain biblical texts is not an exact science. And, as with earlier modes of interpretation, such argument often discloses a desire to prove the Bible "true," meaning here historically reliable. Yet times change. By the century's end, the number of professional historians confident of being able to reconstruct a "period of the Judges," let alone a history of Gideon, was dwindling.

As confidence in the historical "Judges period" was starting to wane, other scholars were turning from history to art – the art of biblical storytelling. In contrast to the "source" analysts, literary critic Barry G. Webb (*Book of the Judges*, 1987, 144–59) reads Judges 6–8 as a unified story in a carefully designed larger story, the "final form" of Judges. He attends to plot, character development, and how plot and character build the story's "theme." The narrative begins and ends at Ophrah, and consists of two movements, the second starting with Gideon's crossing the Jordan. At first Gideon is like Moses (Exod 3:1–4:17) in the way he is called, given authority, protests his inadequacy, and receives a reassuring sign. Stressed are his fearfulness and need of reassurance – he is "a reluctant conscript" relying upon Yahweh, "a model of Mosaic piety." His war is a holy war in which victory is not his achievement but Yahweh's gift (a familiar conclusion). But in the second movement Gideon is different. He presses after Zebah and Zalmunna with "frenzied determination." Yahweh is not involved, and Gideon's diffidence is gone – he treats Succoth and Penuel ruthlessly. Yet offered kingship, Gideon "recoils from the impiety" and asserts that God shall rule – though ironically the offer stems from his exceeding his authority and behaving as a king by crossing the Jordan. Exodus motifs surface also in this movement. Gideon and his followers are in the wilderness, but without manna. He is contrasted with Moses (his vindictive manner) and compared to him (Moses too overreaches in the wilderness and erects a bronze serpent – later an idolatrous cult object (2 Kgs 18:14)). Finally we see that Ophrah, initially home to a clan cult, "a family affair," is now where "all Israel" worships the ephod: so "Gideon, Yahweh's champion against Baal, presides over national apostasy." While one aspect of the initial crisis (Israel versus Midian) is resolved, the fundamental aspect (Israel versus Yahweh) is more acute.

Gideon has always appealed to Christian educators. He is rarely absent from children's Bible storybooks and has been a favorite in Sunday School curricula. Here is the quintessential reluctant hero, an "everyman" who finds faith and bravely delivers his people. The fleece test was regularly retold, though less favored in wide-circulation books for a "liberal" readership. Lapping is usually included, and frequently fudged. The idea that the "alert" were chosen (cf. Smith, above), is popular. The conundrum is sometimes solved by illustration: the chosen, whether kneeling or standing, drink from their hands, while the others drink either directly from the pool (Grainger, *365 Bible Stories and Verses*, 1971) or even from vessels (Taylor, *My First Bible*, 1989). The trumpets are always there. Succoth's elders, Penuel's men, Zebah and Zalmunna – they are usually gone. So too the golden ephod. But Gideon often gets to refuse the crown.

Among some Protestant evangelicals in North America the fleece story is a precedent for seeking an external sign or making a material test to determine God's will, a practice called "putting out a fleece." Better known are the "Gideon Bibles" found in hotels across the land, placed (by the millions) by The Gideons International, an organization of evangelical businessmen with numerous local chapters. At the founding meeting of three men in Beaver Dam, Wisconsin, in 1899, one Will J. Knights rose from prayer declaring "We shall be Gideons" and read aloud from Judges 6–7. The Gideons explain that humility, faith, and obedience marked Gideon's character. He did what God wanted him to do, regardless of his own judgment. So must they.

A different exemplar of faith is the modern Gideon of dramatist "Paddy" Chayefsky (1923–81) in his Broadway comedy (*Gideon*, 1961), later adapted for television. Chayefsky fashions with humorous irony the man who refuses to acknowledge God despite miracles. He is "a comic anti-hero but made so out of the playwright's poignant reflection that part of what it means to be resignedly 'modern' is the knowledge that heroism and faith are inextricable; when faith disappears, heroic self-transcendence disappears soon after" (Jeffrey, *Dictionary*, 1992, 307).

Gideon inspires yet another sense of zeal in the early Zionist memoir *Gideon's Spring: A Man and His Kibbutz*, by Zerubavel Gilead (1912–88) and Doreothea Krook (1920–89). Gilead recalls feeling a "symbolic significance" to his living as a boy "on the banks of the biblical spring where Gideon's men were chosen." The mysterious test was about calling to a mission. Pondering story and place he understood better his own mission to make real the Zionist-socialist dream: "Being distinctly secular-minded, we did not care to think of ourselves as 'chosen'—God's Chosen People, or Gideon's chosen three hundred. Yet the sense of having been called to carry out a great historic task was strong in us, and with it the sense that our every act, indeed our every thought, feeling, and attitude, was a test of our fitness for it" (3–4).

Rabbi Abba Hillel Silver of the Reform congregation Tifereth Israel (The Temple) in Cleveland, Ohio, was a Zionist spokesman before the UN in the 1947 hearings on Palestine. In the chapel of "Silver's Temple" is a stained glass memorial to the congregation's men who died in service. The artist was Arthur Szyk (1894–1951), one of the century's outstanding illustrators and political cartoonists. (A poster version of Szyk's "Gideon" is sold today.) Gideon, who defeated the Midianites, is wrought in gorgeous color and elaborate decoration incorporating repeated stars of David. He stands with spear and armor in a window alongside Samson, who slew the Philistines, and Judah the Maccabee (Judas Maccabeus), who freed his people from the Syrians (PLATE 4.3c; p. 113).

Celebrating Gideon as warrior-hero has always been susceptible to the tension in the story between divine and human leadership. Whose is the victory, and who, indeed, is "king"? Is the point of the lapping to produce 300 stalwarts or 300 cowards? or simply to reduce the many to the few? – so that (as many have professed) God may be the more glorified. For J. Clinton McCann (*Judges*, 2002) the issue of sovereignty pervades Judges, and is highlighted in Gideon's story, perhaps the book's turning point. McCann expresses this traditional emphasis through questions he sees the story asking, "Will Gideon, and will Israel, recognize the priority of God's claim and the centrality of God's will? Or will they slip steadily into the twin sins of idolatry and self-assertion, which inevitably result in chaotic and destructive consequences?"

> The signs which God to Gideon gave,
> His holy sov'reignty made known;
> That he alone has power to save,
> And claims his glory as his own.
> (E. Miller, *Scripture History*, 1833)

Abimelech, a son of Gideon (Gedeon) and a concubine from Shechem (Sichem), persuades his mother's kinsfolk to support his bid to rule. Slaying 70 brothers he becomes king. But Jotham (Joatham) escapes and cries out to the Shechemites a parable ("Jotham's fable"): the trees gathered to anoint a king, most refused to serve, but finally the bramble assented, warning that if they chose in bad faith, it would burn the cedars. He explains: if the Shechemites have honorably chosen Abimelech, well and good, but if not, fire will devour both of them. He then runs away.

After three years an evil spirit from God stirs up strife between Abimelech and the Shechemites. Gaal arrives in Shechem and encourages revolt, boasting that if in charge he would deal with Abimelech. Zebul, the city governor, is not pleased. He urges Abimelech to ambush Gaal. When Gaal realizes he is trapped, Zebul utters the immortal words, "Where is your mouth now?" Defeated, Gaal is expelled. Abimelech takes the city, kills all within, and destroys it. At this news the people of the Tower of Shechem enter a stronghold which Abimelech burns along with about 1,000 men and women.

Finally Abimelech takes Thebez (Thebes) and prepares to burn one remaining tower of refuge. But a certain woman drops an upper millstone on his head. Lest it be said a woman killed him, he demands that his armor-bearer run him through – and the soldier obliges. Thus, concludes the narrator, did God requite Abimelech's wickedness, and "all the evil of the men of Shechem did God render upon their heads, and upon them came the curse of Jotham."

This story has elicited less comment than others in Judges, though from earliest times it has suggested the need for good government. In the seventeenth and eighteenth centuries it joins the argument about legitimately removing rulers. Readers have always admired Jotham's "fable" and found therein an array of lessons. They have also compared the whole narrative to political or historical drama with compelling characters. A recurring question is how divine and human causality interact to drive the plot. Discussion often converges on the fatal millstone. Did the woman drop it of her own accord? Or was she pushed?

Ancient and Medieval

Not surprisingly, few have a kind word for Abimelech, a condemnation made easier because he is not called a judge or said to have been raised up by God. One of his earliest critics is Jewish historian Josephus (37–c.100 CE), concerned that his Greco-Roman readership appreciate the antiquity of his people's laws and their respect for good government. Abimelech is an aberration. He "transformed the government into a tyranny, setting himself up to do whatsoever he pleased in defiance of the laws and showing bitter animosity against the champions of justice" (*Antiquities*, v.233–4 (7.1)).

Josephus's contemporary known as Pseudo-Philo hardly gives him the time of day, confining the story to Jotham's fable, narrated as though actually occurring (37:1–5). Abimelech kills his brothers, whereupon the trees gather. Refusing the leadership, they predict that Abimelech's rule will be short, he will demand blood from Israel, and die by stoning. The bramble notes its own long-standing history, from Adam's thorns and thistles to the thorny thicket which enlightened Moses. Now it will again offer the truth: so it consumes the other trees with fire. Abimelech then rules briefly and is killed by a woman dropping a millstone. (*Midrash Tanhuma B.*, 1:103, connects the trees in the fable to earlier judges – the olive is Othniel, the fig Deborah, the vine Gideon, and the bramble Abimelech.)

Greed brought him a deservedly early end. Indeed, his greed and wicked-ness are in pointed contrast to the piety and generosity of his Genesis name-sake, Abimelech, king of Gerar (*Aggadat Bereshit*, 26:52–4). In his Proverbs commentary, Rashi (1040–1105) approves the haggadic tradition which finds in Prov 26:27 – "Whoever rolls a stone, it will roll back on him" – the poetic justice ultimately visited upon Abimelech who slew his brothers on one stone and died by a stone.

As one might expect of early Christian Fathers, Jotham's speech yields both allegory (an allegory of the allegory) and a lesson about virginity. Methodius of Olympus, bishop of Lycia (d. c.311), tells his maidenly readers that he will show them "written prophecy" from Judges, "where the future reign of chastity was already clearly foretold." Jotham, he explains earnestly, speaks not of real trees, "for inanimate trees cannot be assembled in council to choose a king, inasmuch as they are firmly fixed by deep roots to the earth." This sorted out, the meaning is clear: souls, too deeply luxuriating in transgressions before Christ's incarnation, seek God's mercy, "that they may be governed by His pity and compassion, which Scripture expresses under the figure of the olive" (pro-ducing oil that lights and nourishes). Specifically, the olive "signifies the law given to Moses in the desert, because the prophetic grace, the holy oil, had failed from their inheritance when they broke the law." While the olive is the old law, the bramble is the new, "given to the apostles for the salvation of the world." It leads to salvation because by the Apostles' instruction "we have been taught virginity, of which alone the devil has not been able to make a decep-tive image" (*Banquet of the Ten Virgins*, x.2.1). No doubt Methodius has in mind the bramble's quality of keeping intruders out.

Early Modern and Modern

"Listen to me," cries Jotham to the Shechemites, "that God may listen to you." But does God listen to cries generated by anger or revenge? Calvin (1509–64) is sure that God "hears the complaints of the poor, who find no protector or avenger on earth," the more so if the despoiled bear their wrong patiently. But what if the cry contravenes the command to pray for our enemies? Calvin answers that God does not always approve of prayers he nevertheless answers, as with Jotham's imprecation, which took effect despite being "plainly the off-spring of immoderate anger" (*Last Four Books of Moses*, 1563 [III, 114–15 (on Deut 24:14)]; cf. *Institutes*, 1550 [II, iii.20.15, 870]).

More often, Abimelech's story has drawn readers to its political drama. Renaissance poet Anne Dowriche (c.1550–1638) compares the slaughter of

Protestants in Angiers, one of the "famous bloody broils" of her poem, *The French History* (1589). The Lord, she says, will strike down bloody tyrants, "with all their faithless crew." And whoever betrays his neighbor or seeks deceitfully to slay his brother shall not escape (ll. 2179–86):

> Such cursed bloody men God's plague does follow still,
> For wicked King Abimelech, who was content to kill
> His seventy brothers all the kingdom for to have,
> From just revenge he could not long his cursed carcass save,
> For from a woman's hand a millstone down was sent
> From off a wall, which with the weight his brain pan all to-rent,
> And after by his page was thrust unto the heart
> With sword, lest that a woman's stroke his glory should subvert.

Cleric and writer Joseph Hall (1574–1656) describes the participants as characters in a Shakespeare history (*Contemplations*, 1615 [ix.8, 119–21]). The Israelites are the "pattern of unthankfulness": "They who lately thought a kingdom too small recompense for Gideon and his sons, now think it too much for his seed to live; and take life away from the sons of him that gave them both life and liberty." Hundreds of years later, "when time had worn out the memory of Jerubbaal," the act might have been more excusable. "But ere their deliverer was cold in his coffin, to pay his benefits (which deserve to be everlasting) with the extirpation of his posterity, it was more than savage." The Shechemites who once betrayed their city in yielding to Hamor's suit (Genesis 34) are now "fit brokers" for Abimelech. "To cast off the sons of Gideon for strangers, were unthankful; to admit of seventy kings in one small country, were unreasonable; to admit of any other, rather than their own kinsman, were unnatural."

Abimelech should have seen his brothers as his equals, if not, given his mother's status, his betters. "Those that are most unworthy of honour are hottest in the chase of it; whilst the consciousness of better deserts bids men sit still, and stay to be either importuned or neglected. There can be no greater sign of unfitness, than vehement suit." Hall's account of Abimelech's ambition recalls Macbeth:

> Flattery, bribes, and blood, are the usual stairs of the ambitious. . . . Woe be to them that lie in the way of the aspiring! though they be brothers, they shall bleed; yea, the nearer they are, the more sure is their ruin. Who would not now think that Abimelech should find a hell in his breast, after so barbarous and unnatural a massacre? and yet, behold, he is as senseless as the stone upon which the blood of his seventy brethren was spilt. . . . All sins will easily down with the man that is resolved to rise.

Yet such prosperity is but short and fickle. "A stolen crown (though it may look fair) cannot be made of any but brittle stuff. All life is uncertain; but wickedness overruns nature." Thus the tide turns: "the evil spirit thrust himself into the plot of Abimelech's usurpation and murder." The Shechemites raised Abimelech unjustly to the throne; now, fittingly, "they are the first that feel the weight of his sceptre. The foolish bird limes herself with that which grew from her own excretion."

Hall adopts Rashi: "There now lies the greatness of Abimelech: upon one stone had he slain his seventy brethren, and now a stone slays him: his head had stolen the crown of Israel, and now his head is smitten." As for the king's vain attempt to deprecate the "frivolous" reproach of dying by a woman, our commentator has but scorn. He should have been more troubled at "frying in hell" and begging God's mercy. "So vain fools are niggardly of their reputation, and prodigal of their soul."

Hall's reading raises the question, does the divine agent control the plot? What part is played by the human hand? Puritan poet and politician John Milton (1608–74) is certain that God's providence works through sin, permitting it and often, as with Abimelech and the Shechemites, "inciting sinners to commit sin, hardening their hearts and blinding them" (*Christian Doctrine*, c.1658–60 [i.8.21, 331]). But Milton also believes that human action is indispensable. Royal apologist Salmasius argued (in defence of Charles I) that Judg 9:56, "God paid back the sin of Abimelech," means "God alone is judge and punisher of kings." Responds Milton, mockingly, "But the woman paid it back too, and so did the armor-bearer, over both of whom he boasted his royal rights" (*Defence of the People of England*, 1651, ch. 2 [370–1]).

Milton's case for humans deposing tyrants surfaces during the American War of Independence. In *Defensive Arms Vindicated* (1779), the writer, probably Captain Stephen Case (1746–94), argues similarly against the crown, from Abimelech's example [p. 753]. This usurping tyrant was "disowned by the godly [Jotham] and threatened with God's vengeance," resisted by both his initial supporters and those he subjected, and finally slain by a woman "without resentment" from the rest of Israel. Given such a biblical example, "then must it certainly be duty for a people who had no hand in the setting up such a tyrant to defend themselves against his force." The Rev. Samuel Langdon (1723–97), in *The Republic of the Israelites an Example* (1788), blames the people's "general neglect of government" for allowing this disastrous state of affairs in the first place [pp. 951–3].

If the story is divine warrant for Case's war, it is equally a godsend for French Deist Voltaire (1694–1778), intent on undermining biblical authority (at the risk of fostering anti-Jewish prejudice). Critics, he claims, "rise up against this abominable multitude of fratricides. They say that the crime is as improbable as it is odious" – improbable in a tiny population barely out of slavery, and more horrible that any list of assassinations, including Richard III murdering his nephews. The story thus represents the people being "as savage and idiotic at the same time as any who have sullied and bloodied the earth," though to be sure (facetiously voicing moderation), "the sacred books do not praise this action as they praise those of Ehud and Jael." One critic, he claims, even says that "the story [*fable*] of Abimelech's reign is more of a fable than that of the trees, and of condemnable morality besides, and that one does not know who is the cruelest, Moses, Joshua, or Abimelech." As for the 18 years of oppression, their sixth such servitude after mastering the country with an army of 600,000 men: "There is simply no example of a comparable contradiction in profane history" (*Bible enfin expliquée*, 1776 [138–9]).

As befitted an Anglican, educator Mrs Trimmer (1741–1810), mother of 12, was a less trenchant critic. But if she accepted the story, she challenged both Abimelech and his father. "Gideon had several wives, and a great number of children; as this was the case, his family could not be educated on a very regular plan." Not surprisingly, this family was the scene of envy, jealousy, and discontent, even during Gideon's lifetime. No doubt multiple wives was a custom borrowed from Israel's idolatrous neighbors, for it was "quite contrary" to God's requirement of monogamy (no mention of the problematic patriarchs). The silver lining was that the custom was also a great means of bringing God's judgments upon them! Trimmer sums up Abimelech as a man "of most savage disposition," and Gaal "another vile wretch." Like Hall, she is shocked that the stricken king "spent his last thoughts on a trifling concern for his fame . . . a false notion of honour, founded on pride." Such sentiments continue, "but Christianity teaches better principles, and shews that nobleness of mind consists in supporting disgrace with fortitude and resignation" (*Sacred History*, 1873 [liv, 237–8]).

Nonconformist Esther Hewlett (1786–1851), agreeing about Abimelech's "malignant disposition," takes another educational path. Since Jotham's "parable" is Scripture's first, this method of instruction is worth elucidating. A parable is a "similitude taken from things natural, and applied to things spiritual," a "descriptive picture" conveying an important truth to which the mind was inattentive or prejudiced. Things are thus placed in a stronger light; lengthy reasoning is spared; and the truth is made palpable to reason and conscience. Before self-love makes the worse appear the better argument, the individual judges himself without intending it (*Scripture History*, 1828, 32). Adds the Rev. James Gardner in *The Christian Cyclopedia* (1858), "This is the oldest fable on record and shows with what power the reason and conscience can be addressed through the medium of the imagination." The only problem is, he feels constrained to note, "however appropriate the parable was to the circumstances in which it was spoken, it seems to have failed in its purpose."

A century after Esther Hewlett and another Nonconformist, the Rev. T. Rhondda Williams, in Brighton, England, is also offering a Bible guide for the young in his *Old Testament Stories in Modern Light* (1911). He describes briefly the fate of the "bramble-bush king" and draws a lesson (pp. 80–1):

> He had evidently been a despiser of women, had thought himself a quite superior sort of being, like a good many foolish men before his day, and since. . . . He had forgotten that a woman had given him birth, that a woman had nursed him and done everything for him when he could do nothing for himself, and it was terrible to be reminded in this rude way by a stone on the skull that a woman, after all, must be reckoned with, even in warfare. . . . There is a lesson here for boys. Do not begin the silly delusion of thinking yourselves superior to the girls. You are nothing of the sort. If you do that, you may be sadly taken down some day.

Other readers draw other lessons. In *Portraits of Men of the Old Testament* (1922), Scottish minister Thomas E. Miller (fl. 1900–30), finds three in Jotham's fable, including the need to recognize "the blessings of the sphere we already occupy" (cf. the olive, fig, and vine). "Bramble government" is inevitable if "the best men" refuse office, whether because repelled by graft or too busy pursuing wealth, as witness "Tammany Hall in New York," and "civic corruption in other American cities." The same danger, he says, "faces us in this country." We should also remember that whatever work we are engaged in, "there is room for the highest service." Jotham foresaw the outcome of the unholy alliance between Abimelech and the Shechemites, had the wit to satirize its folly, but not the driving force to act effectively. His moment came and passed. Abimelech's moment came when a woman dropped an upper millstone over the parapet." God and gravitation did the rest" (pp. 93–7).

God and gravitation raises again the issue of agency in the plot. For Reformed (Calvinist) theologian Benjamin Warfield (1851–1921) that millstone precisely illustrates God's governing hand – guiding "a plan broad enough to embrace the whole universe of things, minute enough to concern itself with the smallest details, and actualizing itself with inevitable certainty in every event that comes to pass." Behind every external occurrence "there always lies a Divine ordering which provides the real plot of the story in its advance to the predetermined issue" (*Biblical and Theological Studies*, 1895 [276–7]).

The evil spirit complicates things. Is it divine providence? One view is that good comes from God "directly," evil "somewhat indirectly." The former "awakes vision and valour," the later "produces madness and incites to crime," as with Abimelech and the Shechemites (Loring W. Batten, *Good and Evil*, 1918, 149–50; cf. Loraine Boettner, *Reformed Doctrine of Predestination*, 1932, 245: evil spirits from God "trouble sinners"). Martin Buber (1878–1965) understands the evil spirit as initiating, "from above," punishment which is then worked out through "natural events," since Jotham's political curse required political fulfillment (*Kingship of God*, 1936 [73]).

From evil it is but an easy step to the satanic. Evangelist Arthur W. Pink (1886–1952) sees Abimelech typifying not Christ but the Antichrist – of shameful birth (his mother a concubine), a bloody persecutor of Israel, king during Israel's apostasy, connected with the mountain of curses (Deut 11:29, 27:4; Josh 8:30), a mighty man of violence, slain by the sword (cf. Rev 13:3) (*Antichrist*, 1923, ch. 13; two decades later, Pink did not recommend this book!).

More commonly, readers, like Joseph Hall, have discovered a very human political drama. The moving wood recalls "Birnam Wood come to Dunsinane," in Shakespeare's *Macbeth*, "whose story is very like that of Abimelech, the earlier follower of a false ambition" (*Master Library: Leaders of Olden Days*, I, 1923, 366). Another sees in the fate of Gideon's house suitable material for the tragic poets of fifth-century BCE Greece, and parallels have been drawn with the death of Pyrrhus of Epirus, said to have been killed at Argos with a tile thrown from a roof by a woman (in Plutarch), or the words of Hercules, at his besting by a woman, in the *Trachiniae* of Sophocles.

Buber finds fundamental political philosophies in tension. Jotham's fable, "the strongest anti-monarchical poem of world literature," is the counterpart to Gideon's disavowal of power (8:22–3) and best compared with "certain Taoistic figurative sayings." It teaches that kingship is not a productive calling. "It is vain, but also bewildering and seditious, that men rule over men." Everyone should pursue their proper business so that the aggregate of such manifold fruitfulness will constitute a community which no one needs to rule – except God alone. For this commonwealth an "invisible government" suffices (*Kingship of God*, 1936 [75]).

Buber is definite on the fable's point. So is J. Clinton McCann, except the point is different – directed more against Abimelech than against monarchy. On one level, Judges prepares for the Davidic monarchy; and the larger prophetic canon sees monarchy as legitimate. The Shechemites' mistake is not making *someone* king but making Abimelech king. At issue is not a form of government but whether people deal "in good faith and honor [or integrity]" (9:16). Like Pink, McCann notes that Jotham speaks from Mount Gerizim, where the Israelites were called to covenant obedience, a place of curses for Pink and promised blessings for McCann (Deut. 27:12)" (*Judges*, 2002, 73).

Readers read differently but also similarly. Tammi J. Schneider has echoed the point made by Samuel Langdon in the late eighteenth century and T. E. Miller in the early twentieth. The bramble implies that those who designate the ruler are as responsible as the ruler. "Kingship is described as 'waving over the heads' of others who are too busy producing useful materials to be bothered ruling." Like Buber, too, she sees as a major issue whether the deity should be the supreme leader. Jotham claimed that his family was wronged, but by the deity's rules, the deity was wronged by the hero, his family, and the Israelites (*Judges*, 2000, 139, 150).

Abimelech is universally condemned, Jotham more often applauded, though sometimes with qualification (so Miller, above). Schneider is less appreciative than most, finding little sympathy for Jotham. In the larger story so far, no leader's children have ruled; and Gideon explicitly foreswore such an eventuality. Jotham survived not by fighting to be leader but by running away while his brothers were killed, and by hiding like his father (6:11). He never uses the Israelite deity's distinctive name (Yahweh), but only the generic "Elohim" (divinity). In short, the story stresses the degenerate state of Israel, or its leadership, rather than anything positive about Jotham (p. 142).

On the surface, Abimelech's story shows his seizure of power conflicting with God's sovereignty. That is a common reading. Naomi Steinberg interprets it differently: the central problem is Abimelech's undermining of the "ancient Israelite societal norm of patrilineal kinship," descent traced through the father's line. Abimelech's *coup* also depended upon his mother's lineage, which made him kin to the Shechemites. The story's underlying message: Abimelech dies as punishment for contravening the rules of kinship ("Judges 9 and Issues of Kinship," 1995).

The "chaotic violence" of this story and chapters 17–21 frames the judges succeeding Gideon, showing the nation's "progressive deterioration." Indeed, depictions of chaos and internal violence, Israelite against Israelite, follow or conclude the final three stories of Gideon, Jephthah, and Samson. Chapter 9, therefore, points up Gideon's story as pivotal – specifically, a turn for the worse (McCann, *Judges*, 72).

Illustrations of Judges 9 almost always show Abimelech's death. Occasionally some other subject sneaks through, such as a despondent Jotham standing alone against a dark landscape beside a dying thistle (Hermann Frye, c. 1900, in Horne, *Bible and its Story*, 1908) or Abimelech seated on a bloody sacrificial stone, surrounded by his brothers' corpses (James Tissot, *Old Testament*, 1904; cf. Gustave Doré's depiction, *Sainte Bible*, 1866). But Abimelech's own death predominates. The picture takes one of three forms: a comprehensive view, a close-up of the dying king, and, least commonly, a picture foregrounding the woman with the millstone.

The comprehensive view shows Abimelech at the tower base, usually falling amidst his soldiers, and above a small female figure leaning out, arms extended, hands empty (as in Jan Goeree's exquisite design for Pieter Mortier's "Great Bible" of 1700). There are many small variations. Usually the stone strikes the king's skull, though sometimes it is still in the woman's hands (and the king yet upright), or it lies beside its fallen target. A fine example is by Dutch artist Gerard Hoet (1648–1733) in Pierre de Hondt's folio suite, *Figures de la Bible* (1728). The engraving accurately conjures up the biblical text. Unlike, say, the widely copied design by Matthäus Merian (*Icones Biblicae*, 1626), with an extensive castle and massed attacking forces meeting fierce resistance, Hoet's tower is modest, and most of the soldiers are standing about watching others bringing sticks and sheaves to pile against the door for burning (cf. 9:52). A brazier blazes in the center foreground, and sunlight falls across the fuel-gatherers. Above, in the midground shadow, but outlined against the sky, the woman points down. Only by looking carefully into the shade does the viewer then see, almost merged with the bodies of his soldiers, Abimelech stumbling against the piled wood, struck by a millstone faintly edged with light (PLATE 5.1b).

The close-up view focuses on Abimelech being despatched by his armor-bearer. This is the choice of another Dutch artist, Romeijn de Hooghe (c.1645–1708), whose designs in the style of Rembrandt for a Bible history ('*T Groot Waerelds Tafereel*, 1706) were long influential. Each picture has a central scene surrounded by vignettes of associated episodes. Abimelech is about to be finished off by a pretty youth. Beside them a soldier struggles with the king's rearing horse. Behind looms the tower, on which the woman is glimpsed, pointing down (PLATE 5.1c). The whole design, side scenes included, reappears in a mid-nineteenth-century Bible history for families, *Sunny Sabbaths*. The redrawing is faithfully if less finely executed, though the young man's pantaloons and sleeves have acquired eye-catchingly bold yellow and black stripes, and the woman is no longer obvious (PLATE 5.1d). She disappears, too, from the illustration by celebrated French artist Gustave Doré (1832–83), where the youth has strangely turned into an older bearded and crowned figure, whom the reader could easily mistake for the king. Abimelech entreats him to slay him, while others try to stay him as he draws his sword. Two figures at the edges of the picture, however, look upwards and so indirectly reintroduce the woman (*Sainte Bible*, 1866; *Doré Bible Gallery*, 1879). In other pictures, as in Cassell's popular *Illustrated Bible* (c.1870s), the woman entirely disappears in favor of the armor-bearer plunging his sabre into the dying king's breast. (That picture reappears, e.g., in Dr Northrop's *Charming Bible Stories* of 1894.) The woman

PLATE 5.1 Abimelech's end: (a) Schnorr, 1860; (b) Hoet, 1728; (c) de Hooghe, 1706; (d) *Sunny Sabbaths*, c.1860. (See pp. 130, 132)

is rarely foregrounded. James Tissot (1836–1902), taking us to the top of the wall, depicts her, flanked by two others who peer over, standing in a crenellation, stone held aloft and ready. Abimelech is unseen, below (*Old Testament*, 1904).

Julius Schnorr von Carolsfeld (1794–1872) also takes us above the wall and foregrounds the woman, but retains Abimelech, in his neoclassically styled series of woodcuts (*Bibel in Bildern*, 1860; *Bible in Pictures*, 1869), versions of which appear frequently into the twentieth century (e.g. Northrop's *Charming Bible Stories*). The woman stands, poised like a Fury, aiming the millstone. Behind her cower despairing refugees. Below in the wall's shadow we notice Abimelech on horseback, looking away to his soldiers and waving with an elegantly royal wave. But several of his men stare up in dismay at the woman and impending doom. One reaches out, too late, to warn the oblivious king. Behind, flames rise from buildings. Through a doorway a woman is glimpsed, clutching her baby, and another, trapped on a balcony, waves for help. The picture may move a viewer. Yet the absurdity of the grandly gesturing king may equally well provoke grim laughter. Schnorr aptly captures the fate that Abimelech so abhorred (PLATE 5.1a).

> The raging king, with rising ire,
> Proceeds to set the door on fire;
> When from the top, in open view,
> Part of a rock a woman threw.
> (E. Miller, *Scripture History*, 1833)

After Abimelech's death, two others arise who "judge" Israel: Tola of Issachar and Jair of Gilead (Galaad). Again the Israelites "do evil," serving gods of Moab, Ammon, and Philistia, and their own deity sells them into enemy hands: the Ammonites oppress the Gileadites, east of the Jordan, and cross over against the Benjamites and Ephraimites. At the people's cry for help, God asks why, after being so often rescued, they keep forsaking him for other gods. Why not cry to them instead? The people cry again, put away the foreign gods, and worship him. He takes note. The Ammonites encamp in Gilead, and the Israelites seek a leader.

Jephthah (Jephte) the Gileadite, a warrior, is a prostitute's son; his father is Gilead. But his brothers, sons of other wives of Gilead, expel him lest he share their inheritance. He gathers an outlaw band for raiding. When the Ammonites make war, Gilead's elders seek Jephthah's help. Why, having driven him out, he asks, are they now coming to him? Nevertheless, he strikes a deal – Gilead's headship in return for victory. When the Ammonite king demands back his land east of Jordan, Jephthah claims that Israel's god gave it to Israel; let the Ammonites keep what their own god gave them. The king is unimpressed.

God's spirit comes upon Jephthah. He gathers an army and makes another deal: in return for victory he vows to offer up to the deity whoever/whatever (Hebrew makes no distinction) is first to meet him on returning. He duly wins, but is met by his only child, his daughter. He cannot take back his vow, he says. She asks only for two months in the mountains with her female companions to "bewail her virginity." This done, Jephthah fulfills his vow. It becomes a custom for the daughters of Israel to lament her each year.

The men of Ephraim cross over to Jephthah and upbraid him for excluding them. Jephthah denies their claim, fights, and cuts off their escape at the fords. A test betrays the fleeing Ephraimites: they pronounce the word "Shibboleth" as "Sibboleth." And so they are slain. Jephthah judges Israel six years.

After him, Ibzan (Abesan) of Bethlehem, Elon (Ahialon) of Zebulun (Zahnlon), and Abdon the Pirathonite judge Israel.

If commentary space is any guide to readers' interests, then two questions would seem to have predominated. First, why did Jephthah vow, and why did he not retract? Second, what happened to the daughter? Was she really killed, or did she become a lifelong virgin in recluse? Jephthah is often criticized for his vow, and his daughter's death is regarded as punishment or a salutary lesson. Some find admirable his carrying through with her execution (a vow must be honored); others are horrified that a "rash vow" was not broken. Christian interpreters struggle with Jephthah's being listed among heroes of faith in Hebrews 11. Some readers through the centuries represent the daughter's point of view positively, in lament or in praise of her virginity (especially if she ends in devotional seclusion), or in admiration for her fortitude and loyalty to father and country. Some take the story less kindly, pointing at God's complicity in the daughter's death and at the father's assumed right to dispose of her at will.

Ancient and Medieval

Jewish

"An oblation as was neither conformable to the law nor acceptable to God" (Whiston tr.) is how Jewish historian Josephus (37–c.100) described Jephthah's sacrifice (*Antiquities*, v.266 (7.10)). His near-contemporary, known today as Pseudo-Philo, was of like mind. At Jephthah's vow God grew angry: "Behold Jephthah has vowed that he will offer to me whatever meets him first on the way; and now if a [ritually unclean] dog should meet Jephthah first, will the dog be offered to me?" (*Biblical Antiquities*, 39:10–11). Early rabbinic discussions reflected in Talmudic and Midrashic texts regarded the sacrifice as errant, clearly prohibited by Torah (e.g. *Genesis Rabbah*, 60:3, and *Leviticus Rabbah*, 37:4). The Law provided penance for rash oaths (Leviticus 5) and redemption for inappropriately devoted things, including persons (Leviticus 27). Later medieval scholars such as Moses ben Nahman, known as Ramban (1194–1270), maintained this judgment (commentary on Leviticus, 480–1). (On Jewish interpretation, see Ginzberg, *Legends*, vi, 203–4 n. 109; Bronner, *Eve to Esther*, 1994, 129–34; on Josephus and Pseudo-Philo, see Thompson, *Writing the Wrongs*, 2001, 106–11.)

For many early Jewish interpreters, Jephthah reflected widespread disregard of God in Israel at that time. Josephus sees the tragic vow stemming from a drift to disorder and contempt for God's law (*Antiquities*, v.255 (7.7)). Agreeing, the Targum to Judges criticizes Jephthah for slaughtering the Ephraimites even though they deserved slaughter for worshiping an idol, Sibboleth. So often was this name on their lips, they accidentally said it when asked by Jephthah at the Jordan to say "Shibboleth." Thus were they distinguished and slain (12:6).

Jephthah's critics wonder at his ignorance of the law but also his failure to consult the priest Phineas (cf. 20:27–8), who would properly have annulled the objectionable vow (e.g. *Targum Jonathan* to Judg 11:39; Rashi on 11:39). Some criticize Phineas for not intervening. *Midrash Ecclesiastes Rabbah* (10:15) imagines them haughtily avoiding one another: "Jephthah remarked, 'Shall I, a chieftain and ruler in Israel, go to Phinehas!' and Phinehas remarked, 'Shall I, the High Priest and the son of a High Priest, go to an ignorant person!'" Because "between the two of them the poor girl perished," both men were punished for her blood. Centuries later, Aharon ben Masjiahm (fl. 1692), a Jewish poet in Persia, puts it thus (in Moreen, *In Queen Esther's Garden*, 2000, 144–6):

> Phineas, the leader, was not with him
> To suggest a remedy for his daughter,
> To counsel him according to religion,
> So that he would sacrifice a cow or lamb instead,
> Or give it to the priest to burn it
> In her place. For this they both lost Body and Soul.
> Though Phinehas and Jephthah both magnified
> God, they were afflicted in the end

Both men deserved punishment, many judged. *Ecclesiastes Rabbah* (12:15) reasons that God's spirit left Phineas from here on (cf. 1 Chron 9:20, "previously God was with him"), while Jephthah gradually lost his limbs, buried where they dropped: so Jephthah "was buried in the cities [plural] of Gilead," as Judg 12:7 states (also Rashi on 11:39, adding boils to dismemberment).

Pseudo-Philo (39:11) supplies God's vocal condemnation of the vow. More-over, the daughter's death is Jephthah's punishment. Echoing ironically the sac-rifice of Isaac (Genesis 22) and the slain first-born in Egypt (Exodus 12), God continues: "And now let the vow of Jephthah be accomplished against his own firstborn, that is, against the fruit of his own body, and his request against his only begotten." Thus God remains in control, but at the daughter's expense (cf. Baker, "Transformation of Jephthah's Daughter," 1989, 197–9; Brown, *No Longer Be Silent*, 1992, 96–9).

Yet this ancient version is not oblivious to the daughter. It makes her a sen-tient subject, bearing a name, Seila. Her wisdom and determination contrast with Jephthah's ignorance and rashness. She knows the ancient traditions, comparing herself to Isaac submitting to Abraham. Not that her own accep-tance of death validates the vow: "I am not sad because I am to die," she says, "nor does it pain me to give back my soul, but because my father was caught up in the snare of his vow." Indeed, she knows God has choreographed her sac-rifice to punish Jephthah. "See how I am singled out [*accusor*] but let my soul not have been given in vain," she says in her lyrical lament. Her *planctus* conveys both her determination to proceed and her emotion at curtailing her budding life (Alexiou and Dronke, "Lament of Jephtha's daughter," 1971). She is both sensual and plaintive, imbuing elegy with marriage song (40.6):

> Unquenched is my hunger for my bridal bed, . . .
> My perfume of musk [rdg. *moschi*] I have not used,
> Nor has my soul unfurled its leaves, though my anointing oil is prepared.
> O Mother, in vain did you bear your only daughter,
> For hell is become my bridal bed . . .
> And the white robe my mother sewed, the moths will eat,
> And the flowers of the crown my nurse plaited, in time they will wither,
> And the coverlet I wove all by myself, of hyacinth,
> And my purple robe, the worms will spoil . . .
> For my years are broken off,
> And this season of my life will grow old in the darkness of night.

Unlike Pseudo-Philo, Josephus attends little to Jephthah's daughter. But he finds great virtue in her readily accepting her fate (v.265), "since she should die upon occasion of her father's victory, and the liberty of her fellow-citizens," as Whiston translates (1737, v.7.10). This interpretation of her motives – for father and country – has a long history of readerly approval.

With an eye to his audience, Josephus presents Jephthah as a conquering hero whose fatal flaw alludes to stories well known to Greco-Roman readers (cf. Brown, *No Longer Be Silent*, 119–27). Agamemnon offered his daughter Iphigeneia to appease the goddess Artemis who was preventing the Greek fleet from sailing against Troy (Aeschylus, *Agamemnon*, 458 BCE). In the play by Euripides (*Iphigeneia in Aulis*, 406 BCE), Iphigeneia eventually agrees to the sacrifice for the sake of the Greek army and the honor of Greek women, but at the last minute Artemis substitutes a deer and takes Iphigeneia to be her priestess at Taurus. In another story (cf. Virgil, *Aeneid*, iii), Idomeneus, sailing back from Troy, vowed to offer Poseidon the first living thing to greet him on his return, if the sea god would abate a terrible storm threatening his ship and crew. His son (daughter in some versions) met him and was sacrificed, angering the other gods. These parallels have intrigued readers of the biblical story from earliest times.

Christian

Many early Christian interpreters, like their Jewish counterparts, condemned Jephthah's vow as rash and counter to God's will. The textual scholar Jerome (c.342–420) agrees here with "most Hebrews" on why God failed to intervene: God so ordered events that Jephthah learned the error of his improvident vow by his daughter's death (*Against Jovianus*, i.23; cf. Pseudo-Philo, above). In the Eastern Church, renowned preacher John Chrysostom (c.347–407) takes Jephthah as a prime example of the danger of making oaths. As for God's role, while "unbelievers impugn us of cruelty and inhumanity on account of this sacrifice," it was rather "a striking example of providence and clemency." God allowed the murder that it might be remembered in lamentation and "make all men wiser for the future," so preventing further atrocities (*Homilies Concerning the Statues*, xiv). (For a detailed review, including the Middle Ages, see Thompson, *Writing the Wrongs*, 2001, 111–54.)

In the Western Church, Ambrose (c.339–97) likewise argues that sometimes fulfilling a promise or keeping an oath is contrary to duty: better no promise at all than for Jephthah to fulfill it in his daughter's death (*Duties of the Clergy*, i.l.264). Later in this work, however, he qualifies his criticism. Jephthah's vow was thoughtless, not deliberate, and he did repent: "with pious fear and reverence" he fulfilled his "cruel task," and himself ordered annual mourning. Hence Ambrose cannot blame him for holding to his vow. But the problem remains. Any "necessity" demanding the child's death was surely a wretched one. He reiterates: better no vow than to vow what God does not wish. As Isaac's case shows (Genesis 22), not every promise is always to be fulfilled (iii.xii).

One reading strategy shifts attention from vow to daughter and finds redemption in her. Thus Ambrose cites a well-known story from Cicero about two men willing to die: if what these esteemed men did was full of marvel, how much more glorious was the case of the virgin. "The weeping of her compan-

ions did not move her" and "their grief prevailed not upon her." She returned
to her father, "and of her own will urged him on when he was hesitating, and
acted thus of her own free choice, so that what was at first an awful chance
became a pious sacrifice" (iii.xii).

Ephrem the Syrian (c.306–73) finds in Jephthah's daughter a lesson for
Christian virgins. Her untimely death was a blessing, protecting her virginity:
"her pearl, delivered from all dangers, remained with her and consoled her."
But whereas her virginity was sealed when her father shed her blood, the
Christian woman's virginity is sealed by the blood of Christ. Ephrem exhorts
her to protect it, for "distress will be the companion in death of the woman
whose pearl perishes here" (*Hymns on Virginity*, ii). Jerome, writing from
Bethlehem a decade after Ephrem's death, begs to differ. Jephthah's daughter is
no model for Christian virginity, "For we are not commending virgins of the
world so much as those who are virgins for Christ's sake" (*Against Jovianus*,
i.23).

Virgins for Christ's sake is what Methodius of Olympus (d. 311) has in mind
in *The Banquet of the Ten Virgins Or, Concerning Chastity* (cf. Alexiou and
Dronke 1971: 852). At the end, the virgin saint Thecla leads her companions
in a song praising virginity. Like Jephthah's daughter, the young women have
longed for the mystic marriage to the celestial bridegroom:

> Freshly-slain—
> He, Jephthah, offered to God as a sacrifice his maiden daughter,
>   who knew no man, as a lamb at the altar.
> She, nobly fulfilling the image [type] of your body, O blessed one,
>   bravely cried out:
> I keep myself pure for you,
> And holding my shining lamps,
> Bridegroom, I come to meet you.

According to the apocryphal *Acts of Paul and Thecla* (late second century
CE), the virgin saint ended her life a martyr. In his commentary on John's
Gospel, Origen (c.185–c.254), whose father was martyred and who was himself
to die persecuted, treats the daughter's sacrifice as a martyr's death. Considered
in the "spiritual sense of such sacrifices which cleanse those for
whom they are offered" (in this case, Jephthah), he sees it as akin to the
sacrifice of Jesus, the Lamb of God, on behalf of sinful humanity (vi.276–7
[243]).

Most influential in the long term, as so often, is Ambrose's pupil Augustine
(354–430). He discusses the text extensively in Question 49 of his *Questions on
the Heptateuch* (419) (see Thompson, *Writing the Wrongs*, 2001, 125–30). Jephthah intended something unlawful by the vow. Likely to meet him was hardly

a sheep – sheep generally do not do that sort of thing – but rather a dog, he thinks. Yet a dog was unacceptable for sacrifice. Moreover, the Latin text reads "whoever comes forth," not "whatever." If not his daughter, then, did he expect his wife? But why act so? First, the text does not say God commanded him, as with Abraham; and where Abraham's obedience is praised, there is silence on Jephthah's action, unless one counts Judg 11:29 ("the Spirit of the Lord came upon Jephthah") and Heb 11:32 (he is among the faithful heroes). These texts, argues Augustine, suggest a parallel between Jephthah and Gideon, who also receives the Spirit and errs by testing God and making the golden ephod. The lesson: God also uses those who are flawed.

Also possible is that divine providence imbued wrong actions with prophetic significance. In Gideon's case it was a sign that the Church would supersede Israel (see on Gideon). Jephthah's deed was designed to shock "pious minds" into seeking the true nature of sacrifice, seen in Christ's death. Nonetheless, what God and Jephthah each intended remained morally distinct. Jephthah's ignorant act was rightly punished. Yet God very properly ordained him a type of Christ, who offers up his virginal flesh to redeem believers. As for Jephthah's wife and daughter, they both signify the Church, Christ's "wife" (Eph 5:31–2) and "daughter" (Matt 9:18–25; cf. 2 Cor 11:2, "chaste virgin"). So Augustine, like his teacher, enlists Jephthah's daughter to help rescue the story.

Augustine's interpretations were furthered in the seventh century by Isidore of Seville (c.560–636), who represented Jephthah's daughter as herself a type of Christ's own flesh – that is to say, his humanity – a view long remaining popular. Both Augustine and Isidore on Judges 11 are present in the *Glossa Ordinaria*, the standard commentary from the twelfth century on.

The problem continually besetting medieval commentators is the apparent breach between Judges 11 and Hebrews 11. Various expedients are resorted to (see Thompson, *Writing the Wrongs*, 138–44). Jephthah must have had great faith – even though obscure. His victory, not his vow, was what the Apostle Paul had in mind. He was a faithful man before and after the vow, just not in between! He repented. And, anyway, if Hebrews 11 names him faithful, it is impious to doubt it. Another tactic was to argue, against Augustine, for divine dispensation, indicated by 11:29, where the divine spirit comes upon Jephthah. Dominican theologian Thomas Aquinas (c.1225–74), above all, gathers exonerating arguments, including divine dispensation, while at the same time criticizing Jephthah.

Typologically speaking, Jephthah continues to prefigure Christ, or sometimes God the Father, who offered up his only offspring, and the daughter to prefigure Christ's humanity, or sometimes the Church, offered up during persecution. At the same time, however, Jephthah is generally condemned both for making the vow and for keeping it. Italian poet Dante Alighieri (1265–1321), in his *Paradiso*, pens the lines: "Let mortals never take the vow in sport. Be faithful, and with that be not perverse, as was Jephthah in his first offering, who ought rather to have said 'I did amiss,' than, by keeping his vow, to do worse" (v.64–8).

In all this discussion of vow and sacrifice, the daughter tends to become but a debating point. Yet sometimes she is accorded a voice. Like Pseudo-Philo centuries earlier, and probably influenced by him, Peter Abelard (1079–1142) wrote a lament on the daughter's sacrifice (*Planctus Virginum Israel Super Filia Jeptae Galaditae*; in manuscript only until 1838). His ill-fated romance with Héloïse haunts the poetry. At his behest, Héloïse had allowed herself to be shut away as a nun, a deathly sacrifice on his behalf, to become instead the bride of Christ (see East, *This Body of Death*, 1997).

The young women of Israel, coming together to commemorate the "pitiful victim," condemn the father's rash vow and praise the exalted daughter's noble sacrifice: "O how seldom may a man be found like unto her!" To uphold the vow of her father, through whom God saved the people, "she urges him [to cut] her own throat." Their concluding chorus sharpens the condemnation as they describe her delivering the sword herself on the steps of the kindled altar:

> O frenzied mind of a judge!
> O mad zeal of a prince!
> O father, yet enemy of his kin,
>   Which he destroyed by the slaughter of his only daughter!

The daughter, answering her father, takes charge from the first scene. She presses him to keep his vow. Invoking her counterpart Isaac, she proclaims, "If God did not accept a boy, how much greater glory if he accepts a girl!"

In both poems, ancient and medieval, the daughter's death is a wedding, a "grim parody" (Alexiou and Dronke, 1971, 856). But Abelard's protagonist is silent against the weeping attendants preparing her as a bride of death. Only at the scene's end does she suddenly dispense with the last ornaments and cry out: "Oh it is enough to marry / To perish utterly is too much!" (*Que nupture satis sunt / periture nimis sunt!*).

Death or survival?

In the twelfth century appeared an argument that significantly mitigated Jewish condemnation of Jephthah and eventually had great impact on the story's

Christian reception. Poet and scholar Abraham ben Meir ibn Ezra (c.1092–1167) believed, according to Ramban, that Jephthah did not actually sacrifice his daughter, but built her a house outside the city where she resided in seclusion, a virgin devoted to God for life. To which Ramban countered sarcastically, "Heaven forbid that this be a custom in Israel, to lament the daughter of Jephthah the Gileadite four days in a year because she did not marry and she worshipped God in purity!" He urges his readers not to be misled by ibn Ezra's "empty words" (see Ramban on Leviticus, Bechukothai 29:481–2). Ramban's dismissal notwithstanding, the seclusion (or "survival" as opposed to "sacrificial") argument was destined to live on.

The argument hinges on Hebrew grammar, taking the Hebrew connective (*wᵉ*) as disjunctive (*or*) instead of, more usually, conjunctive (*and*). Rather than requiring the firstcomer to be devoted to God *and* offered as a sacrifice (the usual reading), the vow stipulates *either* devoted to God (if a person) *or* offered as a burnt offering (if an animal fit for sacrifice). This construal appears also in the Judges commentary of outstanding grammarian David Kimchi (c.1160–c.1235), who credits his father, along with two other points: the daughter mourns her virginity, not her death (11:37); and upon return from the mountains, her subsequent seclusion is confirmed by "she did not know a man" (11:39).

The daughter's "survival" comes into Christian interpretation through Nicholas of Lyra (c.1270–1349), an advocate of the "literal sense" of Scripture (*Postilla litteralis*). He cites Jewish support, but not its grammatical basis. Rather, he finds no explicit mention of a sacrifice taking place and envisions the daughter like a nun, secluded, praying, fasting, and performing pious works. The interpretation appealed, because it solved main problems. The vow was not so awful after all, and Hebrews 11 was vindicated. In due course Kimchi's commentary appeared in print (1485), and by the mid-sixteenth century Christian exegetes were deploying the grammatical argument in support of the "new" interpretation.

For medieval manuscript illuminators, the story unquestionably ends in the daughter's death. In an early thirteenth-century *Bible moralisée* (Codex Vindobonensis 2444, fol. 61), Jephthah, wearing a ruler's crown, cleaves his daughter's skull with a sword. Queen Mary's Psalter (BM MS 2.B.VII; early fourteenth century), shows Jephthah speaking with God in one scene and in the other grasping his kneeling daughter's head and preparing to strike her throat with his brandished sword. In the same spirit are early Renaissance depictions in print. A woodcut published in 1491 by Anton Koberger of Nuremberg shows again a kneeling, praying daughter beside a flaming altar. In full plate armor, Jephthah grasps his sword two-handed, ready to decapitate the young woman.

Ironically, in a chapel behind stand the tablets of the Law, neatly dissected by the poised sword (PLATE 6.1b).

Death by the sword is also implied in the first printed Bible to include illustrations of whole scenes (Cologne Bible of Heinrich Quentel, c.1478). The scene, the meeting between father and daughter, is the favorite of illustrators. The composition imitates earlier medieval illuminations and influences subsequent depictions in print. The daughter emerges from the castle gate, playing a small harp. Opposite stands Jephthah, in armor, at the head of his soldiers. He cuts his mantle with his drawn sword. A later composition is similar, but the style now decidedly Renaissance (Lübeck Bible of Stephan Arndes, 1494). Jephthah's serated helmet is stark against the sky. His gaze, arm, and sword point to his daughter, demurely playing her harp. Behind her, two female companions exchanging words do not quite balance out the group of three soldiers, distinct individuals, behind Jephthah. It is a meeting of two worlds, of men and women. Both the imbalance of the composition, weighted to the men's world, and the drawn and cutting sword, implying bloodshed, are ominous signs for the daughter (PLATE 6.1a).

Early Modern and Modern

The rash vow

That the vow was rashly made is a commonplace among Christian readers from early modern Europe on. (For the vow in the Reformation, see Thompson, *Writing the Wrongs*, 2001, 154–78.) Protestant Reformer John Calvin (1509–64), on "Vows; and How Everyone Rashly Taking Them Has Miserably Entangled Himself," points to Jephthah's "hasty fervor" when arguing that celibacy, among rash vows, "holds the first place for insane boldness" (*Institutes*, 1550 [iv.12.3]). The running head to Judges 11 in many Geneva Bibles, long popular in Puritan households, was "Iphtahs rash vow." The vow is rash for Joseph Hall in the seventeenth century ("It was his zeal to vow; it was his sin to vow rashly"; *Contemplations*, 1615), as in the eighteenth for Isaac Watts: Question 58: "What was remarkable concerning [Jephthah]?" Answer: "He made a rash Vow . . ." (*A Short View*, 1730). "Rash" is, likewise, how Esther Hewlett characterizes the vow in the nineteenth century (*Scripture History*, 1828), and Rudolf Kittel (*History of the Hebrews*, 1909) and Thomas E. Miller (*Portraits*, 1922) in the twentieth. Illustrations, especially in the eighteenth and nineteenth centuries, are often labeled "Jephthah's Rash Vow," as in Esther

Judg. XI. Ver. 40. *Went yearly &c.*

The Lamentations of the Daughters of Israel. for the Death of the Daughter of Jephthah.

PLATE 6.1   Jephthah's daughter: (a) Lübeck Bible, 1494; (b) Koberger, 1491; (c) Bankes' *Family Bible*, c.1790. (See pp. 142, 169)

Hewlett's book or Gaspey's *Tallis's Illustrated Scripture History for the Improvement of Youth* (1851).

Jephthah is not condemned out of hand. Joseph Hall (1574–1656), an Episcopalian with Calvinist leanings, approves of his zeal in war: "His hand took hold of his sword, his heart of God; therefore he, whom the Old Testament styles valiant, the New styles faithful [Hebrews 11]." Still, Jacob, Jephthah's forefather, "might have taught him a better form of vow: 'If God will be with me, then shall the Lord be my God.'" Hall is not too sanguine about vows. "It is well with vows, when the thing promised makes the promise good . . . Vows are as they are made, like unto scents: if they be of ill composition, nothing offends more; if well tempered, nothing is more pleasant. Either certainty of evil, or uncertainty of good, or impossibility of performance, makes vows no service to God" (*Contemplations*, 1615 [x.1, 123]).

Nonetheless, condemnation comes aplenty, along with attempts to explain the misdeed. Two centuries later, the author of *Scripture Biography* (1818) sums up: Jephthah's conduct was folly, and he should have sought forgiveness for it. The vow arose out of superstition, "the most inexorable of all tyrants; demanding in every age the sacrifice of human victims, in one form or other, to appease the anger or conciliate the favour of some imaginary deity, whose claims are alike repugnant to the God of justice and mercy" (p. 313). Evangelical preacher F. B. Meyer (1847–1929) is equally harsh. The vow was no less than a bribe. "There is no need to bribe God's help, as Jephthah did, by his rash promise." If we are "right with our fellow men," then God will give gladly and freely what we need (*Our Daily Homily*, I, 1898 [221]).

More sympathetic is self-taught scholar John Kitto (1804–54). Perhaps Jephthah felt insecure, felt that "he had not, like former deliverers, been expressly and publicly called and appointed by God to the work he had undertaken," and so "sought to propitiate heaven by a vow" (*Bible History*, 1841 [213]). Marcus Dods (1834–1909) argues that a vow in itself was not out of place. Anyone can say that Jephthah had "merely a heathen idea of God, as a Being to be bribed." But inadequate ideas of God were common among heathen generals, and still so today. Not having been told about Jephthah's state of mind, we should allow him the benefit of the doubt: he was justified in making some vow, if not this "incomprehensibly rash" one (in Hastings, *Greater Men and Women*, 1914, 488).

Dods is picking up an old line of interpretation. Puritan Richard Rogers (1550–1618) preached (*Judges*, 1615, 569): "This vow, though he meant well, was ill made and in great ignorance, in that he did not make it more distinctly and advisedly." What, he asks (in line with Jewish discussion), would Jephthah have done if met by a dog, unfit for sacrifice, and "if he had thought of his daughter, would he have made that vowe?" (Ironically, in Gerard Hoet's picture of the meeting (1728), Jephthah is indeed met by a dog!). Jephthah's problem, as Isaac Watts puts it in his catechism, was that he was a "Soldier, in those Days of Ignorance" (*A Short View*, 1730). His vow, writes John Cunningham Geikie (1824–1906), was the cry of a "wild soldier," and the ideas of the times were "rude and imperfect" (*Old Testament Characters*, 1884, 163–4).

For Esther Hewlett (1786–1851), among a growing number of women writing for youth, the vow rested at least on "a misapprehension of some precepts in the law of Moses" if not "too great familiarity with the customs of the heathen" (*Scripture History*, 1828, 39; cf. Mrs Trimmer, *Sacred History*, 1783 [lvi, 247]). The author of *Scripture Biography* (1818) was sure that a "better informed" Jephthah would have understood that his vow was unacceptable. Unfortunately "the influence of religion is not to be traced in this part of his conduct." So, too, in the Rev. Darius Mead's *Christian Parlor Magazine* (July 1844 [65–6]), Jephthah was well aware of the true God's power and providence. But of this Being's moral attributes, his law, the acts of devotion pleasing to him, Jephthah "was certainly to some extent—probably to a very great extent—ignorant." His vow was a superstitious attempt to purchase the Almighty's favor.

Indefatigable author and anthologizer, James Hastings (1852–1922) also suspects heathen influence upon an ill-informed and desperate soldier who "wished to feel sure of God." If the vow was hardly out of place in the times, its literal execution "could hardly have taken place had it been undertaken by any one more under moral restraints, even of that lawless age, than the freebooter, Jephthah" (*Greater Men and Women*, 1914, 490). But for all the freebooter's faults (including a "remorseless temper"), doubtless offensive in God's sight, he found pardon – "because, like St Paul, he sinned in ignorance." Here, as so often in Christian reception, Hebrews 11 comes into play. It produces, moreover, the enigmatic conclusion: "In the chief trial of his life he found acceptance, because he displayed faithful obedience" (p. 485).

Appeal to different social contexts is typical of early twentieth-century explanations, especially in churches where "historical criticism" was accepted. The Rev. T. Rhondda Williams (c.1860–c.1940) points out to his young readers that they must make allowance for those "ignorant times" but not think of Jephthah as a good man, "as we want a man to be good now. From our point of view it was perfectly horrible of him to think of sacrificing a human being at all, but at that time people did not understand that it was so horrible; they thought they were doing something very splendid by killing somebody else to the glory of God" (*Old Testament Stories in Modern Light*, 1911, 88).

Even if the vow was made in ignorance, should it have been kept? Many agreed with Dante that keeping it was an equal or worse mistake. Like Calvin, another Reformer, Andreas Bodenstein von Carlstadt (c.1480–1541), uses Jephthah's vow to argue against celibacy. Since Leviticus 5 provides penance for retracting an erroneous vow (in this case, celibacy), it is imperative to repair the wrong. Jephthah's vow, which Jephthah considered good but was in fact evil ("Thou shalt not kill," Exod 20:13), should not have been carried out. He enlists Augustine's support, adding wryly against a common objection, "Do not be disturbed by Scripture saying that the Holy Spirit was with Jephthah [11:29]. In half an hour or much less, one may lose the Holy Spirit by doing what is wrong" (*Regarding Vows*, 1522 [79]). Benedictine scholar Dom Augustin Calmet (1672–1757), in what became known (in many editions) as *Calmet's Dictionary*, agrees: neither the precipitate vow made in ignorance of God nor its literal execution can be justified. Jephthah should have asked forgiveness and accepted, with the high priest's advice, a penalty proportioned to his fault (cf. Taylor's edn, 1837).

Hewlett strongly criticizes both vow and execution. She lists Jephthah's errors: his blind promise irrespective of sacrificial rules; his unwarranted control of his daughter's future life, not to mention usurping the right to take life; his failure to redeem the devoted object, as permitted; and, if celibacy and solitude were the daughter's fate, such a vow was not sanctioned by the Law (*Scripture History*, 1828, 41). Nearly a century on and Hastings (1914) writes that Jephthah's performance of the vow was "no less rash and unhallowed" than the vow itself, both being "doubtless offensive in God's sight."

But not all readers have taken this path. The youth being improved by Gaspey's *Tallis's Illustrated Scripture History* (1851) learned that Jephthah had no choice but to follow through. "Sad was the lot of the parent, sad the lot of the child, but however painful the task of fulfilling it, a solemn vow to the Lord must not be disregarded."

Jephthah's action also draws reluctant admiration from the critical Hastings. "While we shudder at the awful sacrifice, we cannot but admire the grim determination of this half-wild, barbaric chieftain, as he holds to the terms of his terrible vow, and, at the expense of rendering himself childless, proceeds to fulfil it" (1914, 489). His sentiment is shared. Though "a tremendous blunder," allows Scottish minister Thomas E. Miller, Jephthah no doubt thought his action heroic when he poured out his heart to God at Mizpeh, and, indeed, "there is something grandly heroic in seeing it through to the bitter end." Recalling Josephus's description of the sacrifice as neither lawful nor acceptable to God, Miller adds: "From our point of view it was wrong, it was unnecessary, it was criminal. . . . But our point of view was not Jephthah's and we must judge him by the standards of his own time" (*Portraits*, 1922, 107, 113).

Death or survival?

The story's tragic dimensions have always struck a chord with readers. Humanist scholar Erasmus (1466–1536) translated into Latin Euripides' tragedy of Iphigeneia at Aulis (*Iphigenia in Aulide*, 1506), and, although unpublished, the English translation by Lady Jane Lumley (c.1537–77) testifies to widespread interest in the sacrificial daughter (*The Tragedie of Iphigeneia*, 1550). The parallels prompted another humanist, John Christopherson (d. 1558), to write a play on Jephthah in Greek (1504; later a Latin version), as he himself explains. In 1540 George Buchanan (1506–82), a noted Scottish humanist, wrote a dramatic version in Latin (*Jephthes*, published 1554), several times translated into English and influential for a century or more. Shakespeare (1564–1616) likely knew a Latin translation of Euripides' play and certainly the Jephthah story, enough to play on it several times. Hamlet calls Polonius "old Jephthah" and casts his daughter, ill-fated Ophelia, as Jephthah's daughter (*Hamlet*, 1600–1).

The allusion suggests that, whatever the scholars were writing, Shakespeare understood the daughter to have died. So, too, poet Francis Quarles (1592–1644). In an age of fierce religious controversy, Quarles turns the tragedy of the "unhappy Child, and too too cruell Father" against the "presumptuous Sin" of "strict Religion." He throws at victorious Jephthah Dante's accusation that his was a rash-made Vow . . . whose undertaking

> Was ev'n a Sin more odious, then the making:
> 'Twas cruell Piety that taught thee how
> To paddle in thy Daughter's Blood . . .
> ("On Ieptha's vow," *Divine Fancies*, 1632, ii.4 [214])

The seventeenth century is Judges' heyday in England, driven by Puritan convictions about theology and politics, inextricably entangled. But first the text's "plain meaning" had to be clarified. Influencing early Puritan views were the Jewish arguments that the daughter survived (see above). Puritan theologian William Perkins (1558–1602) sided with this view: Jephthah dedicated her, like a Nazirite, "to the end of her daies, to leade her life apart in a single estate" (*Cases of Conscience*, 1606 [ii.98]). Richard Rogers, in contrast, is sure the Hebrew specifies a burnt offering. Also, if virginity were intended, Jephthah would have foreseen it involving his daughter: "For who had bin liker to have first come foorth to meete him than she?" As for the grammatical argument – the firstcomer shall be the Lord's *or* I shall sacrifice it – Rogers sees no reason to take the connective in any other than its common use (*and*), "as they well know that have any understanding in the Hebrew tongue" (*Judges*, 1615). John Milton (1608–74) allows both interpretations possible. Jephthah's misunderstanding of vows led him to suppose that he "could not but oblige his conscience to be the sacrificer, or if not, the jayler of his innocent and onely daughter" (*Doctrine and Discipline*, 1644, Preface [i, 234–5]).

By the eighteenth century the "survival" argument is widespread. Librettist Thomas Morell (1703–84) happily adopts it for a happier ending to the oratorio *Jephtha* (1751) by George Frideric Handel (1685–1759). Jephtha (very precisely) vows: "What, or whoe'er shall first salute mine eyes, / Shall be forever Thine, or fall a sacrifice." But on meeting his daughter, named Iphis (as in Joost van den Vondel's Dutch play of 1659), he laments that she must die, "a victim to the living God"; and Iphis, like her classical counterpart Iphigeneia, is ready to die "a grateful victim" asking only Heaven's blessing "on my country, friends, and dearest father!" As in Euripides' play, however, divine intervention stays the fatal blow. The vow's grammar is revisited: "No vow can disannul / The law of God, nor such was its intent / When rightly scann'd; yet still shall be fulfill'd." Jephtha must dedicate his daughter to God "in pure and virgin state fore'er," since she was "not an object meet for sacrifice." The angel assures Jephtha: "The Holy Sp'rit, that dictated thy vow, / Bade thus explain it, and approves thy faith." And the angel bids Iphis:

> Happy, Iphis, all thy days,
> Pure, angelic, virgin-state,
> Shalt thou live, and ages late
> Crown thee with immortal praise.

Everyone is blessed. "Amen. Hallelujah."

Likewise, in the first presentation of a biblical story at the Paris Opera, in 1732, the heroine Iphise lives on, her sacrifice stopped by a spectacular ball of fire and thunder sent by God (*Jephté: Tragedie lyrique*, composed by Michel Pignolet de Monteclair (1667–1737); libretto by Abbé Simon-Joseph Pellegrin (1663–1745)). The opera was popular, with over 100 performances by 1761, and the audience was assured that the God of love needs no bloody sacrifice. This sentiment, Pellegrin reminds us in his Preface, is shared by many interpreters, Jews as well as Christians.

The scholarly debate continued, however. Isaac Watts (1674–1748), writer of hymns ("When I survey the wondrous cross") and children's books, sums up: "It is a Matter of Doubt and Controversy among the Learned, whether Jephthah, being a Soldier, in those Days of Ignorance, did not really offer his Daughter for a Sacrifice, according to his Vow, as the Scripture seems to express it; or whether he only restrained her from Marriage and bearing Children, which in those Days was accounted like a Sacrifice, and as a Sentence of Death passed on them" (*A Short View*, 1730 [87]).

Some of the "learned" just could not contemplate Paul's exemplary man of faith (Hebrews 11) doing such a deed. "No one without horror and amazement can suppose Jephthah sacrificed his daughter for a burnt-offering," writes the Rev. Samuel Smith in his Family Bible (*Compleat History*, 1752).

> To find a man, and that not a wild barbarian, but an Israelite, offering in a burnt-offering a young, innocent, and no doubt, beautiful and virtuous maid; to find an indulgent father burning the fruit of his own body, his own child, nay, and his dutiful and obedient child, too, the object of his hopes and present comforts; to find him, whom the Apostle lists in the catalogue of the most pious and faithful Worthies, of the Old Testament, vowing to offer an human sacrifice to God, at the very time in which the Scripture says, "The Spirit of the Lord was upon him;" and putting his vow afterwards in execution, though human sacrifices were hateful to the Lord . . . I say, to find all this is very puzzling and unaccountable.

Yet, despite widespread approval of the survival interpretation (John Wesley's view, for example), unease persists. Eighteenth- and nineteenth-century Bible commentaries and dictionaries frequently devote more space to this question than to any other single matter in Judges.

The typical case *against* the daughter's death is made by revivalist preacher, Jonathan Edwards (1703–58), in his *Notes on Scripture* (1722–56), borrowing liberally from the immensely popular commentary, begun in 1666, by Matthew Poole (1624–79). Edwards offers five well-rehearsed reasons. First, since the vow required a lawful offering, he substituted by dedicating his daughter, like a Nazirite. He must have paid the priest the redemption estimate and left her in God's service, as Hannah left Samuel. "And what time she did not spend in duties of immediate devotion, she might spend in making of priests' garments (Ex. 35:25–26), or in other business subservient to the work of the sanctuary, as there might be enough found that a woman might do." Second, to put her to death would have been "so horrid and so contrary to the mind and will of God" that we cannot imagine God allowing it. Nor, being a "pious person" (Heb 11:32), would Jephthah have done so. Moreover, what did transpire was doubtless agreeable to God, who otherwise would not have assisted the daughter to resign herself so readily to it. Third, she bewails her virginity on the mountain, not her untimely end. Fourth, "she knew no man" explains the consequence of what Jephthah did, namely devote her to perpetual virginity; otherwise the clause is otiose, since we already know she bewailed her virginity. Fifth, Jephthah's lament ("Alas, my daughter, thou hast brought me very low") implies not her death but the extinction of Jephthah's family, in those days "an exceeding great calamity." Edwards might have added a sixth reason: a father slaying his daughter ill fits a model of faithfulness and a type of Christ – and Edwards was wedded to typology, serving a Christocentric evangelical faith. Like many others, Edwards badly needed a less heinous outcome.

This "less harsh alternative" enjoyed support for much of the nineteenth century. Several widely read commentaries adopted this view, including that (completed 1826) by Methodist preacher Adam Clarke (1762–1832) who quotes at length from the detailed exposition by William Hales (1747–1831) in *A New Analysis of Chronology* (1809, iii, 319). Likewise the Rev. Richard Watson's (1737–1816) *Biblical and Theological Dictionary* (13th edn, 1861) finds Dr Hales's remarks of "great weight" and decisive against the daughter's death. Still, Watson hedges his bets: should the daughter's immolation be established, there is not the least evidence of God's sanction. Jephthah was manifestly a superstitious and ill-instructed man, an instrument of God's power, rather than an example of his grace.

But the influence of Hebrews on readers was tenacious, as was the desire to find positive qualities in Scripture heroes. For the author of *Uncle Tom's Cabin*, Harriet Beecher Stowe (1811–96), Jephthah appears "a straightforward, brave, generous, God-fearing man." There were noble, God-fearing people living in the period, and she deems improbable "that people like Boaz, Elkanah or Manoah and his wife (and their friends) would have accepted a man guilty of such a crime." She is impressed that a "large and very learned and respectable body of commentators among the Jews, both ancient and modern," deny that Jephthah killed his daughter, and "as appears to us, for the best of reasons." But finally, if historians are divided, "we are never far out of the way in taking that solution which is most honorable to our common human nature, and the most in accordance with our natural wishes" (*Woman in Sacred History*, 1873, 123–6).

Edwards's contemporary, French critic Voltaire (1694–1778), read very differently. The philosopher of tolerance willingly accepted the text's "plain meaning" and wrote often of Jephthah (David and Solomon are other favorites), attacking the Old Testament and its god for barbarous morality and intolerance – a "bloody god," *dieu sanguinaire*, he called him with reference to Jephthah (*Examen important de milord Bolingbroke*, 1761). "God, absolute master of life and death, permitted sacrifices of human blood. He even commanded them. He commanded Abraham to sacrifice his only son, and he received the blood of Jephthah's only daughter" (*Bible enfin expliquée*, 1776 [142]). Voltaire's larger target was not only the anthropomorphic god he saw depicted, but also the authority of the Church which appealed to the Bible. Ironically, his attempts to undermine the Jewish Scriptures as part of the Christian Bible, undertaken at risk to himself, also risked heightening prejudice against Jews.

"The Jews," he writes in *A Treatise on Toleration* (1763), "offered human sacrifices to God." He cites Jephthah's daughter (her death "is plain by the text") and Agag hewed in pieces by Samuel (1 Sam 15:33). In a footnote he sows confusion. Dr Calmet (of *Dictionary* fame), he reports, says that God disapproved of such vows but insisted on their fulfillment to punish those making them and warn others. However, St Augustine and most Church Fathers condemn Jephthah for carrying out the vow. Yet Scripture says he was filled with God's spirit; St Paul in Hebrews praises him; and St Jerome in his Epistle to Julian says that the Apostle "placed him among the saints" for sacrificing his daughter to the Lord. Having pitted scripture against scripture and ancient Christian authorities against each other, Voltaire concludes sardonically: "Here now is a diversity in opinions, concerning which it is not permitted us to pronounce a decision; nay, it is even dangerous to have any opinion of our own" (ch. 12).

The daughter's sacrifice shows Scripture history's immorality, he insists in his *Philosophical Dictionary* (1764–9). Her being a burnt offering ("I am keeping to the text") accords with Levitical law about devoting to destruction ("The Jewish law expressly ordered the immolating of men consecrated to the Lord" (Lev 27:29)). With this event, "human blood sacrifices are clearly inaugurated; no point of history is better verified. One can judge a nation only by its archives, and by what it reports about itself" ("Jephthah or human blood sacrifices," 325–6). Equally sarcastically, he elsewhere dismisses the argument over the daughter's fate: "But what does it matter in the end, to you and me, . . . whether someone, sometime, wrote that a barbarian, in a barbaric war between villages, out of piety [*piété* for *pitié*] cut his daughter's throat!" (*égorger*, cut throat/sacrifice) (*Un Chrétien contre six Juifs*, 1776 [528]); see also *Bible enfin expliquée*, 1776 [142–4]).

While Dr Calmet's view of God's role is more to Mrs Trimmer's liking, she remains unsure about this "very affecting" story which "cannot be read without painful emotions." The vow was inconsiderate, its result a melancholy event. Human sacrifice was forbidden as cruelty displeasing to a God of infinite mercy and resembling "the horrid practice of the idolatrous nations." Perhaps in exile he had learnt heathen practices and "really intended to offer a human victim," since he was unlikely to meet first an animal, an ox or lamb, fit for sacrifice. Hence "God taught him to understand the enormity of this horrid crime, by suffering him to be involved in such extreme distress." The daughter's fate is unclear, whether "she resigned her pious soul as a voluntary sacrifice" for God's mercy towards her father and country, or whether, "as is the general opinion," she relinquished hopes of honorable offspring and passed her remaining days "in solitary sadness" (*Sacred History*, 1783 [lvi, 245–8]).

If Trimmer expresses wistfully her unclarity, John Kitto (*Bible History*, 1841 [214]) cannot disguise his regret that the sacred writer has not expressed in "plain terms" the "dreadful immolation," so opening the matter to dispute. He cites early Christian and Jewish writers, including Josephus, as agreeing that the daughter died, and blames the survival view on "the ingenuity of modern criticism" – though he admits to previously holding it himself (in his *Pictorial Bible*) before being constrained to adhere to "the harsher alternative." His reasons derive from better acquaintance "with the spirit of the time, the state of religion, the nature of the ideas which then prevailed, the peculiarities of the ecclesiastical polity among the Hebrews, and the character of Jephthah himself," whom he describes as superstitious and an "infatuated hero."

For others it was more straightforward. Scottish author George Gilfillan (1813–78) knew a good story when he saw one: clearly "the Iphigenia of Israel" was put to death. "Otherwise, how explain her father's terrible grief when she comes forth to meet him, and what a lame and impotent conclusion to the story had her simply taking the veil been!" (*Bards of the Bible*, 1879, 97).

Clearly principles of interpretation differed. The Rev. Darius Mead's *Christian Parlor Magazine* (1844 [65]) suggests that this unwarranted "fancy" of the daughter's survival came from "a desire to free the Bible from an imputation of sanctioning cruelty; a sanction supposed to be found in the simple absence of any condemnatory remark by the sacred penman." But lack of explicit moral comment is the normal narrative style of the historical books, leaving the reader to judge the nature of the facts narrated. "From the mere absence of expressed condemnation, no inference is to be drawn of the divine approbation of any act." Hence nothing restrains us from judging the sacrifice "according to its real moral character."

By the nineteenth century's close, the survival view was losing its grip. Increasingly, Jephthah's actions were seen as primitive behavior in primitive times, as part of "progressive revelation" – as civilization would progress, so too divine revelation. It was not simply that Jephthah personally was ignorant or the Israelites going through a rough patch. Hence James Orr (1844–1913) is not surprised that in those "rude and barbarous" days God's spirit came upon a man like Jephthah "whose modes of speech and action" (as in his ideas of God, or his vow) show "the rudeness of the times" (*Problem of the Old Testament*, 1906 [473–4]). For the Rt. Rev. Bertram F. Simpson (1883–1971) in the multi-volume *Story of the Bible* (c.1938, 287), the difficulty is not the text's meaning (the daughter dies) but its effect upon readers. Schoolchildren found the incident a source of considerable trouble, convinced that breaking a wrong vow was a lesser evil than slaughtering a human being. Simpson's response: this is a lesson about the development of moral standards. The "sad fact" is, at this stage of history even the Israelites could still imagine that human sacrifice pleased God.

The trend to the "obvious" meaning continued in the twentieth century. A notable dissent is that of David Marcus, who on balance favors survival while allowing the narrator a degree of deliberate ambiguity (*Jephthah and his Vow*, 1986). But by late in the century, as feminist critics rediscovered the story, this alternative ending was all but forgotten.

The story illustrated

Illustrators have always ignored the survival interpretation. Like Gilfillan and the poets, they knew what made a dramatic scene, and sacrificial death beat perpetual solitude for drama. The maiden at the sacrificial altar appears regularly until the end of the nineteenth century. But even as the survival view waned among commentators, changing sensibilities about appropriate illustration, especially for young viewers, led to sacrificial scenes disappearing. Yes, it was a real sacrifice, but no, it was not for general exhibition.

Some books, such as the early Luther Bibles (e.g. Hans Lufft, 1540) or Pieter Mortier's influential "Great Bible" (1700), chose to forgo the scene in favor of the ubiquitous first meeting of father and daughter. The omission is obvious later, too, in such profusely illustrated and influential works as Harper's *Illuminated Bible* (1846), Cassell's *Illustrated Family Bible* (c.1870), and the *Old Testament* (1904) by J. James Tissot (1836–1902). An alternative was to leave the sacrifice implied but not pictured. A full page in the Victorian *Sunny Sabbaths* tells the story, in conventional fashion (cf. de Hooghe, 1706), by clustering cameos around a central scene, here the fatal meeting. Among the cameos we see no sacrifice, but instead the daughter and her companions lamenting on the hillside – and a craggy mountain view with waters rolling down.

From the sixteenth century on, however, fulfillment was depicted, following medieval tradition, as imminent death at the altar. Typically the daughter kneels by an altar on which burns a small fire; her father, a priest, or other executioner is about to kill her. (Kitto considered it "a monstrous conception of the painters" that the high priest was the sacrificer; the "awful deed was probably perpetrated at some old altar" by Jephthah himself (*Pictorial Sunday-Book*, 1845, 187).) In the series *Icones Biblicae Veterae* (1679) by Melchior Küsel (1626–83), the setting is classical with ornate altar and fluted columns. The daughter's executioner, wielding a long-bladed axe, holds her head and, unusually, leans as if speaking to her, while she kneels, hands tied, awaiting the blow. A priest officiates, and a young acolyte looks on. Nearby her father and others writhe in lamentation (PLATE 6.2a). A late eighteenth-century engraving in the Rev. E. Blomfield's *New Family Bible* (1813) still depicts classical antiquity. The engraver throws the scene into dramatic contrasts of light and shadow, highlighting the kneeling woman, the standing, gesturing father, and the altar smoke. This design reappears in *Tallis's Illustrated Scripture History* (1851) (PLATE 6.2b).

A favorite for several generations is one version or another of a painting by Cornish artist and Royal Academician John Opie (1761–1807). Kennicott's *Universal Family Bible* (1793) shows the kneeling daughter, blindfolded, bare-breasted; an aged priest grimly leans over, knife poised to plunge; a young acolyte crouches apprehensively, bowl at the ready. To one side stands a large intact pitcher, symbol of virginity. Behind are two figures, one sorrowfully pinioning the daughter's arms, the other turned away as if unable to look. Fire burns on the shadowy altar to one side; behind, a dark archway. Half a century later, in Tallis's *Family Devotions*, edited by Thomas Gaspey (c.1850), the scene has grown starker, yet set now within a delicately decorated frame. The background figures are gone, heightening the contrast with the young woman's white body, for the archway behind now leads into black darkness, as if into a tomb. Yet the priest's mouth is no longer grimly set, the daughter might faintly smile, and the boy looks on almost eagerly (PLATE 6.2c).

To the viewer who suspects that eroticism played a part in the Opie picture's appeal, a perusal of another Victorian favorite, "Jephthah's Daughter" (1827) by American editor and essayist Nathaniel Parker Willis (1806–67), suggests that such latent sentiments were not rare (cf. Songs 4:1–7, 6:4–9):

> . . . and the wind,
> Just swaying her light robe, revealed a shape
> Praxiteles might worship. . . .
> Her lip was slightly parted, like the cleft
> Of a pomegranate blossom; and her neck,
> Just where the cheek was melting to its curve
> With the unearthly beauty sometimes there,
> Was shaded, as if light had fallen off,
> Its surface was so polished. She was stilling
> Her light, quick breath, to hear; and the white rose
> Scarce moved upon her bosom, as it swelled,
> Like nothing but a lovely wave of light,
> To meet the arching of her queenly neck. . . .
> Her countenance was radiant with love.
> She looked like one to die for it. . . .

PLATE 6.2   Jephthah's daughter: (a) Küsel, 1679; (b) Tallis's *Scripture History*, 1851; (c) after Opie, in Gaspey, *Family Devotions*, c.1850; (d) after Opie, lantern side, c.1900; courtesy George Eastman House; (e) Moser, © 1999 Pennroyal Caxton Press. (See pp. 153–4, 156)

By the turn of the century Opie's picture was still going strong, in an educational lantern slide version. The daughter's breast is more discreetly bared, but now ropes encircle her waist and loosely pin her arms. The two background figures are restored, black-bearded men, one wearing Assyrian head gear. Gone is the gloom, replaced by lush curtains and Egyptian pillars. The pitcher is decoratively wreathed, and a large incense urn now burns in the foreground. The picture has been "orientalized" to add authenticity (and distance), and its starkness tempered (PLATE 6.2d). It remains, nonetheless, a scene foreign to religious education a century later.

Shockingly simple and direct is the head and upper torso of a dark-skinned girl merging into the kindling wood of the holocaust pyre. This post-Holocaust Jephthah's daughter confronts the reader of the recent Pennyroyal Caxton Bible (1999) designed and illustrated by Barry Moser (PLATE 6.2e).

The daughter

While the vow and its fulfillment have dominated commentators' attention, a few readers have also sought to enter into the daughter's experience. Joseph Hall offers an inner monologue as she decides to meet her victorious father, little suspecting what danger lies in "dutiful triumph."

> My sex forbade me to do any thing towards the help of my father's victory: I can do little, if I cannot applaud it. If nature have made me weak, yet not unthankful: nothing forbids my joy to be as strong as the victor's. . . . A timbrel may become these hands which were unfit for a sword: this day hath made me the daughter of the head of Israel; this day hath made both Israel free, my father a conqueror, and myself in him noble: and shall my affection make no difference?

No day in her life seemed as happy as this, yet it "proves the day of her solemn and perpetual mourning." Hall frames the daughter's joy and sadness with a cautionary moral: "It falls out often, that those times and occasions which promise most contentment, prove most doleful in the issue. . . . It is good, in a fair morning, to think of the storm that may rise ere night, and to enjoy both good and evil fearfully" (*Contemplations*, 1615 [x.1, 123]).

"What must be the agony of her mind, when she beheld him turning from her in an agony of distress, and heard him declare her unhappy fate?" wonders Mrs Trimmer (*Sacred History*, 1783 [lvi, 246]) of the daughter who "came forth to meet her honoured parent, with every demonstration of joy and thankfulness to heaven for his success and preservation; expecting to be pressed to his fond bosom, and hoping to reward his toils with assiduous duty!" Echoing

Trimmer, Thomas E. Miller (*Portraits*, 1922, 108–9) portrays a "young and beautiful and innocent Hebrew maiden" going forth with great gladness, only to be met by "a heavy heart and haggard countenance." "Where was the father's welcome embrace and loving kiss? Was not she his only child . . . Wherefore this coldness, this hesitating approach? Had war turned the paternal heart into stone?"

Scottish poet James Grahame (1765–1811) conveys the daughter's shock in a single line ("Jephtha's Vow," 1807 [297–8]). This Jephthah approaches home with troubled steps. Strikingly, he is aware of what he has staked:

> His vow will meet a victim in his child:
> For well he knows, that, from her earliest years,
> She still was first to meet his homeward steps:
> Well he remembers how, with tottering gait,
> She ran, and clasp' his knees, and lisp'd, and look'd
> Her joy. . . .

He hears a song and tries to think the voice is not hers; but she emerges, foremost of the band. "Moveless he stands." He grasps his hilt and quits the hold, "And clasps, in agony, his hands, and cries, / 'Alas, my daughter! thou has brought me low.'—/ The timbrel at her rooted feet resounds."

Illustrations of their meeting sometimes focus on the daughter, sometimes on the father, but more often seek a balance. They signal her joy by her instrument. In the Middle Ages she plays a small stringed instrument, akin to a harp or even a viola, or perhaps two small nakers or kettledrums (Latin *tympanum*) slung across her hips and popularized in the seventeenth and eighteenth centuries by the design by Matthäus Merian (1593–1650) in his famous suite (PLATE 6.3a) (*Icones Biblicae*, 1626; Zetzner's "Merian Bible," 1630). Caspar Luyken (1672–1708) shows a child oblivious to the dramatic confrontation intently beating a single kettledrum, while the daughter gazes directly at her father, her fingers still strumming a lute-shaped drum tucked against her shoulder. Her companion's hands have abandoned her own drum in horror (PLATE 6.3c) (*Historiae Celebriores*, 1708). A triangle makes an occasional appearance, as in Pieter Mortier's classical "Great Bible" of 1700 or Ebenezer Miller's 1839 edition of *Scripture History* for children (PLATE 6.3b). But tambourines (also *tympanum* in Latin) grow in favor, as in Esther Hewlett's *Scripture History* of 1828 (PLATE 6.4a), and dominate nineteenth- and twentieth-century illustration. The trend culminates in James Tissot's portrait (PLATE 6.4c) (*Old Testament*, 1904). A headdress which mimics tambourines crowns the daughter's exotic "Oriental" garb; and her shoulder supports, apparently effortlessly, the largest tambourine in the history of Bible illustration. She

PLATE 6.3 Jephthah's daughter: (a) Merian, 1626; (b) Miller's *Scripture History*, 1839; (c) Luyken, 1708. (See p. 157)

gently smiles at the viewer, perhaps the father, who, unusually, is not in the picture.

Other meetings, especially from the nineteenth century on, show joy through dancing, sometimes tambourine in hand (as in Hewlett). Most celebrated is the dancing daughter of Gustave Doré (1832–83), whose illustrations (*La Sainte Bible*, 1866; *Doré Bible Gallery*, 1879) reappear in numerous publications. Arms upraised in triumph, she steps over a craggy outcrop ahead of her dancing musicians. Another French artist, Jean-Paul Laurens (1838–1921), better known for his (anticlerical) scenes from ecclesiastical history, shows a diaphanous daughter dancing out the door, tambourine in hand, body back-lit, a bare-breasted companion executing a step, and a naked girl waving through a window – all under an (Egyptian) harem guard's watchful eye. An intent to register a dramatic contrast with what is to ensue risks being lost to other viewerly distractions (PLATE 6.4b). The odd naked woman and child also grace Herbert Gandy's 1920s meeting which looks like a scene on a Hollywood set. The daughter herself is amply draped and turbaned, arms extended, flowing flapper-style. She sways with the dancers, but stays center stage ahead of the extras (PLATE 6.4d).

The scene most usually evoking the daughter's emotions is the mountain lament, a nineteenth-century favorite and a vehicle for large doses of pious sentiment. Doré's engraving fits the pattern. The young women languish on a hilltop, daughter at the high focal point, eyes heavenwards. A friend rests her head on the daughter's shoulder and touches her hand. Another popular rendition (it turns up later as a lantern slide) is by Pre-Raphaelite painter Henry O'Neil (1817–80). Again women cluster around the daughter, also gazing up. There is sorrowful languishing, but also perhaps a little conversation, and one companion plays the lyre for her friend. The women touch or lie against each other, and the composition enhances their sad solidarity (in Sparrow, *Joshua to Job*, 1906, 46). Also popular was the simpler group of four companions clustered around a standing daughter by German Romantic painter of the Nazarene circle, Carl Oesterley (1805–91). The young women cling and comfort, while the daughter gazes down and gestures to the valley below (PLATE 6.5c). We might contrast the languid sensuality of an 1876 painting in Oriental mode by French academic classicist Edouard Debat-Ponsan (1847–1913), very similar in composition to O'Neill's group but wholly different in affect. Again male desire undermines the scene's ostensible sentiment of lament. Two older black women, slaves no doubt, gaze sorrowfully; but they seem there mainly for exotic effect and to intensify the whiteness of the maiden's exposed breast and an undraped European body prostrate in the foreground. The daughter stares out under dark eyelids. Does she lament her virginity or perhaps her fate as *femme fatale*

manquée? (PLATE 6.5b). This must be one of the truly low points of Bible illustration.

In stark contrast is the line drawing in the *Oxford Illustrated Old Testament* (1968) by John Bratby (1928–92) (PLATE 6.5a). Here the naked figures startle an unexpectant viewer, but their faces and the strangely tabular setting provoke thought. Does their nakedness signal vulnerability? Is the companions' upward gaze piety or suspicion? With furrowed brow and staring eyes the daughter gazes down – at the altar? Unlike her companions, her lower body is cut off – as her life and sexuality will soon be? Another contrast, and among more moving depictions, is "Jephthah: The Days of Mourning" by Thomas Rooke (1842–1942), exhibited at the Royal Academy in 1882. Rooke produced a series of Old Testament paintings, including also "The Vow's Fulfilment" (exhibited in 1872). In the latter, the hunched-over young woman, head buried in her arms and clearly flinching from the expected blow, kneels atop a pyre. Jephthah, knife in hand, invokes heaven, but whether for a stay of execution or its blessing we do not know. In the mourning scene, the daughter stands apart from her grieving companions, head bent, tucking her cheek against her clasped hands, deep in thought or sadness. Spreading trees offer cover, and plants survive in the parched ground. This daughter is both supported and terribly alone (PLATE 6.5d).

Mostly, comment on the daughter hinges on her acceptance of the vow and its consequence, and bears no small debt to the ever-popular Josephus. She is universally lauded for unhesitatingly performing her duty to religion (even if mistakenly), her country, and her father. For many, her filial devotion defines her and is the source of her resignation and even contentment. Joseph Hall early sets the standard: she "was not more loving, than religious; neither is she less willing to be the Lord's than her father's." "Many a daughter would have dissuaded her father with tears, and have wished rather her father's impiety, than her own prejudice. . . . How obsequious should children be to the will of their careful parents, even in their final disposition in the world, when they see this holy maid willing to abandon the world upon the rash vow of a father! They are the living goods of their parents, and must therefore wait upon the bestowing of their owners" (*Contemplations*, 1615 [x.1, 124]).

As Mrs Trimmer later says, Jephthah's daughter "certainly was possessed of uncommon fortitude of mind," for she calmly submitted to the calamity, "rather than her father should be guilty of impiety." She indulged herself in only a short respite in order to reconcile herself to dying without children, reckoned by Jewish women the greatest disgrace, because every one hoped to bear

---

PLATE 6.4   Jephthah's daughter: (a) Hewlett's *Scripture History*, 1828; (b) Laurens, c.1900; (c) Tissot, 1904; (d) Gandy, c.1920. (See pp. 157, 159)

PLATE 6.5   Jephthah's daughter: (a) Bratby, 1968; (b) Debat-Ponsan, 1876; (c) Oesterley, nineteenth century; (d) Rooke, c.1882. (See pp. 159, 161)

some great deliverer, if not the promised Savior (a common understanding in Trimmer's time). Whatever her precise fate, she is an example of the most exalted filial piety, to be admired by every dutiful child. Those "unmindful of their parents' happiness, and unthankful for the blessings which paternal love dispenses, ought to blush with shame and confusion, when conscience obliges them to draw a comparison between themselves and Jephthah's amiable daughter" (*Sacred History*, 1783 [lvi, 246–8]). Likewise she exemplified patriotism: "To know that her father had triumphed over his enemies and those of his country, was happiness for her, and rejoicing in his glory she was content to die" (Thomas Gaspey, *Tallis's Illustrated Scripture History*, 1851; cf. Kitto, *Bible History*, 1841 [213]). For Alexander Whyte (1836–1921), the power of her example begins with the young women who commemorated her annually. For they "came back to be far better daughters than they went out. They came back softened, and purified, and sobered at heart. They came back ready to die for their fathers, and for their brothers, and for their husbands, and for their God" (*Bible Characters: Gideon to Absalom*, 1905, 31).

Some of the century's great poets also had their view. The succinct lines of Byron (1788–1824) leave little room for doubt as to what so impelled the daughter towards her fate ("Jephtha's Daughter," 1815):

> Since our Country, our God—Oh, my Sire!
> Demand that thy Daughter expire;
> Since thy triumph was bought by thy vow—
> Strike the bosom that's bared for thee now! . . .
> I have won the great battle for thee,
> And my Father and Country are free!
> When this blood of thy giving hath gushed,
> When the voice that thou lovest is hushed,
> Let my memory still be thy pride,
> And forget not I smiled as I died.

Perhaps no one, however, captured better the sentiment of God, country, and father, so congenial to Victorians, than their favorite, Tennyson (1809–92), in "A Dream of Fair Women" (1832). The daughter speaks for herself:

> My God, my land, my father—these did move
> Me from my bliss of life, that Nature gave,
> Lower'd softly with a threefold cord of love
>   Down to a silent grave. . . .
> When the next moon was roll'd into the sky,
> Strength came to me that equall'd my desire.
> How beautiful a thing it was to die
>   For God and for my sire!

> It comforts me in this one thought to dwell,
> That I subdued me to my father's will;
> Because the kiss he gave me, ere I fell,
> Sweetens the spirit still.

The historian, observes Harriet Beecher Stowe, "has set before us a high and lovely ideal of womanhood in the Judaean girl. There is but a sentence, yet what calmness, what high-mindedness, what unselfish patriotism, are in the words! 'My father, if thou has opened thy mouth to the Lord, . . .' How heroic the soul that could meet so sudden a reverse with so unmoved a spirit!" (*Woman in Sacred History*, 1873, 125–6).

A discordant note is sounded by Canadian Charles Heavysege (1816–69) in his long narrative *Jephthah's Daughter* (1865). He quickly draws the parallel with Agamemnon's daughter, but gives Jephthah's daughter a mother who, unlike Clytemnestra, never wavers in denouncing her husband:

> All men are robbers, like the Ammonite—
> Even thou, for thou wouldst rob me of my child;
> Blighted by thee, and, in thy purpose, stolen,
> As altar-fuel, that might shed a flame
> To light thy taper-glory in the field. . . .
> Thou cruel man, as ruthless as fell Ammon,
> Whose children pass to Moloch through the fire,
> Think'st thou Jehovah will accept such a victim?

Jephthah himself passionately oscillates, invokes Isaac's reprieve, and even offers himself – and his wife – to satisfy the religious requirements. The priests, interested in preserving victory, claim to find no alternative. The daughter, who at first eloquently protests, comes to own "There *is* some signal bliss awaiting those / Who perish for their country," and finally speaks as Byron and Tennyson would have her:

> Oh, doom delightful even as 'tis dread!
> Were it not great to die for Israel,—
> To free a father from a flood of woe?
> Father, you shall not say I disobeyed.
> Let me not need now disobey you, mother,
> But give me leave to knock at death's pale gate,
> Whereat indeed I must, by duty drawn,
> By nature show the sacred way to yield.

Yet the poem ends ambivalently. The mother's accusations against the father are not answered, her trust that Jehovah will repudiate the sacrifice appears ill placed, and no word is uttered in the deity's defense. The narrator offers an epitaph to "this ancient Hebrew maid, / Transcendent, and surpassing poets' praise; / Who bowed her to a parent's urgent need, / Enduring irreparable wrong." She died, "self-forgetful; – yet, immortal, lives, / Loved and remembered to the end of time."

As might be expected, *The Woman's Bible* (1898), product of the women's movement in North America, strikes a far more discordant note (ii, 24–6). Elizabeth Cady Stanton (1815–1902) is scathing in criticism of Jephthah, as of Abraham, "these loving fathers" who "thought to make themselves specially pleasing to the Lord by sacrificing their children to Him as burnt offerings." Her own context as a woman fighting for equal rights with men informs her comments.

> The submission of Isaac and Jephthah's daughter to this violation of their most sacred rights is truly pathetic. But, like all oppressed classes, they were ignorant of the fact that they had any natural, inalienable rights. We have such a type of womanhood even in our day. If any man had asked Jephthah's daughter if she would not like to have the Jewish law on vows so amended that she might disallow her father's vow, and thus secure to herself the right of life, she would no doubt have said, "No; I have all the rights I want," just as a class of New York women said in 1895, when it was proposed to amend the constitution of the State in their favor.

Cady Stanton remarks that the daughter is given no name, a sign of being owned absolutely by her father, and sharply contests the lauding of her "beautiful submission and self-sacrifice." "To me it is pitiful and painful. I would that this page of history were gilded with a dignified whole-souled rebellion." She offers the reader a counter-text, the manifesto of an independent and brave young woman who would sternly rebuke her father:

> I will not consent to such a sacrifice. Your vow must be disallowed. You may sacrifice your own life as you please, but you have no right over mine. I am on the threshold of life, the joys of youth and of middle age are all before me. You are in the sunset; you have had your blessings and your triumphs; but mine are yet to come. . . . I consider that God has made me the arbiter of my own fate and all my possibilities. My first duty is to develop all the powers given to me and to make the most of myself and my own life. Self-development is a higher duty than self-sacrifice. I demand the immediate abolition of the Jewish law on vows. Not with my consent can you fulfill yours.

But admiration for daughterly devotion continues into the twentieth century: a "glimpse of obedience as perfect as any the world has known," declares Florence Bone (1892–1986). She wonders whether the modern woman takes her freedom for granted, and sees in Jephthah's daughter a woman "whose nature becomes fine and rare, whose work is achieved, in spite of terrible odds. . . . She had not thought of being daunted, and there was absolutely nothing in her character of the disposition to whine and pity herself. She was entirely brave" (*Girls of the Bible*, c.1915, 52–7).

Occasionally in the nineteenth and twentieth centuries her self-sacrifice prompts typological and Christological interpretation. George Gilfillan (*Bards of the Bible*, 1879, 99) pictures her ascending the mountain, "composed, majestic, moving to lofty purpose" in order to "bewail that she never could entertain the hope of bearing the Messiah, but was only permitted to typify his early and cruel death." "Like her great antitype—Jesus of Nazareth," writes Thomas Miller (*Portraits*, 1922, 115), "she offered herself a willing sacrifice, in the belief that her death was the purchase price of her people's victory." Nor did she die in vain, he adds: the annual lamentation educated the maidens of Gilead "in the deep things of life—obedience, self-surrender, and sacrifice." Even the free-thinking Welsh minister, T. Rhondda Williams (*Old Testament Stories in Modern Light*, 1911), is unreservedly enthusiastic. She comes out splendidly, he says, even if, living in a dark age, her ideas about sacrifice were wrong: the grand thing about her was her willingness to die for the people's good and her father's honor. "That was a touch of the spirit which made Jesus willing to die on the Cross, it is the spirit that sinks self for the good of others. We are called to exercise it, not in dying for the word, but in living for it."

Oddly, this line of thought culminates in feminist criticism later in the century. The classic essay is by Phyllis Trible, "The Daughter of Jephthah: an Inhuman Sacrifice," in her influential *Texts of Terror* (1984). Opposite the essay title is pictured the daughter's gravestone inscribed with an epigraph (cf. Matt 27:46; Mark 15:34): "My God, my God, why hast thou forsaken her?" Trible does not comment upon the picture. Yet it asks a reader to ponder how the daughter's sacrifice relates to that of Jesus, and whether, in a world where men have controlled the writing of Scripture and often its reading, she is forsaken still. Undoubtedly this picture and Trible's essay lie behind Clinton McCann's recent remark: "A male-dominated history of interpretation has sometimes identified the judges, especially Samson, as types of Jesus . . . If there is any type of Jesus in the book of Judges—that is, anyone who embodies God's experience—the most likely candidate is Jephthah's daughter" (*Judges*, 2002).

Recent reception

Late nineteenth- and twentieth-century "historical criticism" generally has more to say about Jephthah than his daughter. One challenge to a long-accepted view concerns his alleged diplomatic skill in treating with the Ammonite king. But his sense of geography is fuzzy, his account of the past muddled (not matching Numbers or Deuteronomy, as long recognized and ignored), and, most startling: "the Ammonite king is likely surprised to be told that his god is Chemosh (who was the god of the Moabites). . . . This is an error, and it hardly impresses the Ammonite king!" (Lawson Younger, *Judges and Ruth*, 2002, 257). Or is the muddle deliberate, after all, designed to ensure that diplomacy ends not in peace but war?

Much discussion has centered on the story's historicity, especially Jephthah's role as leader. Some leading German critics in the nineteenth century (e.g. Wellhausen and Stade) found little of historical value. A century later, on the other hand, Jephthah and the minor judges were viewed as historical figures who proclaimed Israel's own sacral law or transmitted ancient Near Eastern case law (Boling, *Judges*, 1975, 186–7). Yet, by the century's end, many historians of ancient Israel were becoming skeptical again.

"Narrative critics," more interested in the literary qualities of the story in its extant form than its historicity or the history of its composition, have explored especially its connections to, and contrasts with, the other stories in Judges, as well its own internal patterns. For example, the so-called "framework" of Jeph-thah's story (ch. 10) differs noticeably from earlier stories (Robert Polzin, "*The Book of Judges*," 1980, 176–81). For the first and only time the narrator speci-fies Israel's "evil" in the sight of God (listing the gods worshiped) and tells how, after being oppressed, they cried for help, were rebuffed, but repented, put away the gods, and returned to worship the Lord. Here a reader might expect to move explicitly (Ehud, 3:15) or implicitly (Deborah, 4:4) into a deliverance story or, at worst, encounter first a chastising prophet (Gideon, 6:8–10). Instead the narrator reports God's response, ambiguously. The sentence might mean (as traditionally) "and he became indignant over [KJV: his soul was grieved for] the misery of [i.e. suffered by] Israel," or it might be translated, "and he grew short [or impatient] with the trouble [caused by] Israel." The uncertainty reminds a reader that God's deliverance is not assured. By the book's end this will become doubly apparent, even more so when the larger story ends in exile (2 Kings 24–5).

The pattern of the people's rejecting and then returning to God, seeking his help, recurs at the onset of Jephthah's own story (David Gunn and Danna Nolan Fewell, *Narrative in the Hebrew Bible*, 1993, 112–19). Cast off by his own people, Jephthah, become powerful, is sought by them. Initially he responds much as God does (10:11–14) by asking (11:7), Did they not reject him and drive him from his home? Why come to him now when they are in trouble? When the people persist, God responds ambiguously, while Jephthah drives a bargain. Success will return him to his father's house, as head. Another bargain, the vow, will destroy his house. The report that Ibzan of Bethlehem judged after him rubs in the point: Ibzan "had thirty sons; and thirty daughters he gave in marriage outside his clan, and thirty daughters he brought in from outside for his sons" (12:8). As for God, he apparently grants his people what they want, through Jephthah, and we presume that, for the time being at least, they remain his people. Will it always be so?

Phyllis Trible's "rhetorical criticism" analyzes how the story is constructed, word by word, sentence by sentence, and scene by scene (*Texts of Terror*, 1984, 92–116). She notes key words repeated (e.g. "go out/go forth") and narrative patterns, such as "chiasmus" (abccba), where she finds meaning. The unit 11:34–9, for example, opens and closes with narrated discourse (the narrator telling what happens) which "surrounds" direct discourse (the characters' speech). Then in each section of narrated discourse, actions by Jephthah "surround" descriptions of his daughter. Likewise, in direct discourse, two speeches by the father "surround" two speeches by the daughter. Such formal "surrounding" mimics Jephthah's actual "confining" of his daughter. "Design and content show that he confines her, even unto death" (p. 99).

In going out with music and dancing, the daughter shares with "a noble company of women" an Israelite tradition, seen earlier with Miriam after victory over Pharaoh (Exod 15:19–21) and later with Israelite women after David defeats Goliath (1 Sam 18:6–7). Yet she goes out alone, no song on her lips, a difference accenting "the terrible irony of an otherwise typical and joyful occasion" (p. 101). But Danna Nolan Fewell sees a different irony: Jephthah's vow, likely made in public, was perhaps known to the daughter, as her reply suggests. Her tone is not innocent submission but ironic judgment: "Do to *me* what you have said!" She *is* one of his troublers because she takes the place of someone he deemed expendable, a servant or bodyguard. She challenges his bargain for glory; she takes control ("Judges," 1992, 71; cf. *Children of Israel*, 2003, 77–80).

Isaac, another "one and only child" is of good lineage, and Abraham acts in faith at God's behest. The nameless daughter's father is born to a prostitute, and her mother never mentioned. As an only child she evokes pity for herself and sympathy for her father; but when her father blames her for bring him low, he thinks only of himself. "Faithfulness to an unfaithful vow has condemned its victim; father and daughter are split apart in deed and destiny" (Trible, 102). And God says nothing.

Trible sees the daughter compassionately taking charge by holding Jephthah to his vow and asking for a respite. She relegates to a footnote the question of sacrifice or seclusion: either way, "the female is the innocent victim of violence." Like so many before her, she is unsparing of the father: "Hers is premeditated death, a sentence of murder passed upon an innocent victim because of the faithless vow uttered by her foolish father" (p. 104). The daughter reaches out to other women, "her own kind,"and after her death, the English versions translate, "it became a custom in Israel" that maidens lamented her. Better, says Trible, is "*she* became a *tradition*." The finality of Jephthah's faithless vow is tempered by the women's faithfulness. This "postscript," then, shifts the focus "from vow to victim, from death to life, from oblivion to remembrance" (p. 107). (See PLATE 6.1c, p. 143: the commemoration, in Bankes, *Family Bible*, c.1790).

Trible's essay has its own postscript (107–9). Unlike those trying valiantly to make this story and Hebrews 11 congruent, she sets the texts against each other. Jephthah, "who through faith conquered kingdoms, enforced justice," is Jephthah the unfaithful murderer. Voltaire would be proud. Here is a direct attack on conventional views of scriptural authority – from someone taking very seriously the biblical text. For Trible, as for other feminist critics, the problem transcends Jephthah's individual error (oh well, God uses all sorts) and cannot be mitigated by claiming social or religious difference (things were different in those primitive times). This story and the Bible in which it is at home are part of the present, part of the problem of "patriarchy," where men still too often dispose of women's bodies, where the very term "survivor" (used of sexual abuse) points to the problem.

> Like the daughters of Israel, we remember and mourn the daughter of Jephthah the Gileadite. In her death we are all diminished; by our memory she is forever hallowed. Though not a "survivor," she becomes an unmistakable symbol for all the courageous daughters of faithless fathers. Her story, brief as it is, evokes the imagination, calling forth a reader's response. . . . (p. 109; cf. David's lament for Jonathan, 2 Sam 1:19–26)

> The daughter of Jephthah lies slain upon thy high places.
> I weep for you, my little sister.
> Very poignant is your story to me;
>   your courage to me is wonderful,
>   surpassing the courage of men.
> How are the powerless fallen,
>   a terrible sacrifice to a faithless vow!

Israel is enduring 40 years of Philistine oppression when an angel comes to the barren wife of the Danite Manoah (Manue). He promises her a child, stipulating that she consume neither strong drink nor unclean food and that the child be a lifelong Nazirite. Hair uncut, he would "begin to deliver Israel." She tells her husband of the "man of God" and relays the message, minus the prediction about deliverance. Manoah asks God to send this man to him. The angel again appears to the woman, alone in the field, and she fetches Manoah, who queries him about his instructions. Manoah offers to prepare a meal, but the angel declines, suggesting instead an offering to the Lord. He also deflects Manoah's wish to know his name, saying it is "too wonderful." Only when the visitor ascends in the altar's flame do they realize his nature. Manoah thinks he will die, having seen God; his wife is more phlegmatic. Samson is born and grows up, and the spirit of the Lord stirs in him.

Samson goes to Timnah (Thamnatha) in Philistine territory (ch. 14). He sees a woman "who was right [or proper] in his eyes" and persuades his reluctant parents to arrange the marriage. On his way to visit her, he slays a lion and later finds honey in its carcass. This curiosity provides the literal ingredients of a riddle that he poses, with a wager, to his Philistine groomsmen. They in turn force his bride to obtain and reveal the riddle's answer, and Samson angrily leaves the marriage feast. Prompted by the spirit of the Lord, he slays 30 Philistines and pays the wager with their garments.

He returns to reclaim his bride (ch. 15), but her father has given her to another. Vengeful, he catches 300 foxes, ties torches to their tails, and burns the Philistines' grain. They in turn burn the woman and her father, inciting further violence by Samson, who then retreats to the rock of Etam. Bound over to the Philistines by 3,000 men of Judah, the spirit of the Lord again seizes him at Lehi (Lechi), and, ropes melted, he kills 1,000 with the jawbone of an ass.

Samson's visit to a Gaza prostitute (ch. 16) ends with him escaping from the waiting Philistines and carrying off the city gates. In the valley of Sorek he falls in love with Delilah (Dalila), whom the Philistines pay 300 pieces of silver to extract the secret of his strength. Three times she asks him, and three times he lies, each time escaping capture. Pleading by his love for her, she finally pesters the true answer out of the Nazirite. Shorn of his seven locks, Samson is captured, blinded, and bound to grind at a mill. His hair begins to grow back. At a sacrifice to the Philistine god Dagon, Samson is brought out to be tormented. Praying to God for strength, he breaks the temple pillars, killing himself and his enemies. His family takes his body home for burial.

Samson has generated centuries of conflicting interpretation. His legendary strength has supported ethnic pride for the early rabbis, typological interpretation for theologically minded Christians, and a favorite tale for pious children inclined to hero worship. On the other hand, his equally legendary sexual appetites, especially as they involve "foreign" women, have caused consternation.

Given that he is an exemplar of faith in Hebrews 11 and a frequent recipient of the spirit of the Lord, Christian interpreters have striven to find the good in him, often articulating, especially in ancient and medieval interpretation, the many ways he prefigures the life, death, and final victory of Christ. Hence the lion prefigures Satan (or Hell) vanquished. By the seventeenth century, however, not only Samson's moral qualities but the very historicity of his story is in question: for some it becomes an exaggerated tale about how *not* to behave, and certainly has nothing to do with proper (modern) ideas of God.

The theophany (ch. 13) has raised questions about how divinity reveals itself (do Manoah and his wife actually see God in the angel?), and the angel's message taken to advise clean living and temperance for all readers. Meanwhile Samson's parents have received both sympathy and scorn as imperfect models for all parents. Vast quantities of ink have been spilt on both the veracity and the morality of Samson's more outlandish exploits with the foxes (jackals?), the jawbone, and the gates of Gaza. The text notwithstanding, Samson's three women are typically lumped together as evil temptresses, although occasional sympathy is spared for the Timnite bride, caught between countrymen and husband. Delilah, however, is often tarred with the brush of the prostitute. One textual detail does plague visual artists: is it Delilah herself or a Philistine who actually cuts Samson's hair? Recent feminist interpretation points to patriarchal ideology at work in the portrayals of the story's women.

Samson's captivity and death have provoked a wide range of reflection and artistic responses. The loss of his eyes has been aligned with their (mis)use regarding the Timnite woman; there is question about the righteousness of his prayer for vengeance; and, especially, his suicide must be rationalized.

The riddle (ch. 14) has recently received unaccustomed attention. At first typically castigated as a "bad riddle" requiring the special knowledge of Samson's lion and its honey, it has become instead, for some, a key to the whole story. Folklore studies show the sex-laced riddle to be typical of wedding feasts and set the amoral yet heroic Samson within the boundary-crossing tradition of the "trickster." Focus on the trickster's alliance with God, and God's alliance with strange women, highlights the riddle of divine (in)justice.

Ancient and Medieval

Jewish

Samson's reception among early Jewish commentators is mixed. In a backhanded compliment, one tradition compares Samson to Aaron, as it does Gideon to Moses and Jephthah to Samuel, to teach that latter-day leaders, though "the lowliest of the lowly," are as worthy as "the most celebrated of the former celebrities" (*Midrash Ecclesiastes Rabbah*, 1:8; cf. Rashi on 1 Sam 12:11, Deut 19:17; also Yehudah HeChasid (c.1150–1217), *Sepher Chasidim*, 129). Others compare him to Samuel (no razor is to touch their heads: Judg 13:5, 1 Sam 1:11) as a kind of Nazirite for life, which special status might explain why his frequent contact with defiling corpses does not appear to disqualify him (*Y. Talmud Nazir*, 9:6; *B. Talmud Nazir*, 4b).

His birth story invites the ancient Jewish historian Josephus (37–c.100) to elaborate: Manoah is enraptured to distraction by Samson's exceedingly beautiful mother (hence, though childless, he did not divorce her) and so madly jealous of the tall, handsome visitor announcing his wife's pregnancy (*Antiquities*, v.276–84 (8.2–4)). Josephus's contemporary, known today as Pseudo-Philo, has more. Manoah and his wife, Eluma, argued endlessly over who was sterile, until one night, as Eluma prayed, an angel told her that, though she was the one, God had attended to her prayers and tears, and she would bear a son called Samson (*Antiquities*, 42:1–3).

Tradition sees the Danite judge Samson fulfilling Jacob's deathbed blessings on his son Dan: "Dan shall judge [*yadin*] his people as one of the tribes of Israel" (Gen 49:16–18). Jacob's cryptic comparison of Dan to a serpent refers to Samson's underhand attacks on his enemies or his ways with women. The "snake in the way," that "bites the horses's heels, so that his rider falls backward" was an image of Samson between two pillars, fatally pulling down Dagon's temple so that the Philistines on the roof fell to their death (e.g. *Midrash Genesis Rabbah*, 98:13–14; *Midrash Numbers Rabbah*, 14:9; Rashi on Gen 49:17; Ramban, 595–6).

His legendary strength more than matched Goliath's and could be a source of ethnic pride: When other nations are at peace, "eating, drinking, and becoming drunk, and engaging in lewd converse," they point to the Bible and boast (listing non-Israelites), "Who is as wise as Balaam? Who is as rich as Haman? Who is as strong as Goliath?" The house of Israel replies, "Was not Ahitophel wise? Was not Korah rich? Was not Samson strong?" (*Midrash Leviticus Rabbah*, 5:3; so also *Midrash Numbers Rabbah*, 10:3). Indeed, noting Samson's love of Philistine women, legend has it that Samson was the Philistine giant's father (see Ginzberg, VI, 250 n. 29). Yet, as with Goliath, Samson's strength was his greatest weakness: some – David and Judah – increased their strength to their advantage, others – Samson and Goliath – to their disadvantage (*Midrash Ecclesiastes Rabbah*, 1:18).

His greatest weakness was apparently his susceptibility to Philistine women, starting with the Timnite. Marrying her defiled him, as is signaled by his eating honey from the ritually unclean carcass of a lion on the way back from Timnah and also his use of the jawbone of a freshly dead ass to kill his enemies. Indeed, Rabbi Isaac saw Samson "filled with longing for something unclean" (*Midrash Numbers Rabbah*, 9:24). In writing "the way of a fool is straight in his own eyes," Proverbs (21:2) alludes to Samson telling his parents, "Get [the Timnite] for me for she is right [or *pleasing*] in my eyes" (Judg 14:3); Jacob, by contrast, wisely obeyed his father by not marrying a Canaanite. Likewise Samson's disastrous "going down" to Timnah, to marry a "heathen woman," compares with Judah's auspicious "going up" to Timnah (Gen 38:12), leading to the birth of Perez, King David's ancestor (*Midrash Genesis Rabbah*, 59:8, 85:6). Since his purpose in Timnah was marriage, some said that his deterioration truly set in when he "went down" to Gaza to a harlot (*Midrash Numbers Rabbah*, 9:24).

That Samson's weakness lay in his eyes is a commonplace, with Judg 14:3 always cited. Hence he was later punished through his eyes (Judg 16:21). "And God said, 'Behold now Samson has been led astray through his eyes . . . He has mingled with the daughters of the Philistines. . . . Now [his] lust will be a stumbling block for him, and his mingling a ruin. I will hand him over to his enemies, and they will blind him" (Pseudo-Philo, *Antiquities,* 43:5; cf. *Midrash Numbers Rabbah,* 9:24; *Mishnah Sotah,* 1.8; *Tosefta,* 3:15; *B. Talmud Sotah,* 9b–10a; *Y. Talmud Sotah,* 1:8; *B. Talmud Berakoth,* 72). The principle is that God punishes pride through the very thing in which pride is taken (*Mekilta de-Rabbi Ishmael,* Shirata 2 on Exod 15:1).

If the Timnite woman does not fare well among early Jewish readers, neither does Delilah. From earliest times, she is rarely a character of interest in her own right. Often termed a harlot, she represents illicit sex and is Samson's (and men's) problem. Delilah's name is commonly related to the verb "to make weak." She deserved such a name (so *Midrash Numbers Rabbah,* 9:24), because she enfeebled Samson's strength, actions, and determination, whence "his strength went from him" (Judg 16:19) – though perhaps not entirely. *Numbers Rabbah* cites Rabbi Johanan on Samson's grinding at the mill (Judg 16:21): "grinding" is a euphemism for sex, as in Job 31:10. "It teaches that all and sundry brought him their wives to prison so that they might conceive from him. This illustrates the saying current among people: Put wine before him that drinks wine, and a dish of scraped roots before a ploughman." As scraped roots to a ploughman, so was sex to Samson.

The medieval commentator Yehudah HeChasid (c.1150–1217) sums up: Samson was the strongest, David the most devout, and Solomon the wisest man ever. Scripture records their erring through women "to teach us that women have an overpowering hold over men, and that sexual desire overwhelms even the greatest" (*Sefer Chasidim,* [225]).

Christian

Early Christian readers were much taken by Samson, identified in Late Antiquity with Hercules. There grew up a veritable "mass" of patristic literature on him (T. Michael Krouse, *Milton's Samson,* 1949, ch. 3; see chs 4–5 on medieval and Renaissance views). Sometimes the story is simply retold, in the spirit of the literal-grammatical school of Antioch. As early as Clement of Rome (before 100 CE) it is used in homiletical arguments for chastity. Clement points to this consecrated man of great strength, ruined by a woman "with her wretched body, and her vile passion," and asks his (male) reader whether he too may not be such a man. So "know thyself, and know the measure of thy strength" (*Two Letters concerning Virginity,* ii.9). Ambrose (c.339–97) devotes a homily to Samson proving the pitfalls of Christians marrying pagans. Not even his consecration and strength could save Samson from the alien woman (*Epistle* XIX).

Such literal readings usually follow Heb 11:32–8 in considering Samson a saint, an exemplar of faith. They note his birth and mission foretold and the "Holy Spirit" upon him. Origen (c.185–c.254) agrees with the rabbis, moreover, that Jacob prophesies of Samson in Gen 49:16. His faith far outweighed his failures, though he was not always an exemplar. His death, for example, was exceptional, because divinely impelled and no justification for suicide, argues Augustine (354–430) (*City of God*, i.26; cf. Aquinas, *Summa Theologica*, ii.2, q. 64: the Holy Spirit "secretly commanded him"). This is an argument invoked frequently through the centuries to account for the hero's checkered career.

Just occasionally, Krouse notes, a reader wonders whether all the details could be literally true. Could Samson really have killed 1,000 men with an ass's jawbone from which a fountain sprang? (Nilus of Sinai [d. c.430], *Peristeria*, 11.8 (PG 79, 914–15). (In the Latin Vulgate, Judg 15:19 reads, "Then the Lord opened a great tooth in the jaw of the ass and waters issued out of it." English translations, until recently, have followed suit: so Tyndale and Geneva; KJV: "God clave an hollow place that was in the jaw"; contrast RSV: "God split open the hollow place that is at Lehi.")

Allegory and typology, dominating early and medieval Christian interpretation of Samson, had the advantage of sidelining many problems with Samson's "literal" behavior. As prefiguring Christ, the main task he set interpreters was to draw as many abstract parallels as possible between the two figures – and these are many and ingenious.

Samson killing the lion, finding honey in its body, and posing a riddle is a favorite story. As Samson tore apart the lion, death's likeness, so Christ ripped death asunder. Thus the answer to Samson's riddle – "Out of the eater came forth food, and out of the strong came forth sweetness – is that "Christ made the sweet life emerge from its bitterness for human beings" (Ephrem the Syrian (c.306–73), *Hymns*, 13.4). Ambrose exclaims, "O divine mystery! O manifest sacrament! we have escaped from the slayer, we have overcome the strong one. The food of life is now there, where before was the hunger of a miserable death. Dangers are changed into safety, bitterness into sweetness" (*On the Holy Spirit*, ii). One version expresses polemic against Judaism: the slain lion is the lion of Judah in whose body will be found honey, that is, a true remnant destined to become the Church, the body of Christ wherein is stored the honey of true wisdom.

Ambrose's protégé, Augustine, embraces such figurative meaning. What else does the riddle signify, he asks, than Christ rising from the dead? From death issues "that food which said, I am the living bread, who have come down from heaven [John 6:41]." From the dead lion, the body of Christ, came forth a swarm of bees, Christians. As for Samson saying "You would not have found out my riddle unless you had plowed with my heifer" (Judg 14:18), the heifer is also the Church, whose husband revealed to her the secrets of the faith – trinity, resurrection, and so on (*Sermons*, 276–8).

In later medieval picture books like the *Mirror of Human Salvation* (see Ehud) or the *Biblia Pauperum* (see Gideon), the typology relates to Samson astride the lion, tearing apart its jaws. This depiction has a venerable history, possibly back to the Roman legionaries' savior god, Mithras, who slays a death-dealing bull, and certainly forward beyond the Reformation as a commonplace of public sculpture, painting, and Bible illustration in Europe and later America. The pose is even to be found on stove doors in seventeenth- and eighteenth-century German homes and among the Pennsylvania "Dutch" (Mercer, *Bible in Iron*, 1961, figs. 47, 99). In medieval pictures, the lion's prised jaws parallel the devil's jaws into which Christ thrusts a cross, as in a fifteenth-century manuscript *Mirror*, or a monster's jaws, agape and representing limbo, whence the triumphant Christ will lift trapped souls, as in a printed blockbook (*Biblia Pauperum*) from the same period. Samson varies from a beardless youth with flowing locks to a hirsute hulk (PLATE 7.1c, e).

Tying the foxes' tails and sending them burning into the fields taxes Origen's credulity. But he perseveres. "Let us try to knock something out of it, however, as far as we are able: so let us take the foxes as false and perverted teachers" (cf. the foxes in Songs 2:15). Samson, a faithful teacher, catches them with the word of truth and confutes them and their various views by setting each against the other ("tail to tail"). With syllogisms and propositions from their own words he reaches conclusions which send fire into their corn, and with their own arguments burns up all the fruits of "the evil brood" (*Commentary on the Canticle of Canticles*, 260–6; cf. Maximus of Turin, Sermon 41). Augustine helpfully elaborates: the foxes' tails are the heretics' backsides. Their fronts are smooth and deceptive, their backsides bound – that is, condemned, dragging fire to consume the works of those yielding to their seduction. And since the foxes were no doubt burnt up themselves, so judgment will come upon the heretics, impudently unaware (*Sermons*, 278–9).

After visiting a prostitute, Samson carried Gaza's gates up a mountain. What does that mean? "Hell and the love of a woman, scripture joins the two together," writes Augustine. The harlot's house is hell – it turns nobody away,

---

PLATE 7.1   Samson typology: (a) *Types and Antitypes*, c.1886; (b)–(c) and (d)–(e) fifteenth-century blockbooks (*Biblia Pauperum*). (See pp. 176, 178, 182, 193)

PLATE 2

The Birth of Samson foretold

The Annunciation

A man of GOD came unto me, and his countenance was like the countenance of an angel of GOD very terrible; but I asked him not whence he was neither told he me his name; But he said unto me, Behold, thou shalt conceive, and bear a son, And the woman bare a son, and called his name Samson; and the child grew, and the LORD blessed him,

Judges XIII. 6.7.24.

And the angel said unto her, Fear not Mary, for thou hast found favour with GOD And, behold, thou shalt conceive in thy womb, and bring forth a son, and shalt call his name JESUS HE shall be great, and shall be called the SON of the HIGHEST

St. Luke I. 30–31.

draws everyone who enters. After Christ descended into hell, his enemies guarded the place where he was not dead but "sleeping." As Samson rose at midnight, so Christ rose secretly, revealing himself to a chosen few. And, like Samson, Christ removed the gates of hell and ascended on high (*Sermons,* 279–80). Picture books illustrate: Samson supports a gate on one shoulder and carries its pair under his other arm (sometimes they are crossed); while the guards sleep, Christ steps from a medieval graveyard tomb, holding a crosier and raising his right hand in blessing (PLATE 7.1b). Samson stretched out his arms to the Philistine temple's pillars as if on the cross, and while being destroyed himself, he overwhelmed his adversaries in a mystery "clearly fulfilled" by Christ (*Sermons,* 279–80).

Augustine also addresses saintly Samson's failings. Some naysayers will wonder, "And is Christ overcome by a woman's blandishments?" Did Christ go in to a harlot, or have his head shaved? Was he stripped of his strength, bound, blinded, made sport of? But Christ, retorts Augustine, both performed a strong man's feats and suffered as a weak man: in his one person is both Son of God's strength and Son of Man's weakness. Moreover, the Church is Christ's body with Christ at its head – thus comprising both strong and weak members. So Samson did some things (feats of wonder) as head, some (whether wise or foolish) as body, everything, however, in the role of Christ (*Sermons,* 276–8).

Such understanding – Samson a saint of faith, his significance typological – dominates the medieval period. Some, like Rupert of Deutz (c.1075–1129), added to the typological repertory (he interpreted Delilah's various devices to bind Samson), but for centuries changes were minimal. Commentaries were compendia of what had preceded.

Moral and spiritual meanings, however, continued to be discovered. A thirteenth-century guide for anchoresses wishes women, above all, to learn from Samson's foxes who faced away from each other. "We turn our faces happily toward something we love, and away from something we hate." People not loving each other turn their faces, but "are joined by the tails and carry the devil's brands, the fire of lechery." (Is Samson, then, the devil?) But Augustine's influence remains. The tail, says the guide, also represents the end: in their bound tails "shall be set brands, that is, the fires of hell" (*Ancrene Wisse,* iv, 140). As medieval becomes early modern, the Carmelite mystic, John of the Cross (1542–91), understands Samson's captivity in a spiritual sense, as a guide to the soul. When the soul's enemies, the desires, rule it, they first weaken and blind it, then "afflict and torment it, binding it to the mill of concupiscence; and the bonds with which it is bound are its own desires" (*Ascent of Mount Carmel,* i.7).

Delilah's reception among early Christian theologians varies. The rabbinic view that her name means "weaken" is now understood of Delilah's own "impoverishment" (she was a *paupercula*, "impoverished little woman"; cf. Jerome (c.342–420), *Liber interpretationis*, 32 (PL 23, 853)). Samson as a type of Christ suggested Delilah as the Church in its weakness clinging to Christ (e.g. Jerome's commentary on Eph 1:1 (PL 26, 484)). Prior to joining with Christ she fornicated with idols, but afterwards he revealed to her "the hidden things of heavenly mysteries" (Augustine, *Sermons*, 276–8). On the other hand, an anti-Jewish typology saw her as the Jewish "synagogue" conspiring to have Jesus crucified (Rabanus Maurus (776–856), *De Universo*, 3.1 (PL 111, 57)). Or she represents an aspect of humankind, (feminine) flesh betraying (masculine) rational sense (Isidore of Seville (c.560–636), *Quaestiones*, Judg. 8 (PL 83, 389–90); cf. N. Vance in Jeffreys, *Dictionary*, "Delilah").

Normally, however, she is the treacherous temptress who exemplifies also the evils of avarice (cf. Cyril of Alexandria, *De sanctissima trinitate*, 7.641 (PG 75, 1094)). It is to Delilah that Ambrose (c.330–79) turns when warning his clergy readers against "love of money." For money, Delilah deceived "the bravest man of all," who laid his heroic head on the woman's knee and was robbed of hair and might. Money, says Basil, flowed into the woman's lap, and God's favor forsook the man (*Duties of the Clergy*, ii.xxvi).

Increasingly she is blamed for the tragic end to a great man's life. This is apparent in two twelfth-century poems, the monk's tale (ll. 2015–94) in the *Canterbury Tales* of Geoffrey Chaucer (1343/4–1400), and the lament for Samson (*Planctus Israel super Samson*) by Peter Abelard (1079–1142/3) which includes: "O woman, always the greatest ruin of the strong! Woman, created only to destroy!" In late medieval English literature Delilah's censure becomes standard, along with growing disregard for the story's religious significance. Rather, it was "a tragedy in which a great and strong man, lacking in prudence, fell from high to low estate because he fondly loved, and foolishly confided in, a treacherous woman" (Krouse, *Milton's Samson*, 61). John Lydgate (c.1370–c.1450) is typical. His "Fall of the Princes," a "gargantuan" poem written in the monastery of Bury St Edmonds (c.1430–8), has a long section on Samson, 20 stanzas devoted to the treachery of Delilah, Samson's "wife" (W. Kirkconnell, *That Invincible Samson*, 1964, 153). Lydgate laments how devastating is this story for men: "For yiff wyves be founden variable, / Wher shal husbondis fynden other stable?" Lest the point be missed, the poem ends with this advice: "Suffre no nyhtwerm withynne your counsail kreepe, / Thouh Dalida compleyne, crie and weepe!" Such a view likely informed the late fifteenth-century stonemason in Norwich cathedral who carved Delilah about to shear Samson's hair (with sheep shears) on one of the stone roof bosses telling the world's history from Creation to Last Judgment (PLATE 7.9c, p. 221). In short, Delilah gets a bad press.

Early Modern and Modern

Samson in biblical reception is a man of many parts, and artists through the centuries have often captured several of these in the same picture, as in the 1491 woodcut published by Anton Koberger in Nuremberg (PLATE 7.9a, p. 221 – one has to love the lion). Here, however, it is another story.

Typology

Samson as a type of Christ continues into the Reformation, and still has its proponents today. Martin Luther (1483–1546), at least in early writings (see Gideon), was an enthusiastic typologist. Samson, David, Solomon, Aaron, and others "literally and accurately" signify Christ, though he has not time to explain the details (1521, Sermon on Luke 2:33–40 [126]). John Calvin (1509–64) on Matt 2:23, however, suggests an exegetical path from Samson the Nazirite to Jesus of Nazareth (the "Nazarene" – as "spoken by the prophets"). Matthew does not call Jesus "Nazarene" simply because of where he lived. Rather, *nazir* strictly means devoted to God, from the verb "to separate." Fear drove Joseph to Galilee, but God had a higher purpose; for Nazareth was ordained to be Christ's home, that he might bear the name "Nazarene." The prophetic reference is to Samson the "Nazirite," who as deliverer foreshadows Christ's salvation. Samson's honors, then, were intended not for him but for Christ (*Commentary . . . Ezekiel*, 1565 [118]).

Dutch Anabaptist Dirk Phillips (1504–68) exemplifies ongoing typology in the sixteenth-century Reformation. In Christ, the true Nazarene and judge over Israel, Samson is spiritually restored. As Samson took a Philistine wife, Christ chose a congregation from the heathen; as Samson overcame the lion and found honey, Christ overcame Satan and produced grace; victory over the Philistines with a jawbone was fulfilled by Christ's overcoming the "uncircumcized of heart" (the worldly-wise) by means of unlearned apostles whom the world regarded as asses; Samson's thirst quenched prefigures God's gift of living water to thirsty souls; the gates of Gaza signify the gates of Hell; as Samson loved foreign women and fell into enemy hands, so Christ laid aside his divine form to go "outside" through love of "us Gentiles" and fell, by providence, into his enemies' hands; and as Samson brought down the temple upon the Philistines, so Christ in his death has vanquished death. Phillips here deploys age-old anti-Jewish typology, with the Philistines becoming the Jews (no matter that they were previously the Gentiles), punished, scattered, and bearing guilt for not wishing Christ to rule over them (*Enchiridion*, 1564 [316–37, 334–6]). While standing firmly in the typological tradition, Phillips nonetheless distances himself from contemporary "false prophets" using Old Testament "shadows and figures" (typology) to veil their deceptive doctrine. *Caveat lector!*

A departure from the usual (but see *Anchrene Wisse*, above) is relayed by Sir Thomas More (1478–1535). The traditional view of the foxes (cf. Origen and Augustine, above) is recast: Samson now prefigures not Christ but the devil, and while the foxes remain heretics, the cornfields belong to the true Church. More himself finds no fault with those expounding the text as the devil sending his heretics into the cornfield of Christ's Catholic Church with the fire of false words to destroy the corn of true faith and good works. Despite their heads being asunder, the tied (heretic) foxes tend to the same end: namely, the destruction of goodness – though their fiery tails mean that they will never loose the bands of hell. While approving of this "spiritual allegory," More also insists on the event's literal truth. Any who would deny that literal meaning are themselves heretics! (*Answer to a Poisoned Book*, 1533, i.3 [19]).

Samson as type of Christ, however, is the norm. By the end of the sixteenth century, it is how Samson appears in the Elizabethan homilies required to be read by clergy in an attempt to improve lamentable preaching. The Easter Day sermon speaks of Christ's resurrection signified "by Sampson when hee slew the Lion, out of whose mouth came sweetenesse and hony" (*Elizabethan Homilies*, 1623, II. xiv.110–12). Francis Quarles (1592–1644) even addressed a poem "On Iesus and Sampson" to the Virgin Mary. The angel brought news of conception to Manoah's wife: "Did not another Angel, if not He, / Thrice-blessed Virgin, bring the same to thee?" Quarles then, following tradition, matches each aspect of Samson's life with the work of Jesus (*Divine Fancies*, 1632, ii.5 [214–25]).

The seventeenth century saw interest grow in the literal meaning of stories like Samson's and how these events and the characters' behavior were exemplary for the present. If "prefiguring" interpretation waned by comparison, it did not die out. In the next century, revivalist Jonathan Edwards (1703–58) could be relied upon never to let pass a "spiritual" or "prophetical" meaning. "His name, Samson, signifies 'little sun,' well agreeing with a type of the Messiah, that great Sun of Righteousness so often compared in the prophecies to the sun." The type, he stresses, is but a pale imitation of the antitype, a "little light" compared with the "great light" of Christ. Samson's love of Philistine women is "agreeable" to prophecies representing the Messiah as marrying a daughter of Canaan (Ezek 16:3, 8–14), his wedding feast is agreeable to Isa 25:6 and Isa 65:13–14, prophecies of feasting and joy, and so on. The list is long (*Types of the Messiah*, 1747 [254–7]). Edwards's end is always spiritual awakening. Samson's mother was barren like Sarah and Hannah, who also bore children. They therefore "typified the church's bringing forth Jesus Christ spiritually," their barrenness signifying "the barrenness of our souls" until "Christ is born in our hearts" (*Notes on Scripture*, 1722–56 [89–90]).

By the later nineteenth century, typology still has advocates. Samuel Wilberforce (1805–73), bishop of Winchester, is mainly interested in the moral lessons of the hero's life; yet, when imagining Samson's development from infancy, traces "the broken outline of his typical character, as the image of The True Man is forecast upon this uncertain mist-blurred mirror" (*Heroes of Hebrew History*, 1870, 171–2). It does not surprise one to find an illustrated *Types and Antitypes of our Lord and Saviour Jesus Christ* being presented to young John Prince of St Mark's School in Connah Quay, North Wales, "for attention to Bible Study" at Christmas, 1886. John probably made it to the second plate, in which case he learned that Samson's birth foretold was a type of the Annunciation (PLATE 7.1a, p. 177).

Moreover, for evangelist Arthur W. Pink (1886–1952) the Scripture's "typical" significance proved divine authorship. On Samson, the parallels are the usual, concluding with his triumph at Gaza – "a remarkable type of our Lord's resurrection." Like the other types (Abel, Isaac, Moses, David, etc.), Samson is an imperfect representation: each contributes a line or two, but all are needed for a complete picture. Together, though dissimilar personages, they depict a harmonious whole, Christ's complete story. "Beneath the historical we discern the spiritual: behind the incidental we behold the typical: underneath the human biographies we see the form of Christ, and in these things we discover on every page of the Old Testament the 'watermark' of heaven" (*Divine Inspiration of the Bible*, 1917, ch. 6).

> As Sampson bore the doores away,
> Christs hands, though nail'd,
> Wrought our salvation,
> And did unhinge that day.
> (George Herbert, "Sunday," stanza 7, *The Temple*, 1633)

Edifying history

Samson's story came into its own as the drama of a hero veering unevenly between comedy and tragedy. Assessing the moral and religious value of this narrative, understood as edifying history, early modern and modern readers have freely passed judgment on him, from unqualified approval to outright condemnation.

For many Christians, any judgment of Samson must somehow square with the imprimatur of Hebrews 11. As Anabaptist Menno Simons (1496–1561) says, from the heroes listed "you may learn how simple, straightforward, and ordinary, how honest, bold, and obedient, how full of all kinds of virtues and fruits, genuine faith has been from the beginning" (*True Christian Faith*, c.1541 [343, 363]). Moreover, God's spirit periodically came upon him, Martin Luther notes, producing actions holy and obedient to God. While God's spirit acts among the heathen, "this is not sanctifying action" ("Difference between Samson and Julius Caesar," 1533 [79]).

Among seventeenth-century Samsons few are more sympathetically treated than the *Samson Agonistes* (1671) of John Milton (1608–74). At his death (ll. 1728–44), his father Manoa will speedily gather kindred and friends, he says, to solemnly attend him "With silent obsequy and funeral train / Home to his Father's house," there to build "A Monument, and plant it round with shade / Of Laurel ever green, and branching Palm." There he will hang his trophies, and "Thither shall all the valiant youth resort, / And from his memory inflame their breasts / To matchless valor and adventures high." Nonetheless the eulogy falters, ending on a falling note:

> The virgins also shall on feastful days
> Visit his Tomb with flowers, only bewailing
> His lot unfortunate in nuptial choice,
> From whence captivity and loss of eyes.

"[U]nfortunate in nuptial choice," says Milton's Manoa. Unfortunate indeed, might many a critic of Samson have added. Yet that verse lingers – "Then his brethren came down and buried him" (16:31) – and perhaps in the spirit of Milton is Isaac Taylor's powerfully simple depiction of the strong man fallen face down, still shackled to the broken pillars, behind him his family, bearing a litter, come to fetch him home (PLATE 7.10d, p. 225; *Boydell's Illustrations of Holy Writ*, 1820).

Samson's moral behavior is a growing concern in the seventeenth and eighteenth centuries. So, too, is the credibility of the tales. On one side is Sir Thomas Browne (1605–82) in *Religio Medici* (1643, i.2.21). Skeptical inquiry with appeal to Greek and Roman authors as norms has led scholars to "peremptorily maintain the traditions of Aelian or Pliny, yet in Histories of Scripture raise Queries and Objections, believing no more than they can parallel in humane [human] Authors." He confesses that some Scripture stories do "exceed the

Fables of Poets," and none can "carry the Buckler unto Sampson." But he quickly dismisses the problem. It arises from a failure to treat Scripture as a divinely inspired text relating divinely inspired events. To "the weakness of our apprehensions," there are bound to appear "irregularities, contradictions, and antinomies."

On the other side, the eighteenth-century Deists insist on rational measurement against those "humane" norms. Decidedly the credulity of Voltaire (1694–1778) will not stretch as far as Samson's prodigious strength. Assuming an orthodox voice, he observes of Samson's carrying Gaza's gates that such astonishing feats are "miracles" showing God not wanting to abandon his people. As if anticipating the skeptic's objection, he adds the double-edged protestation, "We have said twenty times that what does not happen today happened frequently in that period." And he twists the knife: "We believe this response suffices" (*La Bible enfin expliquée*, 1776 [144–6]).

Voltaire characterizes the stories as "the eternal subject of jokes and incredulity" and lists problems. God enslaves his people for 40 years. A practice more injurious to the Divinity is hard to imagine, and to blame the people's sins is a poor excuse, since the conquerors were worse idolaters. Mocking orthodoxy, he explains that God chastised his children more because he had done more for them – hence they were more criminal. A small difficulty concerns Samson not using the razor on his head since, he says, Jews do not shave – the practice derives from Egyptian priests. Moreover, the Nazirite custom was for a limited time, whereas Samson never shaved, making him a "different kind of Nazirite." Finally, Voltaire says that critics derive Samson's story from the ancient Greek tales of Nisus and Cometho and of Hercules, and date Hercules 79 years before Samson (born c.1110). He gravely invokes other "wise commentators" to restore orthodox opinion: both stories, they argue, could be independently true. After all, every country knows men of extraordinary strength, and the more vigorous they are, the freer they are with women and so cut short their days! Having thus rescued the biblical story's veracity, Voltaire has turned it into but one of a kind.

If the Deists made sport with Samson, they were not alone in their distaste, and perhaps even helped tip the scales of judgment against him. A measure of impatience is a hallmark of this period and later: he just does not fit the moral model sought in Scripture. Certainly Anglican Mrs Trimmer (1741–1810), writing for youth in 1783, held the biblical strong man in small esteem. Had he properly used his extraordinary gift, "what a shining character would he have been!" Rather, he acted "in a very inconsistent manner," concerned little with his principal business of delivering Israel and much with gratifying revenge on his own account. Present-day readers should not expect to imitate

Samson's deeds "because the present state of the world does not require them." Lest this judgment sound too dismissive of Scripture, however, she adds that readers should not find his deeds incredible, since they resulted from the divine Spirit upon him (cf. Browne, above). The same Spirit influences Christians, who should heed Samson's (negative) example and make the most of their own gifts to God's glory (*Sacred History*, 1783 [lxii, 272–3]).

No less disappointed is Nonconformist Esther Hewlett, particularly exercised by Samson's liaisons with women. His singular history shows "that great talents are disgraced and beclouded, when the soul is in subjection to sinful, foolish, and hurtful lusts. The truest greatness of character consists in self-dominion, and the greatest meanness and degradation in the slavery of vice." Yet Hewlett, too, makes concessions: if the recorded circumstances of Samson's moral character are not of a favorable cast, still he probably possessed "many excellencies" not in the design of sacred history to record. As a public person he was truly eminent. He is also among the heroes of faith in Hebrews 11 (*Scripture History for Youth*, 1828, 56).

Like Hewlett, lay scholar John Kitto (1804–54), widely read in Britain and North America, is clear wherein these failings lay – "ungovernable passions" which, nonetheless, were made "the instruments of distress and ruin to the Philistines." Even his being a judge elicits some skepticism, since he scarcely appears to have exercised any authority; but at least for chronological purposes he is counted a judge, for 40 years (*Bible History*, 1841 [216, 220]).

Controlling passions is also the theme of Seventh Day Adventist Mrs E. G. White (1827–1915). To this staunch advocate of Christian temperance, Samson's life read as "dark and terrible." Despite favorable beginnings, he let go of God "under the influence of wicked associates," yielding to temptation. Physically the strongest of men, in "self-control, integrity, and firmness" he was one of the weakest. Many mistake strong passions for a strong character, whereas in truth the person mastered by passions is weak. Though Satan attacks us through our character defects, none need be overcome. Help is at hand for "every soul who really desires it" (*Patriarchs and Prophets*, 1890, 567–8).

Yet some viewed the hero's passions with approbation. Bishop Samuel Wilberforce waxes lyrical. How must the parents of the "God-given, impulsive, solitary boy" have gazed with "awe-struck wonder" upon his moody youth! "How must they have trembled at the dark violence of his passion, stirred almost to madness, like the waves of the deep rock-bound lake, when the roar of the whirlwind lashes suddenly its surges into storm!" Samson's mistakes were intentional, instructive. His "yielding to the voice of sensual appetite" showed that if the people yielded to the sensual inducements of foreign idol worship, they, like Samson in Delilah's arms, would be snared and destroyed.

His final act was revenge and deliverance, but also repentance. The moral: doing God's will requires giving up self-will; and of those to whom much is given, much is required (*Heroes of Hebrew History*, 1870, 170–91).

Samson is often compared with Hercules. For Wilberforce, the pagan story's Hercules was but the inspired record's Samson, "distorted and robbed, by the thick vapours of heathendom, of the moral teaching which breathes everywhere from the history of Manoah's son" (p. 193). (One wonders how Mrs Trimmer might have responded!) By the century's end, interest in the comparative history of religions was rife, and Samson was argued to be originally a mythological (usually solar) figure. Alexander Whyte (1836–1920) disagrees. The story is not to be read with the "mythologists" (comparing it to classical stories) or the "mystics" (seeing Samson as a type of Christ), but as a *tragedy* (cf. Milton). From Samson's tragic flaws flows a lesson – one should use one's talents and strengths in selfless service to God's will (cf. Trimmer and Wilberforce), knowing that success will not always come, but relying on God's grace in the end (*Bible Characters*, 1905, 200–10).

The nineteenth and early twentieth centuries saw a sharp increase in appeals to historical and social relativism – conditions were different in Antiquity – to explain problematic texts. Samson's story is no exception. In his *Greater Men and Women of the Bible* (1914), James Hastings (1852–1922) admits that much about Samson appeals to the (especially youthful) imagination. We wonder at the feats he was "stated" to have performed. Yet (a familiar refrain) so deficient in the qualities of a leader was he that he found no following and betrayed his trust. The reader must realize that the story "partakes of the rough and unmoral character of the times." As with Trimmer, the moral is negative: this "indifferent Nazirite" who squandered "the fairest prospects" exemplifies how *not* to behave. But all is not gloom. His chief value lay, perhaps, "in the one inspiring thought which his prowess awakened – the thought that God was there" (pp. 499, 504–5).

Probably Samson's nadir is reached in a character sketch by Welsh Nonconformist T. Rhondda Williams, author of *Old Testament Stories* (1911), a guide for the young. His chapter opens bluntly: "A schoolboy once wrote an essay on Samson, which he finished by saying that Samson killed an awful lot of Philistines, and though in the end he was also killed himself, he did not mind that." Well, continues the minister, "there is not anything very much better than that to say about Samson, and if you had never heard about him it would be no loss to you, so far as his character is concerned." His best surmise is that the story was included in the Bible because Samson, indeed, killed a lot of Philistines, an outcome well regarded by the Israelites. As for God's prompting Samson, Williams offers some advice: "You must always be on your guard against taking your ideas of God from these old stories." The people thought

God would behave much like them, so the writer "attributes a very mean motive" to Samson's parents and to God, when suggesting that God prompted Samson to seek a wife, and that his parents consented, "simply in order to bring the woman's people into trouble."

Williams is unwilling to dispense entirely with the story, despite his incredulity. Samson's exploits were no doubt exaggerated before being recorded, as the exploits of contemporary strongman, Eugen Sandow, would have been had he lived then. So what is the story's moral? The great thing is not to have strength so much as character, and "if we have strength the greatest privilege is to use it for helping others" (pp. 94–7).

Like others, Thomas E. Miller (*Portraits*, 1922) attempts to remove responsibility for Samson's behavior from God: "The Spirit never clothed himself with Samson; it only moved him 'at sundry times and in divers manners.'" Thus Samson's very success proved a snare, leading him to believe that his great powers, physical and mental (a talent not usually recognized), were unconditionally his own to use at his own behest. His splendid physique being the envy of the boys of his tribe (who probably differed little from those of Britain), he must have risked being spoiled by hero worship. In the age of psychology, Miller wonders also whether Samson's parents may share a little blame. One can be too anxious to shield children from evil, bring them up in too straitlaced a fashion, restrict them; so that later they react, turning liberty to license. This may help account for Samson's inexplicable conduct (pp. 123–40).

In lighter vein is Methodist preacher Clovis Chappell (1882–1972). Jolly Samson was "gifted with a happy disposition." He enjoyed a joke, was full of pranks. He had a laugh before which the blues vanished. Fittingly his name means sunny. At his sparkling eye and cheerful face, "gloom had a way of taking to its heels." He had physical courage, admirable, though not the highest type of courage – after all, "we possess [it] in company with the bulldog." Like Hastings, Chappell locates his story in a rough age, yet, like Miller, he merges ancient and modern. As an athlete, Samson was a hero who appealed to his "half-savage" age. We claim today to measure greatness by head and heart rather than muscle. But that is only partially true in popular esteem. "We soon forget the athlete. But he grips us hard during the days of his glory" (*Sermons*, 1925, 122–3).

More typical mid-twentieth-century response to Samson in "mainstream" Protestantism, however, is still negative. An Anglican scholar, the Rt. Rev. Bertram F. Simpson (*Story of the Bible*, c.1938, I, 288), sums up: "It is a popular story, and poet and musician have conspired to immortalize this strange figure; but neither moralist nor historian will feel that Samson contributes much to the lessons of this Book."

Of course, Samson need hardly worry at bad press from the Rev. Simpson or anyone else. George Frideric Handel (1685–1759) celebrated him in an oratorio, written about 1742 after completing his *Messiah*, with libretto (by Newburgh Hamilton (1715–43)) based on Milton's *Samson Agonistes*. The blinded, captive hero resists Dalila's further persuasions and the taunts of Philistine giant Harapha, before bringing down Dagon's temple. The chorus sings in closing of the heavenly host: "Let their celestial concerts all unite, / Ever to sound his praise in endless blaze of light." He strikes a heroic pose from the outset in the French opera *Samson et Dalila* by Camille Saint-Saëns (1835–1921) – libretto by Ferdinand Lemaire and the composer – completed just after the Franco–Prussian War of 1870–1 (first performed 1877). Before a crowd of cowed Israelites, he declares that the hour of deliverance is at hand. In his heart he hears bounteous God promising liberty. "Brothers! Break our chains and raise up again the altar of Israel's only God!" And if he falls under Dalila's spell, who would not, on hearing her exquisite aria, "Softly Awakes My Heart": "My heart opens to your voice as the flowers open to the kisses of dawn!" Little wonder he cries, "Dalila! Dalila! Je t'aime!"

In popular culture he is better known, and more widely appealed to, than almost any other biblical figure. He has sold numerous products in the age of mass production, from padlocks to luggage, and not forgetting the Samson Visumatic Iron ingeniously powered by electricity, no less, not muscle power. As comic-book hero he enjoys marvelous, extra-biblical adventures: "The remnants of the human race battle for their very existence in a world ruled by mutant monsters . . . 'Samson! Look . . . the Fanged Flyers!' " (*Mighty Samson*, no. 22, 1965). The Grateful Dead have sung his song (since the mid-1970s): "If I had my way / If I had my way / If I had my way / I would tear this whole building down" (*Samson and Delilah*, traditional; cf. Blind Willie Johnson's version, *If I Had My Way*, 1928). At the movies, too, he faces daunting odds in exotic exploits, regularly replacing Italian legendary heroes in the dubbed English versions. But in all this he does not entirely abandon his immortal partner, Delilah. Nor does he for too long escape notice in the press – along with a photograph based on his well-known resemblance to Victor Mature, who played opposite Hedy Lamarr in Cecil B. DeMille's (1881–1959) movie, *Samson and Delilah* (1949) (PLATE 7.2).

DeMille's was one of the first post-World War II "biblical epic" movies (see Forshey, *American Religious and Biblical Spectaculars*, 1992). Paramount's movie gift book describes it as "one of the greatest and tenderest of love stories . . . but it was a strange and terrifying love. For they both knew that one day one must destroy the other" (*Cecil B. DeMille's Masterpiece Samson and Delilah*, 1949). The director, we are assured, has told the story "without contradicting a single fact related in The Bible," even though "he obviously had to write

PLATE 7.2 Popular Samson. (See p. 188)

between the lines, because, if he had not, we would have had no more to see than a string of episodes." One between-the-lines "improvement" was to make Delilah the Timnite woman's sister. Another is to introduce a "local girl," Miriam (who wears blue), whom his mother wants him to marry – she would bring the good out in him. But she's higher above him than the moon, he tells her. It's the Timnite he wants. Exclaims his mother, "Samson, Samson, you're blind!" And so he takes the path to perfidy.

But the movie is also a celebration of the strong man's brute strength, and is cast, in DeMille fashion, as a fable of Man's unquenchable thirst for freedom pitted against the forces of slavery, idolatry, and tyranny. Among other sources the screenplay draws on the authoritarian novel by Revisionist Zionist Vladimir Jabotinsky (1880–1940), who in 1937 founded the armed Irgun Tzvai Leumi and from whom descends the Israeli right-wing Likud party. His Samson is both repulsed by and attracted to the Philistines. Contemplating them, he realizes that his people need two things to succeed: "iron" and "a king." They must have strong weapons and a strong leader – a man who will give a signal "and of a sudden thousands will lift up their hands." In a festival at the temple in Gaza he had seen such a spectacle, glimpsed "the great secret of politically minded peoples" – "thousands obeying a single will" (*Samson the Nazirite,* 1930).

Manoah, his wife, and the angel

Manoah's wife, Samson's mother, is frequently mentioned as a barren woman who conceives and bears a child, like Sarah before her, and afterwards Hannah, Elizabeth, and especially Mary. She is less noticed as a full-fledged character, with notable exceptions. She shares the company of other "strong women," such as Deborah, Jael, Ruth, Abigail, Judith, and Esther, illustrating the talents and virtues of women and serving as models of moral instruction. Print suites of these women became popular. One such was published in Antwerp around 1600 by Philips Galle (1537–1612) from designs by influential Flemish painter Marten de Vos (1532–1603). The inscription says that Samson's mother-to-be (not Manoah's wife) was taught by no less than the voice of Heaven. She sits peacefully, hands clasped in her lap, eyes closed or nearly so, her head bent in contemplation. In the background she kneels with her husband beside the altar from which flames, smoke, and the angelic visitor ascend. Manoah flings wide his arms in amazement. The woman, who knew a divine visitor when she met one, holds her hands in prayer (PLATE 7.3a).

Anglican priest and man of letters Joseph Hall (1574–1656) is one reader who pays her careful attention. He notes that "it was to the woman that the

PLATE 7.3 Samson's mother and the angel: (a) de Vos, c.1600; (b) Cole, c.1720; (c) Goeree, 1700; (d) Luyken, 1708. (See pp. 190, 193, 195)

angel appeared, not to the husband," and wonders why. Perhaps it was because "the reproach of barrenness lay upon her more heavily than on the father"; perhaps because "the birth of the child should cost her more dear than her husband"; or perhaps because "the difficulty of this news was more in her conception than in his generation." Whatever the reason, Hall affirms that God addresses his comforts to hearts most in need. Wondering also at the angel's address – "Thou art barren" – Hall decides it is well intended. "Not that the angel would upbraid the poor woman with her affliction; but therefore he names her pain, that the mention of her cure might be much more welcome" (*Contemplations*, 1615 [x.2, 124–5]).

Two centuries later, Jewish reformist Grace Aguilar (1816–47) also notes that "it was to the WOMAN, not the man, the Most High deigned to send His angelic messenger," both times; the angel addressed Manoah only when addressed by him. As the mother of Israel's future deliverer, she was more important in God's sight than her husband. Aguilar then builds a case for the woman's equality with the man: she was a "perfectly free agent," bound only by the links of love enjoined by marriage; Manoah includes her in all he says and does; she partakes equally in the burnt offering; and her quick intellect reassures her husband (a simple believer), suggesting a social position where such faculties were exercised. But, this said, Aguilar diplomatically warns her young women readers that "however woman may be naturally endowed with superior attainments," still it is "her bounden duty" to never let these gifts jar upon her husband's feelings. "It is woman's province to *influence*, never to *dictate*; to conceal rather than assume superiority" (*Women of Israel*, 1845 [227–36]).

Discussions of the theophany are apt to collapse together the experiences of Manoah and wife. "The wondering mortals fell on their faces, overpowered by a spectacle so astonishing," reports Thomas Gaspey (1788–1871) in *Tallis's Illustrated Scripture History* (1851). "Fear, at first, possessed them, but to this hope and joy soon succeeded." Others read their text more carefully. Mrs Trimmer notes Manoah's apprehension of imminent death but adds, "Manoah's wife had much more composure of mind, and she expressed it with the utmost propriety" (*Sacred History*, 1783 [lviii, 255]). Evangelical writer F. B. Meyer (1847–1929), with a sense of the story's humor, sees here quirks of human personality. "Manoah was a pessimist, given to dark foreboding, fond of anticipating misfortune." Realizing he had seen God's face, "he made sure that his wife and he would die. His wife, on the contrary, was prone to look on the bright side of things, and she must have been an admirable help-meet. How much some of us owe to the temperament of those with whom we live!" Manoah's wife, not Manoah, provides Meyer with his paradigm (*Our Daily Homily*, 1898 [I, 223]).

Illustrations may contribute to the conflation, since the most common picture over the centuries shows the man and woman before the altar as the angel ascends. Sometimes the two are little differentiated, both kneeling or bowing in prayer, and always the scene is "Manoah's Sacrifice." But often a small difference suggests attention to the text's details after all. The wife, occasionally looking up at the angel, is often depicted with hands clasped reverently as in the design by Jan Goeree (1670–1731) in Peter Mortier's "Great Bible" of 1700 (PLATE 7.3c). Manoah, however, usually spreads his arms wide, as he gazes in amazement or fear at the divine visitor ascending (Gaspey and Sturm's *Family Devotions*, c.1850, and elsewhere). The 1641 painting by Rembrandt (1606–69), now in Dresden's Gemäldegalerie, seems at first to elide the difference between the two reactions, showing both figures kneeling with hands clasped. But the woman kneels upright, unfazed, facing the ethereal angel directly, and her hands rest gently against each other. Manoah's hands are tightly knit, and he cringes to one side. Caspar Luyken (1672–1708) even has the kneeling woman shrinking away, arms out, which makes for a dramatic picture, but shifts the biblical text's fear from the husband to the wife (PLATE 7.3d) (*Historiae Celebriores*, 1708).

Occasionally the two are in earlier conversation with the angel, as in a vignette of Romaijn de Hooghe's 1706 illustration, a version of which reappears for English families in the mid-nineteenth-century *Sunny Sabbaths*. The angel points both to heaven and, with a staff, to the woman, while Manoah stands between, one hand on his wife's back and the other crossing that of the angel, as if linking them. In an early twentieth-century lantern slide, all three characters, including a beautifully winged young angel, stand apart but point to the wife's belly. This angel, like de Hooghe's, also points heavenwards. Rarely, as in John Prince's copy of *Types and Antitypes* (PLATE 7.1a, p. 177), the angel appears to the wife alone. An example of some delicacy belongs in a suite of *Two Hundred Historys* engraved by J. Cole, four scenes to a page, bound in with a Bible of 1724. In a bucolic setting, the angel explains, and the wife stands close, listening (PLATE 7.3b).

Temperance advocate Mrs E. G. White also pays Manoah's wife attention, though less as a person of feeling than as a model for a cause. God's plan required regulating both mother and child. Since the mother's habits affect the child, "she must herself be controlled by principle, and must practice temperance and self-denial." Unwise advisers will urge her to gratify her every wish; God solemnly obliges her to exercise self-control. Fathers too are involved. Both parents pass on their dispositions and appetites to their children, and parental intemperance does damage. Liquor-drinkers and tobacco-users transmit "their insatiable craving, their inflamed blood and irritable nerves"; the licentious bequeath "their unholy desires, and even loathsome diseases"; and each generation falls lower and lower. Every father and mother, therefore, should ask, "What shall we do unto the child that shall be born to us?" (Judg 13:8). Many have too lightly regarded prenatal influences and should heed this twice-repeated instruction from heaven. Indeed, every "unclean thing" should be avoided, including "stimulating and indigestible food." In brief, this is a matter having to do with people's "health, their character, their usefulness in this world," and ultimately, "their eternal destiny" (*Patriarchs and Prophets*, 1890, 561; cf. Mary E. Beck, "The story of Samson's mother: a lesson on total abstinence," in *Bible Readings on Bible Women*, 1892, ch. 6).

Mrs White was not, of course, the first to argue for prenatal temperance from this text. Centuries earlier, Sir Walter Raleigh (c.1552–1618) similarly explained the angel's prohibition: "these strong liquors hinder the strength, and as it were wither and shrinke the childe in the mother's wombe." He too was impatient at neglect of the divine counsel: "yet it seemeth that many women of this age have not read, or at least will not beleeve this precept: the most part forbearing nor drinkes nor meats, how strong or uncleane soever, filling themselves with all sorts of wines, and with artificiall drinkes far more forcible: by reason whereof, so many wretched feeble bodies are borne into the world, and the races of the able and strong men in effect decayed" (*History of the World*, 1614, ii.15).

The angel's visit (along with Gideon's theophany, Judg 6:11–24), has provided grist to the mill for angelologists. Angels, says John Calvin (1509–64), dispense and administer God's benefice. Scripture recalls that they keep vigil for our safety, defend us, and direct our ways, as in Judges 13 (*Institutes*, 1550 [I. i.14.6, 166]). He notes how humans experienced dread and wonder when feeling themselves in God's presence, evidenced in the common expression, "We shall die, for the Lord has appeared to us." The lesson: humans only truly appreciate their lowly state after comparing themselves with God's majesty (i.1.3, 39).

Judges 13 also raises questions about human knowledge of God. Martin Chemnitz (1522–86) lays out a paradox. Like Jacob in Genesis 32, when Manoah asks the angel his name, he receives no direct answer ("it is secret"). Elsewhere, God's name is openly explained and expressed (Exod 3:13–15; Deut 6:4; Jer 23:6; etc.). In one sense, the name is hidden, not to be investigated; in another, God wills it known and invoked. That is, in theological inquiry, we should not look into that secret area of God's essence and will which he would have us not know, but rather gain a "brief summary" from what God chooses to reveal in his Word (*Loci Theologici*, 1591, ch. 3 [57]).

Chemnitz understands Manoah, like Gideon, to have beheld God. But the ambiguity (as in Genesis 18, *re* Abraham's visitors) has exercised readers. Is it an angel, or is it God? Calvin finds the wife's use of Jehovah (Heb: Yhwh; "the

Lord") important in arguing against medieval Jewish scholars (Rashi, Ibn Ezra, Kimchi) that the Old Testament evidences the deity of Christ (the Messiah). Whereas other names (e.g. "Elohim") may be only titles or applied broadly to divinity, Jehovah in Jewish tradition signifies God's very being. And Jehovah, argues Calvin, is frequently, as here in Judges 13, "set forth in the person of an angel." Whence it is (implicitly) but a short trinitarian step to God in the person of Christ (a step hardly likely to have swayed Rashi!).

The issue is perception. John Milton believes that people *thought* they had seen God, since angels bore the likeness of the divine glory and person and God's very words (*Christian Doctrine*, c.1658–60 [i.5.38, 236–8]). But the question of the name persists, often arising, as with Chemnitz, in speculation on the nature of God and how God may be known. Nineteenth-century Jewish apologist Grace Aguilar would have agreed with Milton (*Women of Israel*, 1845 [232–3]). The Christian trinitarian argument is persuasive only "to a mere superficial thinker." God's word to Moses in Exod 33:20, "no man shall see me and live," settles the question: the angel is an angel. When Manoah says that he has seen God, he is mistaken. (And if Exod 24:10–11 and 33:11 seem to contradict 33:20, they are either a wrong translation or an attempt to convey God's glory to the multitude, and in any case cannot outweigh God's own words.)

For Bible illustrators, the problem seems not so much whether the angel is God, as whether the viewer will recognize the angel as an angel. Wings are the answer. (Manoah and his wife just did not notice them at first.) And are angels male or female? Here the answer is androgyny. (First, be rid of that beard.) Nevertheless, some illustrators, alert to the text, make the visitor look like an ordinary human, even when ascending in smoke and flame (cf. Tissot with Gideon's 'angel). Thus Jan Goeree's elegantly rising angel in Mortier's "Great Bible" of 1700 is an elderly man of gravitas (PLATE 7.3c, p. 191).

The woman of Timnah

Samson's marriage is a focal point of Reformation interest. Luther returns to it several times on the topic of parental consent. Sparring with the Pope, he argues against fathers compelling their children to take a particular partner. Marriage should be arranged, as with Rebecca in Genesis 24, subject to the child's willingness (nonetheless, children must be obedient). Again, contrary to the Pope (he asserts), while a father has authority to break up a marriage made without or against his will, he should be prepared to bend a little. So Manoah and his wife "permitted their son Samson to plead with them to get him a woman as wife who pleased him but not his parents" (1521, on Matt 2:1–12 (*Sermons*, II, 219)). But children also have a responsibility to not become engaged without their parents' knowledge. So Samson says, "I have seen a young maiden whom I love. Dear parents, get me this girl for a wife" (1520 (*Christian in Society*, I, 11–12)). Luther later approves Ambrose's admonition against following Rebecca's example, and Samson's choice goes unmentioned (1530 (*Christian in Society*, III, 269)).

Joseph Hall a century later also finds Samson appropriately dutiful and his parents suitably flexible. Even in Israel's deplorable state, "children durst not presume to be their own carvers: how much less is this tolerable in a well guided and Christian commonwealth?" Though Samson's intent ("Get her, for she pleases me") can plead no reason but appetite, "yet the good parents, since they cannot bow the affection of their son with persuasion, dare not break it with violence." As it "becomes not children to be forward in their choice," neither should parents "be too peremptory in their denial." On the one side lies disobedience, on the other tyranny (*Contemplations*, 1615 [x.3, 127–8]).

The impediment, for the parents, was marriage to a Philistine unbeliever. Hall construes their astonishment and remonstrances. Had they been so scrupulous about his eating no unclean thing, and now consent to a heathenish match? Well they knew the "inconveniences of an unequal yoke: corruption in religion, alienation of affections, distraction of thoughts, connivance at idolatry, death of zeal, dangerous underminings, and lastly, an unholy seed." Who could blame their reluctance? Why not a woman of his brethren or all God's people? If religion be more than a cipher, dare we disregard it in our most important choice? Was it simply that she was a "fair Philistine?" (Later, Milton's chorus in *Samson Agonistes* (1671) will wonder: "Why thou shouldst wed Philistian women rather / Than of thine own Tribe fairer, or as fair, / At least of thy own Nation" [ll. 215–17]). Hall responds: "To dote upon a fair skin, when we see a Philistine under it, is sensual and brutish."

But what if God were involved? The parents "knew not that it was of the Lord" (Judg 14:4); yet Hall imagines Samson saying: "It is not mine eye only, but the counsel of God that leads me to this choice. The way to quarrel with the Philistines is to match with them." Surely God who commanded Hosea to marry a harlot, could appoint his Nazirite to marry a Philistine. (Again, Milton's Samson echoes Hall's: "what I motion'd was of God; I knew / From intimate impulse, and therefore urg'd / The Marriage on; that by occasion hence / I might begin Israel's Deliverance" (ll. 222–5)). But whether truly permitted, Hall cannot determine. Nor would it excuse Samson's following inordinately his passions, "nothing but the eye." Hall prefers to think that God intended "to make a treacle of a viper," fetching good out of Samson's evil, rather than approve as good in Samson what was in itself evil.

The Philistine alliance has troubled many. Anabaptist preacher David Joris (1501/2–56) believed that God prompted the marriage, just as Moses took a Midianite wife (Exod 2:21). But Joris, after a disastrous Anabaptist revival of (biblical patriarchal) polygamy in Münster, was anxious to reassert orthodoxy in marriage, including that between believers and unbelievers, and Samson's was an awkward case. So he falls back on traditional interpretation. Although instigated by God, much of the event happened as "an image" (type or allegory). Rather, God-fearing men must take no "heathenish, uncircumcised wives" but be inclined to good and saintly women (*Response to Hans Eisenburg*, 1537 [161]).

Centuries later, Mrs Trimmer argues that God inspired Samson to go to Timnah to use his strength against the Philistines, but Samson allowed the Timnite woman to divert him. His indiscretion, however, could not counteract God's will: the marriage itself became the occasion sought. If God thus ordained it, the parents were still not off the hook. Less charitable than Hall, Mrs Trimmer sternly judges them "indulgent to a faulty degree" (*Sacred History*, 1783 [lix, 258]). Esther Hewlett likewise finds Samson's project wrong, but overruled by God "whose province it is to educe good out of evil" (cf. Hall). Still, marriage with unbelievers, sacrificing principle to passion, remains wrong, and many hopeful and pious young people need to know, emphatically, that Samson sets them no example. The remonstrance of Samson's "tender parents" could well be addressed to them, lest they risk shipwreck of domestic comfort, parental usefulness, and piety itself (*Scripture History*, 1828, 50–1). Mrs E. G. White bypasses altogether God's involvement. Nor does she urge the virtue of obedience to parental authority. It was not his parents but God whom Samson disavowed. The rot set in during his youth in Zorah. Had he obeyed God's commands like his parents, a nobler destiny would have been his. But living near Philistines, he mingled with them; intimacies with idolaters corrupted him, darkening his whole life. "How many are pursuing the same course as did Samson! How often marriages are formed between the godly and the ungodly, because inclination governs in the selection of husband or wife!" Too often the motives leading to this union are not in keeping with Christian principles. By arousing such "unsanctified passions," Satan does his work (*Patriarchs and Prophets*, 1890, 563).

A new century sees Thomas E. Miller making the same point about the Philistine marriage but with noticeably more brevity and less passion: "The religious side of the question weighed as little with Samson as it does with many professedly Christian people to-day. This imprudent marriage was the beginning of Samson's downward career" (*Portraits*, 1922, 126).

Readers' reception of the Timnite woman herself has run the gamut from sympathy to outright condemnation. As usual, Joseph Hall is thoughtful

(*Contemplations*, 1615 [x.3–4, 130–1]). "I do not wonder that a Philistine woman loved herself and her father's family more than an Israelitish bridegroom." If she gave priority to her parents, that differed little from Samson equating her with his ("I have not told it my father or my mother, and should I tell it thee?"). Still, Hall is also impressed with her (stereotyped) role as the woman who betrays her man. "Whom the lion could not conquer, the tears of a woman have conquered. Samson never bewrayed [revealed] infirmity but in uxoriousness." Like Adam, the most perfect man, and Solomon, the wisest man, Samson, the strongest man, is betrayed by the flattery of his "helper." "So woe be to him that is matched with a Philistine!" Still, Hall considers her actions in context, avoids blanket condemnation, and couples criticism of her with criticism of him. "I can no more justify Samson in the leaving of his wife, than in the choosing her: he chose her, because she pleased him; and because she despised him, he left her. Though her fear made her false to him in his riddle, yet she was true to his bed. That weak treachery was worthy of a check, not a desertion."

Some of Hall's mixed feelings may be present in Rembrandt's famous painting of the wedding feast (1638), now in Dresden's Gemäldegalerie. But Rembrandt's Timnite may be read even more sympathetically. Light falls full upon her as she sits in white finery, her hands folded neatly above her belly (anticipating a baby perhaps), a faint smile of satisfaction on her face. She stares directly at the viewer, oblivious to the laughter and flirting and Samson's riddle telling. It is as though they have nothing to do with her. The light partly connects her to Samson, but he is turned away, his face shadowed. She is the arresting figure in the picture, and we know the story will come to rest upon her, but in ways she cannot begin to guess. Her serenity will be shattered. Her lit figure, too, may remind a viewer of her fiery end. It is a painting of great pathos (PLATE 7.4b).

Pathos is not Jonathan Edwards's style. The woman was false. She "represents" – for purposes of spiritual struggle – those lusts which infatuate men. They promise them much, "but never afford 'em anything." They are "like a pleasing shadow at a distance, that do us a great deal of damage in the pursuit; and when we come nigh them, and hope to embrace them, and to be paid for our damages, they afford us nothing but disappointment" (*Notes on Scripture*, 1722–56 [361]). Others are a mite less categorical. Mrs Trimmer, like Hall, at least recognizes the part fear might play in the Timnite's story. And although unwilling to justify her conduct, Trimmer allows that "she belonged to one of those nations in which all kinds of wickedness were practised, whose inhabitants educated their children according to their own bad principles." Several pages later her terrible fate is a grim warning to all of God's judgments on treachery and deceitfulness (*Sacred History*, 1783 [lix–lx, 259, 264]). After Edwards and Trimmer, John Kitto's account comes as a relief: "She put in prac-

PLATE 7.4   (a) Samson's foxes: Armytage, c.1850; (b) The Timnite woman: Rembrandt, 1638. (See pp. 198, 205)

tice all the little arts by which women have ever carried their points with men usually weak" (*Bible History*, 1841 [217]).

The lion

Joseph Hall, like others earlier (e.g. Anabaptist Balthasar Hubmaier, *A Simple Instruction*, 1526 [316]) reads Samson's encounter with the lion as an allegory of the Christian life (*Contemplations*, 1615 [x.3, 128–30]). God exercises his champions with initiatory encounters: both Samson and David must first fight with lions, then with Philistines; and Christ meets the wilderness lion on the threshold of his ministry. So God prepares matches for every Christian, a pledge of victory over spiritual Philistines. Yet Hall has a strong sense of the literal lion: "The beast came bristling up his fearful mane, wafting his raised stern, his eyes sparkling with fury, his mouth roaring out knells of his last passage, and breathing death from his nostrils, and now rejoicing at so fair a prey." Later, Nonconformist preacher John Bunyan (1628–88), in the preface to a book penned from prison to his congregation, writes of enclosing "a drop of that honey, that I have taken out of the carcase of a lion (Judg. 14:5–9). I have eaten thereof myself also, and am much refreshed thereby. (Temptations, when we meet them at first, are as the lion that roared upon Samson; but if we overcome them, the next time we see them, we shall find a nest of honey within them.) The Philistines understand me not" (*Grace Abounding*, 1666).

Typological interpretation of the lion, however, is unstable. Usually the lion is the foe overcome, prefiguring death and Satan overcome by Christ. But a focus on the honey, the sweet food emanating from the slain body, however, may lead in an opposite direction. Francis Quarles (1592–1644) captures this alternative (cf. Ambrose, Augustine) in his poem, *The Historie of Samson*. Having recounted the lion slain, the riddle composed, and Samson set against the Philistines, Quarles pauses to address Christ, the lamb, as the slain lion, whose death yields saving doctrine.

> Great Saviour of the world; Thou Lambe of Sion,
> That hides our sinnes: Thou art that wounded Lyon:
> O, in thy dying body, we have found
> A world of hony; whence we may propound
> Such sacred Riddles, as shall, underneath
> Our feet, subdue the power of Hell and Death.
> (1631, Meditation 9 [147–8])

John Howard (1795–1868) instructs his young readers along more familiar familiar lines (cf. Ephrem the Syrian, or *Elizabethan Homilies*). As Samson conquered the lion, so the Redeemer conquered Satan. Understanding this, we find heavenly food, just as Samson found honey in the wild beast's carcass (*Illustrated Scripture History*, 1840 [136]). Temptation, notes F. B. Meyer (1847–1929), may well be compared to the lion's attack. Going back later, Samson obtained meat and sweetness. "How apt the parable! Every conquered temptation yields these two things—strength and sweetness." God's Word is sweet, and full of sweetness is the life hid with Christ in God (*Our Daily Homily*, 1898 [I, 224]). Likewise evangelist Charles Spurgeon (1834–92) preaches on Samson the lion-slayer, holding out hands "laden with masses of honeycomb and dripping with honey," as a type of Jesus, "conqueror of death and hell," who "stands in the midst of his church with his hands full of sweetness and consolation." To those believing in him "he gives the luscious food which he has prepared for us by the overthrow of our foes; he bids us come and eat that we may have our lives sweetened and our hearts filled with joy" (*Hands Full of Honey*, 1883).

From a literal-historical viewpoint in the eighteenth and nineteenth centuries, Samson's bare-handed defeat of the lion betokened the conquests he might expect by Divine assistance, and the honey an assurance that his courage would not go unrewarded (so Trimmer, *Sacred History*; cf. Howard, *Illustrated Scripture History*). The story had its detractors, of course, including Voltaire. He relates the bees in the lion's carcass to an ancient and erroneous notion (cf. Virgil, *Georgics*, iv) that bees could be produced from a corpse (*Philosophy of History*, 1765, ch. 45 [213]). Then again, defenders appear. John Kitto appeals to detailed knowledge of the Holy Land. Custom decreed at least a month's gap between a proposal and the marriage celebration. In that climate jackals and vultures speedily devour carcasses, so that Samson found only a clean skeleton, partially covered with the undevoured hide. "In the cavity thus formed a swarm of bees had lodged and deposited their honey" (*Bible History*, 1841 [216]).

Visually speaking, the lion *is* Samson. No collection of Old Testament stories is complete without the tale and Samson depicted atop the beast, grasping its jaws. Sometimes he straddles, sometimes, as in de Hooghe's design (1706) his knee pins the lion's body (PLATE 7.5a). Almost always his hands are on its jaws. Often, in the eighteenth and nineteenth centuries, a couple passes by in the background, either unaware of the feat or, more usually, startled. This conventional image of Samson astride the lion has endured. Even Cecil B. DeMille, directing *Samson and Delilah* (1949), recreates the pose.

Occasionally an illustration stands out. Unexpected is the convention's reversal by Dutch artist Gerard Hoet (1648–1733) in de Hondt's 1728 *Figures de la Bible* (PLATE 7.5b). Hoet's Samson has upturned the beast and stretches apart its hind legs, exposing its "virility" about to be rendered useless. "Samson tears the lion in pieces," says the rubric. This is going to be a very nasty tearing. Another rendering follows convention except that this straddling Samson with his winsome curls has shed his clothes. The 1891 painting in the polished "academic" style by French artist Léon Bonnat (1833–1922) proved extraordinarily popular, despite (or because of) its homoerotic overtones (PLATE 7.5c). Versions promptly appeared in Bible storybooks, and it was regularly included in volumes on the Bible in art (e.g. A. G. Temple, *Sacred Art*, 1898, or Clifton

PLATE 7.5   Samson's lion: (a) de Hooghe, 1706; (b) Hoet, 1728; (c) Bonnat, 1891; (d) *A Child's Story*, 1898. (See pp. 201, 203)

Harby, *The Bible in Art*, 1936). Before the decade was out it was decorating the cover of *A Child's Story of the Bible* (1898) from the reputable Henry Altemus Company of Philadelphia (PLATE 7.5d). But a decade later Altemus had decently added a loincloth (J. H. Willard, *What is Sweeter Than Honey* in Altemus's Beautiful Stories Series), and a century on and times had indeed changed. Samsons in children's storybooks, though hardly overdressed (loincloths are still fashionable), do usually keep some clothes on.

Foxes and fire

Allegorical and historical-critical reading of the foxes also coexisted. The literal details dealt with, Matthew Henry (1662–1714) recalls the allegory of the foxes as the Church's adversaries (cf. Origen, Augustine, More), pulling in different directions but bringing a firebrand to waste the Church and kindle the fire of division (*Exposition*, 1708). John Owen (1616–83) is more specific. The "dividers and troublers of church unity" are called Quakers, joined with others "seduced into Socinianism" in "opposition to the holy Trinity." "Knit together by the tail of consent in these firebrand opinions," they "jointly endeavor to consume the standing corn of the church of God" (*Brief Declaration and Vindication*, 1669).

For literal readers, the foxes have occasioned much head-scratching. Two concerns are the deed's practicality and morality. On the former, Puritan scholar Matthew Poole (1624–79) is confident. While "infidels are much offended at this history, and pretend it incredible that Samson could catch so many foxes together," it is not said that Samson caught all by himself, at one time; and God could well have so disposed things that they might be caught (*Annotations*, 1685). The learned Flemish Jesuit, Cornelius à Lapide (1567–1637), is of like mind. Surely God, perhaps through an angel, could have arranged the gathering and capture, as with Noah's animals (*Commentaria*, 1681). Such explanation cuts no ice with Voltaire. He reports (with mock horror) the "reckless indecency" of one skeptic's view: the story is absurd, and would amuse not even the most imbecilic children. It is impossible, at a given time, to find and attach together at the tail 300 foxes; there never was a fox-catcher who could do this (*Bible enfin expliquée*, 1776 [145]).

Voltaire's skepticism was clearly shared. "Much has been said by the Deists in ridicule of this part of the sacred history," complains the Rev. Henry Southwell in his *Universal Family Bible* (1775), "for they pretend to wonder, how, or where Sampson could find so many foxes?" His answer, increasingly common, is to appeal to the Levant of his day. "It is certain that, in those countries, foxes were very numerous; and in this age, some of our modern travellers have asserted, that they go in droves of two or three hundred." Moreover, Samson as a great man could command many assistants; his acting on his own is merely a figure of speech, as when a king is said to gain a battle. Hence, "the objection falls to the ground."

It is hardly surprising that Mrs Trimmer is troubled by Samson's method of revenge, "very difficult to account for, though some of the learned have endeavoured to reconcile it by various arguments" (*Sacred History*, 1783 [lx, 262]). She refers her young reader to Dr Sharpe's *Introduction to Universal History* (1755), where the Hebrew word translated "foxes" is thought better rendered "wheat-sheaves," a likely means of communicating conflagration. This slight emendation of the Hebrew text is generally attributed to eminent Hebraist Benjamin Kennicott (1718–83), although the "improved" edition of his own *Universal Family Bible* (1793) suggests that the proposal "will not stand the test of critical enquiry." Henry Southwell, dedicated to preserving orthodoxy, vehemently opposes the emendation: "nothing in the world can be more false." Half a century on, in John Kitto's *Cyclopaedia* (1846), the argument is still being discussed in detail (by Colonel Hamilton Smith) if only to be rejected: "three hundred shocks of corn would not make two stacks, and therefore the result would be quite inadequate" (II, "Shual" (Foxes)).

Even if the deed's practicality be established by the learned, for Mrs Trimmer the problem of its barbarity remained, soluble only by appeal to the higher justice of divine purpose. As Kitto says, "any other man who did this would deserve to be hanged" (*Daily Bible Illustrations*, 1850 [II, 392–5]).

But why foxes? The answer, Kitto supposes, is that foxes run to cover when in trouble. Dogs, in contrast, would "scour the open road." Why, then, tied tail to tail? Would they not run in opposite directions and so not run at all? Well, foxes have highly suitable bushy tails, which, if lit singly, would drag on the ground and extinguish the fire but, tied, would be "sustained at tension by their mutual exertions." Moreover, so tied, the foxes could not retreat into their holes. As for pulling in different directions, Kitto wishes someone would simply try a five-minute experiment instead of writing large dissertations on the subject. As it happens, he lately saw two dogs tied by the tail. "They certainly did pull in opposite directions, and wasted some minutes in rather awkward movements. But finding the futility of their efforts, they inclined their heads to each other, and after a hasty consultation, turned round so as to bring their bodies parallel to each other, and then ran off with considerable speed." Given that foxes "have not the reputation of being duller than dogs," Kitto has no doubt that they would have hit upon the same solution, while their longer tails would have both given them more room and widened their path of destruction. In short, Samson's was no senseless or ill-considered device.

But were the "foxes" really foxes? Kitto himself elsewhere calls them jackals, and this is usual in nineteenth-century Bible dictionaries and encyclopedias.

Missionary W. M. Thomson (1806–94) thought jackals were intended, since these were "even now extremely numerous. I have had more than one race after them, and over the very theatre of Samson's exploits. When encamped out in the plain, with a part of Ibrahim Pasha's army, in 1834, we were serenaded all night long by troops of these hideous howlers" (*Land and the Book*, 1860, 552). The Rev. J. G. Wood (1827–89) reports a certain Signor Pierotti's anecdote. He was caught, one night in January 1857, stuck on horseback in the middle of a "small torrent." Alas, the only things attracted by his calls, "were numbers of jackals, who remained at a certain distance from me, and responded to my cries, especially when I tried to imitate them, as though they took me for their music-master." The traveler thus had good opportunity, during this "most uncomfortable night," to ascertain that another Samson "would have had no difficulty in finding more than three hundred jackals, and catching as many as he wanted in springs, traps, or pitfalls" (*Wood's Bible Animals*, 1872, 58–9).

The episode's accuracy vindicated, Wood reflects on the foxes' fate, a matter little remarked upon. While Mrs Trimmer – whose celebrated story of Pecksy, Flapsy, Robin, and Dick (*Fabulous Histories*, 1786 – later *History of the Robins*) taught children to be kind to animals – speaks of the deed's "great barbarity," it is not clear that she has the foxes in mind. Wood, however, is clear and has an explanation. Obviously the "wretched animals" were burned to death after suffering "a prolonged torture." But such a consideration would not have deterred Samson. "The Orientals are never sparing of pain, even when inflicted upon human beings, and in too many cases they seem utterly unable even to comprehend the cruelty of which they are guilty." The clarification would have sounded a chord with many a reader, well schooled in the (alleged) immorality of the Orient. Given a Western reader-ship so averse to cruelty, it is curious that the foxes' fate is mostly a matter of indifference.

Yet E. Armytage's Samson, crouching with two foxes, one held on his thigh and peering out like a pet, gives pause. This Samson looks timid, fearful almost, as though wondering what (or who) is driving him, as though wishing simply to go home (PLATE 7.4a, p. 199) (in Stackhouse's *History*, new edn, 1857).

By the close of the nineteenth century, the episode was often compared to the Roman Cerealia festival (Ovid, *Fasti*, iv.679–712), where foxes with lighted torches tied to their tails were released in the Circus for ceremonial hunting. Long noted (e.g. Cornelius à Lapide, Voltaire), the similarity raised questions of historicity. Earlier scholars normally decided in the Bible's favor (so Matthew Poole says that the Roman custom derived, through the Phoenicians, from Samson's "history"), but this changed as historical criticism took hold, and interest in myth, legend, and folklore heightened. Thus students reading the Rev. G. W. Thatcher (1863–1950) on Judges were simply informed that the episode was "folklore which cannot be criticized seriously" (*Judges and Ruth*,

Century Bible, 1910). Oxford scholar G. A. Cooke (1865–1939) tells his high-school readers that the Cerealia custom symbolized the fires "fatal to the ripe corn in the heat of the Dog-days," and was linked to Samson not through history but through ritual and folklore, possibly an exorcism practised by Canaanites or even Israelites in the Danite district. Samson became associated with it in "popular story" (*The Book of Judges*, 1913). Examining "mythical" elements in Samson's story, the Rev. C. F. Burney (1868–1925), also of Oxford, claims that the key to the Cerealia is red, the color of sun, foxes, and fiery torches, and also of red-colored blight, rust, thought in ancient times to arise from hot sun upon damp corn-stalks. Given the connection of Samson's name (*shimshon*) to "sun" (*shemesh*), it is a "reasonable certainty" that he "plays the part of the Sun-god with his fiery heat, letting loose the destructive plague of rust which burns up the standing corn of the Philistines" (*The Book of Judges*, 1918, 393–5; cf. Smythe-Palmer, *The Samson-Saga and its Place in Comparative Religion*, 1913, 101–11).

As the twentieth century waxed and waned, so did enthusiasm for the Cerealia and the mythological meaning of Samson and his foxes. J. Alberto Soggin notes a competing explanation: torching fields is a typical military, especially guerilla, tactic (*Judges*, 1981; also Boling, *Judges*, 1975; cf. earlier, Lias, *Book of Judges*, 1906). The classical parallel is Hannibal at Lake Trasimene in 217 BCE, when he sent oxen with burning torches between their horns into the fields in order to cause the Romans to panic (Livy, xxii.16).

For many readers, however, the question remained: How *did* Samson manage to capture all those foxes, tie their tails, place the torches, and release them into the cornfields? Illustrators, unintentionally, underscore the problem. Numerous pictures show Samson sending off a few foxes (or jackals?), all obligingly heading into the waving grain. Elgers's design in Mortier's "Great Bible" (1700) even introduces a few kennels: released from one by Samson, a pair of foxes hot-tail it towards the crops. But where are all the others? Fortunately, the prolific illustrator J. James Tissot (*Old Testament*, 1904) comes to the rescue, though whether with a sense of humor is hard to tell. At any rate, while our hero lights the tied tails of one pair, there they are, the other foxes (well some of them) – patiently awaiting their turn (PLATE 7.6a).

Voltaire, we might imagine, must still be laughing.

Slaughter at Lehi

Voltaire could not resist a joke when it came to Samson slaughtering 1,000 Philistines with but the jawbone of an ass. In mock dismay he reports (he claims) a scholarly skeptic's sarcasm, "as insolent as it is impious": "He goes so

PLATE 7.6   Samson's exploits: (a) Foxes by Tissot, 1904; (b) Slaughter at Lehi by Doré, 1866; (c) Gates of Gaza, English Bible, 1746; (d) Samson with jawbone by de Jode, 1585. (See pp. 206, 209–10)

far as to say (we repeat it with horror) that the only ass's jawbone in this story is that of the author who made it up" (*Bible enfin expliquée*, 1776 [146]).

Earlier readers took the incident in high seriousness. It informs, for example, discussion of the legitimate use of force. Martin Luther views force as the prerogative of rulers doing their Christian duty, not individuals in their own cause, even to punish evil. Samson, he admits, is an exception, acting under God's special grace. "First become like Samson, and then you can also do as Samson did" (*Temporal Authority*, 1523, 104; cf. *An Open Letter on the Harsh Book*, 1525, 83). John Milton, on the other hand, invokes Samson as justification for war precisely against a ruler, the "tyrant" Charles I. Attacking royal apologist Salmasius, he argues that despite the reproach of his countrymen, "who did not balk at slavery," Samson, whether prompted by God or by his own valor, thought it not impious but pious to kill, single-handed, a host of his country's tyrannical masters (*Defence of the People of England*, 1651, ch. 4 [399–400, 402]; cf. *Samson Agonistes*, 1671 [ll. 255–76]). Joseph Hall is more concerned with proportional response, and commends the pagan Philistines for their moderation. Affronted by Samson, they do not fall upon the whole tribe of Judah, but call for satisfaction from the one offender. Hall feels sure that the same hand of God which "wrought Samson to revenge, restrained them from it." He reserves his scorn for the men of Judah, willing to "make friends to their tyrants, and traitors to their friends" (*Contemplations*, 1615 [x.4, 132]).

Francis Quarles (*Historie of Samson*, 1631) is less concerned with excess violence – "Heaven's high vengeance," after all, and "the secret pleasure" of God's sacred will – than the conundrum, the Nazirite steeped in blood. "May a Nazarite, then, / Embrue and paddle in the bloods of men?" His question is simply answered. Who are we to question God our maker? If God bids a Nazirite to kill, then kill he may, and a Nazirite still remain (Meditat. 13 [153]). Voltaire's conundrum was how a true history could claim that the Israelites were slaves when Samson needed only an ass's jawbone to kill 1,000 Philistines and God operated by his hands "the most astonishing prodigies" (*Philosophy of History*, 1765, ch. 41 [184]).

The episode's exact understanding challenged historians, but Calmet's famous *Dictionary of the Bible* (6th edn, 1837) was up to the task of explaining its obscurities. What did it mean that Samson smote the enemy "hip and thigh"? "Hip under thigh, say some; leg under thigh, say others; or, leg against thigh, or leg over, or upon, thigh; as the words literally express: horse and foot, say others; *i.e.* the foot trusting to their *legs*, are alluded to as *leg* men; the horsemen sitting on their *thighs*, are alluded to as *thigh* men." Mr Taylor, the editor, comes to the rescue. Wrestling, as "now performed by the Turks," was probably the same as "anciently used in the Olympic games"; whereupon he supplies a splendidly detailed account of wrestling in Algiers. The point is, "Do not these challengers well deserve the description of leg-and-thigh-men, or shoulder-and-thigh-men?" Accordingly we can now make an accurate translation: Samson "smote the *hip-and-thigh-men*; or the *arm-and-leg-men*; or the *hip-and-shoulder-men*; *i.e.* their best prize-fighters, with a great stroke."

At any rate, he clearly smote a great many of them, whoever they were, as the illustrators show. While not a favorite scene, the jawbone-wielding hero piling up corpses appears often enough. Indeed, his traditional signature in early modern portraits is usually the jawbone, as in Gerard de Jode's (1509–91) late sixteenth-century suite of "The Judges" (PLATE 7.6d). The problem of the one against so many is alleviated by showing any Philistines in Samson's vicinity either dead or fleeing. Massed spears behind those vainly attempting to escape depict the enemy numbers, but Samson does not actually have to fight anyone. So it appears in the first Luther Bible of 1524, in Matthäus Merian's influential *Icones Biblicae* of 1626 (and Zetzner's Luther Bible, 1630), in Nicholas Fontaine's *History* of 1690 (borrowing from Merian), and in Pieter Mortier's "Great Bible" of 1700 (although here not all Philistines flee – some stand apart, in shock, as Samson batters some unfortunate laggard). In the same spirit, Julius Schnorr von Carolsfeld (1794–1872) fills his picture with Samson and corpses, leaving the background to a few stragglers (*Bibel in Bildern*, 1860; *Bible in Pictures*, 1869).

A simpler solution shows Samson alone with the corpses, as in J. James Tissot's *Old Testament* (1904). Earlier depictions of the aftermath often show the victor drinking water issuing from the jaw (see above, on Vulgate and KJV), whether in Melchior Küsel's sophisticated "Biblical Images" (1679) or in the little picture illustrating Esther Hewlett's *Scripture History* (1828).

Finally, there is Gustave Doré's bold stratagem of upending conventional solutions (*Sainte Bible*, 1866). Panning back, he fills the page with a myriad tiny bodies, some plunging into a ravine. There is Samson, perched above the cliff, jawbone brandished aloft. But he, too, is small, and the crowds dense. Just what is happening? Perhaps the Philistines crushed each other to death, or kept falling off the edge. Certainly, in such a crowd in such a place was no place to be. Samson seems like the least of the Philistines' problems (PLATE 7.6b).

Gaza

Gaza enjoys a typological life well into modern times. In the eighteenth century Jonathan Edwards links the episode with prophecies "representing" the Messiah as loving a harlot – that is, a sinful people – and desiring such a people to be his spouse (Hosea 1–3; Ezekiel 16; Jeremiah 3, 30–1). Samson's gate carrying, too, prefigures the Messiah, encompassed by enemies, "rising from the sleep of death and emerging out of the thick darkness of his sorrows and sufferings, spoiling his enemies, and ascending into heaven and leading captivity captive" (*Types of the Messiah*, 1747 [257]). A century later, Charles H. Spurgeon (1834–92), eminent preacher, invokes this tradition. The woman of Gaza is the straying Church, and Gaza the guarded tomb. The gates represent sin and the cross Christ bore. Thus the sins of God's people "are as clean removed as ever the gates of Gaza were,—posts, gates, bar, and all." With Samson at Gaza so recalled, Spurgeon finally exhorts: "Prisoner, the prison doors are open. . . . Christ hath redeemed you" (*Our Champion*, 1864 [459–67]).

The typological meaning of Gaza was traditionally depicted by Samson carrying the gates, and the scene has continued to be a favorite even when its meaning was simply a literal show of strength. The gate rivals the lion in popularity, and pictures abound. Occasionally Samson rips a gate off its jamb, as in Harper's *Illuminated Bible* of 1846. But although Harper's Bible set a fashion, this picture failed to supplant the customary Samson trudging uphill. Over the centuries the gates have tended to grow bigger, and Samson presumably stronger. But there he remains, stuck like Sisyphus on that hillside, doomed to toil and never to arrive (PLATE 7.6c; Verdeir's design, in an English Bible, 1746).

As literal-historical interpretation increases, so does focus on Samson's visit to the woman. Joseph Hall "cannot wonder more at Samson's strength, than his weakness." Having cast away his love upon a Philistine woman, he now misspends himself upon Philistine harlots: "he did not so much overcome the men, as the women overcame him." Yet, though he capitulated to "lewd desires," he foresaw his predicament, and "his bed of fornication could hold him no longer than midnight." The moral: God's mercy holds us fast. "That bountiful hand leaves us rich of common graces, when we have misspent our better store" (*Contemplations*, 1615 [x.5, 134]).

One way to mitigate the Nazirite's visit was to claim the woman was an innkeeper, not a prostitute: while Hebrew *zonah* usually means a woman of ill repute, here it means one who sells meals and takes in strangers (cf. *Calmet's Dictionary*, 1722–8). Thus the American Sunday School Union's *Scripture Biographical Dictionary* (1833): Samson fearlessly went to the Philistine stronghold "and took up lodgings for the night." Another way, especially for youth, was to avoid the "lodging" altogether and highlight the feat of strength. "Perhaps," ventures Mrs Trimmer, "it was in defiance of the Philistines," that Samson went to Gaza (*Sacred History*, 1783 [lxi, 267]; cf. Gaspey, *Tallis's Illustrated Scripture History*, 1851). She understands, though the text is not explicit, that the Spirit of the Lord enabled Samson's feat and likely prompted him to anticipate the Philistine attack. He was "warned by heaven of his peril," agrees another who himself warns his young readers to beware of being asleep to life's dangers and so prone to the Spirit of Evil (Howard's *Illustrated Scripture History*, c.1840). Elsewhere, a ditty instructs youth that divine inspiration was front and foremost (Fletcher's *Scripture History*, 1839):

> Strong in the strength which God supplied,
> To humble Gaza's growing pride;
> In wait till midnight, Samson lay,
> Then arose, and bore its gates away.

In Romantic vein, the summoning voice for Thomas Carlyle (1795–1881) is not so much "heavenly" as "inward," the "prophetic voice of our whole soul and world," saying "thou canst do!" Often enough, one must go right in the teeth of things, "the gates of Gaza," as it were, which a "right Samson," having duly surveyed their strength and his own, must carry away on his shoulder (*New Letters*, 1842, I, 253).

Mostly, however, Samson's dalliance dogs the story's telling, and as the century turns, the pleas in mitigation continue. James Orr (1844–1913) reminds us not to make too much of an individual's moral lapses or even of the prevailing practice of a time, "else it would go hard with ourselves [i.e. Christians] under a higher and purer dispensation." Samson's conduct is not the measure of Israel's values. Mosaic Law stands for a "a high ideal of sexual morality" given its purest expression by the prophets (*Problem of the Old Testament*, 1906 [470–1]).

More down to earth, though not free of euphemisms, is Methodist Clovis Chappell (1882–1972). Samson, suggests the preacher, "had simply grown tired of being good." As judge "he had been quite decent for many years." But it got on his nerves. "He had an eagerness for laughter, a passionate hunger for pleasure." He could no long endure "his treadmill round of duties." He needed to "go on a lark." That desire to break away, Chappell assures his audience, "is a very normal desire." Have they never felt like throwing aside restraints and doing "something mean?" Samson was also an egotist, sure of himself after so many victories; indeed, the Gaza's danger "would add an extra tang to his pleasure." Not that Chappell approves of going among enemies to have a "good time," but that was Samson. "He hunted for temptation. He found it and played with it and laughed in its face and said: 'I can enjoy this sin, or I can let it alone. I am my own master'" (*Sermons*, 1925, 125–6).

Delilah

Delilah is one of history's "bad women." She falls into, and helps constitute, the cultural stereotype of the *femme fatale*, dear to patriarchal societies.

Delilah's problem, as Erasmus (1466–1536) put it, starts with her tongue, the "agent of treachery" and "source of ruinous counsels." Such were the tongues also of Joab and Judas (*The Tongue*, 1525 [340]). Next comes greed, as she "redoubled her wiles, which had been mocked by Samson's guile" ("Elegy, Against a Greedy Rich Man," c.1490, ll.37–8 [218–19]). Above all, there is love. "Love conquers all: he unbars adamantine doors, and iron chains are broken like straw by Love." Love conquered the unconquerable, Hercules and great-hearted Achilles. "And then, what has the whole wide world ever produced that was stronger than Samson? Single-handed, Love was able to lay him low" ("Cupid with his Quiver," c.1487, ll.19–20, 27–8 [230–3]).

Anabaptist David Joris (1501/2–56) gives Delilah's actions a metaphorical turn while associating her with the evils of fleshly desire. He urges his (male) readers to "let your beards grow and your strength increase in Christ which you, in the first Adam, have allowed the woman (your own flesh) to shave off." They have gone the way of Samson, bound with bands of darkness. "Do not let your beard be cut off," he entreats. "Do not look upon the beauty of the woman, nor upon her temptation and enchanting, so that you not be softened to her covetousness. . . . Do not be imprisoned by the lusts of the prostitutes and concubines. Beloved," he insists, "take heed" (*Wonderful Working of God*, 1535 [117–18]).

By the close of the sixteenth century, many in England had heard Delilah named from the pulpit as simply "the strumpet" with whom Samson fornicated, through fatal idleness (*Elizabethan Homilies*, "Against Idleness," II.19.1–136; as William Gurnall later says, Samson lost his strength "in the lap of sloth and negligence"). While fornication is not explicit in the text, it quickly came to mind for many readers, especially following Samson's Gaza visit. For Sir Walter Raleigh the story's moral was clear: "Whom no force could over-master, voluptuousnesse overturned" (*History of the World*, 1614, ii.15). So Delilah comes to signify carnality. Indeed, to Lutheran mystic Johann Arndt (1555–1621) she represents the world, to which Christians must die lest it overcome them as Delilah overcame Samson (*True Christianity*, 1605–21 [76]). Yet carnality has its good points! John Owen (1616–83) explains with what delight Christ reveals his secrets, his mind, to his saints and enables them to reciprocate. So (typologically) Samson's carnal delight in Delilah led him to reveal his mind to her, though it cost him his life. It is only a bosom friend to whom we will unbosom ourselves (*Of Communion with God*, 1657). To Joseph Hall, however, the carnal in this story is lust, and Delilah the strumpet of the official homily (*Contemplations*, 1615 [x.5, 134–5]). He castigates both Samson, "drunk with the cup of fornications," and "his harlot": "It is no marvel if she, which would be filthy, would be also perfidious." Lust "bewitched" Samson. How, otherwise, could he have been so stupid? Diverted by his harlot, his heart was effeminate. "All sins, all passions, have power to infatuate a man, but lust most of all. Never man, that had drunk flagons of wine, had less reason than this Nazarite. Many a one loses his life, but this casts it away; not in hatred of himself, but in love to a strumpet."

In *Paradise Lost* (1667), Milton's Adam and Eve also find sensory pleasure: in a bed of flowers, they took largely "thir fill of Love and Love's disport." But on waking, naked, their pleasure yields to guilty shame. "So rose the Danite strong / Herculean Samson from the Harlot-lap / Of Philistean Dalilah, and wak'd / Shorn of his strength, They destitute and bare / Of all thir virtue . . ." (ix, ll.1039–66 [402–3]).

In *Samson Agonistes*, too, Delilah's lap is fatal:

> Then swoll'n with pride into the snare I fell
> Of fair fallacious looks, venereal trains,
> Soft'n'd with pleasure and voluptuous life;
> At length to lay my dead and hallow'd pledge
> Of all my strength in the lascivious lap
> Of a deceitful Concubine who shore me
> Like a tame Wether, all my precious fleece,
> Then turn'd me out ridiculous, despoil'd,
> Shav'n, and disarm'd among my enemies.

The chorus takes up Hall's refrain: it was not wine that brought low the Nazirite but the desire of a woman (ll. 521–46 [564]).

Handel's oratorio *Samson* (1741), which adapted Milton's poem, has Dalila visit the captive Samson to make amends and win back his love (II. 2): "But hear me, hear the voice of love!" (and the chorus agree). She invokes the favorite argument of poetry's male lovers, *carpe diem* (seize the day): "To fleeting pleasure make your court, / No moment lose, for life is short! / The present now's our only time / The missing that our only crime." But Samson rejects her: "I know thy warbling charms, / Thy trains, thy wiles, and fair enchanted cup." Yet her response evokes pathos – "Let me approach at least, and touch thy hand" – and, even if ironically unaware of the awful truth in store, she retains her dignity: Why should she sue for peace, thus scorn'd,

> When in this land I ever shall be held
> The first of womankind, living or dead.
> My praises shall be at solemn feasts,
> Who saved my country from a fierce destroyer

A century later, Mrs Trimmer takes us back to Erasmus. For her, too, Delilah represents greed: "a mercenary wretch, who lived with him from interested views, such an one could not resist a bribe." Like Hall, she wonders how Samson did not guard better against Delilah's "artifices," but spares some thought for his subsequent suffering: "What mortifying reflections must have arisen. . . . And what agonies must have torn his wretched bosom!" But she is not swayed: it was "an inexcusable fault" repeatedly to "form connexions with the Philistine women." The lesson of Delilah is plain. Men must "be on their guard against the artifices which are usually practiced by wantons; these unprincipled females, having no affection for those who are weak enough to waste their tenderness upon them, are ready to betray or ruin them whenever it will answer any mercenary views of their own" (*Sacred History*, 1783 [lxi, 268–9]). Or, in Matthew Henry's aphorism: "If we sleep in the lap of our Lusts we shall certainly wake in the hands of the *Philistines*" (*Exposition*, 1708).

Not all accounts of Delilah are in perfect accord. Esther Hewlett offers familiar views tempered with restraint. Delilah's beauty "bewitched" Samson, and her "insinuating wiles" at length prevailed over his strength. Yet whether she was an Israelite or a Philistine, and Samson's connection with her "permanent or temporary, lawful or otherwise, we are not informed" (both accurate observations). Even of her greed, Hewlett notes that it is "generally supposed" she was a mercenary woman (*Scripture History*, 1828, 54). As for her identity, John Kitto is forthright: "she was probably of Israel, although Josephus, to save the credit of his countrywomen, makes her a Philistine" (*Bible History*, 1841 [218]).

No nineteenth-century writer more stringently denounces "Delilah the Destroyer" than Harriet Beecher Stowe (1811–96), of *Uncle Tom's Cabin* fame (*Woman in Sacred History*, 1873). Pictures of biblical womanhood, she explains, "are not confined to subjects of the better class." Moreover, as there is always deep shadow to bright light, so "there is in bad women a terrible energy of evil which lies over against the angelic and prophetic power given to them, as Hell against Heaven." Delilah is one of a few representations of "loathsome vice and impurity" left in the sacred records to show the utter corruption of the nations the Jews were commanded to exterminate. "Incurable licentiousness and unnatural vice had destroyed the family state, transformed religious services into orgies of lust, and made woman a corrupter, instead of a saviour." Here Stowe shares the widespread belief that Canaanite religion was rife with sexual license (see above on Judges 1–3). Sacred history, she writes, reveals no greater danger than "the bad power of bad women, and the weakness of men in their hands." Idolatry's introduction always stems from "the arts and devices of heathen women." This story is thus a graphic warning to even the dullest mind. "Delilah! not the frail sinner falling through too much love; not the weak, downtrodden woman, the prey of man's superior force; but the terrible creature, artful and powerful, who triumphs over man, and uses man's passions for her own ends, without an answering throb of passion." She who cannot love, since love brings weakness, has her wants – money, power – "and men are her instruments; she will make them her slaves to do her pleasure." So good-natured Samson, eyes wide open, succumbs. So too Hercules became "the scoff and slave of Omphale," and Anthony "the tool and scorn of Cleopatra." The story is for all time, and even today is repeating itself. Stowe ends with the Bible's classic warning against the "strange woman":

> She hath cast down many wounded,
> Yea, many strong men hath she slain;
> Her house is the way to Hell,
> Going down to the chambers of Death
> (Prov 7:26–7)

So Delilah lives on as the Philistine "temptress," and Samson the man who lies in her coils, as James Hastings (1852–1922) puts it, because he "dallies with temptation." Such a man, as Proverbs affirms, is doomed. Still, Hastings lets slip some admiration for her as he describes Samson "supine upon the breast of the ablest, the most patriotic, and the most fascinating of Philistine women" (*Greater Men and Women*, 1914, 514, 517). "Able" and "patriotic," however, generally yield to "fascinating." "How could Samson, primitive man as he was, resist this primitive woman with her beauty, lures and blandishments?" ask the marquess and marchioness of Aberdeen and Temair. He was "easily caught by womanly arts," so the "snares of Delilah enticed him and he walked into her net." Yet Delilah was not without feeling, even if it proved fatal: "Something of love entered her heart, to trouble her when it was too late, to make her allurements more persuasive. . . . 'Softly wakes my heart,' breathed Delilah's lips the more entrancingly in that her heart was indeed awakening" (they borrow from Saint-Saëns's opera). Small wonder that the authors end, like Harriet Beecher Stowe, with an epitaph: "The wise man spoke truly when he said, 'I find more bitter than death the woman, whose heart is snares and nets, and her hands as bands'" (*Women of the Bible*, 1927 [39–43]).

Bible illustration confirms Delilah as traitorous temptress. Her scene, above all, is the hair cutting, when she signals to the Philistines as the scissors snip. Less commonly, in the aftermath, she watches Samson being blinded. Either way, the scene is betrayal. She is alert and in charge; he is vulnerable. A long-standing, though not universal, tradition has (at least) her breasts exposed, signifying temptress. The variations rung on the theme are, of course, endless, but the cumulative effect is the same.

PLATE 7.7   Samson and Delilah: (a) Harper's *Illuminated Bible*, 1846; (b) Hoet, 1728. (See p. 217)

Many outstanding artists have painted the scene. Andrea Mantegna (1431–1506) sits her under a tree, up which a vine snakes. Carved on the trunk is a Latin proverb linking woman with the devil and evil/apple (*mala*), a traditional allusion to Eve as the woman who causes the Fall. Between her knees slumps sleeping Samson, whose hair she clips. Delilah is thus the archetypal woman who brings sin and death (cf. Stowe, above).

Different portrayals suggest different motivation. Is she a prostitute? Does she act from greed? Two works by Peter Paul Rubens (1577–1640), one now in the National Gallery, London, the other in the Alte Pinakothek, Munich, place her in settings suggesting a brothel. Disheveled bedclothes, along with disarrayed attire in one painting and no attire in the other, perhaps conjure lovemaking prior to Samson's sleep. As for greed, "she looks as if she could use the money the Philistines offer her," remarks J. Cheryl Exum (*Plotted, Shot, and Painted*, 1996, 192; see on Rubens and other artists, visual and verbal, ibid. 175–237).

Greed is in plain view in Gerard Hoet's engraving of the aftermath (in de Hondt's folio, *Figures de la Bible*, 1728). In a sumptuous hall he foregrounds a tangle of bodies disclosing Samson pinned down as his eye is gouged out. A telltale lock of hair lies before him, and to one side a young man with scissors clutches rather more than seven locks. Behind and central, light catches Delilah, *décolettée*, receiving a box of coins (PLATE 7.7b). Earlier, in Mortier's 1700 "Great Bible" (O. Elgers is the designer), greed is less immediately apparent. Delilah sits on a canopied bed's edge while a young man cuts Samson's hair. Her breasts are bare; Samson is dressed. She beckons to entering Philistines. The viewer has to discern in the gloom the bags of money they hold out (PLATE 7.8d). Elgers' design, then, both indicates greed and, by contrasting the exposed woman with the clothed man, clothes Delilah with sexual temptation and exposes the man as vulnerable.

Widely imitated was the scene's composition by Merian (1626, 1630), as at the end of the eighteenth century in a beautifully executed little picture in Thomas Bankes' *Family Bible* (c.1790) (PLATE 7.8c). In 1846 a version appears in Harper's *Illuminated Bible* (PLATE 7.7a) (borrowed in turn – such is the story of illustration – from a French edition of Fontaine's *Histoire*, 1835). Unlike Mortier's Delilah, in these versions she is very properly dressed. There is neither exposed flesh nor money, no obvious sex or greed – in short, no obvious motivation. This, during the seventeenth, eighteenth, and nineteenth centuries, was how many readers encountered Delilah.

Illustrations differ in an obvious detail (Judg 16:19). In Mortier's scene a young man kneels to cut Samson's hair. In Merian's design Delilah, alone with Samson, cuts his hair herself. Curiously, in the Harper's version, an older woman acts as barber, delicately separating a lock and snipping. The gesture is

PLATE 7.8 Samson and Delilah: (a) Ardizzone, 1961; (b) Lantern slide, c.1900; courtesy George Eastman House; (c) Bankes's *Family Bible*, 1790; (d) Elger, 1700; (e) Armitage, nineteenth century. (See pp. 217, 219–20)

borrowed from Rubens' National Gallery painting, only there a man cuts while an old woman stands alongside, holding a candle. Harper's woodcut thus merges Merian's engraving and Rubens' painting to the exclusion of the painter's sexual interpretation. Instead of an erotic temptress, two modestly clothed and maternally demeanored Delilahs are now doing the deed. Harper's Bible was lavishly produced, but the stereotyping process meant that many more copies were printed than previously. Within a few years, possibly more people would have seen Harper's motherly Delilah than had seen Rubens' voluptuous Delilah over much of the painting's lifetime.

Who cuts Samson's hair? The alternatives stem from varying texts. The ancient Greek and Latin versions are ambiguous: she summoned "a man" (LXX[B]) or "the barber" (LXX[A], Vulgate), and she or he shaved his locks. The Hebrew text has Delilah shave even though she summons "the man." What was he doing, if Delilah was shaving? To solve the problem, the Protestant Geneva Bible makes the verb causative (against common use): she called a man and "made him to shave" (whence KJV (1611) and later English versions, e.g. RSV). The seventeenth-century Douai–Rheims translation, authoritative for English Catholics, follows the Vulgate: "she called a barber and shaved." This makes Delilah the subject, but leaves open the implicit meaning that the barber shaved for her. Elsewhere, in Luther's German translation, the summoned man does the deed. That illustrators differ on this crucial detail is hardly surprising.

The late nineteenth century is reticent in depicting Delilah. Gustave Doré downplays overt sexual appeal, merely hinting with a bare arm, bent knee, and rich attire as his Delilah stands listening impassively to Samson explain his secret (*Sainte Bible*, 1866; *Doré Bible Gallery*, 1879). Though widely reproduced over the next half-century, the picture is one of a diminishing number showing Delilah with Samson. Even in earlier Scripture histories for youth, such as Hewlett's, Gaspey's (*Tallis's*), or Howard's, she is missing. Nor does she make much of an appearance in twentieth-century illustrated Bible stories, though Edward Ardizzone (1900–79) contributes a gentle Delilah with a weary Samson to Walter de la Mare's *Stories from the Bible* (1961) (PLATE 7.8a).

Yet the late nineteenth century sees no few free-standing paintings of Delilah eroticized as *femme fatale* (e.g. Jean Paul Laurens, Henri Motte, or Solomon J. Solomon), some soon reproduced in volumes of "Bible and art" but rarely in books designed for family or youth. Delilah is painted lying with Samson ("beguiling"), at his seizure, and also watching him turn the millstone in prison, thus joining his Philistine tormentors, though the Bible mentions no such visit (cf. Maurice Mitrecey in A. G. Temple's *Sacred Art*, 1898). In a mid-Victorian painting by Royal Academy member E. Armitage (often reproduced as an engraving, later a color plate in *Bibby's Annual*, 1913), an overseer readies the lash. Delilah, amid a motley crowd of mockers, gazes and points disdain-fully. Light falls across her half-open robe to remind the viewer of her sexual charm (PLATE 7.8e). "Samson beguiled by Delilah" is a recurring title, as in an early twentieth-century magic lantern series, "Old Testament Bible." Samson leans back on the pillows, wine goblet in hand, like a young Greek god. Delilah snuggles and smiles up at him, and insinuates her hand down his tucked leg. Both are naked, if partially draped (and he keeps his sandals on). There is little reticence here – and not much art (PLATE 7.8b).

With a wholly different imagination, Edwina Sandys, at the century's end, turns precisely the beguiling *femme fatale* into a *femme forte*, a strong woman, like a Renaissance Deborah, or Jael, rather (*Women of the Bible*, 1986). The stereotypical message associated with Delilah is that the woman who allures brings death. Sandys sardonically strips her of her allure – and the male viewer of his titillation – and presents her starkly as a fatal woman, pure and simple. She *is* the scissors. She brings death between her legs. And she holds her head up proudly as she looks forward to the next man. It is as though Delilah has said to Rubens, "If this is what you believe about me, then forget that volup-tuous body – here I am." By an ironic turn, Sandys reclaims Deborah as a woman in her own right (PLATE 7.9d).

Captivity and death

Samson, captured, loses his eyes. As in ancient Jewish commentary, the irony of Samson's being "eyeless in Gaza" (Milton) is not lost on readers. His eyes, writes Joseph Hall, "were the first offenders, which betrayed him to lust; and now they are first pulled out, and he is led a blind captive to Azzah [Gaza], where he was first captivated to his lust." Better Samson blind in prison than abusing his eyes in Sorek; "yea, I may safely say, he was more blind when he saw licentiously, than now that he sees not; he was a greater slave when he served his affections, than now in grinding for the Philistines." Until he lost his eyes, he saw not his sin (*Contemplations*, 1615 [x.5, 135–6]).

In prison, he grinds at the mill, and in the East grinding, as *Calmet's Dictionary* informs us, was women's work, so severely degrading – a view often repeated. Such vindictive contempt was the height of Philistine contumely, "a vilely fit employment for Dalilah's deluded lover!" Thus Samson was "worse used than Job [31:10] supposes his wife might be" (6th edn, 1837). Calmet's

---

PLATE 7.9   (a) Samson's exploits, Koberger, 1491. (b)–(d) Delilah cuts Samson's hair: (b) Hayes, 1978; (c) Norwich Cathedral, c.1460s; (d) Sandys, 1986. (See pp. 180, 220, 230)

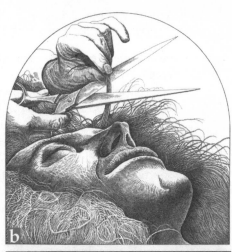

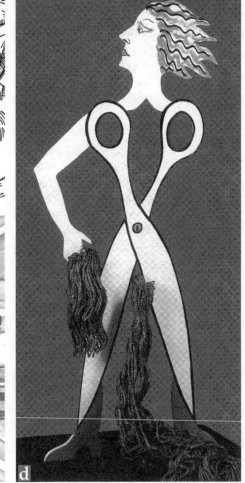

older contemporary and fellow dictionary-writer, the philosopher Pierre Bayle (1647–1706), passes over Samson's history ("everyone knows it") but does pause at something "quite odd." Some scholars think Samson's "grinding" is a euphemism, as in Job 31:10 (see *Numbers Rabbah*, above, p. 174.) That is, the Philistines "made him lie with their women, in order to have posterity from such a courageous man." Bayle confesses himself hardly persuaded of such good-natured Philistines who would so revenge themselves on their hated scourge. After all, Samson greatly loved women. He would have had to be treated like "the stallions of a stud-farm." The only thing he would have had to worry about would have been "how stiffly constrained he was [*la contrainte*]" (*Dictionnaire historique et critique*, 1697).

For the young mid-nineteenth-century reader of *Tallis's Illustrated Scripture History* grinding means grinding. Highlighted, rather, is the brutality with which Samson, poor sightless fettered captive, is treated as an object of cruel sport in the house of Dagon. "But a greater God than Dagon observed the vile doings of these wicked revellers." In an instant, that abode of idolatry, scene of "unhallowed merriment," became "a spectacle most dreadful to behold." The voice of joy was "lost in the shrieks and groans of the wounded and the dying." Pride should remember that, in a moment, God's power can exalt the humble and bring upon the oppressor helpless ruin (Gaspey, 103–4).

Samson's cry at his end has provoked much discussion: "Strengthen me, O God, that I may take vengeance on the uncircumcised" (Judg 16:28). John Calvin recognizes the problem. Despite its righteous zeal, this prayer expressed a "vicious longing for vengeance." May prayer made for the wrong reasons still obtain its effect? Calvin's response sounds familiar: individual examples do not abrogate universal law; special impulses have been imparted to a few men; and the prayers God grants do not always please him. But Scripture teaches that he helps the miserable and hearkens to the unjustly afflicted, even if they are unworthy to receive even a trifle (*Institutes*, 1550, II.iii.20.15 [870]).

More often Samson's death raises the question of suicide. Sir Thomas More (1478–1535) joins a debate over Samson "salvation." Did he act upon divine impulse? The Philistines by mocking Samson scorned God, who thus likely "gave him the mind" to bestow his life in revenge for the displeasure done to God. Several times the text says that God's power rushed into Samson, suggesting that his strength was not inherent in his hair or always at hand, but rather to have "at such tymes as it pleasid god to give it hym." Hence he must have pulled down the house with God's gift of strength and spirit in him (*Dialogue of Comfort against Tribulation*, 1534, ii.16, ll.6–15 [140–1]). This explanation is often repeated. "Thou shalt not kill" applies broadly, argues Lutheran Martin Chemnitz (1522–86), and killing oneself is no exception. But Samson seeks to punish the Philistines publicly for mocking God, through him. As a ruler who risks death in a lawful war does not sin, neither did Samson. Anyway, he was a type of Christ, who in dying must destroy death. Hence his end was "in the hidden guidance of the Holy Spirit." Chemnitz is satisfied: "So much for this question" (*Loci Theologici*, 1591, viii.B.2 [409–10]). A century later, Italian Puritan Francis Turretin (1623–87) agrees. Samson's "self-murder (*autocheiria*)" came not from a private impulse but from God who claims our lives as he pleases. Turretin also finds support in typology and, finally, Hebrews 11. If Paul lists Samson as an exemplar of faith, then he must not have violated the law (*Institutes of Elenctic Theology*, 1682 [II, 14; cf. 117]).

Making the same case, Joseph Hall exposes Samson's inner thoughts when, moved by zeal, not malice, he sues to God for power to revenge God's wrongs more than his own. "His renewed faith tells him, that he was destined to plague the Philistines; and reason tells him, that his blindness puts him out of the hope of such another opportunity." Knowing he must die, "he re-collects all the forces of his soul and body" that his death may vindicate God. Having vindicated Samson's suicide, however, Hall beats a familiar retreat: "All the acts of Samson are for wonder, not for imitation." And Hall, too, finds comfort finally in typology: "So didn't thou, O blessed Saviour, our better Samson, conquer in dying" (*Contemplations*, 1615 [x.5, 135–6]). Hall's contemporary, Francis Quarles, expresses this view in Samson 's prayer (*Historie of Samson*, 1631, sect. 23 [168]):

> Lord, the wrong is thine:
> The punishment is just, and onely mine:
> I am thy Champion, Lord; It is not me
> They strike at; Through my sides, they thrust at thee.

He urges,

> Revenge thy wrongs, great God; O let thy hand
> Redeem thy suffring honour, and this land:
> Lend me thy power; Renew my wasted strength,
> That I may fight thy battles; and, at length,
> Rescue thy glory.

His hands upon the pillars, he exclaims, "Thus with the Philistines, I resigne my breath; / And let my God finde Glory in my death." Yet in "On Iesus and Sampson," Quarles sounds a less triumphant note:

> In this they differ'd; Iesus' dying Breath
> Cry'd out for Life; But Sampson's cald for Death:
> Father forgive them did our Iesus crye;
> But Sampson, Let me be reveng'd and dye:

Since then, sweet Saviour, 'tis thy Death must ease us,
We flye from Sampson, and appeale to Iesus.
(*Divine Fancies*, 1632, ii.5 [214–15])

Despite some anxiety, then, about how he dies, Samson's destruction of the house of Dagon is favorably received. Against temptations that ordinary means cannot master, readers should draw out the long sword of "extraordinary prayer," advises William Gurnall (1617–79). Such was Samson's prayer, enabling him "to pull down the devil's house upon his head." He set his hands to the pillars; so prayer needs to be backed up by action. "He that hath bid thee pray against thy lust hath bid thee shun the occasions of it. . . . Certainly, he that would not have his house blown up will not have set his gunpowder in the chimney-corner" (*Christian in Complete Armour*, 1655–62 [ii.11 [750]]).

As we have seen, for typological readers Samson is a positive exemplar. Jonathan Edwards (1703–58) explains that the Philistines, "the devils," thought to make sport with God's people when they captured Samson. But he, who represented Christ as well as his brethren, gave them "a most dreadful overthrow" (*Notes on Scripture*, 1722–56 [73–4]). Not given to typologizing, Edwards's contemporary Mrs Trimmer was more concerned with Christian character through a literal-historical reading of Scripture. Here a repentant captive Samson acts out of higher motives. "The heavy calamities which fell upon Samson awakened his conscience, and he acknowledged that the punishment was justly inflicted, for slighting the gift of God." Still, she cannot pass over the vengeful prayer lightly. Samson very reasonably resented his injuries, and since he was not living "under the mild Dispensation of Christianity, which alone teaches universal charity and forgiveness of enemies," we must not hastily condemn him for desiring revenge. Then the argument takes a familiar turn: also, he most likely wished to vindicate God. So, bowing his head in "humble resignation to the Divine will, which had ordained him to punish the Philistines," he did his final duty (*Sacred History*, 1783 [lxii, 271–2]). One might imagine Trimmer approving of the illustration in Esther Hewlett's *Scripture History*, simply composed and with a minimum of death and destruction (PLATE 7.10b, adapted from a popular eighteenth-century design), even more so the child's ABC, where S is for Samson, no bodies in sight (*Routledge's Scripture Gift-Book*, c.1866; PLATE 7.10c).

Sometimes the message of Samson's end is decidedly mixed. The Rev. Alexander Fletcher (1787–1860) informs *his* young readers in no uncertain terms that Samson's calamitous end was brought on by his misdeeds, especially dalliance with unsuitable women. On the opposite page, however, the ditty accompanying the picture of his end celebrates his valor (*Scripture History*, 1839, I):

PLATE 7.10 Samson's end: (a) Doré, 1866; (b) Hewlett's *Scripture History*, 1828; (c) *Scripture Gift Book*, c.1866; (d) Taylor, 1820. (See pp. 183, 224, 227)

> Scorn'd, and insulted, and depriv'd of sight,
> The valiant Samson cries to Heaven for might;
> Then all his strength against the Pillars throws;
> And slays at once himself and Israel's foes.

The divine answer is explicit in Gaspey's *Tallis's Illustrated Scripture History* (1851):

> "One moment be my strength restor'd,"
> The blind betrayed mock'd Samson cries.
> His prayer is granted by the Lord;
> The temple falls, avenged he dies.

The theme of repentance in captivity and death has captured many an imagination wishing for a heroic end. James Hastings (1852–1922) recapitulates in the twentieth century the sympathetic readings of Hall and Milton in the seventeenth. Blinded, Samson begins to recover "inward sight," becoming "a patriot once again, with a patriotism purged of the dross of ambition and self-interest." At the song exalting Dagon (16:23–4), inspiration comes: one deed will undo his injury to his God and people. His Nazirite strength is upon him, old convictions surge, "till his whole being is flooded with the tide of sacred passion." We see him "erect at last in the dignity of his new-won manhood, his face fronting the mocking faces that he could not see—Samson Agonistes!" Imagination still sees him – "the tragic, stately form bowing itself against the central pillar, the shuddering building, the gaping roof, the appalling avalanche of wood and stone." So Samson keeps his vow and redeems his story. "Nothing in his life became him like the leaving of it," writes Hastings, borrowing from *Macbeth*. "The penitent heroism of its end makes us lenient to the flaws in its course"; we leave this last of the judges sleeping in his grave, "a true soldier of God" (*Greater Men and Women*, 1914, 518–20).

Thomas Miller (*Portraits*, 1922, 132–8) also responds to Milton's portrait (*Samson Agonistes*, 1671) in which the fallen hero's words of penitence and self-reproach evince pity and sympathy: "Nothing of all these evils hath befallen me / But justly; I myself have brought them on, / Sole author I, sole cause" and

> The base degree to which I now am fall'n
> These rags, this grinding, is not yet so base
> As was my former servitude, ignoble,
> Unmanly, ignominious, infamous,
> True slavery, and that blindness worse than this
> That saw not, how degenerately I served.

Similarly in Saint-Saëns's opera (*Samson et Dalila*, 1872/77), Miller finds most moving the erstwhile strong man working as a slave: "His song of penitence, while grinding out the corn, has a touch of infinite sorrow and moves the heart to pity and sympathy and regret." Yet Miller's reading of Samson's earlier "degeneration," with conscience dethroned and appetite in its place, tempers his judgment. He quotes Milton's Manoa: "Nothing is here for tears, nothing to wail / Or knock the breast, no weakness, no contempt, / Dispraise or blame, nothing but well and fair, / And what may quiet us in a death so noble." Miller is not so sure: "These are generous words, perhaps too generous." Instead, like Hastings, he turns to *Macbeth* for Samson's epitaph: "he died / As one that had been studied in his death, / To throw away the dearest thing he ow'd, / As 'twere a careless trifle."

Occasionally a writer decides that readers might better skip the ending altogether – so Gertrude Smith in *Robbie's Bible Stories* (1905, 84–6). Papa relates Delilah's wicked ploy and poor Samson's capture. "Oh, papa," interjects Robbie, "little Virginia is crying! She doesn't like the story!" But Papa replies, "Wait, little girl, and do not cry." Poor Samson knew, as he sat in the dark prison house, that his strength had gone because he let the wicked Delilah woman make him forget God. So he was sorry and prayed, and his hair grew back, and his wonderful strength returned. And Robbie's mother said: "I think that is a good place to end your story of Samson, papa." And Robbie's father said: "Yes, I think I have told you quite a long story to-day, dear children." And Robbie and little Virginia ran down to the edge of the little lake and watched the six big white geese floating about on the water.

No doubt Robbie's mother would have regarded Gustave Doré's endlessly reproduced depiction of Samson's end amidst massive mayhem as likewise not for universal exhibition (PLATE 7.10a).

The riddle of Samson

> Out of the eater came something to eat,
> Out of the strong came something sweet.

For centuries, readers have considered Samson's riddle a bad one, impossible to answer without knowing his unique experience. "Lion and honey" is assumed to be the answer. After all, the companions reply: "What is stronger than a lion? What is sweeter than honey?" Little in biblical interpretation is new under the sun, but some readers are seeing Samson's riddle in a new light.

The story starts at least with early twentieth-century "form critics" seeking component "forms" or literary genres of the Bible and asking about their original social context (*Sitz im Leben*). Herman Gunkel (1862–1932) saw the Philistines' answer to Samson's riddle as itself a riddle, both originally independent sayings ("Simson," in *Rede und Aufsätze*, 1913). Hugo Gressman (1877–1927) decided that the original answer to Samson's riddle was "vomit" – the result, at a wedding feast, of excess drinking and eating of sweet things (*Die Anfänge Israels*, 1914, 250–1). As for the Philistines' riddle, it originally demanded the answer "love" – Gunkel agreed – in view of similarities with Song of Songs 2:3 (the lover's fruit is sweet) and 8:6 (love is as strong as death, jealousy as cruel as Sheol). For Otto Eissfeldt (1887–1973) the solution of Samson's riddle was originally "semen," since he saw a sexual metaphor like Prov 30:20 ("This is the way of an adulteress: She eats, and wipes her mouth, and says, 'I have done no wrong'") ("Die Rätsel in Jud 14," 1910, 134). The riddle then lost its meaning in its new context because it demanded an answer ("lion and honey") available only to Samson.

Observing that the response is itself a riddle, James Crenshaw saw both riddle and response as requiring the answer "sex" or preferably "love," which answer logically connects them (*Samson*, 1978, 112–20). Philip Nel agreed that the keywords "strength" and "sweetness" in the Philistine's response referred to love, and saw the response as a popular proverb or "folkloristic riddle" which Samson's riddle was designed to evoke. Samson's ingenuity lay in his ability to compose a new riddle of sex demanding the old riddle as its solution. What he did not bargain on was that the Philistines would break the rules of the game. The author constructed the lion and honey episode as a kind of "narrative prelude" to the riddle telling ("Riddle of Samson," 1985). Claudia Camp and Carole Fontaine revisited sexual connotations of both riddle and response, showing how they can be read sexually of both male and female. Riddles, they point out, are customary at wedding feasts, both to entertain and to dissipate social problems (such as disparities of power). Like any good riddle, Samson's contains grammatical and metaphorical features providing both clues and blocks to the correct answer. Samson, in a potentially dangerous situation (an Israelite among Philistines), exercises his verbal skills and knowledge of custom in a diplomatic way. Ironically, these irenic skills produce the "occasion against the Philistines" (14:4) God has sought all along ("Words of the Wise," 1990).

Once Samson's riddle is understood as soluble (by "sex" or "love"), the narrator's own game with the reader is exposed: the lion and honey are not just a "prelude" but themselves a block, which for latter-day readers has proved too effective! Because of it, most believe the riddle's answer is "lion and honey," literally, and so view the riddle as insoluble (and unfair). But if lion and honey block the reader, they are unknown to the Philistines in the story. So why could they not find a (fair) solution? Were they (as all Israelite readers already knew) not very clever? Or is the question a problem for the solution?

The riddle is given another turn by Edward Greenstein ("Riddle of Samson," 1981, 247–51) when he suggests that the reader "apply the riddle formula to the story of Samson itself." The whole story is a "virtual riddle to be solved, a code to be cracked." We should ask: "Who strays after foreign women, acts on impulse, and neglects his cultic obligations?" The answer is Israel.

Readers for centuries have eagerly faulted Samson for his sexual urges. J. Cheryl Exum concurs, but understands his sexual desire in terms of the patriarchal society producing the text, where woman's sexuality is feared and hence regulated (*Fragmented Women*, 1993, ch. 3; cf. Mieke Bal, *Lethal Love*, 1987, ch. 2). The text dissociates sexuality from the "good" model of womanhood, Manoah's wife, and associates it with the "bad" models, the Timnite, the prostitute, and Delilah. Women are either mother or whore. Exum also shows the story fashioned from binary oppositions, good woman versus bad woman but also male versus female, Israelite versus Philistine, clean versus unclean, and own kind versus foreign. By constantly crossing and confusing these boundaries, Samson shows their fragility. In Exum's view, the story teaches that death comes to such boundary-crossers.

Susan Niditch, however, understands a category confuser like Samson to be one of folklore's "tricksters" whose outrageous behavior, contravening moral norms, society accepts as a corrective to a too rigid order favoring the powerful. The theme is "the marginal's confrontation with oppressive authority." His birth as a hero, adventures with women and assailants, and death "all emphasize the victory of the weak over seemingly implacable forces." Samson's tale "is a powerful statement of hope and vindication" ("Samson as Culture Hero," 1990, 624).

Folklorists say that trickster stories remind their listeners, if only subliminally, that life encompasses more than moral and social standards, that chaos needs somehow to be incorporated into the social order. Samson's story might then be ambiguous, both subverting and supporting the society producing it. Claudia Camp develops this view by focusing on "strangeness" here and in other "wisdom" texts concerned with such identity-shaping oppositions as Exum lists (*Wise, Strange and Holy*, 2000, 94–143). Samson the trickster makes even God end up in the company of the "strange." God finds "occasion" against the Philistines, not through the "good" mother or the men of Judah, but through the Philistine woman of Timnah and Delilah, the archetypal "strange woman." Readers for centuries have found the story's morality and its depiction of God's justice (theodicy) highly problematic, and have expended many words trying to make the problem go away. The point, suggests Camp's analysis to the contrary, is that the problems are part of the picture. They are not to be "solved."

Camp's analysis of the riddle suggests that sex and love are confused categories creating confusion in Samson's life. Samson as bawdy trickster is also

Samson the ordinary lover. She reads him, therefore, as neither buffoon nor national hero but as tragic trickster.

> If Woman is what is sweet and strong, Samson is a strong seeker of sweetness. If his search leads to the death of a Strange Woman, this is mythically balanced by the survival of two others. If his search joins him to the Strange Woman in death, it is only because he has found God, and her sweetness if not necessarily healing to the body. If you have found honey, eat only enough for you, or else, having too much, you will vomit it (Prov 25:16).
>
> Samson dies, with his bride, for the love of sweetness. But Delilah bears witness that they do not die, like Romeo and Juliet, caught blindly in the snare of the patriarchal ideology that constructs them, but as tricksters, both eyes avenged, watching their predestined tragedy unfold. (p. 138)

Camp's sympathy for Samson finds an echo in Marvin Hayes's stark drawing of Samson's vulnerability. He takes up the detail linking Rubens' *Samson and Delilah* and Harper's *Illuminated Bible*, the detail at the heart of the pictures: namely, the delicate execution of the hair cutting itself. Hayes has stripped away the context and left us only with Samson's head amid a mass of hair, and someone's fingers gently holding up a few strands between open scissor blades. His life hangs on a thread. Samson's whole story comes down to this – a gentle squeeze of the scissors (PLATE 7.9b, p. 221).

The story begins with no formula of evildoing and its consequences. Micah (Michas), in the hill country of Ephraim, owns to having stolen money from his mother, and restores it. She uses some to have two images made and installed in a shrine of Micah's making, along with an ephod and teraphim, and with his son as priest. A young Levite from Bethlehem, seeking a position, arrives, is hired as priest, and becomes like a son to Micah, who now believes that God will prosper him. The tribe of Danites are also seeking a place to live. Five spies stay at Micah's house, recognize the Levite, ask for an oracle about their journey, and receive a favorable response. Continuing on, they observe the quiet and unsuspecting people of Laish. Returning to their brethren, they urge them to attack Laish and settle in its land of plenty. God, they say, has given it into their hand. Six hundred armed Danites set out for Micah's house. The spies rob the sanctuary of its sacred objects and tell the remonstrating priest to join them. The priest's heart is glad. Micah, however, with neighbors, pursues the Danites and protests: they have robbed him of his gods and priest. They suggest that if he continues raising his voice, some injury may befall him. He desists. The Danites, with their booty, descend upon Laish, kill everyone and burn the town. Rebuilding it, they dwell there and call it Dan. They also erect the graven images. The priest – now named as Jonathan the son of Gershom, son of Moses – and his descendants serve there until the exile.

This is one of the less favored stories in Judges, though from time to time it has received attention. It has, for example, been the key to revising the book's apparent chronology, since at least the first century. Probably the dominant issue, argued most virulently in the early Reformation, has been the legitimacy of images in Christian worship. Proponents of "right worship" have also scrutinized whether the Levite provides an acceptable model for clergy. In the nineteenth and twentieth centuries, professional historical critics found evidence here for source and redaction theories of the book's composition. They also encouraged the distinction, commonly drawn, between the "rude" manners of the times and modern "civilized" behavior and belief. Readers in all periods have puzzled at "strange and irregular transactions," to borrow the apt words of *Sunny Sabbaths* (c.1860). How to understand them? By the close of the twentieth century, among scholarly readers at least, the emerging lens was irony.

Ancient and Medieval

From early on, Jewish tradition – though not always (Pseudo-Philo; *Seder 'Olam*, 12) – assigns these events, along with the Gibeah outrage and aftermath (chs 19–21), to the beginning of the Judges' period, the days of Othniel (ch. 3). Micah's Levite (17:7) is identified with the priest of Dan (18:30) named as Jonathan, grandson of Moses, suggesting a time soon after Joshua. (A curiosity of the Masoretic Hebrew text of 18:30 is a letter "n" (*nun*) inserted into but above the word Moses (*mosheh*), the case of the suspended nun! The traditional explanation: out of respect for Moses, the priest is described instead, symbolically, as the grandson of Manasseh (*m^enasheh*), since both were idolaters.)

Medieval commentator Rashi (1040–1105) elaborates (see on Judg 17:1). The Danites accepted Micah's graven image while the house of God was in Shiloh (18:31), a period he reckons to start 14 years after the Jordan crossing. Also, in the next story (ch. 19) the travelers bypassed Jebus (Jerusalem) as a city of heathens, implying that it had not yet been captured by Judah (1:8). Locating these final chapters chronologically at the beginning goes back at least to Josephus (c.37–c.100 CE), who omits, however, all reference to Micah. He starts with Judges 1–2 (*Antiquities*, v.120–35 [ii.1–7]), tells at length of the rape and civil war (136–74 [2.8–12), and briefly of the Danites' resettlement (175–8 [3.1]). He then picks up with Judges 3. The rearrangement has been followed by numerous accounts of biblical history well into modern times, normally with Micah included.

Micah's mother (Pseudo-Philo calls her "Dedila") was sometimes thought to be Delilah because of her eleven hundred pieces of silver (the sum offered to Delilah, 16:5). Rashi disagrees (on 17:3), since on his view Micah long preceded Samson. Though chronologically separate, these stories were set side by side, he explains, because of the equal amounts of wicked silver, both being silver of misfortune (cf. *Targum Judges* and David Kimchi on 17:2).

The silver idols have usually intrigued and often bothered readers. Ancient historian Pseudo-Philo conveys the problem by raising the stakes (*Biblical Antiquities*, 44): Micah makes the idols not from silver but from a hoard of gold. His mother further suggests an altar and a golden column, and a detailed price list for sacrifices. He is to be called priest and worshiper of the gods. He fashions various images (boys, calves, lion, eagle, dragon, and dove), each appropriate for relaying the divine response to a particular type of request. "And his wickedness was manifold and his impiety was full of guile." Lest the point of this tale of extravagant idolatry be missed, a long speech from God laments the people's failure since Sinai to observe the commandment against graven images, not forgetting adultery and lusting after foreign women (one of the author's abiding concerns). Finally, in a charming ending, God promises to deliver Micah to fire and his mother to rotting in his sight while still alive; and he pronounces doom on all who sin against him.

Speculation linked Micah with events prior to entry into Canaan. Some connect him with the making of the golden calf (Ginzberg, VI, 209 n. 126); some tell of the Israelites bringing an idol from Egypt, and at least one source identifies this idol with Micah's (*Talmud Sanhedrin*, 103b). Given his reputation as idol maker, he is not surprisingly named "father" of King Jeroboam, who made two golden calves for Bethel and Dan (1 Kgs 12:26–33), an even more sinful deed than his (*Sanhedrin*, 101b). Likewise, Rashi reports a tradition (see *Targum Jonathan*) about the prophetic voice in Jer 4:15. Exile will befall Judah because they worshiped the calf in Dan and subordinated themselves to Micah's image in Ephraim.

But at least Micah kept an open house, which earned him credit when the angels stood up against him for judgment before God (*Sanhedrin*, 103b).

If the rabbis were not overly interested in Micah, early and medieval Christian commentators were sufficiently less so as to have virtually nothing to say about him in the main extant sources.

Early Modern and Modern

"In those days there was no king in Israel and every man did what was right in his own eyes" (17:6; cf. 18:1, 19:1, 21:25). The narrator's comment frequently appears in defenses of ordered and stable government. Lutheran Martin Chemnitz (1522–86), in his *Loci Theologici* (1591), is very specific: the problem in those days was Micah's idolatry. Since a ruler's first concern is for his subjects' religion, government officials must support and protect churches and schools as they endeavor to instruct the people in true doctrine and worship (viii.2 [II, 400]).

A century later, Puritan Samuel Slater (d. 1704) preached on the duty of magistrates "for the suppressing of profaneness." This was a matter of urgency necessitating coercion, otherwise "sad and doleful experience hath made it evident to the world, that hell will immediately break loose, the flood-gates of wickedness will be all drawn up, and an inundation of the blackest villanies will follow and drown a land." In Judges in those days, he notes, every man did what was right in his own eyes; "and you need not doubt but a great deal of that was wrong and odious in God's eyes" (1690 [487–8]).

Reflecting just prior to World War II on "every man's doing right in his own eyes," Jewish scholar Martin Buber (1878–1965) reads Judges as a book of opposing political declarations (*Kingship of God*, 1936 [77–8]). Chapters 17–21 form a "monarchical book," set against the staunchly theocratic, anti-monarchical book of judges (chs 1–16). The "theocratic chronicle" tells of ever-returning periods of cultic defection and political weakness, but also finds in the loose political structure "a sufficient security for internal order, and in the 'judges' dependable and superior guardians." The pro-monarchical chapters try to rectify this picture with two counterexamples (lying outside the chronological sequence) showing "what a mischief and outrage the famed kinglessness had produced." The comment framing chapters 17–21, that there was no king and every man did right in his own eyes, was a slogan of the anti-theocratic party. It meant plainly: "That which you pass off as theocracy has become anarchy," and "Only since this people, as is fitting for human beings, took unto itself a human being for a king, has it known order and civilization."

Perhaps the heyday of Micah's story in the Protestant Christian tradition comes with its popularity in the seventeenth century as grist to the mill in controversies with Roman Catholics over sound worship, notably the legitimacy of images in churches.

Already in the late sixteenth century, the Leyden professor of theology Jacobus Arminius (1560–1609) draws from the story in a public disputation on the use of images (of Mary, the saints, the Last Supper, relics, etc.) in churches and worship. He denies the distinction made by the "papists" (exemplified by Jesuit theologian Cardinal Bellarmine) between an idol, the likeness of something false, and a religious image, the likeness of something real. Biblical examples show, he argues, that this distinction does not hold. He includes Micah's image, called an idol, yet set up to Jehovah (Judg 17:4, 18:31). Arminius concludes sarcastically that the distinction, purely an invention of the human brain, "is itself the vainest idol, nay one of the veriest of idols" (1588 [Disputation xxiii, 651–6]).

Joseph Hall (1574–1656), moderate Calvinist, finds idolatry in the story even before images are mentioned: the god of Micah's mother was silver itself, "ere it did put on the fashion of an image"; otherwise, "she had not so much cursed to lose it, if it had not too much possessed in the keeping." Micah stole out of wantonness, not necessity, since his mother was rich. And he was beggarly towards the needy Levite: "He that could bestow eleven hundred shekels upon his puppets, can afford but ten to his priest; so hath he at once a rich idol, and a beggarly priest." Hall scorns, too, the Danites for stealing from Micah a god which could be stolen and not look after itself, which could be won by theft and not devotion! As for Micah after the Levite's arrival, despite a glimpse of his error in appointing his son priest, he still could not see the faults of his ephod and images. "The carnal heart pleases itself with an outward formality, and so delights to flatter itself, as that it thinks if one circumstance be right, nothing can be amiss." Hall's conclusion draws on imagery of fire and plague very real to his own times: "Thus the wild-fire of idolatry," previously confined to Micah's private house, "now flies furiously through all the tribe of Dan, who, like the thieves that have carried away plaguy clothes, have insensibly infected themselves and their posterity to death. Heresy and superstition have small beginnings, dangerous proceedings, pernicious conclusions" (*Contemplations*, 1615 [x.6, 137–9]).

John Milton (1608–74) sums up the Protestant view: "Idolatry means making or owning an idol for religious purposes, or worshipping it, whether it be a representation of the true God or of some false god." Referring to Micah's behavior, he concludes: "the worship of the true God in the form of an idol is accounted no less grave a sin than the worship of devils" (*Christian Doctrine*, c.1658–60 [ii.5.24, 690–2]).

While the argument over images was directed at actual practices of Christian worship, the language of idolatry lent itself to other controversies of religion and politics, inseparable in seventeenth-century England. Puritan William Gurnall (1616–79), in his still-popular *Christian in Complete Armour* (1655–62), uses the metaphor to speak politically under cover of ambiguity. Reflecting on the Christian struggle to keep Christ on the throne of one's life and to shun the powers and principalities of this world (Eph 6:12), he asks his reader, who claims Christ as prince, "Whose law dost thou freely subject thyself unto?" All too readily, he suspects, his reader-courtier yields himself to do the pleasure of the other prince. "Alas, for thee, thou art under the power of Satan, tied by a chain stronger than brass or iron; thou lovest thy lust. . . . If Christ should come to take thee from thy lusts, thou wouldst whine after them, as Micah after his gods" (ii.2 [95]).

Very different is the self-deprecating and appropriately ironic adoption of Micah's lament for his stolen gods by Richard Baxter (1615–91). In *The Saints' Everlasting Rest* (1650), initiated during a serious illness while a chaplain to Cromwell's New Model Army in 1647, he ruminates on desire as an affection to be excited in heavenly contemplation: "O the incomprehensible glory! O the transcendent beauty! O blessed souls that now enjoy it! When I am so far distant from my God, wonder not what aileth me if I now complain: an ignorant Micah will do so for his idol, and shall not my soul do so for the living God?" (ch. 14.2.2).

Baxter, who tried to steer a middle path, suffered under the Restoration of Charles II, spending two years in prison at age 70. Milton, of more combative temperament, was another person drastically affected, not least because of his reply to a book, *Eikon basilike*, which appeared in 1649 just after Charles I's execution, purporting to be the king's account of his "solitudes and sufferings" at the hands of Parliament. Micah's Levite comes to Milton's aid. Charles's complaint that he lacked his chaplains in prison draws a scathing response. "A chaplain is a thing so diminutive, and inconsiderable, that how he should come heer among matters of so great concernment, to take such room up in the Discourses of a Prince, if it be not wonderd, is to be smil'd at. . . . Yet heer he makes more Lamentation for the want of his Chaplains, then superstitious Micah did to the Danites, who had tak'n away his houshold Priest." Micah took as great a care that his priest be "Mosaical" as the king that his be "Apostolical"; but both were mistaken, since priests were not to officiate in household devotions, and kings were allowed to offer public prayer (so David, Solomon, and Jehoshaphat). The scorn grows withering: "What aild this King then that he could not chew his own Mattins . . . ? Yet is it like he could not pray at home, who can heer publish a whole Prayer-book of his own, and signifies in some part of this Chapter, almost as good a mind to be a Priest himself, as Micah had to let his Son be." Doubtless, says Milton, there was some other matter in it, making him so desirous to have about him his chaplains, "who were not onely the contrivers, but very oft the instruments also of his designes" (*Eikonoklastes*, 1649, ch. 24).

A century later, another great writer, Deist critic Voltaire (1694–1778), turns Micah's story against those using Scripture to enforce orthodoxy. With typical irony he adduces the text not as a dire warning against idolatry but as "incontestable proof" of "extensive toleration and liberty of conscience allowed among the Jews." Tongue in cheek, he simply recounts how Micah made images, hired the Levite, and cried, "Now I know that the Lord will do me good!" The words others normally took to show that Micah (mistakenly) believed his worship legitimate, Voltaire claims at face value as scriptural validation of just such unorthodox belief. "And what is more remarkable," he adds to cap the case, "Jonathan, the grandson of Moses, was a priest of the temple, wherein the God of Israel and the idol of Micah were both worshipped at the same time" (*Treatise on Toleration*, 1763, ch. 12). Indeed, he remarks elsewhere, Micah and his mother fell into precisely the same sin as Aaron and the Israelites in the wilderness (Exodus 32, *re* the golden calf) "without the God of Israel paying it the least attention" (*Bible enfin expliquée*, 1776 [147–50]). As for the Danites, he has only scorn, describing them as pillagers, thieves, and ravagers; and he mocks the "chaplain" for blessing them. But by now his point has shifted from praise of tolerance to condemnation of the quality and instability of early Israelite religion (*Un Chrétien contre six Juifs*, 1776 [524]; see also Ages, "Voltaire's Critical Notes," 1963, 192–4).

The necessity of orthodoxy, however, is exactly the message many English-speaking readers in the eighteenth and nineteenth centuries draw from Micah's story. Right worship is now less a defining issue of religious and political struggle (Protestant versus Catholic or Anglican versus Puritan) than a matter of well-being, whether that of the state, the internal condition of a religious community, or, increasingly with the onset of the Romantic age, the individual's right relation with God – that is, a matter of personal piety.

Neglect of "the worship of the true God as prescribed in the law" was the main cause of disorder and misery in newly independent America. That was the view of the Rev. Samuel Langdon (1723–97), earlier president of Harvard, and a New Hampshire state delegate in 1788 when he preached on "The Republic of the Israelites an Example to the American States." Langdon offers Micah and the Danites (along with Gideon and his ephod) as prime examples of what befalls those who fail to maintain prescribed religious practice – wrongly believing, as they did, "that all kinds of religion came much to the same thing, and whether precisely agreeable to the command or not, would be acceptable, if they were sincere" [p. 954].

The difference between outward forms of religion and true "inward" religion concerns the American revivalist, later president of Oberlin College, Charles Grandison Finney (1792–1875). In his *Lectures on Revival* (1835), Finney remarks how reluctantly people give up outward forms. Change comes by degrees. "Now, how came people to suppose a minister must have a gown or a wig, in order to preach with effect? . . . How is it that not one of these things has been given up in the Churches, without producing a shock among them?" But in fact they have been given up, one by one, to the distraction, for a time, of many congregations. People felt they could not worship God without them. "And when these things were taken away, they complained, as Micah did: 'Ye have taken away my gods'" (Lecture 14).

In England, Esther Hewlett (1786–1851) draws a message about core religion, for youth. A woman of strong Nonconformist (Baptist) convictions, she warns that while conscientious obedience to divine commands uniformly tends to advance holiness, "additions to what is prescribed, or willful neglect of what is enjoined us, as uniformly tend to idolatry on the one hand, or utter profaneness and contempt of religion on the other." She wonders whether the Levite was not paid his tithes regularly, but suspects he preferred a wandering life, away from priestly supervision. Between them, Micah and the Levite were mightily satisfied with their efforts and expected God's blessing. "Alas! how binding and besotting are sin and idolatry! and how important the injunction, —'Little children, keep yourselves from idols!'" The story's moral: "Let us ever beware of turning from the express commands of scripture, either to the right or the left;—for we 'see how great a matter a little fire kindleth'" (*Scripture History*, 1828, 4–9).

The Rev. M. Officer (1823–74) would have agreed. As a missionary in Africa, he attempted to persuade a West African chief that rather than adding "a few items of the Christian faith and practice" to his religion, "a medley of religious creeds and forms," he should receive Christianity entire. "But he argued that such a course would be manifestly unwise, since by receiving only the one, he would be confined to the excellencies of one, while by accepting them all, he would secure their combined virtues." Sadly, it reminded Office of Micah's "senseless and idolatrous scheme: but this instance shows how easily men are led astray in the matters of religion" (*African Bible Pictures*, 1859, 63–5).

Indeed, the story shows how a low moral and spiritual condition can easily lead to practices of "an idolatrous tendancy" corrupting worship and betraying God (*Sunny Sabbaths*, c.1870, 129–32). And since the priest appears to Moses' grandson, the account also supplies a melancholy illustration that true piety is not a hereditary quality. Still, parental influence can be both a powerful restraint and a mighty agency. "Let Christian parents not cease to instruct, exhort, and warn the children, and train them up in the way wherein they should go" (PLATE 8.1).

It is the soul's craving for God that ultimately matters, not the adequacy of the priesthood, writes another Baptist, preacher and evangelist F. B. Meyer (1847–1929). From Judg 17:10 ("Dwell with me, and be unto me . . . a priest") he draws two lessons. First, "men crave for a priest," and we should beware of any religion attempting to eliminate this office. Such attempts "reduce the worship of God to a system of high-thinking, but fail to deal with man's

PLATE 8.1   Micah and the Danites: *Sunny Sabbaths*, c.1860. (See p. 238)

consciousness of sin, and his yearning for a settled basis of peace." Second, "human priests must ultimately fail." God has put them aside, "setting up the priesthood of the blessed Lord." Moving then to 18:24 ("Ye have taken away my gods"): "whatever can be taken from us has the mark and signature of man upon it" and cannot supply "the immortal cravings of the soul which, having come from God, craves for God" (*Our Daily Homily*, I, 1898 [227–8]).

Other readers have drawn direct comparisons between Micah's relationship to the Levite priest and the social situations of clergy in more recent times. Hard to match is a piece penned by politician and historian T. B. Macaulay (1800–59), drawing on John Eachard's satire (1670) on the chaplain in a late seventeenth-century English country house.

> The coarse and ignorant squire, who thought that it belonged to his dignity to have grace said every day at his table by an ecclesiastic in full canonicals, found means to reconcile dignity with economy. A young Levite—such was the phrase then in use—might be had for his board, a small garret, and ten pounds a year, and might not only perform his own professional functions, might not only be the most patient of butts and of listeners, might not only be always ready in fine weather for bowls, and in rainy weather for shovel-board, but might also save the expense of a gardener or of a groom. Sometimes the reverend man nailed up the apricots, and sometimes he curried the coach horses. He cast up the farrier's bills. He walked ten miles with a message or a parcel. He was permitted to dine with the family, but he was expected to content himself with the plainest fare. He might fill himself with the corned beef and the carrots; but as soon as the tarts and cheese-cakes made their appearance, he quitted his seat, and stood aloof till he was summoned to return thanks for the repast, from a great part of which he had been excluded. (*History of England*, 1848, I.iii)

Also in comparative vein, writing on Micah's "bastard church," the Rev. Thomas E. Miller of Dunfermline, Scotland, describes the Levite as a mendicant priest "not of a very high type," who reminds him of former times in Scotland "when the chiefs had their own private chaplains, as poorly paid as this Levite and treated with even less respect." While the Levite was a son to Micah, "in the house of the Scottish nobles the clergyman had to take his place at table 'below the salt' along with dependents, inferiors, and poor relations." The migration of the 600 Danites, on the other hand, recalls the Mayflower pilgrims seeking a home across the Atlantic. Yet, unlike the Danites, they had no warlike purposes, no desire to dispossess anyone; and their vitality and influence stemmed from the religion that dominated their every thought and action. "They did what the Danites failed to do, they rendered obedience to the Ten Commandments and applied the whole Law of Moses to their everyday life." The story of Micah, Miller concludes, is a "sordid story," yet not wholly removed from the contemporary world: "Religious superstition is not dead" (*Portraits*, 1922, 150–5).

Historical criticism, gaining ground in the nineteenth century, encouraged readers to distinguish between the "primitive" cultural practices and religious ideas of the ancient text and the normative customs and values of modern (European) "civilization." To historian Rudolf Kittel (1853–1929), Judges not only reflects "the highly primitive state of things which we otherwise know actually prevailed in that pre-monarchic age," but as a literary work is "completely artless." He takes Micah's story at face value: the narrator's failure to criticize, explicitly, the Danites reflects the moral baseness of the times (*History of the Hebrews*, 1896, [II, 20]). Such scholarly distinctions between ancient and modern culture appear also in books for enquiring lay readers. *The Story of the Bible* (c.1938) discusses Judges 17–18 in a section entitled "Moral standards of the conquerors," by Rev. J. C. Ormerod. Chivalry is absent from the deliverers' method of making war; butchery in cold blood, assassination, treachery, are standard; but the most startling picture of moral standards and practices are in the historically reliable "appendices," and "in Chapters xvii to xix they stagger us by their unrelieved barbarity" (III, 303).

From the late nineteenth century on, historical critics found Judges 17–21 to be composed from two separate sources, though confidence ebbed over attributing these to Pentateuchal sources J and E. Thus in his scholarly commentary (*Judges*, 1895), George F. Moore (1851–1931) is sure that "where the text is redundant and confused it is possible to disengage two strands of narrative," but he admits that there are often "no criteria to determine" which source they belong to; "every attempt at a reconstruction in detail must at best be one of several possibilities."

In his Anchor Bible *Judges* (1975), Robert G. Boling still maintains a two-source theory for chs 17–18, but believes the account to be an editorial "supplement" to the main book. It stems from the "Deuteronomistic Historian" (who fashioned Deuteronomy to Kings), intent on denigrating the northern shrine of Dan in the interests of Jerusalem. Boling reads the text as *implicitly* critical, and to help make the point, spells out Micah's name (Who is like Yahweh?), in his translation: "There was a man of the Ephraimite hill country whose name was Yahweh-the-Incomparable. . . . and his mother took two hundred of silver and gave it to the smith, and he made of it a molten figure. There it was, in the house of Yahweh-the-Incomparable!" (17:1–4). The redactor appears to be saying, "Think of it. Images! And with a name like that!"

Recognition of irony becomes a notable shift in reading strategy. J. Alberto Soggin speaks of redactors' "marked ironical thrusts, even if they are sometimes ambiguous," against the Danite sanctuary" (*Judges*, 1981), while Lillian R. Klein more systematically details the case for a critical and ironic reading

(*Triumph of Irony*, 1989). J. Clinton McCann reads "a comedy of errors." The irony of Micah's name is that "absolutely no one in chapters 17–18 knows what God is like!" Within the space of only five verses, "Micah and his mother have broken at least half of the Ten Commandments." However the story developed, in its present context ("final form"), the behavior of Micah and his mother, not to speak of the "priest-for-hire" and the "might makes right" Danites ("Shut up, or we'll kill you"), is nothing short of "ludicrous." Here culminates the deterioration that began with Gideon. Of course, things will get worse in chapters 19–21, McCann adds, "but the story of Micah and his mother is not a bad way to start" (*Judges*, 2002).

A sense of irony takes E. John Hamlin in a different direction. He notes how similarly to Laish Ezekiel describes Israel: "the land of unwalled villages; . . . the quiet people who dwell securely" (Ezek 38:11). In Ezekiel the people are targets of Gog's, but God will come to their aid. No such divine aid is afforded the Laishites. "Are we to conclude," asks Hamlin, "that what was wrong for Gog was permissible for the Danites?" (*Judges*, 1990).

Hamlin's question is rhetorical. But it may take a reader further along this path. As sometimes noted, the Danite story alludes to the earlier account of Israel's conquest of Canaan. Like Israel in the wilderness, the Danites are still wandering. Their spies recall those sent by Moses (Numbers 13). Their report of a land of plenty recalls the land flowing with milk and honey. Their urging attack on a weak people, on the other hand, contrasts with Moses' spies (except Caleb) urging caution in the face of strength. Joshua, too, sends spies (Joshua 2), who in Jericho treat with "the harlot" Rahab. Like the Levite "priest," she assures the spies: "the Lord has given you the land." And after destroying Jericho, Joshua sends the spies to "the harlot's house" to take her from it. The "silver and gold, and the vessels of bronze and of iron," they take from the city and place in the treasury of "the house of the Lord." And Rahab and her descendants "dwelt in Israel to this day" (Joshua 6). Is the Danite story, then, a parody of the conquest of Canaan? And as we reread the book of Joshua, how can we not think of Laish? Does Judges 17–18, then, subvert the very foundation story of Israel's possession of Canaan?

Hamlin's path takes a parallel track. "Modern Land-Grabbers" is his rubric. "We might find in the Danites a mirror image of the Spanish conquerors of Latin America who 'totally dislodged the Indian culture by eliminating its leaders, destroying its institutions, and subverting its economic infrastructure.'" He cites José Miguez Bonino (*Toward a Christian Political Ethic*, 1983) on the effect of imposing religion, "spiritual 'genocide,'" as an instrument of domination. He concludes: "Similar mirror images could be identified in South Africa, North America, the Philippines, Palestine, and elsewhere."

A Levite of the hill country of Ephraim went to Bethlehem to retrieve his wife (*pelegesh*, secondary wife or "concubine") who had run off to her father's house. On the way back they were given lodging at Benjamite Gibeah (Gabaa) by an Ephraimite living there. During the night, men of the city sought to rape the Levite, who put his woman out for them to assault instead. In the morning he found her apparently dead. He cut her up into 12 pieces which he sent throughout Israel demanding action.

The Israelites gathered at Mizpah (Maspha) and, after the Levite recounted the outrage, agreed to act. Asked to give up the "sons of Belial" of Gibeah for execution, the Benjamites refused and mustered against the rest of Israel. The Israelites consulted the oracle and twice went into battle unsuccessfully, with great loss of life. The third time they fasted and offered sacrifices and were successful. They slaughtered the Benjamites until only 600 men remained.

Suddenly the Israelites realized they had nearly exterminated one of their tribes. Moreover, they had sworn not to give their daughters to the Benjamites. What were they to do to restore the tribe of Benjamin? Well, no one from Jabesh-gilead (Galaad) had aided the Israelites, so the Israelites slaughtered everyone save 400 young virgins. These they gave to the now reconciled Benjamites. But they were still 200 women short. A remedy was found that honored the oath. The young women of Shiloh (Silo) went out to dance in a festival. The Benjamites themselves were instructed to seize them as wives. This they did, and the problem was solved.

While these chapters are not widely discussed by ancient and medieval writers, they clearly raised problems from early on. The rape at Gibeah has elicited universal condemnation of the rapists, but a decidedly mixed response to the actions of the Ephraimite host and the Levite, not to speak of the fate of the Levite's wife. Likewise, the slaughter at Jabesh-gilead and the abduction of the daughters of Shiloh have troubled readers, uncertain whether these are events to emulate or abhor. In all periods, readers have asked why God allowed the Israelites to be first defeated (and slaughtered) in their war against the Benjamites and to wonder at the wisdom (or folly) of the Israelites' vow-making.

Early modern and modern readers have continued to struggle with the violence of Gibeah, Jabesh-gilead, and Shiloh, becoming increasingly inclined to condemn the Israelites, as well as the Gibeahites, for wanton behavior. In the seventeenth and eighteenth centuries, chapter 20 was hotly debated. When is war justified, especially civil war? And what role does religion play in the prosecution of a just war? The question of how the story treats women, always a concern to some, gains ground in the nineteenth and twentieth centuries, as views of women and women's rights were changing. It is voiced most strongly by feminist critics in the late twentieth century, one of whom dubbed the narrative one of the Bible's "texts of terror."

Like Micah's story, the events of Judges 19–21 are often set early in the Judges' period (see on Micah).

Ancient and Medieval

The rape at Gibeah

At the story's heart is an unnamed woman. Understanding her has partly depended upon which text is read. In English, the dominant King James Version (KJV) of 1611, following the popular Geneva Bible, translates the Hebrew, "his concubine played the whore against him, and went away from him." But the Latin Vulgate, the medieval Church's Bible, terms her the Levite's "wife" (*uxor*) and reads simply, "she left him (*reliquit*)" and returned. That matches an ancient Greek text (LXX[B]), "she left him (*eporeuthe ap'autou*)" and went away. Another Greek text (LXX^A), however, has "she was angry with him (*orgisthe*)" and went away, similar to both the ancient Aramaic Targum, where the woman "despises" or "scorns" the Levite, and Josephus's *Antiquities of the Jews*, where the couple are at odds because she did not return his affection. "At last, the woman was so disgusted at these quarrels, that she left (*katalipousa*) her husband, and went to her parents"(v.137 (2.8)).

In classical Jewish sources, the rabbis generally fault the husband's harsh nature. Unbearable treatment led his wife to run away, teaching that "one must not attempt to overawe the members of his family," for this man's severity led to bloodshed, unchastity, and desecration of the Sabbath (*Gittin* 6b; *Targum Judges* 19.2).

The parallels between Gibeah and Sodom (Genesis 19) have struck many readers over the centuries. To Jewish scholar Ramban (1194–1270), the latter attains a higher degree of evil. The men of Sodom, everyone from every quarter, sought to stop people coming among them; whereas the "wicked ones" of Gibeah were certain "rulers and strong men" ("masters [*ba'aley*] of Gibeah," Judg 20:5) steeped in immorality, and though desiring sex with the wayfarer were satisfied with the woman. Because they were rulers, others did not protest (on Genesis, *Vayeira* 19:8).

Three main problems have troubled readers: first, the men of Gibeah desire to rape the male guest; second, the householder offers his daughter and the woman to be raped instead; third, the Levite (or the householder) actually puts the woman outside for the men.

Jewish historian Josephus (c.37–c.100 CE) removes all mention of homosexual rape by making the concubine the original object of the men's lust – they saw her in the market place and "admired her comeliness." The householder, obliged to protect his guests, offered his daughter only when threatened with death. While he implored the men to commit no iniquity, they (not he or the Levite) seized the desired woman and carried her off "to sate their lewdness all night long." Finally, "outworn," she returned and, "out of grief at what she had endured and not daring for shame to face her husband" – since she thought he would be inconsolable at her fate – "she succumbed and gave up the ghost." Her husband, meanwhile, supposing her in a deep sleep and "suspecting nothing serious" tries to awake her "with intent to console her by recalling how she had not voluntarily surrendered herself to her abusers." Only when finding her to be dead is he "chastened before the enormity of the wrong," though how chastened, exactly, Josephus does not tell us (*Antiquities*, v.143–9 (2.8)).

Another ancient Jewish writer, known as Pseudo-Philo, deals with the problems more radically. He simply has the men entering the house by force and dragging out both Levite and concubine but then "casting off" him before abusing her. Her death is not a problem: she had transgressed against her man once by committing sin with the Amalekites, whence God delivered into sinners' hands (*Biblical Antiquities*, 45.3). Why the Amalekites is not clear, though it fits with the author's evident aversion to intermarriage with foreigners.

Ramban, centuries later, argues that the householder offered his daughter knowing they would not want her or harm her, which is why they refused to listen and, with the concubine in their grasp, ceased molesting him. As for the concubine's disposal, Ramban notes the male guest's priority (for both host and guest!) and the woman's lacking "the status of a man's wife." Besides, he continues, she had already played the harlot against him (on Genesis, Vayeira 19:8).

Among early and medieval Christian writers the story is hardly a favorite, though they occasionally comment. No account of Gibeah would be complete without a glimpse of the woman at the threshold, as seen by Ambrose (c.339–97), bishop of Milan: "Overcome by this cruelty or by grief at her wrong, she fell at the door of their host where her husband had entered, and gave up the ghost, with the last effort of her life guarding the feelings of a good wife so as to preserve for her husband at least her mortal remains" (*Duties of the Clergy*, iii.xix.114).

Franciscan Nicholas of Lyra (c.1270–1349), in a literal reading, notes that the Hebrew text describes the woman as "playing the harlot" and suggests that either her husband sent her away or she left with another man, which in no way excuses the rape or the host's putting her out to the mob. The moral lesson: reason should rule sensuality, just as husband should rule wife. Allegorically, the Levite seeking out his wife represents God seeking out the Jews after they worshiped other gods (i.e. "fornicated"). Typologically (and remarkably), the woman's suffering prefigures the sufferings of the apostles and saints; and just as her fate was broadcast throughout Israel, so should that of the martyrs be broadcast throughout the church, encouraging the faithful (*Postilla litteralis*, 1471–2, on Judges).

A century later, Denis the Carthusian (1402–71) defends the Vulgate: the woman was angry on account of some "excess" of her husband. Nor would she have dared to return to her own father's house "with a lover in tow." Moreover, the host and Levite are culpable: if committing a venial sin to preserve someone else from a mortal sin is wrong, how much more is it wrong to "expose someone else to adultery or rape" (on Judges; cited in Thompson, *Writing the Wrongs*, 2001, 204–5; see pp. 179–221 for further discussion through the Reformation).

The Benjamite war

The Israelites responded "as one man" to the Levite's story, gathered by the thousands against Gibeah, and demanded that the Benjamites give up the men of Gibeah to be put to death. Josephus, however, stressing the importance of law to Jews, reports a more measured response. While the people were sorely moved by the tale of violence and "impatient to rush to arms," the elders urged them "not so hurriedly to make war on their brethren," but to act lawfully by sending an embassy and attempting to bring the "supposed evildoers" to repentance (cf. Deut 20:10). So a delegation was sent, "in obedience to the law," but the Gibeahites scorned to bow out of fear, and the other Benjamites joined in the (mistaken) belief "they were repelling aggressors" (v.150–4 (2.9)).

A common question about the Benjamite war concerns the initial Israelite setbacks. What had they done to warrant defeat? In Pseudo-Philo, when the priest Phineas asks this question of God, the deity tells a parable about a lion who neglects to guard other animals' young but creates uproar over one small incident. That is, Micah's graven images led all astray, "and you were silent like that wicked lion." Now, on seeing how this woman of "wicked deeds" died, everyone is disturbed and wants God to hand over Benjamites. "And now I have destroyed you, who were silent then. And so I will take my revenge on all who have acted wickedly" (*Antiquities*, 47:7–8; so also *Pirke deRabbi Eliezer*, 38; cf. *Sanhedrin*, 103b; Rashi on Hos 10:10; Ramban on Genesis, Vayeira 19:8).

Ramban, however, criticizes the specific actions taken. Benjamin should have judged its "constituents," and Israel failed to consult with Benjamin before issuing demands (cf. also Rashi, on Hos 10:10). Both parties deserved punishment. Asking God who should go first (Judg 20:18) shows that Israel had already decided on war and was simply settling a contentious detail. So God answered – saying Judah is always first – without actually granting permission for the battle. Yet neither did he forbid them, since the Benjamites merited punishment. Hence, left to "natural circumstances," the courageous Benjamites defending their own cities won against the combined tribes trusting purely in their own strength. But not content to drive their opponents from Gibeah, Benjamin instead slaughtered too many and compounded its error. Now realizing their own mistake, the Israelites sought divine permission, but failed to ask whether they would win, thus showing them still relying on superior numbers. Hence another defeat; permission to fight did not guarantee victory. Finally they decreed a fast, as required by law, offering burnt offerings to atone for their self-reliance and peace offerings as thanks for having escaped the sword. Now they could fight and win. Despite Benjamin's near annihilation, Ramban finds a silver lining: namely, a measure of equity in the punishment of the two groups. He calculates the slaughter at some 40,000 each, including men, women, and children (*Vayeira* 19:8).

The Benjamite massacre elicits various responses. For church leader and theologian Ambrose (c.339–97), the slaughter is of scant concern. What matters is that 40,000 drew the sword against their brethren "in their desire to avenge the wrong done to modesty, for they would not endure the violation of chastity." As for their reverses, "they disregarded the sorrow the avenging of chastity cost them. They rushed into the battle ready to wash out with their own blood the stains of the crime that had been committed" (*Duties of the Clergy*, iii.xix.116). Much later, Nicholas of Lyra will find more to question. The slaughter of the women of Benjamin is "deplorable," the more so since God did not prescribe it (*Postilla litteralis*).

The aftermath

Chastity concerned the rabbis also. The massacre at Jabesh-gilead raised its own special question: How were the spared women determined to be virgins? "They made them sit upon the mouth of a wine-cask. [Through anyone who had] had previous intercourse, the odour penetrated; through a virgin, its odour did not penetrate." But this was the wrong test; they should have passed before the priest's font-plate! (*B. Talmud Yebamot*, 60b). As for the slain inhabitants, *Pirke de Rabbi Eleazar* (38) views death as just punishment for refusing the national call to arms. Denis the Carthusian, however, considers at least the children innocent; and no doubt many women were displeased by the Gibeah crime. Still, he agrees with Rabbi Eleazar: punishing the men through their wives and children was appropriate. In any case, those innocent children and displeased women would not have gone to hell (on Judges; see Thompson, *Writing the Wrongs*, 205).

Nor are too many tears shed for the raped women of Shiloh. Ambrose is sure the Shiloh expedient gave "fitting punishment for the violation, since [the Benjamite men] were only allowed to enter on a union by a rape, and not through the sacrament of marriage. And indeed it was right that they who had broken another's intercourse should themselves lose their marriage rites" (*Duties of the Clergy*, iii.xix.110). Of the women, he has nothing to say.

Like Rabbi Eleazar, Athanasius of Alexandria (c.296–373), Ambrose's older contemporary, sees the benefit to the nation as a whole. He has in mind the Christian community. In a circular letter of 339 to fellow ministers, after being ejected by Arian opponents, he writes of the Levite's sending out his wife's body parts to show that such injury extended to all alike. So all came together, as if themselves the sufferers, and destroyed the perpetrators. Since the story is well known, he need not rehearse the details. The important point is that it relates "to our present circumstances," even worse than those of old; on comparing them, his readers will be filled with "greater indignation." Then, but a single woman was injured and one Levite wronged. "Now the whole Church is injured, the priesthood insulted, and worst of all, piety is persecuted by impiety." Then, the tribes were astounded at the woman's body; now "the members of the whole Church are seen divided from one another, and are sent abroad" bringing word of the injustices suffered. So let all lend their aid, urges Athanasius, that God may speedily amend what is amiss and the Church be avenged on her enemies (*Circular Letter*). The daughters of Shiloh have disappeared in the interests of the great cause.

For Rashi, however, the daughters are not so easily subsumed but retain their tangibility. Tradition has it that Saul was one of the Benjamites told to get a wife by capturing one of them (21:21); but shy by nature, he had not the courage to approach the dancing maidens. One, however, attracted by his beauty, pursued him so that he should capture her (Rashi on 1 Sam. 20:30). And so the problem of the rape is solved. Nicholas of Lyra adopts a similar solution: the plan was justifiable, and the abducted virgins "probably" consented to marry before they were "known" by their captors. So, really, there was no problem (*Postilla litteralis*).

Early Modern and Modern

The rape at Gibeah

This was a time "when there was no king in Israel" (19:1), echoing 18:1 and matched in turn by the the the story's closing lines: "In those days there was no king in Israel; every man did what was right in his own eyes" (21:25). Readers have often found in this framing the story's theme: absence of sound government descends into anarchy.

Writing of magistrates in his *Institutes of Christian Religion* (1550), Protestant Reformer John Calvin (1509–64) claims general assent for the principle, "no government can be happily established unless piety is the first concern." Scripture praises kings who restored proper worship or took care that religion flourished unblemished. The opposite condition is anarchy, and "the Sacred History places anarchies among things evil: because there was no king in Israel, each man did as he pleased [Judg. 21:25]" (IV.20.9).

The threat of war and anarchy was never far away in seventeenth-century England. Around 1628, a young English cleric, Robert Gomersall (1602–c.1646), shared his aversion to the prospect of civil war in his "poetical meditations" upon Judges 19 and 20 (*The Levite's Revenge*, 1628).

> They had no King: as well the fools as wise
> Did all what did seem right in their own Eyes.

And Sodom's crime seemed right to some: to see
When every man will his own monarch be,
When all subjection is ta'en quite away,
And the same man does govern and obey. . . .

A century and a half on, Rev. Samuel Langdon (1723–97) preached on this text to the Massachusetts Bay Colony Congress (1775): "And now we cannot wonder if courts of justice ceased when the higher powers of government were wanting. These courts, which should have been continued in every walled city, dwindled away and came to nothing; crimes were unpunished, and the most abominable vices spread their infection through all ranks." In the case of the Levite there is evidently no judicial system, and no national authority to which recourse could be had. The Levite was obliged to take drastic steps in order "to excite the indignation of the other tribes" ("The Republic of the Israelites an Example to the American States" [953]).

Across the Atlantic in that same age of revolution, Anglican educator Mrs Trimmer (1741–1810) also draws a lesson about the benefits of sound and stable government. Clearly the excellent form of government ordained by Moses, at God's command, was disregarded. The stories showed what ill effects came from want of a regular settled government, "when there was no king in Israel, and every man did that which was right in his own eyes." This was God's way of teaching people "to feel the sad effects of their presumption and self-dependance." How thankful, then, should those be who live in a kingdom blessed with laws and a good king and magistrates to execute them. In such a case, let people not indulge a wish to do everything they think right in their own eyes; "lest, enticed by faction, impelled by mistaken zeal, or hurried on by tumultuous passions," they subvert religion and the peace of society, and provoke God's judgments. "War with a foreign enemy is a great evil, but lawless riot and intestine division are productive of the greatest misfortunes that can happen to any country, of which may we never be even spectators!" (*Sacred History*, 1783 [xlviii, 208–11]).

As the nineteenth century wears on, evangelist F. B. Meyer (1847–1929) finds in these opening words a different resonance. This "terrible chapter" shows "the depths of depravity to which man may sink apart from the grace of God. Where Christ is not enthroned as King, drunkenness, impurity, cruelty, selfishness, are supreme, and pursue their ravages unchecked" (*Our Daily Homily*, I, 1898 [229]).

The ancient argument about what the woman did and who was to blame continued. In 1644, Puritan John Milton (1608–74) picked up this debate while defining fornication in connection with divorce (Matt 19:9). He cites Grotius

(*Annotationes*, 97), as saying that in Scripture fornication means "such a continual headstrong behavior, as tends to plain contempt of the husband," adducing as proof Judg 19:2, "where the Levites wife is said to have playd the whoor against him; which Josephus, and the Septuagint, with the Chaldaean [Targum] interpret only of stubbornnes and rebellion against her husband." Milton adds that Kimchi and other rabbis agree: had it been "whoordom," reasons Ben Gersom, a Jew and Levite would have disdained to fetch her back. Indeed, Milton contributes, she would not have run to her father's house, "it being so infamous for an hebrew woman to play the harlot, and so opprobrious to the parents." Fornication in this text, then, means stubborn disobedience against the husband, not adultery (*Doctrine and Discipline of Divorce*, 1644 [ii.18, 335–6]; see also *Christian Doctrine*, c.1658–60 [i.10.45, 378]).

For others, the matter is more straightforward – fornication is fornication. With Tyndale's Old Testament (Joshua to 2 Chronicles, 1537), the Hebrew text of 19:2 enters English Bibles in the form, "which concubine played the whore in his house," and the possibility of taking "whoring" metaphorically (as frequently in the Bible) is largely overlooked. So for Joseph Hall (1574–1656) the downward progression at the story's outset was simple: "The law of God allowed the Levite a wife; human connivance, a concubine. . . . She, whom ill custom had of a wife made a concubine, is now, by her lust, of a concubine made a harlot" (*Contemplations*, 1615 [x.11, 139–40]). Esther Hewlett (1786–1851), like Mrs Trimmer writing for youth, sees it as simply as Hall, but noticeably tempers her language: "The subordinate wife of a Levite near mount Ephraim, having been guilty of infidelity, went from him," and stayed in her father's house. "The Levite, retaining a strong affection for her, and probably having received some intimation of her penitence, followed her, and spoke kindly to her; a reconciliation was effected" (*Scripture History*, 1828, 9–10).

Usually commentators view the father's welcome of the Levite with approbation. Some are less than overjoyed at his errant daughter's reception. Joseph Hall is puzzled. If the penalty for adultery (reading the Hebrew and English texts) was death, why was she only dismissed. And "why would her father suffer his house to be defiled with an adulteress, though out of his own loins?" At least Hall can appreciate the "good nature" of the Levite whose exercise of mercy is a credit to his Levitical status. Besides, if he were to wait for her to importune him before taking her back, "half the thanks were lost"; better to make a voluntary offer of favor, and she is obliged forever (*Contemplations*, 1615 [x.11, 140]).

The Rev. Thomas Lye (1621–84), however, is not puzzled. He is outraged. The Puritan preacher's theme is "That the indulgence of parents is the bane of children, a pander of their wickedness, the asylum of their vanity," and the object of his vast scorn is the luckless father. As he puts it, "When the looseness of youth knows where to find pity and toleration, what mischief can it forbear?" Where else to flee but "to her own dear father's house," where no doubt he'll open his heart to her. Well, home she speeds, but does her good old father receive her? Does he suffer his house to become a brothel-house, to be defiled with an adulteress? "Methinks I hear him in a just indignation thus accosting her: 'Why, how now, impudence? what makest thou here? Dost thou think to find my house a shelter for thy sins? The stews are a fitter receptacle for thee. Whilst thou wert a faithful wife to thy husband, thou wert a beloved daughter to me: but now thou art neither. . . . Get thee home, therefore, to thy husband.'" Her husband's forgiveness craved and his love redeemed by modesty and obedience, then "my doors shall not be shut." In the mean time, "'know, I can be no father to a harlot.' Thus methinks I should have heard him say."

Lye interweaves his own voice with the biblical character's voice, reminding us of Hall's common resort to the interior monologue or soliloquy in order to lay out interpretive choices. Here, however, Lye cleverly uses irony to prejudice the decision from the start. His reader is left little choice but to construe the father's reception as indulgence, though the text explicitly makes no such judgment. Now he embarks on an extended simile comparing, in a *tour de force* of gender reversal, the father's welcome to Jael's reception of Sisera: "'Turn in, my dear child, turn in to me.' He brings her into his house; covers her with a mantle; instead of water, gives her 'a bottle of milk'; yea, he 'brings forth butter in a lordly dish'; treats her at the kindest rate, and that for four whole months." But remember that this courting Jael proved a most fatal executioner! Who knows, had the concubine's father been more severe, "he might have prevented her fate." Indulgence is a syren, that first sings and then slays; "worse than Jael: her hammer and nail destroy only the body; but this destroys the soul, and that even by its lullabies, when the unhappy fondling sleeps and snores in the parent's bosom" (1682, "What May Gracious Parents Best Do . . . ?," [168–9]).

A century later and Anglican vicar and pioneer novelist Laurence Sterne (1713–68), in "The Levite and his Concubine," develops this rhetoric into a yet more complex dialogue of voices – preacher, commentators (implicit and personified), and character. His end is the opposite of Lye's, a plea not for rash judgment and censure, but for careful and courteous inquiry. He blesses those, like the Levite, who would practise mercy, and embraces the father's rejoicing. He starts with the woman leaving: "—Then shame and grief go with her, and whereever she seeks a shelter, may the hand of justice shut the door against her. —Not so; for she went unto her father's house in Beth-lehem-Judah, and was with him four whole months.—Blessed interval for meditation upon the fickleness and vanity of this world and it's pleasures!" He turns to the Levite: "I see the holy man upon his knees,—with hands compressed to his bosom, and with uplifted eyes, thanking heaven, that the object which had so long shared his affections, was fled." But then he interposes, "The text gives a different picture of his situation" and recites the Levite's journey and warm reception. "A most sentimental group! you'll say: and so it is, my good commentator, the world talks of every thing: give but the outlines of a story, —let *spleen* or *prudery* snatch the pencil, and they will finish it with so many hard strokes, and with so dirty a colouring, that *candour* and *courtesy* will sit in torture as they look at it." Soon, however, he begs leave to stop "and give the story of the Levite and his Concubine a second hearing: like all others much of it depends upon the telling; and as the Scripture has left us no kind of comment upon it, 'tis a story on which the heart cannot be at a loss for what to say, or the imagination for what to suppose—the danger is, humanity may say too much" (*Sermons of Mr Yorick*, 1766 [167–8]).

Taking Sterne as his linchpin, Stephen Prickett (*Origins of Narrative*, 1996, ch. 3) has argued that the rise of the novel in eighteenth-century England influenced readers to treat biblical narrative with the same attention to the motives and feelings of characters as they would any secular novel, with the proviso that Scripture recounted the ways of human characters and God not as fiction or conjecture but as reality. His case for an intimate connection is well made, but he underestimates how much earlier such reading had its roots, at least as far back as Joseph Hall – who, incidentally, was widely read in the eighteenth and nineteenth centuries.

The Levite's refusal to lodge in Jebus (Jerusalem) because it was a city of foreigners is an irony often eliciting comment. Alas, laments Esther Hewlett, that in Gibeah, an Israelite city, there should be found "inhumanity and unfeeling disregard" to a brother in need, "which would have disgraced, which probably would not have been experienced, in the heathen city they had just passed" (*Scripture History*, 1828, 10). It is the subsequent rape at Gibeah, however, that dominates discussion.

"Gibeah was a second Sodom," avers Joseph Hall (cf. Ramban, above). "These villains had learned both the actions and the language of the Sodomites: one unclean devil was the prompter to both; and this honest Ephraimite had learned of righteous Lot, both to entreat and to proffer." Yet Lot fared better than the Levite: "there the guests were angels, here a sinful man; there the guests saved the host, here the host could not save the guest from brutish violence; those Sodomites were stricken with outward blindness, and defeated; these Benjamites are only blinded with lust, and prevail" (*Contemplations*, 1615 [xi.1, 142]).

In a different age, Deist critic Voltaire (1694–1778) uses the "extraordinary" resemblance between the two stories to throw doubt on the Bible's veracity and morality. He invokes English philosopher Lord Bolingbroke:

He said that it was almost pardonable for epicurean Greeks, perfumed youth, to abandon themselves in a moment of debauchery to most condemnable excess which, in mature age, one would regard with horror; but he contends that it is hardly possible that a married priest, who would consequently have a large beard as do Orientals and Jews, arriving from a distance on his ass accompanied by his wife, and covered in dust, could inspire a whole town to lewd desires.

There is nothing, so Bolingbroke, in the most revolting stories of all Antiquity, that resembles such an unlikely act of infamy.

Voltaire will not let it go at that. While the Sodomites refused Lot's daughters, the Gibeahites gratified their brutish passion on the priest's wife, to the point of her dying. "It is to be presumed that they beat her after having dishonored her, at least that this woman did not die of an excess of shame and indignation, which she must have felt, for there is no example of a woman who died on the spot from an excess of intercourse" (*Bible enfin expliquée*, 1776 [151]).

As already observed, this episode's readers have been troubled by the facts that the initial object of rape is a man, the daughter and visitor's wife are offered as replacements, and the latter is actually thrown to the pack.

On the Levite's treatment of the woman, the usually compassionate Joseph Hall hardly falters in his enthusiasm for the man's noble character. The trump card is hatred of "unnatural wickedness." As Hall sees it, "if he had not loved her dearly, he had never sought her so far, after so foul a sin; yet now his hate of that unnatural wickedness overcame his love to her; she is exposed to the furious lust of ruffians, and, which he misdoubteth, abused to death." And the woman's death turns out to be no problem after all, for the Almighty Judge is always just. Having not suffered for her sin ("because she smarted not"), she is called by God to reckoning and punished with her own sin. "She had voluntarily exposed herself to lust, now is exposed forcibly. Adultery was her sin; adultery was her death." Hall is struck by the irony (*Contemplations*, 1615 [xi.1, 142]).

A century later, Thomas Morgan (d. 1743), sees likewise. It is plain the woman before her elopement had been "a common Whore," and he wonders how the couple behaved themselves to "raise such a Mob about them." Her ravishers simply gave her "too much of what she had liked but too well before" (*Moral Philosopher*, 1737 [276]). And this view of her fate as retribution continues well into the nineteenth century in the long-lived commentary of Thomas Scott (1747–1821), who makes clear, in a forgiving sort of way, that God's justice was displayed even by the men's enormous wickedness. "Adultery was punishable by death: this woman having committed adultery, was about to escape; but in this dreadful manner her iniquity found her out, and she was punished in kind; yet this by no means implies that she did not repent and find mercy" (*Holy Bible*, 1788–92). Others, if not overly concerned about the woman, could not so easily condone the Levite's action: "that was also a grave sin that he turned her over to their lewd desires, for which as punishment he had to bear her loss," though he did thereby spare the old man's daughter (J. S. Bach, *Calov Bible*, col. 1338 [fac. 91]).

Two writers for youth clearly have a problem. Mrs Trimmer passes over the whole scene ("many outrages committed") in order to arrive expeditiously at the outcome, the "most cruel murder of the Levite's wife" (*Sacred History*, 1783 [xlviii, 209]). Several decades later, Esther Hewlett provides both a clue to the homosexual rape ("instigated by the vilest dispositions") but also a decoy ("and probably enraged with the old man for exercising that hospitality which they had withheld") in explaining why the men of the city "demanded that the traveller should be given up to their fury." Avoiding the question of agency, she concludes, "He [the Levite] was preserved from their designs, but the unhappy wife became their victim: —being cruelly abused by them, she expired before morning-light" (*Scripture History*, 1828, 10). John Kitto (1804–54), a learned and popular commentator, recounts simply that the house was besieged "after the same fashion and for the same purpose, as that of Lot had been, when he entertained the angels in Sodom," and that "as a last resource, the Levite, in the hope of diverting them from their abominable purpose, put forth his wife into the street," where she was "grievously maltreated by this vile people" (*Bible History*, 1841 [194]). For Kitto, the threat of homosexual rape understandably determines the Levite's action.

The women's movement leader Elizabeth Cady Stanton (1815–1902) is not interested in excuses. The woman's "fate was terrible and repulsive," she says bluntly. "There are many instances in the Old Testament where women have been thrown to the mob, like a bone to dogs, to pacify their passions; and women suffer to-day from these lessons of contempt, taught in a book so revered by the people" (*Woman's Bible*, 1898, II, 16).

The campaign for women's rights was having its effect. A few decades later, Scottish minister Thomas E. Miller is typically unwilling to exonerate the Levite: "sad to say, the Levite, to save his own skin, was coward enough to sacrifice his concubine." Miller finds it strange that the sacred historian fails to condemn the dastardly act. "We must, therefore, infer that at this period in ancient Israel women had no rights—that their position was even worse than it is in heathen countries to-day." And if the Levite felt remorse on finding the body, stronger was his passion for revenge, a sentiment Miller holds in no high regard (*Portraits*, 1922, 162). "The low view regarding women shocks the modern reader," writes Congregationalist professor J. C. Ormerod in *The Story of the Bible* (c.1938). The Levite callously drives out his concubine "simply in fulfilment of the law of self-preservation." And it is not the deed of corporate lust that demands punishment, "but the violation of the law of property in women, and of the obligation of hospitality." To top it off, the measures the Levite takes to initiate punishment, cutting up and despatching the woman's corpse, "horrify us by their savagery" ("Religion and Ethics," 303).

The Levite's method of summoning an assembly has often occasioned some remark. "Himself puts on cruelty to the dead, that he might draw them to a just revenge of her death," Hall observes. "Actions notoriously villanous, may justly countenance an extraordinary means of prosecution" (*Contemplations*, 1615). "A method shocking to humanity," says Langdon, but necessary to provoke action in the absence of regular national authority ("The republic of the Israelites," 1788). A "strange expedient" as Trimmer puts it (*Sacred History*, 1873). "A rather mysterious custom" employed by "a man of obviously peculiar character," writes Kitto (*Bible History*, 1841).

The action is sometimes compared to Saul's summoning of the tribes to battle by cutting up and sending out pieces of oxen (1 Sam 11:7). For his part, Miller also draws attention to "the practice in the highlands of Scotland in sending round the fiery cross dipped in blood, to summon the various clans to battle" (*Portraits*, 1922). And we all know where that practice ended up.

If Mrs Trimmer had a problem writing about the woman's rape and dismemberment, the more so did Bible illustrators in picturing it. The usual solution was to do as she did and pass it over.

There are, of course, notable exceptions, from as early as an unusual thirteenth-century French picture book in the Pierpont Morgan Library (see Cockerell, *Old Testament Miniatures*), which never shrinks from gruesome details (PLATE 9.1d). The influential series in Pieter Mortier's (1661–1711) great print Bible of 1700 also includes a scene, but, unlike the French picture where entrails spill from the severed corpse of a woman, Mortier's designer, O. Elgers, depicts a curiously empty, almost bloodless carcass, of uncertain gender. It is as though he has dared the picture, but shied away from the fundamental detail, that this is a man chopping up his wife (PLATE 9.1e).

The rape scene itself is equally avoided, though again not entirely. A 1683 Dutch edition of Josephus shows the woman being dragged violently from the house, mouth agape, vainly gesturing back. Her husband (or the servant) clings to her robe, but is pushed back by an assailant, while another raises a club to beat him. This detail accords with Josephus, who has it that the woman was

---

PLATE 9.1   The Levite and his wife: (a) Dutch *Antiquities*, 1682; (b) Clarke's *Compleat History*, 1737; (c) Harper's *Illuminated Bible*, 1846; (d) Medieval picture-book; (e) Elgers, 1700. (See pp. 256, 258)

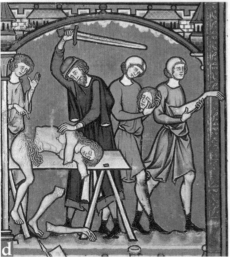

from the beginning the object of the men's lust. A torch-bearer lights the scene and beckons the rapists to follow as they carry her off to their homes, as Josephus tells it (PLATE 9.1a).

More often, though still infrequently, the woman lies at the door, hands on the threshold. Her husband has opened the door and is gazing with surprise or grief, or both. Behind him is usually the old host. Sometimes a donkey is being readied. Such a scene appears in Laurence Clarke's *Compleat History of the Holy Bible*, 1737 (PLATE 9.1b). Artist and engraver Caspar Luyken (1672–1708) shows the Levite trying to lift the woman, the old man behind with hands raised in horror, and a lad with a donkey awaiting the burden. The Levite looks at the boy, perhaps for help, but the boy is transfixed by the woman (PLATE 9.2b) (*Historiae Celebriores*, 1708). The threshold scene gains favor in the nineteenth century, perhaps influenced by the painting of French artist Auguste Couder (1790–1873), now in the Louvre (reproduced in Shaw Sparrow, *Old Testament in Art*, 1906, and Clifton Harby, *Bible in Art*, 1936). Light picks out the Levite's dramatic gestures and appalled gaze, and also finds the head, bare shoulder, and arms of the woman at his feet. What these pictures mask is the husband's complicity in the woman's death and his words, "Get up, let us be going!" Couder's painting focuses on the man's grief, while the woman's pose, more fashionably languid than awkwardly dying, helps not at all. A freely rendered (and less languid) version appears in an 1835 French edition of Fontaine's *Histoire*, a German Bible of the time, and in America in Harper's extravagant *Illuminated Bible* of 1846 (PLATE 9.1c). Another French artist, Gabriel Guay (b.1848), a pupil of the orientalizing Jean-Léon Gérome, shows the kneeling husband clutching his head, distraught, and with the other arm ensuring that his well-fleshed wife is posed suitably as an odalisque (*Le Lévite d'Ephraim*, 1884, now in Grenoble). This painting appeared for English viewers in Charles F. Horne's *The Bible and its Story*, originally issued as a serial with numerous reproductions of paintings and engravings (1908–9).

At the century's turn, yet another Frenchman, (Jacques) James Tissot (1830–1902), illustrated a complete Old Testament in English (1904). He devotes several scenes to Judges 19–21, including "The Levite's Wife Dies at the Door." She lies alone on the cobble stones, eyes open, staring or dead. Another scene borrows from a painting of "The Levite and his Dead Wife," by Jean-Jacques Henner (1829–1905), which won a Medal of Honor at the 1898 Salon.

Henner depicts the woman supine and naked on a slab, her body deathly white against surrounding darkness. Behind her, merging into the gloom, the Levite broods. One critic sees here the artist brooding over the fate of his native

PLATE 9.2   The Levite and his wife: (a) Rembrandt, 1645; (b) Luyken, 1708. (See pp. 258, 260)

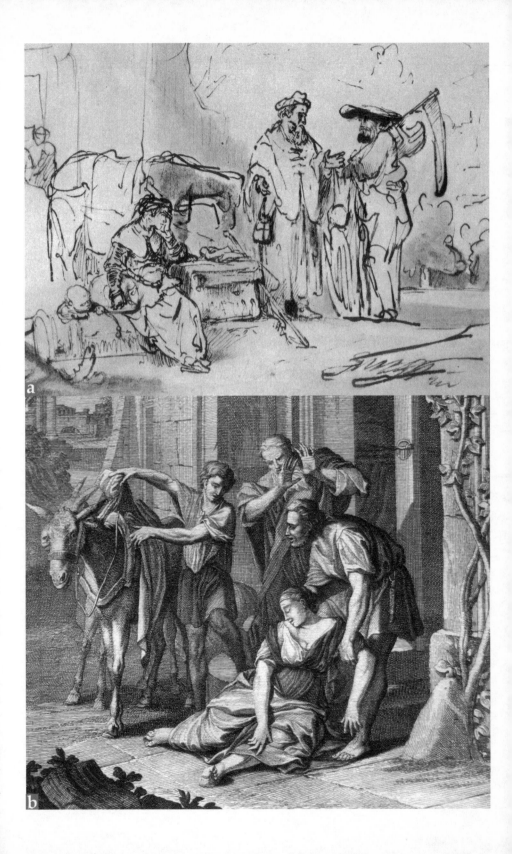

Alsace-Lorraine, lost to France after the Franco–Prussian War (1870–1). In the Levite's loss and desire for retribution, the artist saw "a parallel with the feelings of those whose homeland was dismembered" (R. Mühlberger, *Bible in Art*, 1991, 115). The woman has become, then, a cipher for national politics. Tissot's version is both more mundane (no dramatic lighting) and more brutal. Now the Levite stands between viewer and laid-out body, an apron pulled around his waist, like a butcher. He leans on the table, head bent forward, the fingers of his right hand resting just an inch from a long butcher's knife. A shallow bowl comes into focus in the foreground (PLATE 9.3a, p. 268).

Tissot also shows the woman sitting glumly in the Gibeah square, while the old man invites the Levite. Again she stares, ignoring their conversation. The painting may owe a debt to a 1645 drawing (pen and wash), by Rembrandt (1606–69), now in the British Museum. While the Levite and the Ephraimite talk, the woman sits wearily resting her head against her hand, elbow propped on a large trunk. A toddler peers over the valise on which she sits. The talking men, the tired woman lost in her thoughts, the luggage, and the child are all part of an ordinary world. It would be a touching scene by itself. But Rembrandt has framed it with a textual world that lies outside it. For the viewer who knows what is to come, this is probably the most awful picture of all (PLATE 9.2a).

The Benjamite war

Seventeenth-century English commentators often reflect directly on contemporary politics. Robert Gomersall sharply edges with irony the rape's consequence (*The Levite's Revenge*, 1628) (PLATE 9.3c, p. 268). Voicing the contrived eloquence with which the messenger sent to Judah delivers his missive, Gomersall sardonically narrates:

> But he that unto princely Judah went,
> Carrying the head of the dismembered corse,
> With such a voice which sorrow had made hoarse,
> (Lest he should rave too highly) thus begins!
> "Is there an heaven? and can there be such sins?
> Stands the earth still? . . ."

Whereupon, after many passionate words, the people of Judah themselves fall into a passion. Like a raging river, that sweeps all before it, "Such was the people's fury. They're so hot / That they will punish what we credit not, / And be as speedy as severe. . . ."

There follows, however, a counterpoint to the strains of war. Some elders would urge caution against a rush to judgment, some "Who loathed the bloody accents of the drum—/ Who thought no mischiefs of that foulness are, / But that they gain excuse, compared with war, / And war with brethren. . . ." Stay, says one, "and be advised before you be undone." He counters furious haste by conjuring war's realities – neglect, insecurity, destruction, death, and rape: "Are then your sisters, daughters, wives too chaste?" He responds to critics of restraint – "Do I excuse them then to please the time, / And only make an 'error' of a crime? / Am I sin's advocate?" – with sarcasm: "Far be't from me / To think so ill of war as sodomy!" But yes, he calls the crime "sodomy," since that was the intent. He has reached a crux:

> But whose intent? O pardon me, there be
> Benjamites spotless of that Infamy.
> Shall these be joined in punishment? a sin
> You'd war against? O do not then begin
> To act a greater, as if you would see
> Whether injustice equaled luxury!

The poem ends with a recognition of its whimsy, that:

> Kings might put up their swords,
> And every quarrel might conclude in words:
> One conference would root out all debate
> And they might then most love, who now most hate,
> The most sworn foes: for show me, where is he
> Would seek revenge without an injury?

With civil war but a few short years away, these lines have, in hindsight, a kind of sad prescience. A decade or so later and Gomersall's vision of restraining voices among the Israelites is a vain echo from the past. England has enjoyed its Civil War as the Israelites had enjoyed theirs in Judges.

In the war's aftermath, John Milton appeals to Judges 19–21 in very different vein. In January 1649, following Charles I's execution, a book appeared purporting to be the king's memoir (*Eikon Basilike*). Its success in portraying a royal martyr prompted Parliament to ban it and commission a rebuttal by Milton. *Eikonoklastes* appeared within months. Ten years later, on the eve of the Restoration, Milton's own book was burned by the public hangman; Milton was imprisoned and narrowly escaped execution.

Charles charges that Parliament's undue severity exacerbated the Irish Rebellion and deserved a curse such as Jacob's upon Simeon and Levi (Gen

49:7) for slaughtering the Shechemites in retaliation for their sister Dinah's rape (Genesis 34). Milton finds the king little concerned for those who had lost fathers, brothers, wives, and children through the rebels' cruelty and deems retaliation not, as the king supposes, "unevangelical." His trump card is Judges 19–21: "Did not all Israel doe as much against the Benjamits for one Rape committed by a few, and defended by the whole Tribe? and did they not the same to Jabesh Gilead for not assisting them in that revenge?" (*Eikonoklastes*, ch. 13).

Milton here draws on established Puritan argument on just war and holy war, going back at least to the sermon, "Of war" by Henry Bullinger (1504–75), required reading for Elizabethan clergy. It extends standard Augustinian just war theory to include the magistrate's duty "to make war upon men which are incurable, whom the very judgment of the Lord condemneth and biddeth to kill without pity or mercy." Like Moses against the Midianites and Joshua against the Amalekites, the Benjamite war is of the sort properly waged against those who, rejecting all justice and equity, stubbornly "persist in their naughtiness." Such were the Benjaminites. "Such are at this day those arrogant and seditious rebels which trouble commonweals and kingdoms" (*Fiftie Godlie and Learned Sermons*, 1577).

Within two years, Milton was again Parliament's apologist, against another defense of Charles I (Salmasius, *Defensio Regia*), funded by his heir. Milton returns to just war and Judges 20–1. Assailing Charles as wholly accountable for the Civil War's bloodshed and destruction of families, he defends both the restraint of the magistrates and people against the king's provocations and their eventual prosecution of the war, "civil" though it be.

> What teachings of law or religion ever instructed men to consider their own ease and the saving of money or blood or life more important than meeting the enemy? Does it matter whether the enemy be foreign or domestic? Either one threatens the state with the same bitter and ruinous destruction. All Israel saw that without much shedding of blood she could not avenge the outrage and murder of the Levite's wife; did they think that for this reason they must hold their peace, avoid civil war however fierce, or allow the death of a single poor woman to go unpunished? (*Defence of the People of England*, 1651, ch. 5)

That the death of "a single poor woman" not go unpunished is hard to gainsay. Gomersall turned the crime broadly to "sodomy"; Milton focuses sharply on a wife's murder. Yet place Milton's argument in Gomersall's poem, against the voices of restraint, and it is less compelling. At issue in the argument is proportion. At issue in the reading of the biblical text is tone. Gomersall is reading a text that satirizes prejudice and excess, Milton a text that maps civil behavior.

The Benjamite war was in vogue during another civil war, which became the American War of Independence (1775–83). Like Milton, the text's users mostly took it at face value, without allowing that its tone might be sardonic. The only question was, Who were the Israelites and who the Benjamites?

In Pennsylvania in 1775, on a July fast-day appointed by the Continental Congress, Baptist minister David Jones (1736–1820) preached that war was a legitimate Christian course of action in defense of freedom against tyranny. All would not be easy, but "let us not be discouraged; for so it was with Israel in their first battles with Benjamin, but in the third battle the whole tribe of Benjamin is cut off, save six hundred men" (*Defensive War in a Just Cause Sinless*, 1775). Several years later, a treatise dedicated to General Washington (possibly by Captain Stephen Case (1746–94)) appealed to the Bible to show "the approven duty of defensive arms against oppressing rulers." Not only did the Israelites under Gideon rightfully avenge themselves against Midianite cruelty, they were morally justified in waging war against Benjamin, since "there is a command [Deut 13:12, 15] to punish every city of party, making apostacy unto idolatry"; and "if people are to bring to condign punishment idolatrous apostates, much more ought they to resist all tyrants, seeking to destroy all religion and liberty, for they are twins. Where the spirit of the Lord is, there is liberty. As I said before, destroy the one and the other cannot live" (*Defensive Arms Vindicated*, 1779 [763]).

But the story has another side. Across the Atlantic, a clergyman friend of John Wesley, John Fletcher (1729–85), states the matter plainly: the colonists are in the wrong and God is not on their side (*Bible and the Sword*, 1776). Fletcher affirms a royal proclamation for a fast throughout England, seeking pardon for sins and imploring God's intervention to deliver "our loyal subjects" [p. 569]. The fasts in the colonies were much mocked, but Fletcher urges that the field of national prayer not be left to "our revolted colonies." His warrant is another "bloody civil war," against Benjamin [pp. 570–1]. For it was after the Israelites fasted and offered sacrifices that they were successful. He draws an analogy.

"Certain sons of Belial, belonging to the city of Boston, beset a ship in the night, overpowered the crew, and feloniously destroyed her rich cargo." On being informed, the government was justly incensed against the rioters and requested the unjust city to make up the loss "or deliver up the sons of Belial who had so audaciously broken the laws of the land." But instead of pressuring the inhabitants of Boston to act justly, the other colonists "gathered themselves together unto Boston to go out to battle against the sons of Great-Britain," an act of felony and high treason.

God did not forbid the Israelites to use force against their obstinate brethren and even offered directions for the battle. To be sure, there were grievous losses at first, "But alas! the righteousness of a cause, and the divine approbation, do not always ensure success to those who fight in the cause of virtue." Then came the weeping and fasting before the Lord and thereupon victory.

> And the few Benjamites that escaped the edge of the vindictive sword, lamented the obstinacy, with which their infatuated tribe had taken up arms for the sons of Belial, who had beset the house, in the inhospitable city of Gibeah. And so will the revolted colonies one day bemoan the perverseness, with which their infatuated leaders have made them fight for the sons of Belial, who beset the ship in the inhospitable harbour of Boston. [p. 571]

The story shows, says the preacher, that "the most bloody civil war is preferable to the horrible consequences of daring anarchy." Yet he ends by soliciting regard in their fasting and praying also for his audience's "American brethren" [p. 577]. Many of these, after all, "have been deceived by the plausible and lying speeches of some of their leaders." Or, seized by "the epidemical fever of wild patriotism," they are unaware of its dreadful consequences and "already repent of their rashness." In its concern for individual culpability, it is an argument that would appeal to the naysayer of Gomersall's poem.

John Fletcher's address of 1776 was fashioned in the thick of conflict. The war and the loss of the colonies to Britain took place in the years just prior to Sarah Trimmer's publication of her *Sacred History*. She makes no direct allusion to the struggle and the acrimonious rhetoric it generated (and by which it was generated!). She reads the Benjamite story like Milton, as a textual guide to civic behavior, but with Gomersall's unease regarding the question of disproportion. That disquiet leads her distinctly away from the sharp lines drawn by the Puritan to a very Anglican "middle way": "In the war between the Benjamites and the other tribes, great losses were sustained on both sides; neither party had any reason to hope for the protection and assistance of GOD, and they were made instruments of punishment to each other" (xlviii, 210).

The meaning of the initial Israelite defeats is a recurring topic. That a just cause does not necessarily bring easy victory is generally agreed. There is also assent to viewing the setbacks as punishment. Some commentators reach back centuries for support. Thomas Scott notes that "some Jewish writers observe, with great justice, that it was their failure to punish the idolatry of the Danites while being so zealous to punish the lewdness of the Benjamites that brought these disasters upon them" (*Holy Bible*, 1788–92). Nicolas Fontaine (1625–1709), as usual, draws his lessson from the Fathers (cf. Ambrose). They have "admired the Depths of God's Judgments in this History": while "never was there a War more holily undertaken," the initial defeats show God's wish to teach us how pure we need to be if we undertake to punish the faults of others (*History*, 1670/90). Commonly accepted is that the initial defeats and slaughter are deserved since the outcome is in God's hands, and God only acts justly.

Martin Luther (1483–1546) returns to this text several times to argue that princes should not trust in their own power and reason; God will not suffer it. "The children of Benjamin slew forty-two thousand [*sic*] Israelites because the latter relied on their own strength" (cf. Ramban, above). Perhaps this is why the bloodthirsty Julius II is now so prominent – because France, the Germans, and Venice relied upon themselves (*To the Christian Nobility of the German Nation*, 1520 [124–5]). Writing of the war against the Turks, he urges that Emperor and princes remember Israel's initial defeats, "despite the fact that God bade them fight and that they had the best of right." Their boldness and presumption were their downfall. It is true that, if possible, one should have horses and men and weapons and everything needed for battle, so that one does not tempt God. But having them, one must not be bold lest God be forgotten or despised, since it is written (1 Macc 3:19), "All victory comes from heaven" (*On War Against the Turks*, 1529 [191]).

Joseph Hall, too, conveys Ramban's argument. The Israelites miscarried because God was against them. They fought in a holy quarrel, but with confidence in themselves. Presuming victory, they asked God not about their success but "who should be their captain." The moral: "even good zeal cannot bear out presumption"; and "victory lies not in the cause, but in the God that owns it." For their part, the Benjamites begin to think that God is on their side: "Those swords, which had been taught the way into forty thousand bodies of their brethren, cannot fear a new encounter." Finally, in fasting, weeping, and sacrifice, the Israelites make good and ravage their foes. Hall restates the moral: "It is seldom seen, but that which we do with fear prospereth; whereas confidence in undertaking, lays even good endeavors in the dust" (*Contemplations*, 1615 [xi.2, 143]).

On the other hand, among those seeking human agency in the success of the Benjamites against huge odds is John Kitto, who supposes that the tribe's reputation for "indomitable courage" had an effect on the other Israelites, as did their "peculiar skill in the use of the sling" (*Bible History*, 1841 [195]).

Readers often accept the slaughter of the Benjamites as a necessary consequence of the war. Some, however, approve of it as just punishment, while others attack it as overreaction or senseless revenge.

For seventeenth-century Puritan preacher Elias Pledger, stark justice characterizes the episode. Benjamin is the exemplar of the sinner whose sin has finally caught up with him. "O the horror and amazement they were struck withal, when they could not stand before the face of the tribes which were before them, and they saw their city all on a flame behind them! O, said they, "Now is evil come upon us"; and "they were trodden down as dirt" ("Of the Cause of Inward Trouble," 1661 [315]). But Thomas Scott, a century later, is adamant that "this indiscriminate slaughter cannot be vindicated; for none but Canaanites, and *idolatrous* cities in Israel, were to be thus punished." The people acted too hastily, but the Lord allowed it as an "awful example to future ages of his vengeance against those who commit, and those who countenance and protect others in such abominations" (*Holy Bible*, 1788–92). For Voltaire, the only awful example is the story itself. "Listen to this nice adventure," he begins sarcastically. The brutality of the "few Benjamites" at Gibeah (cf. Gomersall's naysayer) should have led to the culprits being punished. "Not at all." The other tribes massacred most of Benjamin. And sarcasm laces the rest of his recounting, the "extermination" of Jabesh-gilead and the seizing of its girls for the Benjamite survivors (*Sermon of the Fifty*, 1762 [15–16]).

Less scathing but still critical, the Rev. H. C. Adams (1817–1899) includes the story among his tales for Sunday reading, *The Judges of Israel* (1866, 85–101). He has a surviving Benjamite, Eliab, admit the offense at Gibeah but assert that punishment was for Benjamin to pursue, not others to dictate. He describes as "the cruelty of man" the merciless slaughter he escaped, the loss of his family and of Azubah, to whom he was to be betrothed that evening. "Mrs. Mason. What a dreadful tale that massacre of the Benjamites is. I scarcely think all history can match it for horror!" Young Clement wonders at the Divine guidance given the Israelites, and George at the intial defeats. Mary cannot think God commanded all the women, innocent children, and cattle killed. "Papa, they had no commandment to do that, had they? Mr. Mason. I do not see that they had." Their conduct, he explains, was faulty. They first failed to ask God whether they should fight at all, they then failed to humble themselves, and finally, though promised victory, they were not instructed to refuse quarter to, much less slay, women, children, and cattle. "In fact, they appear to have acted throughout in a spirit of blind indignation and fury."

Thomas Miller (*Portraits*, 1922, 165) is equally disparaging: "moved by a senseless spirit of revenge, the victors swept over the territory of Benjamin, burning cities and villages and ruthlessly slaying the women and children." Young Mary would have reminded him of the cattle.

The aftermath

Often commentators are content to paraphrase the Benjamite massacre and pass on. So too with the slaughter of Jabesh-gilead, though some take pause at the killing of women and children and the seizure of the 400 virgins. Of more interest is the Israelite's vow and abduction of the daughters of Shiloh.

The Shiloh abduction is often illustrated (until the twentieth century), perhaps in part because its classical parallel, the rape of the Sabine women (Livy, i.9–10), is a familiar subject of artists from the Renaissance onwards. Without a text, viewers might sometimes wonder which ancient rape they were viewing, as with the classical setting by Melchior Küsel (1626–83) in his *Icones Biblicae Veterae* (1679). Here the women seem lost in the design's intricacies and the pleasure of bodies and flowing robes against the sharp lines of the architecture. More often grape vines or a secondary scene of young women dancing help identify the subject, as in the neoclassical tangle of bodies by Julius Schnorr von Carolsfeld (1794–1872) from his famous series of wood-cuts (*Bibel in Bildern*, 1860; *Bible in Pictures*, 1869).

The women's plight is variously depicted. In a 1630 Luther Bible (Lazarus Zetzner, Strassburg) illustrated by Matthäus Merian (1593–1650), much imitated, fear in the faces of a central group spells coercion, while a man and a woman moving in unison into the foreground suggest also compliance (PLATE 9.3d). The illustrator of *Sunny Sabbaths* simplifies for Victorian family viewers Romaijn de Hooghe's complex 1706 design, but retains the patent dismay of waving arms and clutched foreheads ("The Maiden of Shiloh Surprized," PLATE 9.3b). Gustave Doré (1832–83) is another notable illustrator of the scene. His women swoon or gaze heavenwards, as they are dragged or carried off in men's arms from among the broken vines, or thrown atop a camel (*Sainte Bible*, 1866; *Doré Bible Gallery*, 1879). A striking exception to twentieth-century avoidance of the scene is the pen and ink drawing by John Bratby (1928–92) in the *Oxford Illustrated Old Testament*, 1968. He graphically displays the disparity of power: the Shiloh women are naked, the Benjamite men clothed in black armor, their swords drawn (PLATE 9.3e).

The Israelites' decision to deny women to the surviving Benjamite men (21:1), explains Joseph Hall, was a revenge on men deemed "unworthy to receive comfort by that sex to which they had been so cruel." It was a punishment second to death, since the Israelites held marriage and progeny "a very great blessing" (*Contemplations*, 1615 [xi.2, 143–4]).

Puritan Richard Steele (1629–92) is one of few finding a positive lesson. He directs his sermon at "the uncharitable contentions" between the members of the body politic whom he begs to "forbear biting and devouring one another." After all, what if all their present adversaries were ruined and gone, just like the Benjamites, save 600, who were maintaining a bad cause, moreover? In the event, when the Israelites' hot blood was cooled, "they used all their wits and policy to restore that tribe again." Does not that suggest how feelings may change? ("Uncharitable and Dangerous Contentions," 1689 [243–4]).

PLATE 9.3 Aftermath: (a) Levite with dead wife by Tissot, 1904; (b) Daughters of Shiloh, in *Sunny Sabbaths*, c.1860; (c) From Gomersall's *Poems*, 1633; (d) Merian, 1630; (e) Bratby, 1968. (See pp. 260, 267)

Thomas Scott, however, sees nothing positive here. Yes, the Israelites bewailed the consequences of their action, but had they truly repented they would not have behaved as they did to Jabesh-gilead. The heart of the problem was their uncommanded slaughter of the women, "who could not reasonably be supposed to approve the conduct of the men of Gibeah, or refuse to give them up to be punished," and of the children, "who had committed no fault, and ought not to have been put to death for the crimes of their parents." Though this was commanded against the idolatrous Canaanites, the Benjamites were a very different case (*Holy Bible*, 1788–92).

Among the dissatisfied, of course, are the Deists. Voltaire cites Jean Meslier's condemnation of the Jabesh-gilead slaughter and, pretending indignation at this criticism of Scripture, offers in mocking rebuttal a standard argument from Scripture's defenders: "We admit that this expedient for re-establishing the tribe of Benjamin is a singular barbarity; but God did not command it. It is never he who ought to be taken to task for all the crimes which his people commit. This was a time of anarchy" (*Bible enfin expliquée*, 1776 [154]).

Some small measure of disagreement occurs over the vow and the people's dismay before God at Bethel. Joseph Hall is hardly sympathetic: he discerns poor judgment and want of wisdom. "If the oath were not just, why would they take it? and if it were just, why did they recant it? If the act were justifiable, what needed these tears?" Even a just oath may be taken rashly and end in lamentation. It is bad enough in our civil actions to do what we later want to reverse, "but in our affairs with God, to check ourselves too late, and to steep our oaths in tears, is a dangerous folly." They expostulate with God, moreover, as if somehow their predicament were God's fault and not their own (*Contemplations*, 1615 [xi.2, 144]). John Kitto, on the other hand, admits the hasty vow but is more sympathetic: given "the vile propensities exhibited by the people of Gibeah, it was quite natural that in the first excitement such a vow should have been taken" (*Bible History*, 1841 [196]).

Thomas Miller, in the age of psychology, is intrigued by the implications of the vow's binding nature. This takes him in a different direction. "And to-day persons who gamble may be unscrupulous, having no qualms of conscience in defrauding their neighbour, even in starving wife and children, but gambling debts must be paid." That is a curious fact, and we might well try to find what underlies this odd sense of honor and direct it to higher ends. Miller is also intrigued to know how the 400 were distributed: probably they cast lots to determine the prize-winners, or perhaps they allowed the maidens to choose for themselves, a more romantic method. Whatever the case, "it was a simple and novel way of solving the problem" (*Portraits*, 1922, 166–7). So much for the inhabitants of Jabesh-gilead!

For some readers national considerations are paramount. Despite Joseph Hall's deep reservations about Israel's behavior, he opts for the demands of unity, which he interprets in ecclesiastical terms (*Contemplations*, 1615 [xi.2, 144]). "Jabesh-Gilead came not up to aid Israel, therefore all the inhabitants must die. To exempt ourselves, whether out of singularity or stubbornness, from the common actions of the church, when we are lawfully called to them, is an offense worthy of judgment. In the main quarrels of the church, neutrals are punished." Yet, rare among commentators before late modernity, Hall takes offense at the fate of the maidens who "have lost parents, and brethren, and kindred, and now find husbands in lieu of them."

> An enforced marriage was but a miserable comfort for such a loss: like wards, or captives, they are taken, and choose not. These suffice not; their friendly adversaries consult for more upon worse conditions. Into what troublesome and dangerous straits do men thrust themselves, by their unjust or inconsiderate vows!

We now arrive at the final episode, and the end of Judges, the seizure of the daughters of Shiloh.

Martin Luther assumes both the abduction's necessity and the women's compliance. Marriage by force is invalid, he argues, even after consummation, and no different from rape. Yet, persuading the woman to let it pass and stay with the man, as she would have to do in Turkey, is much better, for it now becomes a true marriage through her consent. So the Romans write that their ancestors' wives, robbed from the Sabines, did; so too the maidens of Shiloh – although for a different reason, "for they were not carried off wantonly but out of great need, as the text there states" (*On Marriage Matters*, 1530 [307–8]).

Joseph Hall is again troubled. He owns some conscience on the part of both Israel and the surviving Benjamites, in venturing this remarkable expedient rather than turning to marriage with foreigners (infidels, the heathen). Yet he is disturbed by the nature of these unions: "Stolen marriages are both unnatural and full of hazard; for love, whereof marriage is the knot, cannot be forced; this was rather rape, than wedlock." And to forestall an argument he brings up the dance. Indeed the virgins were dancing, and "How many virgins have lost themselves in dances?"– to be sure, "wanton gestures, and unchasted touches, looks, motions, draw the heart to folly." But this sport at Shiloh was not immodest. Clearly the virgins danced by themselves, else men would have been at hand to rescue them. Finally, having considered the daughters, he moves to the parents who he supposes took their loss heavily. "There cannot be a greater cross than the miscarriage of children: they are not only the living goods, but pieces of their parents; that they should, therefore, be torn from them by violence, is no less injury than the dismembering of their own bodies" (*Contemplations*, 1615 [xi.2, 144–5]).

Facilitating young readers' reflection on Jabesh-gilead's women and Shiloh's daughters was not Mrs Trimmer's interest (*Sacred History*, 1783 [xlviii]). They are passed over in decent silence. As she says in her Preface (vol. I), "Great care is required in selecting for [young persons] such parts of the Sacred Writings as are suited to the progressive improvement of youth; and it was my experience of the inconveniences attending an *indiscriminate use* of the SCRIPTURES, when educating my own children, that first suggested to me the design of [the *Sacred History*]."

Esther Hewlett, on the other hand, offers her young readers a middle way between Hall and Luther, offering just a glimpse of her distaste. Having devised, she recounts, a new expedient to circumvent the vow, "little less exceptionable than the other," the Benjamite men seized every man a wife and carried her home. They relied on reconciliation with her and her parents, helped by the Israelites' intercession. "From such marriages no great happiness was likely to result" (*Scripture History*, 1828, 14). The Rev. H. C. Adams offer some relief, too. Eliab, who had gone to Shiloh under orders and "much against his own will," returned full of joy. Among the maidens, he had discovered his lost Azubah, miraculously delivered from the flames of Aiath. "None disputed the prize with him" (*Judges of Israel*, 1866, 94).

Later, Thomas Miller (*Portraits*, 1922, 168) echoes Luther, as he imagines this "day of excitement": alarm, fear, protest by the daughters. But when they realized what it meant, "the partnership and protection of a husband in exchange for the shelter of their parents' home," no doubt the number of unwilling victims was small. A nagging doubt survives, however – the morality of this scheme. That did not disturb the elders of Israel, if thereby they could keep their religious vow. But it "raises the question of the relation between morality and religion, a question of present-day importance." How often since have church leaders acted on this principle "and sacrificed morality on the altar of religion?" Shiloh's daughters have vanished, more or less willingly, into a debate between religion and morality.

Nonetheless, Miller (p. 160) is clear about the horror of the Gibeah story as a whole, "a sad and gruesome tale," and not so sanguine as to imagine it belonging only to a distant past (even if he chooses not to look too closely at Britain's recent history): "recent events have shown that such brutality and immorality are not yet banished from the world."

We have evidence through official documents that like cruelties and immoralities were practised by the German soldiery upon the innocent people of Belgium. And the Turkish atrocities in Armenia give us a glimpse into a similar inferno, with deeds as cruel and inhuman as those of the lawless youths of Gibeah three thousand years ago.

Recent reception

Historical-critical studies found much of interest besides the moral issues of rape and war. Did the text offer evidence for the history of early Israelite tribal institutions? And what was its history of composition, what "hands" had it passed through? John Edgar McFadyen (1870–1933), of Knox College, Toronto, summed up at the turn of the century. A mainly "early" story has "passed through a very late redaction": Israel's unanimity contrasts with only tribal action elsewhere in Judges; numbers are impossibly high and facts incredible (Benjamin, without loss, decimates a vastly greater army), marks of later exaggeration; the language (e.g. "congregation") is that of the late Priestly document. But the story's "kernel" is old "and of much historic interest and value" (*Messages of the Prophetic and Priestly Historians*, 1901, 125). George F. Moore (1851–1931), of Andover Theological Seminary, agreed about both the "prodigious numbers" and the "singular unity." The latter conveyed more the action of a church assembly (under the "elders of the congregation") than of a nation, and was characteristic of post-exilic material in the Hexateuch (Genesis–Joshua) and Chronicles. As for waging war directed by divine oracle and interspersed with religious exercises, this differs entirely from the judges' wars in the rest of the book. "It is not history, it is not legend, but the theocratic ideal of a scribe who had never handled a more dangerous weapon than an imaginative pen" (*Judges*, 1895, 404, 431).

Nonetheless, the historical "kernel" persisted. McCormick Theological Seminary professor Robert G. Boling (d. 1995) tells us the story "is a rich mine of data on Israel's premonarchical organization, and the most explicit in the book." He cites German scholar Martin Noth, whose theory that the Israelite tribes were organized around a shrine like an ancient Greek "amphictyony" held sway for decades. Noth treated the events "as accurately reflecting a military expedition of the twelve-tribe organization against one of its members, in the clearest narrative depiction we have of Israel in the pre-Davidic days." On the other hand, Noth "failed to grasp the tragicomic vein" in which the narrative of these early events was recast during the Babylonian exile (*Judges*, 1975).

Even as Boling was writing, the claim to a "historical kernel" was being challenged, and by the century's end many agreed that the history of the "Judges period" lacked reliable textual evidence. Boling's characterization of the story in Judges 19–21 as "tragicomic," however, has undergone a different fortune.

In "Guest and Host in Judges 19" (1984), Stuart Lasine, a Jewish literary critic, views the often noticed elements shared with Genesis 19 (Lot at Sodom) and 1 Samuel 11 (Saul rescues Jabesh-gilead) as showing this world in which "every man does what is right in his own eyes" to be an "inverted world," where actions are often "ludicrous, absurd, and self-defeating." The Levite casting out the woman contrasts with the divine guests rescuing Lot. The dismembering of the woman's body ends in a bloody civil war and a massacre at Jabesh-gilead, while Saul's dismembering of the oxen leads to victory over the Ammonites and Jabesh-gilead's deliverance. Moreover, the story's most bizarre features, such as the Levite's "callous behavior toward his concubine and his distorted report to the assembled people," belong to the same design, showing the ludicrous and "topsy-turvy" nature of this world of excessive selfishness. (The irony of the Sodom parallel is further developed by Lillian R. Klein, *Triumph of Irony*, 1989, ch. 9.)

Lasine's interpretation has a tone like Robert Gomersall's seventeenth-century poem. Because the author does not explicitly condemn the Levite's brutality, modern readers should not suppose that his behavior was less offensive to an allegedly unrefined ancient audience. That, argues Lasine, is to miss entirely the author's condemnation by irony and absurd humor (pp. 38–9).

If reading for irony in Judges 19–21 marks one scholarly trend of the late twentieth century, reading "as a woman" marks another (though the two may overlap). Most influential (cf. Jephthah's daughter) is the feminist essay by Phyllis Trible, a Christian literary critic, in *Texts of Terror* (1984, like Lasine's essay). Trible makes the woman central and draws her own reader to confront the story's horror. She also seeks some word of liberation, in part by invoking Christological (redemptive) overtones. Accompanying the essay is a picture of a gravestone for an unnamed woman, "Concubine from Bethlehem." The epitaph reads, "Her body was broken and given to many" (p. 64; cf. Mark 14:24). She sums up how the story "justifies the expansion of violence against women" – who are increasingly betrayed, raped, tortured, murdered, and scattered – to the point where "Israelite males have dismembered the corporate body of Israelite females." Again she invokes the Gospel: "Inasmuch as men have done it unto one of the least of women, they have done it unto many" (pp. 83–4; cf. Matt 25:40).

Trible also calls for readers to speak out about what they read. Historical-critical scholarship – long dominant in academia and concerned with historical kernels, tribal movements, political and military organization, and redactional history – has had little to say about the raped and murdered women. Like many scholars, then, Trible seems unaware to what extent readers through the centuries have been shocked by the woman's story and tried to speak for her. She does so eloquently herself for her own time.

> Truly, to speak for this woman is to interpret against the narrator, plot, other characters, and the biblical tradition because they have shown her neither compassion nor attention. When we direct our hearts to her, what counsel can we take? What word can we speak? What can we, the heirs of Israel, say in the presence of such unrelenting and unredeemed terror?

First is to recognize the story as ours: "misogyny belongs to every age." Violence and vengeance infect the "community of the elect" to this day. "Woman as object is still captured, betrayed, raped, tortured, murdered, dismembered, and scattered." The reader who takes to heart this ancient story will confess: "The story is alive, and all is not well" (pp. 86–7).

Trible reads with Milton, taking the story straight, not with Gomersall and Lasine, reading for irony. Lasine might well have included Trible among his criticized critics. A feminist critic could well respond that reading the woman's treatment through ironic eyes does not necessarily dispense with the horror seen through women's eyes or experience. Even the ironic text, then, not only risks being read straight but also risks unintended hurt. Still, for many recent readers, an ironic reading is indeed one that speaks for the woman, and the women, of Judges 19–21.

If the woman has no voice, neither has she a name. Feminist critic Mieke Bal (like Pseudo-Philo) accords her one, so allowing her "subjectivity" (*Death & Dissymmetry*, 1988, 89). Several feminist critics follow suit, including J. Cheryl Exum, who calls her Bat-shever (daughter of breaking) – "a name that recalls her treatment by the men of Gibeah and her subsequent dismemberment by her husband." The word also refers to interpretation, as in the "breaking of a dream" (Judg 7:15). "Thus the name also signifies the role feminist interpretation plays in breaking open the text's androcentric ideology and exposing the buried and encoded messages it gives to women" ("Whose interests are being served?" 1995, 83–8; cf. *Fragmented Women*, 1993, 176–7).

Exum explores how ideologies, value systems undergirding everyday thought and action, are modified or reinforced by texts, even when not explicitly the text's "message." Bat-shever's crucial action is to return to her father's house, acting autonomously and so, in the narrator's eyes, "playing the harlot." At an ideological level, then, Judges 19 is about "male ownership of women's bodies, control over women's sexuality." This ideology determines the story's shape. In the end, the mob rapes the woman, and her husband dismembers her. That is to say, her sexual "misconduct" (freedom) receives "narrative punishment." Unlike Bat-shever, the host's virgin daughter has committed no sexual offense against male authority. Therefore she is spared. In short, "decoded," the story's message for women is that any claim to sexual autonomy "has horrendous consequences."

Postscript

What shall we think? What shall we say at the conclusion of this book? Shall we, like the pious sons of Noah, go backward with reverence to throw a veil over the nakedness of this selected people of God, chosen to be a kingdom of priests, and an holy nation? shall we palliate, excuse, or cover folly and ingratitude, wickedness and idolatry? No! Let us not endeavour to set aside that characteristic and indubitable mark of the veracity, and more than human spirit, of the holy scriptures: those sacred writings which relate the most extraordinary things done by God himself for this people. . . . (*Holy Bible with Mr Ostervald's Observations*, Newcastle upon Tyne, 1788)

. . . and at the close, in ornate letters, the word "*Finis*," which you were told meant *The End*, although, after wearily reading it through, you did not know whether it was the end of the book or the end of you. (Rev. T. DeWitt Talmage, Introduction to Buel's *The Beautiful Story*, 1887)

Ancient and Medieval

Jewish

The Midrash Rabbah. 1977. Ed. H. Freedman and Maurice Simon, 5 vols. London: Soncino Press.

The Babylonian Talmud, ed. I. Epstein, 35 vols. London: Soncino. Also *The Soncino Talmud* (on CD). Chicago: Davka Corp.

Targum Jonathan of the Former Prophets. 1987. The Aramaic Bible, X, ed. Daniel J. Harrington and Anthony J. Saldarini. Wilmington, Del.: Michael Glazier.

Talmud Yerushalmi. 1982–93. *English: A preliminary translation and explanation*, tr. Jacob Neusner et al., 35 vols. Chicago: University of Chicago Press.

The Zohar. 1931–4. Tr. Henry Sperling and Maurice Simon, 5 vols. London: Soncino.

Alexiou, Margaret, and Peter Dronke. 1971. The Lament of Jephthah's daughter: Themes, traditions, originality. *Studi Medievali* 12/2, 819–63.

Baker, Cynthia. 1989. Pseudo-Philo and the transformation of Jephthah's daughter. In Mieke Bal (ed.), *Anti-Covenant*, Sheffield: Almond Press, 195–209.

Bronner, Leah. 1994. *From Eve to Esther: Rabbinic Reconstructions of Biblical Women.* Louisville, Ky.: Westminster/John Knox.

Brown, Cheryl Anne. 1992. *No Longer Be Silent: First Century Jewish Portraits of Biblical Women.* Louisville Ky.: Westminster/John Knox.

Ginzberg, Louis. 1911/1913/1928. *The Legends of the Jews.* III, IV, VI. Philadelphia: Jewish Publication Society.

HeChasid, Yehudah [Judah ben Samuel]. 1997. *Sefer Chasidim,* tr. Avrah Yaakov Finkel. Northvale, N.J.: Jason Aronson.

Ibn Ezra, Abraham ben Meir. 1986. *The Commentary of Abraham Ibn Ezra on the Pentateuch,* tr. Jay F. Shachter. Hoboken, N.J.: KTAV.

Josephus, Flavius. 1934. *Jewish Antiquities.* Loeb Classical Library. London: Heinemann; New York: Putnam.

Kimchi, David. 1983. *The Commentary of Rabbi David Kimhi on the Book of Judges,* ed. Michael Celniker. Toronto: Celniker Book Committee.

Kimchi, Joseph. 1972. *The Book of the Covenant of Joseph Kimchi,* tr. Frank Talmadge. Toronto: Pontifical Institute of Medieval Studies.

Lauterbach, Jacob Z. [1933] 1961. *Mekilta de-Rabbi Ishmael,* I–II. Philadelphia: Jewish Publication Society.

Maimonides, Moses. 1881–5. *The Guide of the Perplexed of Maimonides,* tr. M. Friedlander. New York: Hebrew Publication Co.

ben Nahman, Moses (Ramban). 1974. *Commentary on the Torah: Genesis.* New York: Shilo Publishing Co.

—— 1974. *Commentary on the Torah: Leviticus.* New York: Shilo Publishing Co.

Pseudo-Philo. 1985. *Liber Antiquitatum Biblicarum.* In James H. Charlesworth (ed.), *The Old Testament Pseudepigrapha,* I, Garden City, N.Y.: Doubleday & Co., 297–377.

—— 1996. *A Commentary on Pseudo-Philo's* Liber Antiquitatum Biblicarum *with Latin Text and English Translation,* by Howard Jacobson. Leiden: E.J. Brill.

Rashi. 1998. *Complete Tanach with Rashi.* (on CD). Chicago: Davka Corp./Judaica Press.

Christian

CCEL = *Christian Classics Ethereal Library* of Grand Rapids, Mich.: www.ccel.org.

ANF = Philip Schaff (ed.), *Ante-Nicene Fathers.* Grand Rapids, Mich.: William B. Eerdmans. Also at CCEL.

N&PNF, 1st ser. = Philip Schaff (ed.), *Nicene and Post-Nicene Fathers,* 1st ser., 14 vols. Grand Rapids, Mich.: William B. Eerdmans. Also at CCEL.

N&PNF, 2nd ser. = Philip Schaff and Henry Wace (eds.), *Nicene and Post-Nicene Fathers,* 2nd ser., 14 vols. Grand Rapids, Mich.: William B. Eerdmans. Also at CCEL.

PG = J. P. Migne (ed.), *Patrologia graeca.* Paris.

PL = J. P. Migne (ed.), *Patrologia latina.* Paris.

Abelard, Peter. *Planctus Israel super Samson* and *Planctus Virginum Israel super Filia Jeptae Galaditae* PL 178.

Alighieri, Dante. 1973. *The Divine Comedy – Purgatorio*. Princeton, N.J.: Princeton University Press.

—— 1975. *The Divine Comedy – Paradiso*. Princeton, N.J.: Princeton University Press.

Ambrose of Milan. On the duties of the clergy. In N&PNF, 2nd ser., vol. 10, 1–89. CCEL.

—— On the holy spirit. In N&PNF, 2nd ser., vol. 10, 91–158. CCEL.

—— On the mysteries. In N&PNF, 2nd ser., vol. 10, 315–25. CCEL.

—— Treatise concerning widows. In N&PNF, 2nd ser., vol. 10, 389–407. CCEL.

—— Epistle XIX (To Vigilius), PL 16.

Ancrene Wisse (Guide for Anchoresses) 1997. New York: Paulist Press.

Anthony of Padua. *Sermo in Purificatione Sanctae Mariae*. PL 85.

Aquinas, Thomas. 1955. *The Summa Theologica of Saint Thomas Aquinas*. Chicago: Encyclopaedia Britannica.

Athanasius of Alexandria. Circular letters. In N&PNF, 2nd ser., vol. 4, 91–6. CCEL.

—— Four discourses against the Arians. In N&PNF, 2nd ser., vol. 4, 303–447. CCEL.

Augustine, Aurelius. 1995. *Sermons*. New York: New City.

—— *The City of God*. In N&PNF, 1st ser., vol. 2, 1–511. CCEL.

—— On original sin. In N&PNF, 1st ser., vol. 3, 237–55. CCEL.

—— *Quaestiones in Heptateuchum*. PL 34.

Cassian, John. Conference of Abbot Paphnutius. In N&PNF, 2nd ser., vol. 11, 319–30. CCEL.

—— Conference of Abbot Theodore. In N&PNF, 2nd ser., vol. 11, 351–61. CCEL.

Chaucer, Geoffrey. 1996. *The Canterbury Tales*, ed. Helen Cooper, 2nd edn. Oxford: Oxford University Press.

Chrysostom, John. Homilies concerning the statues (Homily 14). In N&PNF, 1st ser., vol. 9, 431–8. CCEL.

Clement of Rome. Two letters concerning virginity. In ANF, vol. 10, 229–56. CCEL.

Cyril of Alexandria. *De sanctissima trinitate*. PG 75.

Cyril of Jerusalem. 1955. *Cyril of Jerusalem and Nemesius of Emesa*, ed. William Telfer. Philadelphia: Westminster Press.

East, W. G. 1997. This body of death: Abelard, Heloise and the religious life. In Peter Biller and A. J. Minnis (eds), *Medieval Theology and the Natural Body*, Rochester, N.Y.: York Medieval Press, 43–59.

Ephrem the Syrian. 1989. *Ephrem the Syrian*, ed. Kathleen McVey. New York: Paulist Press.

Fowler, David C. 1976. *The Bible in Early English Literature*. Seattle & London: University of Washington Press.

Geoffrey of Monmouth. 1958. *History of the Kings of Britain*. New York: Dutton.

Henry, Avril. 1987. *Biblia Pauperum: A Facsimile and Edition*. Ithaca, N.Y.: Cornell University Press.

Isidore of Seville. *Quaestiones* [Judg. 8]. PL 83.

Jeffrey, David Lyle, ed. 1992. *A Dictionary of Biblical Tradition in English Literature*. Grand Rapids, Mich.: W.B. Eerdmans.

Jerome. Against Jovinianus. In N&PNF, 2nd ser., vol. 6, 346–416. CCEL.

—— Letter LVIII. (To Paulinus). In N&PNF, 2nd ser., vol. 6, 119–23. CCEL.

—— *Liber Interpretationis*. PL 23.

John of the Cross. 1987. *Ascent of Mount Carmel.* New York: Paulist Press.

Krouse, F. Michael. 1949. *Milton's Samson and the Christian Tradition.* Princeton, N.J.: Princeton University Press.

Lydgate, John. 1924. *Lydgate's Fall of Princes, Part I & II.* London: Oxford University Press.

Maurus, Rabanus. *De Universo.* PL 111.

Maximus of Turin. 1989. Sermon 41. In Boniface Ramsey (ed.), *The Sermons of St. Maximus of Turin,* Ancient Christian Writers 50, New York: Newman, 101–4.

Methodius of Olympus. Banquet of the ten virgins. In *ANF,* vol. 6, 309–55. CCEL.

Moffatt, James. 1923. *The Bible in Scots Literature.* London: Hodder & Stoughton.

Nicholas of Lyra. 1471–2. *Postilla litteralis super totam bibliam.* Rome.

Nilus of Sinai. *Peristeria.* PG 79.

Origen. 1957. *Commentary on Canticle of Canticles,* tr. R. P. Lawson. Westminster, Md.: Newman.

Origen. 1998. *Origen: Homilies on Jeremiah; Homily on 1 Kings 28,* ed. John Clark Smith. Washington, D.C.: Catholic University of America Press.

Thompson, John L. 2001. *Writing the Wrongs: Women of the Old Testament among Biblical Commentators from Philo through the Reformation.* Oxford: Oxford University Press.

Van Loon, Hendrik Willem. 1923. *The Story of the Bible.* New York: Boni & Liveright.

Early Modern and Modern

CCEL = *Christian Classics Ethereal Library,* Grand Rapids, Mich.: www.ccel.org.

—— [1525] 1991. To the Assembly of the Common Peasantry. May 1525. In Michael E. Baylor (ed.), *The Radical Reformation.* Cambridge: Cambridge University Press, ch. 8.

—— [1623] 1997. *The Elizabethan Homilies,* ed. Ian Lancashire. University of Toronto Library (www.library.utoronto.ca/utel/ret/elizhom.html).

—— 1649. *Eikon Basilike, the pourtraicture of His Sacred Majestie in his solitudes and sufferings.* London.

—— 1788. *Holy Bible with Mr Ostervald's Observations.* Newcastle upon Tyne.

—— 1818. *Sacred Biography. Chronologically Arranged.* Bungay: Brightly & Childs.

—— 1833. *Holy Bible with Mr. Ostervald's Observations.* 10th rev. edn. London: J. G. & F. Rivington.

—— 1833. *Scripture Biographical Dictionary.* Philadelphia: American Sunday School Union.

—— 1837. *Calmet's Dictionary.* 6th edn, rev. by Charles Taylor. London.

—— c.1860. *Sunny Sabbaths or Pleasant Pages for Happy Homes.* London: James Hagger.

—— c.1870. *Teacher's Pictorial Bible.* London: Ward, Lock, & Co.

—— 1878. *The Sunday at Home: A Family Magazine for Sabbath Reading.* London: Religious Tract Society.

—— 1911. *Bible Stories and Character Building.* New York: University Society.

—— 1924. *The Great Stories of the Bible*. New York: World Syndicate Co.

—— c.1938. *The Story of the Bible. I: Genesis to Daniel*. London: Fleetway House.

—— 1949. *Cecil B. DeMille's Masterpiece Samson and Delilah*. Paramount Pictures.

—— 1965. *Mighty Samson*, no. 22. Western Publishing Co.

Aberdeen and Temair, marquess and marchioness of [1927] 1937. *Women of the Bible*. London: Lutterworth.

Adams, H. C. 1866. *The Judges of Israel*. London: Frederick Warne & Co.

Ages, Arnold. 1963. Voltaire's critical notes in the Old Testament portion of *La Bible enfin expliquée* (Ph.D. diss. 1963, Ohio State University).

—— 1967. Voltaire and the Old Testament. In *Travaux sur Voltaire et le huitième siècle*, 55, Geneva: Institute et Musée Voltaire.

Aguilar, Grace. [1845] 1880. *Women of Israel*. New York: D. Appleton & Co. (See www.graceaguilar.info.)

Alexander, Archibald. 1928. *Feathers on the Moor*. Garden City, N.Y.: Doubleday, Doran.

Alexander, Cecil F. 1867. Gideon's fleece. In Baynes (ed.), *Illustrated Book of Sacred Poems*, 301–3.

Alter, Robert. 1981. *The Art of Biblical Narrative*. London: George Allen & Unwin.

Amit, Yairah. 1987. Judges 4: its contents and form. *Journal for the Study of the Old Testament* 39, 89–111.

Arminius, James. [1588] 1956. *The Writings of James Arminius*, III. Grand Rapids, Mich.: Baker Book House.

Arndt, Johann. [1605–21] 1979. *True Christianity*. New York: Paulist Press.

Athearn, W. T., ed. 1923. *The Master Library, I: Leaders of Olden Days*. Cleveland: Foundation.

Bach, Johann Sebastian. 1985. *The Calov Bible of J. S. Bach*, ed. Howard H. Cox. Ann Arbor, Mich.: UMI Research Press.

Bal, Mieke. 1987. *Lethal Love*. Bloomington: Indiana University Press.

—— 1988. *Death & Dissymmetry*. Chicago and London: University of Chicago Press.

—— 1988. *Murder and Difference*. Bloomington: Indiana University Press.

Balfour, Clara Lucas. [1847] 1851. *The Women of Scripture*, 3rd edn. London: Houston & Stoneman.

Bankes, Thomas. 1790. *The Christian's New and Complete Family Bible*. London: J. Cooke.

Batten, Loring W. 1918. *Good and Evil: A Study in Biblical Theology*. New York: Fleming H. Revell Co.

Baxter, Richard. [1650] 2001. *The Saints' Everlasting Rest*. CCEL.

Bayle, Pierre. 1697. *Dictionnaire historique et critique*. Rotterdam.

Baynes, Robert, ed. 1867. *The Illustrated Book of Sacred Poems*. London and New York: Cassell, Petter & Galpin.

Beck, Mary E. 1892. *Bible Readings on Bible Women*. London: S. W. Partridge & Co.

Bellarmine, Robert. [1614] 1989. *The Mind's Ascent to God by the Ladder of Created Things*. New York: Paulist Press.

Boettner, Lorraine. 1932. *The Reformed Doctrine of Predestination*. Phillipsburg, N.J.: Presbyterian & Reformed Pub. Co.

Bohn, Babette. 2005. Death, dispassion and the female hero. In Mieke Bal (ed.), *The Artemesia Files*, Chicago: University of Chicago Press.

Boling, Robert G. 1975. *Judges*. Garden City, N.Y.: Doubleday & Co.

Bond, Alvin. 1872. *Young People's Illustrated Bible History*. Norwich, Conn.: H. Bill.

Bone, Florence. c.1915. *The Girls of the Bible*. London: Pilgrim.

Bonino, José Miguez. 1983. *Toward a Christian Political Ethic*. Philadelphia: Fortress.

Boston, Thomas [1737] 2001. *The Crook in the Lot*. CCEL.

Bottigheimer, Ruth B. 1996. *The Bible for Children from the Age of Gutenberg to the Present*. New Haven: Yale University Press.

Brooke, Stopford. 1896. *The Old Testament and Modern Life*. London: Ibister & Co.

Brown, John, Rev. [1769] 1859. *A Dictionary of the Holy Bible*, rev. edn. Glasgow: Blackie.

Browne, Sir Thomas. [1643] 2001. *Religio Medici*. CCEL.

Buber, Martin. [1936] 1967. *Kingship of God*. 3rd edn, tr. Richard Scheimann. London: Allen & Unwin.

——1949. The Song of Deborah. In *The Prophetic Faith*, New York: Macmillan, 8–12.

——1973. *On Zion: The History of an Idea*. New York: Schocken Books.

Buchanan, George. [1540] 1966. *Jephthé ou, le voeu*. In Donald Stone (ed.), *Four Renaissance Tragedies*, Cambridge: Cambridge University Press.

Buel, J. W. [1887] 1889. *The Beautiful Story*. Richmond, Va.: B. F. Johnson & Co.

Bullinger, Henry. 1577. *Fiftie Godlie and Learned Sermons*. London: Ralph Newberie.

Bunyan, John. [1678] 2001. *The Pilgrim's Progress*. CCEL.

——[1666] 1999. *Grace Abounding to the Chief of Sinners*. CCEL.

Burney, C. F., Rev. 1918. *The Book of Judges*. London: Rivington.

Byron, G. G., Lord. 1905. *The Poetical Works of Lord Byron*. London: John Murray.

Calvin, Jean. [1549] 1948. *Commentary on Hebrews*. Grand Rapids, Mich.: William B. Eerdmans.

——[1550] 1960. *Institutes of the Christian Religion*, I–II. Philadelphia: Westminster.

——[1551] 1950. *Commentaries on the Twelve Minor Prophets*, III. Grand Rapids, Mich.: William B. Eerdmans.

——[1556] 1948. *Commentaries on the Epistles to Timothy, Titus, and Philemon*. Grand Rapids, Mich.: William B. Eerdmans.

——[1559] 1950. *Commentaries on the Book of the Prophet Jeremiah and the Lamentations*, IV. Grand Rapids, Mich.: William B. Eerdmans.

——[1563] 1948. *Commentaries on the Four Last Books of Moses*. Grand Rapids, Mich.: William B. Eerdmans.

——[1565] 1948. *Commentaries on the First Twenty Chapters of the Book of the Prophet Ezekiel*. Grand Rapids, Mich.: William B. Eerdmans.

Camp, Claudia V. 2000. *Wise, Strange and Holy: The Strange Woman and the Making of the Bible*. Sheffield: Sheffield Academic Press.

——and Carole R. Fontaine. 1990. The words of the wise and their riddles. In Susan Niditch (ed.), *Text and Tradition*, Atlanta, Ga.: Scholars Press, 127–52.

von Carlstadt, Andreas Bodenstein. 1995. *The Essential Carlstadt: Fifteen Tracts*. Scottsdale, Pa.: Herald.

Carlyle, Thomas. [1842] 1904. *The New Letters of Thomas Carlyle*. London: John Lane.

—— 1843. *Past and Present.* New York: Charles Scribner's Sons.

Case, Stephen (?). [1779] 1783. Defensive arms vindicated and the lawfulness of the American War made manifest, by a moderate whig. In Sandoz (ed.), *Political Sermons*, 711–70.

Chappell, Clovis G., Rev. 1925. *Sermons on Old Testament Characters.* New York: Harper & Brothers.

Chayefsky, Paddy. 1961. *Gideon.* New York: Random House.

Chemnitz, Martin. [1591] 1989. *Loci Theologici*, II. St. Louis: Concordia Pub. House.

Cheyne, T. K. 1903. Gideon. In T. K. Cheyne and J. Sutherland Black (eds), *Encyclopaedia Biblica*, London: Adam & Charles Black.

Christopherson, John. [1544] 1928. *Jephthah*, ed. F. H. Fobes and W. D. Sypherd. Newark, Del.

Clarke, Adam. [1810–26] 1833. *Holy Bible with a Commentary and Critical Notes*, II. New York: B. Waugh & T. Mason.

Clarke, Laurence. 1737. *A Compleat History of the Holy Bible.* London.

Cobbin, Ingram, 1876. *Commentary on the Bible for Young and Old*, II. New York: Hess.

—— 1881. *The Pictorial Bible Commentator.* Philadelphia: Bradley, Garretson & Co.

Cody, H. A. 1908. *An Apostle of the North: Memoirs of Bishop W. C. Bompas.* New York: E. P. Dutton.

Coggins, R. J., and J. L. Houlden. 1990. *A Dictionary of Biblical Interpretation.* London: SCM Press; Philadelphia: Trinity Press International.

Cooke, G. A. 1913. *The Book of Judges.* The Cambridge Bible for Schools and Colleges. Cambridge: Cambridge University Press.

Cowper, William. [1765–73] 1910. Jehovah-Nissi. The Lord My Banner. In *The Poetical Works of William Cowper*, IV. London: George Bell & Sons.

Crenshaw, James L. 1978. *Samson: A secret betrayed, a vow ignored.* Atlanta, Ga.: John Knox Press.

Cressy, David. 1980. *Literacy and the Social Order: Reading and Writing in Tudor and Stuart England.* Cambridge: Cambridge University Press.

—— and Lori Anne Ferrel, eds. 1996. *Religion and Society in Early Modern England.* London and New York: Routledge.

Dabney, Robert L. 1879. The public preaching of women. *Southern Presbyterian Review* (Oct. 1879).

Davidson, Thain, Rev. 1896. Gideon. In Dean Farrar, et al. (eds), *Biblical Character Sketches*, London: James Nisbet & Co., 45–53.

DeMille, Cecil B. 1949. *Samson and Delilah* [movie]. Paramount Studio.

Dowriche, Anne. [1589] 1999. The French history. In Marion Wynne-Davies (ed.), *Women Poets of the* Renaissance, New York: Routledge, 18–58.

Duncan, Sara Jeannette. 1894. *Vernon's Aunt: being the Oriental Experiences of Miss Lavinia Moffat.* London: Chatto & Windus.

Edwards, Jonathan. [1741] 1972. The distinguishing marks of a work of the Spirit of God. In C. C. Goen (ed.), *The Great Awakening*, IV, New Haven: Yale University Press, 213–88.

—— [1742] 1972. Some thoughts concerning the present revival of the religion in New-England. In C. C. Goen (ed.), *The Great Awakening*, 289–530.

—— [1747] 1993. Types of the Messiah. In Wallace E. Anderson (ed.), *Typological Writings*, New Haven: Yale University Press, 187–328.

—— [1722–56] 1998. *Notes on Scripture*, ed. Stephen J. Stein. New Haven: Yale University Press.

Egermeier, Elsie E. [1922] 1927. *Bible Story Book*. Anderson, Ind.: Gospel Trumpet Co.

Ehrstine, Glenn. 2002. *Theater, Culture, and Community in Reformation Bern*. Leiden and Boston: Brill.

Eissfeldt, Otto. 1910. Die Rätsel in Jud 14. *Zeitschrift für die alttestamentliche Wissenschaft* 30, 132–5.

Enfield, William, Rev. 1777. *Biographical Sermons*. London.

Erasmus, Desiderius. [c.1487] 1993. Cupid with a quiver. In Harry Vredeveld (ed.), *Poems* [*Works*, 85]. Toronto: University of Toronto Press, 230–5.

—— [c.1490] 1993. Elegy, against a greedy rich man. In *Poems*, 216–25.

—— [1522] 1985. The Writing of Letters. In J. K. Sowards (ed.), *Literary and Educational Writings*, 3 [*Works*, 25], Toronto: University of Toronto Press, 1–255.

—— [1525] 1989. The Tongue. In Craig R. Thompson (ed.), *Literary and Educational Writing*, 7 [*Works*, 29], Toronto: University of Toronto Press, 249–412.

Evans, Robert Wilson, Rev. 1835. *Scripture Biography*. London: J. G. & F. Rivington.

Exum, J. Cheryl. 1985. "Mother in Israel": a familiar figure reconsidered. In Letty Russell (ed.), *Feminist Interpretation of the Bible*, Philadelphia: Westminster Press, 73–85.

—— 1990. The centre cannot hold: thematic and textual instabilities in Judges. *Catholic Biblical Quarterly* 52, 410–31.

—— 1990. Murder they wrote: ideology and the manipulation of female presence in biblical narrative. In Alice Bach (ed.), *The Pleasure of Her Text*, Philadelphia: Trinity Press International, 69–95.

—— 1993. *Fragmented Women: Feminist (Sub)Versions of Biblical Narratives*. Valley Forge, Pa.: Trinity Press International.

—— 1995. Feminist criticism: whose interests are being served? In Yee (ed.), *Judges and Method*, 65–90.

—— 1996. *Plotted, Shot, and Painted. Cultural Representations of Biblical* Women, JSOTS 215. Sheffield: Sheffield Academic Press.

Fewell, Danna Nolan. 1992. Judges. In Carol A. Newsom and Sharon H. Ringe (eds), *The Women's Bible Commentary*, London and Louisville, Ky.: SPCK/Westminster/John Knox, 67–77.

—— 1995. Deconstructive criticism: Achsah and the (e)razed city of writing. In Yee (ed.), *Judges and Method*, 119–45.

—— 2003. *The Children of Israel: Reading the Bible for the Sake of Our Children*. Nashville, Tenn.: Abingdon Press.

—— and David M. Gunn. 1990. Controlling perspectives: women, men, and the authority of violence in Judges 4 and 5. *Journal of the American Academy of Religion* 56, 389–411.

Finney, Charles G. [1835] 2001. *Lectures on Revival*. CCEL.

Fletcher, Alexander, Rev. 1839. *Scripture History, Designed for the Improvement of Youth*. London: George Virtue.

Fletcher, John. [1776] 1991. The Bible and the sword. In Sandoz (ed.), *Political Sermons*, 559–78.

[Fontaine, Nicolas] (Sieur de Royaumont). [1670/1690] 1699. *The History of the Old and New Testament Extracted Out of Sacred Scripture and Writings of the Fathers*. London. [Orig. French edn./English trans.]

—— [1670] 1780. *The History of the Old and New Testament, Interspersed with Moral and Instructive Reflections chiefly taken from the Holy Fathers*, tr. Joseph Reeve. London.

Forshey, Gerald E. 1992. *American Religious and Biblical Spectaculars*. Westport, Conn., and London: Praeger.

Forsyth, James S. 1896. *The Women of the Bible: A Series of Biographies*. London: Robert Banks & Son.

Fuchs, Esther. 1985. Who is hiding the truth? In Adela Yarbro Collins (ed.), *Feminist Perspectives on Biblical Scholarship*, Chico, Calif.: Scholars Press, 137–44.

Gardner, James, Rev. 1858. *The Christian Cyclopedia*. Glasgow: Blackie & Son.

Garstang, John. 1931. *The Foundations of Bible History: Joshua Judges*. New York: R. R. Smith.

Gaspey, Thomas. 1851. *Tallis's Illustrated Scripture History for the Improvement of Youth*. London and New York: John Tallis & Co.

—— and C. C. Sturm. c.1850. *Family Devotions*. London: J. & F. Tallis.

Gaster, T. H. 1969. *Myth, Legend, and Custom in the Old Testament*. New York: Harper.

Geikie, Cunningham. 1884. *Old Testament Characters*. London and New York: Cassell & Co.

Gibbon, John. [1661] 1981. How may we be so spiritual, as to check sin in the first rising of it? In Nichols (ed.), *Puritan Sermons*, I. v, 87–111.

Gilead, Zerubavel, and Doreothea Krook. 1985. *Gideon's Springs: A Man and his Kibbutz*. New York: Ticknor & Fields.

Gilfillan, George, Rev. 1879. *The Bards of the Bible*, 7th edn. London and Glasgow: Hamilton, Adams, & Co.

Gilmour, Richard, Rev. [1869] 1904. *Bible History*. New York, Cincinnati, and Chicago: Benziger Bros.

Gomersall, Robert. [1628] 1633. The Levite's Revenge. In *Poems*, London.

Gottlieb, Freema. 1981. Three mothers. *Judaism* 118, 194–203.

Grahame, James. [1807] 1856. Jephthah's vow. In George Gilfillan (ed.), *The Poetical Works of Henry Kirke White and James Grahame*, Edinburgh: James Nichol, 297–8.

Greenstein, Edward. 1981. The riddle of Samson. *Prooftexts* 1, 237–60.

Gressman, Hugo. 1914. *Die Anfänge Israels. (Von 2. Mosis bis Richter und Ruth)*. Göttingen: Vandenhoeck & Ruprecht.

Gunkel, J. H. H[ermann]. 1913. Simson. In *Rede und Aufsätze*, Göttingen: Vandenhoeck & Ruprecht, 38–64.

Gunn, David M., and Danna Nolan Fewell. 1993. *Narrative in the Hebrew Bible*. Oxford: Oxford University Press.

Gurnall, William. [1655–62] 2001. *The Christian in Complete Armour*. CCEL.

Gutjahr, Paul C. 1999. *An American Bible. A History of the Good Book in the United States, 1777–1880.* Stanford, Calif.: Stanford University Press.

Hackett, Jo Ann. 1985. In the days of Jael. In Clarissa Atkinson et al. (eds), *Immaculate and Powerful,* Boston: Beacon, 15–38.

Hales, Dr. [1809] 1830. *A New Analysis of Chronology and Geography, History and Prophecy.* London: C. V. G. & F. Rivington.

Hall, Joseph. [1615] 1844. *Contemplations on the Historical Passages of the Old and New Testaments,* rev. edn. Edinburgh: Thomas Nelson.

Hamlin, E. John. 1990. *At Risk in the Promised Land: A Commentary on the Book of Judges.* Edinburgh: Handsel.

Handel, G. F. [1742] 1880. *Samson: An Oratorio.* London & New York: Novello, Ewer.

Hastings, James, ed. 1902. *A Dictionary of the Bible.* Edinburgh: T. & T. Clark.

——ed. 1911. *The Great Texts of the Bible: Genesis to Numbers.* Edinburgh: T. & T. Clark.

——ed. 1914. *The Greater Men and Women of the Bible: Moses–Samson.* London: T. & T. Clark/Waverly Book Co.

Hauser, Alan J., and Duane F. Watson. 2004. *A History of Biblical Interpretation, I. The Ancient Period.* Grand Rapids, Mich.: William B. Eerdmans.

Hawk, L. Daniel. 1991. *Every Promise Fulfilled: Competing Plots in Joshua.* Louisville, Ky.: Westminster/John Knox Press.

Hayes, John H. 1999. *A Dictionary of Biblical Interpretation.* Nashville, Tenn.: Abingdon.

Heavysege, Charles. 1865. *Jephthah's Daughter.* Montreal.

Henry, Matthew. 1708. An *Exposition of the Historical Books of the Old Testament.* London.

Herbert, George. 1633. *The Temple.* CCEL.

Hewlett, Esther. 1828. *Scripture History for Youth,* II. London: H. Fisher, Son & P. Jackson.

Hodges, Turner, ed. 1956. *The Bible Story Library,* II. New York: Educational Book Guild.

Horder, W. Garrett, ed. 1889. *The Poets' Bible: Old Testament Section.* London: Wm. Isbister.

Horne, Charles F., ed. 1908–9. *The Bible and its Story,* III. New York: Niglutsch.

Horton, Robert F. 1899. *Women of the Old Testament.* New York: Thomas Whittaker.

Howard, John, Rev. [c.1840] c.1865. *The Illustrated Scripture History for the Young,* I. New York: Virtue & Yorston.

Hoyland, John. [1812] 1814. An *Epitome of the History of the World,* I, 2nd edn. York: W. Hargrove.

Hubmaier, Balthasar. [1524] 1989. Theses against Eck. In H. Wayne Pipkin and John H. Yoder (eds), *Balthasar Hubmaier, Theologian of Anabaptism,* Scottdale, Pa.: Herald, 49–57.

——[1526] 1989. A simple instruction. In *Balthasar Hubmaier,* 314–38.

Hughes, Edward. [1853] 1862. *Outlines of Scripture Geography & History.* London: Longman, Green, & Roberts.

Hurlbut, Jesse Lyman. [1904] 1932. *Hurlbut's Story of the Bible for Young and Old.* Chicago, Philadelphia, and Toronto: John C. Winston Co.

Inglis, John. 1890. *Bible Illustrations from the New Hebrides*. Edinburgh.

Jabotinsky, Vladimir. 1930. *Samson the Nazirite*. London: M. Secker.

James, Fleming. 1939. *Personalities of the Old Testament*. New York: Scribner's Sons.

Jefferies, Richard. [1867] 1896. *Jefferies Land: A History of Swindon and its Environs*, ed. Grace Toplis. London: Simkin, Marshall, Hamilton, Kent & Co.

Jeffrey, David Lyle, ed. 1992. *A Dictionary of Biblical Tradition in English Literature*. Grand Rapids, Mich.: W. B. Eerdmans.

Jenks, William. 1835. *Comprehensive Commentary*. Boston: Shattuck & Co.

Jeter, Joseph R., Jr. 2003. *Preaching Judges*. Preaching Classic Texts. St. Louis: Chalice.

Jones, David. 1775. *Defensive War in a Just Cause Sinless*. Philadelphia.

Joris, David. [1535] 1993. The wonderful working of God. In Gary K. Waite (ed.), *The Anabaptist Writings of David Joris*, Scottdale, Pa.: Herald, 109–25.

—— [1537] 1993. Response to Hans Eigenburg. In *The Anabaptist Writings*, 157–75.

Kennicott, Benjamin. 1793. *The Universal Family Bible*. Dublin: Zachariah Jackson.

Kirby, William. 1880. *Canadian Idyls, IV. Stony Creek*. Toronto: Briggs.

Kirkconnell, W. 1964. *That Invincible Samson*. Toronto: University of Toronto Press.

Kittel, Rudolf. [1892] 1909. *A History of the Hebrews*, II. London: Williams & Norgate.

—— 1925. *Great Men and Movements in Israel*. London: Williams & Norgate.

Kitto, John. [1841] 1867. *The Bible History of the Holy Land*. London: George Routledge & Sons.

—— 1844. *The Pictorial History of Palestine and the Holy Land*, I. London: Charles Knight.

—— 1845. *The Pictorial Sunday-Book*. London: Charles Knight.

—— ed. 1846. *The Cyclopaedia of Biblical Literature*, II. New York: Mark H. Newman.

—— [1850] 1857. *Daily Bible Illustrations, II: Moses and the Judges*. New York: Robert Carter & Brothers.

Klein, Lillian R. 1989. *The Triumph of Irony in the Book of Judges*. Sheffield: Almond.

Knox, John. [1554] 1895. Certain questions concerning obedience to lawful magistrates. In David Laing (ed.), *The Works of John Knox*, III, Edinburgh: Banntyne Club, 217–26.

—— [1558] 1895. The first blast of the trumpet against the monstrous regiment of women. In *Works*, IV, 349–422.

Kook, Abraham Isaac. [1950] 1978. Lights of holiness. In *The Lights of Penitence, et al.* New York: Paulist Press, 189–239.

Krouse, T. Michael. 1949. *Milton's Samson and the Christian Tradition*. Princeton, N.J.: Princeton University Press.

Langdon, Samuel, D. D. [1788] 1991. The republic of the Israelites: an example to the American States. In Sandoz (ed.), *Political Sermons*, 943–67.

à Lapide, Cornelius. [1681] 1891. *Commentaria in Scripturam Sacra*, III. Paris: Vivès.

Lasine, Stuart. 1984. Guest and host in Judges 19. *Journal for the Study of the Old Testament* 30, 37–59.

Lias, J. J. 1906. *The Book of Judges*. Cambridge: Cambridge University Press.

Long, Burke O. 2003. *Imagining the Holy Land: Maps, Models, and Fantasy Travels*. Bloomington: Indiana University Press.

Luther, Martin. [1513–15] 1976. *First Lectures on the Psalms* [10], ed. Hilton C. Oswald. Philadelphia: Fortress Press.

—— [1520] 1966. Treatise on good works. In James Atkinson (ed.), *The Christian in Society*, I [44], Philadelphia: Fortress Press, 15–114.

—— [1520] 1966. To the Christian nobility of the German nation. In *The Christian in Society*, I, 115–217.

—— [1521] 1974. The Gospel for Christmas Eve [Luke 2: 1–14]. In Hans J. Hillerbrand (ed.), *Sermons*, II [52], Philadelphia: Fortress Press, 7–31.

—— [1521] 1974. The Gospel for the festival of the epiphany [Matt. 2: 1–12]. In *Sermons*, II, 159–286.

—— [1521] 1974. The Gospel for the Sunday after Christmas [Lk. 2: 33–40]. In *Sermons*, II, 102–48.

—— [1523] 1962. Temporal authority: to what extent it should be obeyed. In Walter I. Brandt (ed.), *The Christian in Society*, II [45], Philadelphia: Muhlenberg, 75–129.

—— [1525] 1967. Against the robbing and murdering horde of peasants. In Robert C. Schultz (ed.), *The Christian in Society*, III [46], Philadelphia: Fortress Press, 57–85.

—— [1525] 1967. An open letter on the harsh book against the peasants. In *The Christian in Society*, III, Philadelphia: Fortress, 57–85.

—— [1529] 1967. On war against the Turks. In *The Christian in Society*, III, 155–205.

—— [1530] 1967. On marriage matters. In *The Christian in Society*, III, 261–320.

—— [1532] 1958. Infiltrating and clandestine preachers. In *Church and Ministry*, II. Philadelphia: Muhlenberg, 379–94.

—— [1533] 1967. The Difference between Samson and Julius Caesar. In Helmut T. Lehman and Theodore G. Tappert (eds), *Table Talk* [54], Philadelphia: Fortress, 79.

Lye, Thomas, Rev. [1661] 1981. How are we to live by faith in Divine Providence? In Nichols (ed.), *Puritan Sermons*, I.xviii, 369–400.

—— [1682] 1981. What may gracious parents best do for the conversion of those children whose wickedness is occasioned by their sinful severity or indulgence? In Nichols (ed.), *Puritan Sermons*, III.vii, 154–84.

Macaulay, T. B. [1848] 1979. *The History of England from the Accession of James II*. London: Penguin.

Manning, Samuel, Rev. 1890. *Those Holy Fields: Palestine Illustrated by Pen and Pencil*. London: Religious Tract Society.

Manton, Thomas, Rev. [1661] 1981. How may we cure distractions in holy duties? In Nichols (ed.), *Puritan Sermons*, I.xix, 400–15.

Marcus, David. 1986. *Jephthah and His Vow*. Lubbock, Tex.: Texas Tech.

Marvell, Andrew. [1665] 1951. The first anniversary of the government under his Highness the Lord Protector. In H. M. Margoliouth (ed.), *The Poems & Letters of Andrew Marvell*, Oxford: Clarendon Press, 108–19.

Matheson, George. 1903. *Representative Men of the Bible*. London: Hodder & Stoughton.

McCann, J. Clinton. 2002. *Judges*. Interpretation: A Bible Commentary. Louisville, Ky.: John Knox Press.

McFadyen, John Edgar. 1901. *The Messages of the Prophetic and Priestly Historians*. New York: Charles Scribner's Sons.

—— 1928. *Old Testament Scenes and Characters*. London: James Clarke & Co.

McKenzie, John L. 1966. *The World of the Judges*. Englewood Cliffs, N.J.: Prentice-Hall.

McKillop, Archibald. 1860. The Bible. In *Temperance Odes and Miscellaneous Poems*, Quebec.

Mead, Darius, Rev., ed. 1844–5. *The Christian Parlor Magazine*. New York: S. W. Benedict & Co.

Meyer, F. B. [1898] 2000. *Our Daily Homily*, I: *Genesis–Ruth*. CCEL.

Miller E. 1833/1839. *Scripture History, for the Improvement of Youth*, I. London: T. Kelly.

Miller, Thomas E. 1922. *Portraits of Men of the Old Testament*. London: H. R. Allenson.

Milton, John. [1667] 1957. Paradise Lost. In *John Milton – Complete Poems and Major Prose*, New York: Odyssey.

—— [1671] 1957. Samson Agonistes. In *Complete Poems*.

—— [1671] 1957. Paradise Regained. In *Complete Poems*.

—— [1644] 1959. Doctrine and discipline of divorce. In *Complete Prose Works of John Milton*, II, New Haven: Yale University Press, 217–356.

—— [1649] 1962. The tenure of kings and magistrates. In *Complete Prose*, III, 190–258.

—— [1649] 1962. *Eikonoklastes*. In *Complete Prose*, III, 335–601.

—— [1651] 1966. *A Defence of the People of England* [*Pro populo anglicano defensio*, 2nd edn]. In *Complete Prose*, IV, 285–537.

—— [c.1658–60] 1973. *Christian Doctrine*, tr. John Carey. In *Complete Prose*, VI.

Moffatt, James. c.1923. *The Bible in Scots Literature*. London: Hodder & Stoughton.

Moore, George F., Rev. 1895. *Judges*. International Critical Commentary. Edinburgh: T. & T. Clark.

More, Thomas. [1533] 1963. *The Answer to a Poisoned Book*. New Haven: Yale University Press.

—— [1534] 1963. *A Dialogue of Comfort against Tribulation*. New Haven: Yale University Press.

Moreen, Vera Basch, ed. 2000. *In Queen Esther's Garden: An Anthology of Judeo-Persian Literature*. New Haven: Yale University Press.

Morgan, Thomas. [1737] 1999. *The Moral Philosopher*. Chicago: University of Chicago.

Mosher, Jennie M., Mrs. 1894. *Story of the Bible in Rhyme*. Independence, Iowa: Independence Book Co.

Le Moyne, Pierre. 1652. *Gallery of Heroick Women*, tr. the marquesse of Winchester. London.

Nel, Philip. 1985. The Riddle of Samson [Judges 14, 14–18]. *Biblica* 66, 534–45.

Nichols, James, ed. 1981. *Puritan Sermons, 1659–1689*, 6 vols. Wheaton, Ill.: Richard Owen Roberts, Publisher.

Nicholas of Lyra. 1471–2. *Postilla litteralis super totam bibliam*. Rome.

Niditch, Susan. 1989. Eroticism and death in the tale of Jael. In Peggy L. Day (ed.), *Gender and Difference in Ancient Israel*, Minneapolis: Fortress Press, 43–57.

—— 1990. Samson as culture hero. *Catholic Biblical Quarterly* 52, 608–24.

Northrop, Henry Davenport, D. D. 1894. *Charming Bible Stories Written in Simple Language*. New York: A. D. Porter.

Noth, Martin. 1930. *Das System der Zwölfstämme Israels*. Stuttgart: W. Kohlhammer.

Ormerod, J. C. c.1938. Religion and ethics in the days when the Judges ruled. In *Story of the Bible*, 301–5.

Orr, James. [1906] 1922. *The Problem of the Old Testament*. New York: Charles Scribner's Sons.

Owen, John. [1657] 2000. *Of Communion with God*. CCEL.

—— [1669] 2000. *A Brief Declaration and Vindication of the Doctrine of the Trinity*. CCEL.

Patrick, Symon. [1702] 1732. *A Commentary upon the Historical Books of the Old Testament*, II, 4th edn. London.

Perkins, William. [1606] 1970. The whole treatise of the cases of conscience. In *The Complete Works of William Perkins*, Abingdon (Berks): Sutton Courtney.

Phillips, Dirk. [1564] 1992. The Enchiridion. In Cornelius J. et al. (eds), *The Writings of Dirk Phillips 1504–68*, Scottdale, Pa.: Herald, 51–425.

Pink, Arthur W. 1917. *The Divine Inspiration of the Bible*. Swengel, Pa.: Bible Truth Depot. CCEL.

—— 1923. *The Antichrist*. Swengel, Pa.: Bible Truth Depot. CCEL.

Pledger, Elias, Rev. [1661] 1981. Of the cause of inward trouble. . . . In Nichols (ed.), *Puritan Sermons*, I.xv, 306–30.

Polzin, Robert. 1980. The Book of Judges. In *Moses and the Deuteronomist*, New York: Seabury Press, 146–204.

Poole, Matthew. [1685] 1688. *Annotations upon the Holy Bible*. London.

Prickett, Stephen. 1996. *Origins of Narrative*. Cambridge: Cambridge University Press.

Quarles, Francis. [1631] 1880. Historie of Sampson. In *The Complete Works in Prose and Verse of Francis Quarles*, ed. Alexander B. Grosart, Edinburgh: Edinburgh University.

—— [1632] 1880. Divine Fancies. In *Complete Works*.

Raleigh, Sir Walter. 1614. *The History of the World*. London.

Ransom, Reverdy C. [1897] 1999. Deborah and Jael. In Anthony B. Pinn (ed.), *Making the Gospel Plain*, Harrisburg, Pa.: Trinity, 75–85.

Robert, Colin H., and T. C. Skeat. 1983. *The Birth of the Codex*. London: British Academy.

Robinson, Thomas, Rev. [1790] 1804. *Scripture Characters: Or, A Practical Improvement of the Principle Histories in the Old and New Testament*, 5th edn. London.

Rogers, Richard. 1615. *A Commentary on Judges*. London. Repr. Edinburgh: Banner of Truth Trust, 1983.

Rogerson, John. 1984. *Old Testament Criticism in the Nineteenth Century*. Philadelphia: Fortress Press.

Ruskin, John. [1885–9] 1997. Praeterita. In *The Complete Works of John Ruskin*, New York: E. R. Dumont, 379–459.

Saint-Saëns, Camille. [1872/77] c.1982. *Samson and Delilah: An Opera in Three Acts*. Orig. French text by Ferdinand Lemaire. English version by Nathan Haskall Dole. New York: G. Schirmer.

Sandoz, Ellis, ed. 1991. *Political Sermons of the American Founding Era: 1730–1805*. Indianapolis: Liberty.

Schneider, Tammi. 2000. *Judges*. Berit Olam. Collegeville, Minn.: Liturgical Press.

Scott, Thomas. [1788–92] 1830. *The Holy Bible Containing the Old and New Testaments*, 5th edn. Boston: Samuel T. Armstrong.

Shakespeare, William. [1598] 1939. *Love's Labour's Lost.* Boston and New York: Harcourt.

Shaw, Jane. 1989. Constructions of woman in readings of the story of Deborah. In Mieke Bal (ed.), *Anti-Covenant*, Sheffield: Almond Press, 113–32.

Simons, Menno. [c.1541] 1986. The true Christian faith. In Harold S. Bender (ed.), *The Complete Writings of Menno Simons*, Scottdale, Pa.: Herald, 321–405.

Simpson, Bertram F. c.1938. It came to pass in the days when the Judges ruled. In *Story of the Bible*, 281–9.

Slater, Samuel, Rev. [1690] 1981. What is the duty of magistrates, from the highest to the lowest, for the suppressing of profaneness? In Nichols (ed.), *Puritan Sermons*, IV.xv, 481–530.

Smiles, Samuel. [1871] 1874. *Character*, new edn. London: John Murray.

Smith, George Adam. 1896. *The Historical Geography of the Holy Land*, 4th edn. London: Hodder & Stroughton.

Smith, Gertrude. 1905. *Robbie's Bible Stories.* Philadelphia: Henry Altemus.

Smith, Hamilton, ed. 1914. *Gleanings from the Past, I: Extracts from the Writings of William Gurnall.* London: Central Bible Truth Depot.

Smith, Samuel, D. D. 1752. *The Compleat History of the Old and New Testament: Or, a Family Bible.* London.

Smith, William, and Rev. J. M. Fuller, eds. 1893. *A Dictionary of the Bible*, 2nd edn. London.

Smyth, Lindley. 1908. *Happy Sundays with the Bible.* Philadelphia: Uplift Pub. Co.

Smythe-Palmer, A. 1913. *The Samson-Saga and its Place in Comparative Religion.* London: Sir Isaac Pitman & Sons.

Soggin, J. Alberto. 1981. *Judges: A Commentary.* Old Testament Library. Philadelphia: Westminster Press.

Southwell, Henry, Rev. 1775. *The Universal Family Bible.* London: J. Cooke.

Spinoza, Benedict (Baruch). [1670] 2001. *Theologico-Political Treatise.* Indianapolis: Hackett Publishing Co.

Spurgeon, Charles H. [1864] 1978. Our champion. In *Spurgeon's Expository Encyclopedia – Sermons by Charles H. Spurgeon.* Grand Rapids, Mich.: Baker Book House.

—— [1873] 1978. Hands Full of Honey. In *Spurgeon's Expository Encyclopedia – Sermons.*

Stackhouse, Thomas. 1742. *A New History of the Holy Bible.* London.

Stanton, Elizabeth Cady. 1898. *The Woman's Bible*, part II. New York: European Publishing Co.

Steele, Richard, Rev. [1689] 1981. How the uncharitable and dangerous contentions that are among professors of the true religion, may be allayed. In Nichols (ed.), *Puritan Sermons*, IV. iii, 215–53.

Steig, Jeanne. 1990. *The Old Testament Made Easy.* New York: Farrar, Straus & Giroux.

Steinberg, Naomi. 1995. Social scientific criticism: Judges 9 and issues of kinship. In Yee (ed.), *Judges and Method*, 45–64.

Sterne, Laurence. [1766] 1996. The Levite and his concubine. In *The Sermons of Mr. Yorick*, III, iii. In Melvin New (ed.), *The Sermons of Laurence Sterne*, IV, Gainesville, Fla.: University Press of Florida, 167–76.

Stoddart, Jane T. 1913. *The Old Testament in Life and Literature*. London: Hodder & Stoughton.

Stowe, Harriet Beecher. 1873. *Woman in Sacred History: A Series of Sketches*. New York: J. B. Fort.

Stricklands, Susanna. 1831. Gideon's fleece. In *Enthusiasm; and Other Poems*, London: Smith, Elder, & Co.

Taylor, Jeremy. 1822. Of the rule of conscience. In Reginald Heber (ed.), *The Whole Works of Right Rev. Jeremy Taylor, D. D.*, XII, London: Ogle, Duncan, & Co.

Tennyson, Alfred Lord. [1832] 1987. Buonaparte. In *The Poems of Tennyson*, I, London: Longman, 385.

Thatcher, G. W. 1910. *Judges and Ruth*. Century Bible. London: Caxton Pub. Co.

Thomson, W. M., D. D. 1860. *The Land and the Book*. London and New York: T. Nelson & Sons.

Thompson, John L. 2001. *Writing the Wrongs: Women of the Old Testament among Biblical Commentators from Philo through the Reformation*. Oxford: Oxford University Press.

Trible, Phyllis. 1984. *Texts of Terror: Literary-Feminist Readings of Biblical Narratives*. Philadelphia: Fortress Press.

Trimmer, [Sarah], Mrs. [1783] 1810. *Sacred History, Selected from the Scriptures; with Annotations and Reflections, Particularly Calculated to Facilitate the Study of the Holy Scriptures in Schools and Families*, II, 6th edn. London: J. Johnson, F. & C. Rivington.

Turretin, Francis. [1682] 1994. *Institutes of Elenctic Theology*, II. Phillipsburg, N.J.: P&R Publishing.

van den Vondel, Joost. 1660. *Samson, of Heilige Wraeck, Treurspel*. Amsterdam.

Vermigli, Peter Martyr. 1994. *Creed, Scripture, Church*. Kirksville, Mo.: Sixteenth Century Journal Publishers.

——1999. *Life, Letters, and Sermons*. Kirksville, Mo.: Sixteenth Century Journal.

Voltaire, Francois. 1880 (reprint 1967). *Oeuvres Complètes de Voltaire*. Paris: Garnier Frères, Libraires-Éditeurs.

——[1749] 1863. *Sermon of the Fifty*, tr. J. A. R. Séguin. Jersey City: R. Paxton.

——[1761] 1880. *Examen important de milord Bolinbroke*. In *Oeuvres Complètes*.

——[1763] 1994. *A Treatise on Toleration and Other Essays*, ed. Joseph McCabe. Amherst, N.Y.: Prometheus.

——[1764–9] 1962. *Philosophical Dictionary: A–I*, tr. Peter Gay. New York: Basic Books.

——[1765] 1965. *The Philosophy of History*. New York: Philosophical Library.

——[1776] 1880. *Un Chrétien contre six Juifs*. In *Oeuvres Complètes*, XXIX.

——[1776] 1880. *La Bible enfin expliquée*. In *Oeuvres Complètes*, XXX.

Wallace, Robert Burns. 1929. *An Introduction to the Bible as Literature*. Philadelphia: Westminster Press.

Warfield, Benjamin B. [1895] 1952. *Biblical and Theological Studies*. Philadelphia: Presbyterian & Reformed Publishing Co.

Warren, John L. 1889. In W. Garrett Horder (ed.), *The Poet's Bible*, 315.

Watson, Richard, Right Rev. 1861. *A Biblical and Theological Dictionary*. London: John Mason.

Watts, Isaac. [1730] 1769. *A Short View of the Whole Scripture History*, 9th edn. London: J. Buckland & T. Longman.

—— *The Psalms and Hymns of Isaac Watts*. CCEL.

Webb, Barry G. 1987. *The Book of the Judges: An Integrated Reading*. Sheffield: JSOT.

Wells, John. c.1670s. How we may make melody in our hearts to God in singing of Psalms. In Nichols (ed.), *Puritan Sermons*, II.ix, 71–81.

Whately, E. J., Miss. 1878. Use and abuse of pictures on sacred subjects. In *Sunday at Home*, 346–50.

White, Annie R., Mrs. 1896. *Easy Steps for Little Feet: From Genesis to Revelation*. N.p.: L. A. Martin.

White, E. G., Mrs. 1890. *The Story of Patriarchs and Prophets*. Mountain View, Calif.: Pacific Press Publishing Association.

Whyte, Alexander. 1905. *Bible Characters: Gideon to Absalom*. Edinburgh: Oliphants.

Wilberforce, Samuel. 1870. *Heroes of Hebrew History*. London: Strahan & Co.

Willard, J. H. 1906. *What is Sweeter Than Honey: The Story of Samson*. Philadelphia: Henry Altemus.

Williams, Isaac, Rev. [c.1860] 1909. *Female Characters of Holy Scripture in a Series of Sermons*. London: Longmans, Green, & Co.

Williams, Raymond. 1978. The press and popular culture: an historical perspective. In George Boyce et al. (eds), *Newspaper History from the Seventeenth Century to the Present Day*, London: Constable, 41–50.

Williams, T. Rhondda. 1911. *Old Testament Stories in Modern Light: A Bible Guide for the Young*. London: James Clarke & Co.

Willis, Nathaniel Parker. [1827] 1844. Jephthah's daughter. In *The Poems, Sacred, Passionate, and Humorous of Nathaniel Parker Willis*, New York: Clark & Austin, 24–8.

Wood, J. G., Rev. 1872. *Wood's Bible Animals*. Philadelphia: George Brooks.

Yee, Gale A. 1995. *Judges and Method: New Approaches in Biblical Studies*. Minneapolis: Fortress Press.

Yonge, Charlotte M. [1875] 1898. *Aunt Charlotte's Stories of Bible History for Young Disciples*, rev. edn. Philadelphia, Chicago, and Toronto: John C. Winston. [1875. *Aunt Charlotte's Stories of Bible History for the Little Ones*. London: Marcus Ward & Co.]

Younger, K. Lawson, Jr. 1999. Early Israel in recent biblical scholarship. In David W. Baker and Bill T. Arnold (eds), *The Face of Old Testament Studies: A Survey of Contemporary Approaches*, Grand Rapids, Mich.: Baker Books, 176–206.

—— 2002. *Judges and Ruth*. The NIV Application Commentary Series. Grand Rapids, Mich.: Zondervan.

Graphical

—— 1630. "Merian Bible" [Luther version]. Matthäus Merian, illus. Strassburg: Lazarus Zetzner. [See W. L. Phelps, ed., *Matthew Merian's Illustrated Bible*, New York: Morrow, 1933; *The Bible in Word and Art*, New York: Arch Cape, 1988.]

—— c.1650. *Afbeeldingen Der Voornaamste Historien*. Amsterdam: Nicolaus Visscher.

———— 1700. "Great Bible." *Historie des Ouden en Nieuwen Testaments.* Amsterdam: Pieter Mortier.

———— 1708. *Historiae Celebriores Veteris Testamenti.* Nuremberg: Christophorus Weigel.

———— c.1840. *Historic Illustrations of the Bible.* London: Fisher, Son, & Co.

———— 1846. *The Illuminated Bible.* New York: Harper & Brothers.

———— c.1860. *Sunny Sabbaths or Pleasant Pages for Happy Homes: A Sunday Book of Bible History and Literature Profusely Illustrated with Coloured Engravings.* London: James Hagger.

———— c.1866. *Routledge's Scripture Gift-Book.* London: George Routledge & Sons.

———— c.1870. *Cassell's Illustrated Family Bible.* Springfield, Mass., and Chicago: Cassell.

———— 1881. *Pleasant Pages and Bible Stories.* Boston: Estes & Lauriat.

———— 1884. *The Child's Bible.* New York: Cassell Publishing Co.

———— 1886. *Types and Antitypes of Our Lord and Saviour Jesus Christ.* London: SPCK.

———— 1888. *Scripture Narratives for the Education and Entertainment of the Young.* Philadelphia: Carson & Simpson.

———— 1898. *A Child's Story of the Bible.* Philadelphia: Henry Altemus Co.

———— 1924. *The Great Stories of the Bible.* New York: World Syndicate Co.

———— 1949. *Cecil B. DeMille's Masterpiece Samson and Delilah.* Paramount Pictures.

———— 1956. *The Bible in Art.* London: Phaidon Press.

———— 1964. *The Children's Bible in Colour.* London: Hamlyn.

———— 1966. *Mighty Samson*, no. 21. Western Publishing Co.

———— 1968. *The Oxford Illustrated Old Testament, with Drawings by Contemporary Artists*, II. London: Oxford University Press.

———— 1979. *Rembrandt Bible Drawings.* New York: Dover Publications.

———— 1987. *Outrageous Tales from the Old Testament.* London: Knockabout Publications.

———— 1995. Samson. In *Samson Comics*, 1/2. New Port Richey, Fla.: Flashpoint Studios.

———— 1999. *Pennyroyal Caxton Bible, Designed and Illustrated by Barry Moser.* London: Viking.

Ardizzone, Edward, illus. 1961. In Walter de la Mare, *Stories from the Bible*, New York: Alfred A. Knopf.

Bankes, Thomas. c.1790. *The Christian's New and Compleat Family Bible.* London: J. Cooke.

Blomfield, E. 1813. *A New Family Bible . . . Embellished with Fifty Beautiful Engravings*, I. Bungay: Brightly & Childs.

Boyd, James P. 1893. *Young People's Bible History.* Philadelphia: American Pub. House.

Christie-Murray, David. 1976. *The Illustrated Children's Bible.* London: Hamlyn.

Cockerell, Sydney C. [n.d.] *Old Testament Miniatures.* New York: George Braziller.

Cole, J. c.1720. *The Historical Part of the Holy Bible . . . exactly and completely describ'd in above Two Hundred Historys.* London.

Doré, Gustave, illus. 1866. *La Sainte Bible.* Tours: Alfred Mame et Fils.

———— 1879. *The Doré Bible Gallery.* New York: Fine Arts Publishing Co.

[Fontaine, Nicolas] Le Sieur de Royaumont. [1690] 1699. *The History of the Old and New Testament Extracted out of Sacred Scripture and Writings of the Fathers.* London.

———— 1835. *Histoire de l'Ancien et du Nouveau Testament.* Paris: L. Curmer.

Friedländer, Max V. 1923. *Die Lübecker Bibel.* Munich: R. Piper & Co.

Galle, Philips. c.1600. *Celebrated Women of the Old Testament.* Antwerp: Philips Galle.

Gaspey, Thomas. c.1850. *Family Devotions,* II. London: J. & F. Tallis.

——1851. *Tallis' Illustrated Scripture History.* London and New York: John Tallis & Co.

Grainger, Muriel. 1971. *365 Bible Stories and Verses.* London: Hamlyn.

Griffith, William. 1925. *Great Painters and their Famous Bible Pictures.* New York: Wm. H. Wise & Co.

Hadaway, Bridget and Jean Atcheson. 1973. *The Bible for Children.* London: Octopus.

Harby, Clifton. 1936. *The Bible in Art.* Garden City, N.Y.: Garden City Pub. Co.

Hayes, Marvin, illus. 1978. In James Dickey and Marvin Hayes, *God's Images,* New York: Seabury.

Henry, Avril. 1987. *Biblia Pauperum.* Ithaca, N.Y.: Cornell University Press.

Hewlett, Esther. 1828. *Scripture History for Youth,* II. London: H. Fischer, Son & P. Jackson.

Holbein, Hans. 1538. *Historiarum Veteris Testamenti Icones.* Lyons.

de Hondt, Pierre. 1728. *Figures de la Bible.* The Hague. (The plates from Gerard Hoet's paintings first pub. in *Tafereelen der Heilige Geschiedenissen,* Amsterdam: Halma, 1706.)

Horne, Charles F., ed. 1908–9. *The Bible and its Story,* III. New York: Niglutsch.

de Hooghe, Romeijn. [1706] 1715. *'T Groot Waerelds Tafereel,* 8th edn. Amsterdam: J. Lindenberg.

Howard, John. c.1850. *Scripture History for the Young.* New York: Virtue & Yorston.

de Jode, Gerard. 1585. *Thesaurus: Sacrarum Historiarum Veteris Testamenti.* Amsterdam.

Josephus, Flavius. 1682. *Al de Werken von Flavius Josephus.* Amsterdam: Jan Jacobsz.

Kitto, John. 1845. *The Pictorial Sunday-Book.* London: Charles Knight.

——c.1850. *The Pictorial Bible,* new edn, II. London: W. & R. Chambers.

Klink, J. C. [1959] 1967. *Bible For Children,* tr. Patricia Crampton. London: Burke.

Küsel, Melchior. 1679. *Icones Biblicae Veteris et Novi Testamenti: Figuren Biblischer Historien Alten und Neuen Testaments.* Vienna. [Repr. Hildesheim: Olms, 1968.]

Labriola, Albert C., and John W. Smeltz. 1990. *The Bible of the Poor [Biblia Pauperum].* Pittsburgh: Duquesne University Press.

Lowden, John. 2000. *The Making of the Bibles Moralisées, I: The Manuscripts.* University Park, Pa.: Pennsylvania State University Press.

Martyn, S. T., Mrs. 1868. *Women of the Bible.* New York: American Tract Society.

Mercer, Henry. C. 1961. *The Bible in Iron: Pictures, Stoves and Stoveplates of the Pennsylvania Germans,* 3rd rev. edn. Doylestown, Pa.: Bucks County Historical Society.

Merian, Matthäus. 1626. *Icones Biblicae* [Part II]. Frankfurt: De Bry. [See *Iconum Biblicarum.* Wenatchee, Wa.: AVB Press, 1981.]

Miller, E. 1833/1839. *Scripture History, for the Improvement of Youth,* I. London: T. Kelly.

Miller, Olive Beaupré. 1940. *Heroes of the Bible.* New York: Standard Book Co.

Mühlberger, Richard. 1991. *The Bible in Art: The Old Testament.* New York: Portland.

Northrop, Henry Davenport, D. D. 1894. *Charming Bible Stories Written in Simple Language.* New York: A. D. Porter.

Officer, Morris. 1859. *African Bible Pictures.* Philadelphia: Lutheran Board.

Poortman, Wilco C. 1983/1986. *Bijbel en Prent*, I–II. Gravenhage: Boekencentrum.

Rose, Martial, and Julian Hedgecoe. 1997. *Stories in Stone. The Medieval Roof Carvings of Norwich Cathedral*. London: Herbert.

Sandys, Edwina. 1986. *Women of the Bible: Sculptures*. Syracuse, N.Y.: Everson Museum of Art.

Schmidt, Ph. 1977. *Die Illustration der Lutherbibel, 1522–1700*. Basel: Friedrich Reinhardt.

Schnorr von Carolsfeld, Julius. 1860. *Die Bibel in Bildern*. Leipzig: Georg Wigands. Eng. edn: *The Bible in Pictures*, London: Blackie & Sons, 1869.

Schramm, Albert. 1923. *Luther und die Bibel*, I: *Die Illustration der Lutherbibel*. Leipzig: Karl W. Hiersemann.

Sears, Robert, ed. 1844. *Bible Biography*. New York: Sears & Walker.

Sparrow, Walter Shaw. 1906. *The Old Testament in Art: Joshua to Job*. London: Hodder & Stoughton.

Stackhouse, Thomas. 1857. *A History of the Holy Bible*, new edn. Glasgow: Blackie & Son.

Stepanek, Stephanie L., ed. 1981. *Woodcuts [of Lucas Van Leyden]: The Illustrated Bartsch*, 12. New York: Abaris Books.

Stowe, Harriet Beecher. 1873. *Women in Sacred History*. New York: J. B. Ford.

Strachan, James. 1957. *Early Bible Illustrations*. Cambridge: Cambridge University Press.

—— 1959. *Pictures from a Medieval Bible*. London: Darwen Finlayson.

Strauss, Walter L., ed. 1980. *Netherlandisch Artists: Hendrik Goltzius. The Illustrated Bartsch*, 3. New York: Abaris Books.

—— and Carol Schuler, eds. 1982/1985. *German Book Illustrations before 1500, Part IV: Anonymous Artists 1481–82/Part VIII: Anonymous Artists 1489–1491. The Illustrated Bartsch*, 83/87.

Szyk, Arthur. www.szyk.org.

Taylor, Isaac, Jr. 1820. *Boydell's Illustrations of Holy Writ*. London: Hurst, Robinson.

Taylor, Kenneth N. 1989. *My First Bible: In Pictures*. Wheaton, Ill.: Tyndale House.

Temple, A. G. 1898. *Sacred Art*. London: Cassell.

Tissot, J. James. 1904. *The Old Testament: Three Hundred and Ninety-Six Compositions Illustrating the Old Testament (Part II)*. Paris, London, and New York: Mike Brunoff.

Wilson, Adrian, and Joyce Lancaster Wilson. 1984. *A Medieval Mirror: Speculum humanae salvationis. 1324–1500*. Berkeley: University of California Press.

Worringer, Wilhelm. 1921. *Die Altdeutsche Buchillustration*. Munich: R. Piper & Co.

—— 1923. *Die Kölner Bible*. Munich: R. Piper & Co.

Illustrations

Glossary

Biblical Texts and Versions

The **Masoretic Text** (MT) of the Hebrew Bible was produced by Jewish grammarians in the sixth to tenth centuries CE, introducing vowel points, accents, and detailed marginal instructions for later copyists. It became the standard Hebrew text.

The **Septuagint** (LXX) is the ancient Greek version of the Hebrew scriptures, used by New Testament writers and Church Fathers to the late fourth century CE. A tradition says it was ordered by Egyptian ruler Ptolemy Philadelphus (285–246 BCE) for his library at Alexandria and was the single text produced by 72 translators working separately. The evidence shows, rather, different translators using different methods.

Targums were Aramaic interpretative translations of the Bible used in synagogue worship when Hebrew was no longer the spoken language. The Targums of Onkelos (on the Pentateuch) and Jonathan (on the Prophets) emerged in Babylonia in the third century CE.

The **Vulgate** (Vg.), Jerome's fourth-century Latin Bible translation, was widely used in the West and pronounced the only authentic Latin text of Scripture by the Catholic Church's Council of Trent in the mid-sixteenth century.

The **Geneva Bible** (GB) ("Breeches Bible," from 1560, many editions) was a Bible translation of the English Reformation with marginal notes in Calvinist vein. The Bible
of the Puritans and the New England settlers.

The **King James Version** (KJV) or Authorised Version of 1611, ordered by James I to
counter the Geneva Bible, which it eventually supplanted. Based on Hebrew and
Greek manuscripts, it was influenced by the earlier Wycliffe version and "Bishops
Bible."

Douai–Rheims (or Rheims–Douai) version, the standard Roman Catholic translation
of the Bible into English until the mid-twentieth century. The Old Testament
appeared in 1610. Later editions followed Challoner's 1749–50 revision.

Rabbinic Texts

Midrash was a mode of biblical interpretation in the rabbinic academies of Palestine
and Babylonia. Midrashic writings show the results of these endeavors (from second
to eighth centuries CE) to explain gaps and apparent contradictions, harmonize, and
apply the teaching of the Torah to daily life, justifying the distinctive rabbinic world
view.

The **Mishnah**, attributed to Rabbi Judah ha-Nasi (early third century CE), is a written
collection of previously oral *halachic* (legal) material presented in six divisions: Seeds
(agriculture), Festivals, Women (marriage laws), Impurities (civil and criminal laws),
Holy Things (ritual laws), and Purifications. It was later supplemented by largely
haggadic (narrative) traditions to produce the **Tosefta**. These texts form the basis of
the **Palestinian Talmud** or *Yerushalmi* (fifth century) and **Babylonian Talmud** or
Babli (sixth century). These extensive compilations of traditional rabbinic commentary have become core texts for Jewish legal and moral understanding.

Interpretation

Some methods of interpretation may be unfamiliar. **Christian typology**, for example,
has had a long life but become lost to many "mainstream" Protestants. It works by
treating the Old Testament text as coded to yield a Christian meaning, so that
Samson's life, for example, is understood to prefigure Christ's saving deeds, and Jael's
killing of Sisera to signify the saving role of Mary. It may sometimes seem arbitrary,
but however imaginatively conceived, it will have some anchor in the text – which
may require some pointing out. For details, the reader may conveniently turn to the
section on the typology of Samson or consult the pictorial representation of Ehud
and Gideon as types of Christ in the relevant chapters. Similarly, **allegory** seeks figurative meanings of spiritual or moral import. Samson's foxes point to false teachers or heretics whose inflammatory words will consume them when confronted by
the teacher of truth. Or Samson's captivity is a guide to the soul ruled and blinded
by desires.

Early Jewish commentary may also puzzle some. A few principles may help. Scripture is usually treated as a self-contained, coherent system of meaning, so that one biblical text may be elucidated by another, not at random (as it might appear to many modern readers) but through defined links such as shared words, names, or contexts (and a host more). Further, both literal and extended meanings can be derived from grammar and word choice: when debating where Samson went wrong, it could be argued that his deterioration truly set in when he "went down" – literally and metaphorically – to Gaza to a harlot (*Midrash Numbers Rabbah*, 9:24). Debate itself is crucial to interpretation, as is knowledge of the tradition to which it belongs; many possibilities need to be heard. And just as Christian exposition seeks by means of the text to make moral and religious sense of contemporary life, so too does Jewish intepretation.

Protestant Events and Movements

The Protestant **Reformation**, a sixteenth-century movement to reform the Catholic Church, advocated acceptance of the Bible as the sole source of revealed truth, the doctrine of justification by faith alone, and the universal priesthood of all believers. On these bases proposals were advanced for societal and political reform.

Anabaptism refers to a variety of sixteenth-century groups which sought to go beyond the partial reformations of the Lutheran and Calvinist churches. Fundamental was believers' (not children's) baptism and the establishment of Christian communities based on the New Testament. They advocated everything from violent social and political reform (Thomas Müntzer, c.1489–1525) to pacifism and common ownership of property.

The **Puritans** were English Protestants who considered the sixteenth-century Reformation in England incomplete and demanded stricter adherence to Scripture in doctrine and practice, on the model of Calvin's Geneva, and civic freedom. Opposed by the crown, they were briefly successful due to the Civil War. The term encompasses a wide range of parties, including Presbyterians and Independents, often at odds with each other politically.

The **English Civil War** (1642–60) was a struggle over religious and political differences between supporters of Charles I (1600–49) and Parliament. It led to the temporary removal of the Church of England as the state church, the king's execution in 1649, and the triumph of Parliament, the Puritans, and Presbyterianism, lasting until 1660, when Charles II (1630–85) was restored to the throne.

Nonconformists were those in seventeenth-century England refusing to accede to the rules of a state-established church. The term became used of all **Dissenters** (opposed to established churches in principle): for example, English Presbyterians, Congregationalists, Baptists, Quakers, Methodists. In Scotland, Free Church Presbyterians likewise broke with the established (Presbyterian) Church of Scotland.

The first **Great Awakening** was an American religious revival which reached a high point in early 1740s New England. Closely associated with the preaching of Jonathan

Edwards and George Whitefield, it emphasized visible signs of conversion and possession of inward grace.

Deism refers to a system of natural (as opposed to supernatural) religion developed in England, notably with John Toland's *Christianity not Mysterious* (1696). Later forms advocated belief in a Creator God whose further interventions in creation were denied as contrary to God's omnipotence and unchangeability. Politically, socially, and religiously, it was viewed as hostile to the traditional order of monarchy, stratified society, and Catholicism. Such views were shared by Voltaire in France and Thomas Jefferson and Benjamin Franklin in the United States.

Abbey, Edwin Austin (1851–1911), American illustrator, painted murals for the new Boston Public Library.

Abelard, Peter (1079–1142/3), controversial French philosopher and theologian, remembered for his abortive love affair with his student, Héloise.

Aberdeen and Temair, **Ishbel Majoribanks**, marchioness of (1857–1939), established the Victorian Order of Nurses.

Aberdeen and Temair, **John Gordon**, marquess of (1847–1934), Governor General of Canada.

Adams, Rev. Henry Cadwallader (1817–99), wrote popular stories for boys in England.

Agrippa, Henricus Cornelius (c.1486–1535), German occult philosopher.

PLATE 10.1   Portraits: (a) Joseph Hall, 1574–1656; (b) John Milton, 1608–74; (c) Laurence Sterne, 1713–68; (d) Voltaire, 1694–1778; (e) Mrs Trimmer, née Sarah Kirby, 1741–1810; (f) Jonathan Edwards, 1703–58; (g) Grace Aguilar, 1816–47 (© Michael Dugdale, Aguilar Collection, 2004); (h) John Kitto, 1804–54; (i) Esther Hewlett, née Beuzeville, 1786–1851; (j) Harriet Beecher Stowe, 1811–96; (k) Gustave Doré, 1832–83; (l) Elizabeth Cady Stanton, 1815–1902.

Aguilar, Grace (1816–47), born in England of Sephardic parents, composed midrashic poetry, wrote on Jewish history, and urged religious reform (better received in the USA than England). She earned posthumous popularity for her domestic fiction and historical romances.

Alexander, Archibald (fl. 1928), British devotional writer.

Alexander, Cecil Francis (1818–95), born Fanny Humphrey, wrote in Ireland the verse for such still popular hymns as "All things bright and beautiful" and "Once in royal David's city."

Alighieri, Dante (1265–1321), Italian poet and political writer.

Alter, Robert, comparative literature and Hebrew Bible scholar.

Ambrose (c.339–97), bishop of Milan, fought Arianism and defended church independence against the Western Roman Emperors.

Amit, Yairah, biblical studies professor in Tel Aviv.

Anthony of Padua (1195–1231), Franciscan "Hammer of the Heretics."

Aquinas, Thomas (c.1225–74), philosopher and theologian in Paris, best known for his *Summa Theologica*.

Ardizzone, Edward (1900–79), World War II artist, gained repute as book illustrator and lithographer.

Arminius, Jacobus (1560–1609), anti-Calvinist professor at Leyden.

Armitage, E. (fl. 1890s), Royal Academy painter.

Armytage, E. (fl. 1840s), English artist.

Arndt, Johann (1555–1621), Lutheran mystic.

Athanasius (c.296–373), anti-Arianist Bishop of Alexandria.

Augustine, Aurelius (354–430), bishop of Hippo, prolific writer, including *Confessions* and *City of God*.

Bal, Mieke, literary theorist, art critic, Hebrew Bible scholar.

Balfour, Clara Lucas (1808–78), prominent Anglican supporter of the 1850s temperance movement in England.

Bankes, Rev. Thomas (fl. 1790), Anglican vicar whose *Universal Geography* made available the images and reports of Captain Cook's Pacific voyages.

Basil of Caesarea (c.330–79) helped organize Eastern monasticism.

Bawden, Edward (1903–89), printmaker, graphic designer, painter, noted for large-scale linocuts.

Baxter, Richard (1615–91), English Nonconformist writer on piety.

Bayle, Pierre (1647–1706), French Deist, famous for his historical *Dictionary* (1695–7).

Baynes, Robert H. (1831–95), Anglican priest, poet, hymn writer, editor.

Bellarmine, Robert (1542–1621), Jesuit Counter-Reformationist and spiritual writer.

Blomfield, Rev. Ezekiel (fl. 1800), produced maps as well as his Family Bible.

Bohn, Babette, art historian of Italian Baroque, women artists.

Boling, Robert C. (d. 1995), American seminary professor, specialist in Jordanian archaeology.

Bompas, W. C. (1834–1906), Anglican missionary in Northwest Canada and first bishop of Yukon diocese.

Bone, Florence (1892–1986), English poet, author of children's books.

Bonino, José Miguez, Protestant Latin American liberation theologian.

Bonnat, Léon (1833–1922), French Academic painter of religious themes and society portraits.

Boston, Thomas (1677–1732), influenced English and Scottish Presbyterians.

Bratby, John (1928–92), English realist artist of the "Kitchen Sink School," called his Bible illustrations "reserved," given the text's "rape, violence, sadism, and cruelty."

Brooke, Stopford A. (1832–1916), poet and critic, sometime chaplain to Queen Victoria.

Brown, John (1722–87), Scottish Free Church professor, preacher, writer, popular long after his death.

Browne, Sir Thomas (1605–82), physician and moralist.

Buber, Martin (1878–1965), Jewish religious thinker, influenced many with *I and Thou* (1923).

Buchanan, George (1506–82), Scottish Reformer, tutored Mary Queen of Scots and James VI.

Buel, James William (1849–1920), prolific writer, especially on the American West.

Bullinger, Henry (1504–75), Protestant Reformer, Zwingli's successor at Zurich.

Bunyan, John (1628–88), fought for Parliament, remembered for his allegorical *Pilgrim's Progress* (1678).

Burney, Rev. Charles Fox (1868–1925), Old Testament and Semitics scholar at Oxford.

Byron, George Gordon, Lord (1788–1824), Romantic poet and adventurer.

Calmet, Dom Augustin (1672–1757), Benedictine, praised by Protestants and Catholics for his compendious "literal commentary."

Calvin, John (1509–64), French Reformer, wrote major works of theology and biblical commentary, and led a theocratic regime in Geneva.

Camp, Claudia, American feminist biblical scholar.

Carlstadt, Andreas Bodenstein von (c.1480–1541), radical Protestant Reformer.

Carlyle, Thomas (1795–1881), celebrated English essayist and historian.

Case, Stephen (1746–94), militia captain in New York State.

Cassian, John (c.360–c.435), wrote a rule-book of Eastern monastic life.

Chappell, Rev. Clovis C. (1882–1972), Methodist, Southerner, immensely popular preacher and writer.

HeChasid, Yehudah (Judah ben Samuel) (c.1150–1217), rabbi in Regensburg.

Chaucer, Geoffrey (1343/4–1400), translator and narrative poet.

Chayefsky, Sydney "Paddy" (1923–81), New Yorker, acclaimed television scriptwriter, playwright, and novelist.

Chemnitz, Martin (1522–86), pastor, theologian, consolidated Lutheran practice.

Cheyne, Rev. T. K. (1841–1915), Oxford scholar, author, editor.

Christopherson, John (d. 1558), English Catholic scholar, imprisoned by Elizabeth.

Chrysostom, John (c.347–407), bishop of Constantinople, famed orator.

Clarke, Adam (1762–1832), born in Ireland, became a Wesleyan, wrote an 8-volume commentary widely used in Britain and America.

Cobbin, Rev. Ingram (1777–1851), wrote for young people and against Catholics.

Cole, James (fl. 1750), English engraver, publisher.

Cooke, Rev. G. A. (1865–1939), Anglican, professor of oriental languages at Oxford.

Couder, Louis-Charles-Auguste (1790–1873), French Romantic painter, known to Americans for his *Siege of Yorkstown* (1781).

Cowper, William (1731–1800), English poet, hymnist (with John Newton), letter writer.

Crenshaw, James L., American Hebrew Bible scholar.

Cromwell, Oliver (1599–1658), Puritan army commander for Parliament against the Royalists, became Lord Protector, and suppressed dissent in Scotland and Ireland.

Cyril (c.315–87), bishop of Jerusalem, wrote of early Church practice and doctrine.

Dabney, Robert L. (1820–98), American seminary theology professor and ethicist.

Davidson, Rev. John Thain (1833–1904), English Presbyterian.

Debat-Ponsan, Edouard (1847–1913), French, painted historical events.

DeMille, Cecil B. (1881–1959), American, directed lavish "sword and sandal" epics.

Denis the Carthusian (1402–71), theologian, mystic, biblical scholar, editor.

Dods, Rev. Marcus (1834–1909), Scottish Free Church commentator.

Doré, Gustave (1832–83), versatile French artist, illustrated over 200 books with numerous plates, often reproduced.

Dowriche, Anne (c.1550–1638), née Edgcumbe, gentlewoman, broke with (gender) convention to write a long dramatic poem on a political topic.

Duncan, Sara Jeannette [Mrs Everard Cotes] (1861–1922), wrote novellas of India.

Edwards, Jonathan (1703–58), American Calvinist theologian, evangelical preacher, supported the 1740s Great Awakening, and wrote on human depravity.

Egermeier, Elsie (b. 1890) wrote children's Bible stories, still sold.

Eissfeldt, Otto (1887–1973), German professor, known for his Old Testament *Introduction*.

Ephrem the Syrian (c.306–73), wrote biblical commentary, defended orthodoxy.

Erasmus, Desiderius (1466–1536), renowned humanist and textual scholar.

Euripides (c.480–406 BCE), prolific Greek playwright of tragi-comedy and the anti-hero, was tried in Athens for impiety.

Evans, Robert Wilson (1789–1866), Cambridge scholar and (edifying) novelist.

Exum, J. Cheryl, American feminist biblical scholar and cultural critic.

ibn Ezra, Abraham ben Meir (c.1092–1167), grammarian, commentator, philosopher, wrote many ethical treatises and biblical commentaries of lasting importance.

Farrar, Frederic William (1831–1903), evangelical dean of Canterbury.

Fewell, Danna Nolan, Hebrew Bible professor, feminist literary critic.

Finney, Charles G. (1792–1875), revivalist preacher, Oberlin College president.

Fletcher, Rev. Alexander (1787–1860), Presbyterian, popular in London for children's sermons. His *Family Devotions* sold over 70,000 copies.

Fletcher, John (1729–85), French Swiss, vicar in Shropshire, friend of the Wesleys.

Fontaine, Carol, American seminary professor, feminist ancient historian.

Fontaine, Nicolas ["Sieur de Royaumont"] (1625–1709), teacher, wrote in the Bastille a biblical history for children, popular in English for over a century and in French (for Catholics) much longer.

Fuchs, Esther, American feminist biblical scholar.

Gaiman, Neil, British writer, acclaimed for the horror-weird comic series, *Sandman* (1988–96), also wrote for children *The Day I Swapped My Dad For Two Goldfish* (1998).

Galle, Philips (1537–1612), bookseller, publisher, and among the greatest engravers of the Antwerp graphics school.

Gandy, Herbert (fl. 1920), painter.

Gardner, Rev. James (fl. 1850s), wrote on beliefs and practices of the world's religions.

Garstang, John (1876–1956), University of Liverpool, founding director of the British School of Archaeology in Jerusalem.

Gaspey, Thomas (fl. 1840–60) taught English in Heidelberg, wrote a long-lived textbook for German students, and translated Sturm's popular devotional writing for English readers.

Geikie, John Cunningham (1824–1906), Anglical evangelical writer on Scripture "in the light of modern discovery and knowledge."

Geoffrey of Monmouth (c.1100–55) wrote the first history of the Britons prior to the Saxons.

Gibbon, Rev. John (1629–1718), English preacher.

Gilead, Zerubavel (1912–88), Israeli poet, came as a child to Palestine from Bessarabia (Moldova). He wrote the Palmach (assault force) anthem.

Gilfillan, Rev. George (1813–78), Scottish Free Church Presbyterian, wrote much on the Bible, also on workers' rights.

Goeree, Jan (1670–1731), Dutch artist and book illustrator.

Goltzius, Hendrick (1558–1617), Dutch printmaker, naturalist painter.

Gomersall, Robert (1602–c.1646), English cleric and poet, who also wrote *The tragedie of Lodovick Sforza, duke of Millan* (1628).

Gottlieb, Freema, writes on Jewish folk art and midrash.

Grahame, James (1765–1811), Scottish poet, satirized in Byron's *English Bards and Scotch Reviewers* (1808) and, worse, hailed by McGonagall.

Greenstein, Edward, professor at Jewish Theological Seminary, New York.

Gressman, Hugo (1877–1927), Old Testament professor at Berlin.

Guay, Julien Gabriel (b. 1848), French painter, trained in the studio of Gérôme.

Grotius, Hugo (1583–1645), Dutch legal scholar, philosopher, poet.

Gunkel, Hermann (1862–1932), German professor, developed the study of biblical literary forms ("form criticism").

Gunn, David M., antipodean, literary and cultural critic of the Hebrew Bible.

Gurnall, Rev. William (1617–79), Puritan, remained an Anglican, earning opprobrium. His *Complete Armour* long outlived his critics.

Hackett, Jo Ann, American feminist biblical historian.

Hales, William (1747–1831), professor of Oriental Languages at Trinity College, Dublin.

Hall, Joseph (1574–1656), moderate Calvinist, was chaplain to James I and tutored Prince Henry, became bishop of Norwich, an object of Parliament's attacks on the bishops (imprisoned in the Tower), ejected from his cathedral, and deprived of his income. A fine pulpit orator, in earlier years his satiric verse was among the first in English (*Vergidemiarum*, 1597–8) and he introduced the satiric "character" into English prose – earning Milton's scorn later.

Hamilton, Newburgh (1715–43), of Old Bond Street, "who assisted me in adjusting words for some of my Compositions" (Handel's will).

Hamlin, E. John, taught for many years in Singapore and Thailand.

Handel, George Frideric (1685–1759), originated English oratorio, best remembered for his *Messiah* (1741).

Hastings, Rev. James (1852–1922), Presbyterian, founded *The Expository Times* and edited major dictionaries of Bible and religion.

Hayes, Marvin, artist in egg tempera painting and copperplate etching, digital image archiving.

Heavysege, Charles (1816–69), a woodcarver born in Yorkshire, wrote poetry in Canada (*Jephtha's Daughter* and *Saul*).

Henner, Jean-Jacques (1829–1905), French Academic painter.

Henry, Matthew (1662–1714), born in Wales, studied law but became a Nonconformist minister in Chester. His *Exposition*, the work of a "sound and ripe scholar" (1st American edn, 1828), remains unrivaled in popularity.

Hewlett (later Copely), **Esther** (1786–1851), née Beuzeville, of Huguenot descent, a Baptist, wrote in England for children, on domestic economy for working-class readers (*Cottage Comforts* saw many editions), and *A History of Slavery and its Abolition* (1836) which also deplored the British apprenticeship system.

Hoet, Gerard (1648–1733), Dutch painter, one of the first to incorporate the romantic ruins and antique statuary he had seen in Italy.

Holbein, Hans, Jr. (1497–1543) book illustrator, painter to the court of Henry VIII.

Holland, Richard (fl. 1450), Scottish poet, cleric, diplomat.

Hollings, Julie, contemporary British comic creator.

de Hondt, Pieter (fl. 1720s), bookseller and publisher, The Hague.

de Hooghe, Romeijn (c.1645–1708), Dutch engraver, combined allegorical elements with real personalities in a continuous story.

Horder, W. Garrett (1843–1922), edited volumes of hymns and religious poetry.

Horton, Rev. Robert F. (1855–1934), English author.

Howard, Rev. [Henry Edward] **John** (1795–1868), son of the earl of Carlisle. His *Scripture History* did well in the USA.

Hoyland, John (1750–1831), of Sheffield, a Quaker, noted for his call for better treatment of Gypsies in England (1816).

Hubmaier, Balthasar (c.1425–1528), German Anabaptist.

Hughes, Edward, F.R.G.S. (fl. 1850), headmaster of the Royal Naval School, Greenwich.

Hurlburt, Rev. Jesse Lyman (1843–1930), popular American religious writer.

Inglis, John (d. 1914), Scottish Presbyterian missionary.

Isidore of Seville (c.560–636), bishop, a prolific writer on secular and religious subjects.

Jabotinsky, Vladimir (1880–1940), Zionist leader, writer, orator, journalist, and soldier.

James, Fleming (1877–1959), Old Testament professor at Yale.

Jenks, William (1778–1866), missionary to seamen, a founder of the American Oriental Society.

Jerome (c.342–420), papal secretary, translated the Bible into Latin (Vulgate).

Jode, Gerard de (1509–91), Dutch publisher, engraver, cartographer, famous for his atlas, *Speculum Orbis Terrarum* (1578).

John of the Cross (1542–91), influential Carmelite mystic.

Jones, David (1736–1820), Baptist minister in New Jersey, (failed) missionary to the Shawnee, army chaplain.

Joris, David (1501/2–56), Dutch Anabaptist mystic.

Josephus, Flavius (c.37–c.100), Jewish general and Roman Imperial pensioner, wrote on the Jewish War with Rome and a history of the Jews, enormously influential. Whiston's English translation (1737) supplanted others, being constantly reprinted.

Kennicott, Benjamin (1718–83), Hebraist, noted for his edition of the Hebrew Bible.

Kimchi, David (c.1160–c.1235), Jewish lexicographer and grammarian, set the standard for such works in the Middle Ages.

Kimchi, Joseph (c.1105–c.70), David's father, grammarian and literal interpreter, translated Arabic scientific works.

Kirby, William (1817–1906), Canadian novelist and poet.

Kittel, Rudolf (1853–1929), German professor, historian, and text critic, famous for his edition of the Hebrew Bible.

Kitto, John (1804–54), with scant formal education, overcame poverty and deafness to become one of the best-known commentators, in Britain and North America, on biblical history and customs (drawing on extensive travels).

Klaasse, Piet (1918–2001), Dutch artist, illustrator.

Klein, Lillian R., American scholar of biblical narrative.

Knox, John (c.1513–72), architect of the Scottish Reformation.

Koberger, Anton (c.1445–1513), established Nuremberg's first printery (1470), pioneered illustrated book production.

Kook, Abraham Isaac (1865–1935), Zionist philosopher, writer.

Krook, Dorothea (1920–89), taught English literature at Cambridge and at Hebrew University in Jerusalem.

Küsel, Melchior (1626–83), illustrator, Merian's son-in-law.

Landelle, Charles (1812–1908), French painter, traveled in North Africa and Egypt. His biblical portraits were often reproduced.

Langdon, Rev. Samuel (1723–97), New Hampshire Congregationalist, president of Harvard.

à Lapide, Cornelius (1567–1637), Flemish Jesuit, wrote commentaries on most of the Catholic canon.

Lasine, Stuart, American Hebrew Bible scholar.

Laurens, Jean-Paul (1838–1921), French academic artist, noted for historical paintings, director of the Fine Arts school in Toulouse.

Lemaire, Ferdinand (fl. 1870s), Creole poet, librettist for Saint-Saëns.

Le Moyne, Pierre (1602–71), French Jesuit, poet.

Leyden, Lucas van (1494–1533), Dutch painter, master copperplate engraver, rival of Dürer.

Lias, J. J. (1834–1923), conservative English biblical scholar, theologian.

Livy (64/59 BCE–17 CE), Roman historian.

Lufft, Hans (1495–1584), Wittenberg, printed the first complete German Bible in Luther's translation, 1534.

Lumley, Lady Jane (c.1537–77), used Erasmus's edition to translate Euripides' *Iphigeneia in Aulis*, the first English version of a Greek drama.

Luther, Martin (1483–1546), German Reformation founder, commented extensively on the Bible.

Luyken, Caspar (1672–1708), Dutch engraver, son of engraver and poet-mystic Jan Luyken, is famous for his collection of costume plates (1694).

Lydgate, John (c.1370–c.1450), English poet, religious writer.

Lye, Rev. Thomas (1621–84), expelled from the Anglican Church, became a Presbyterian, known for his instruction of children.

Macaulay, Lord [Thomas Babington] (1800–59), politician, administrator, historian, essayist, poet.

Mackenzie, Sir George (1636–91), wrote one of Scotland's first historical romances.

Madox Brown, Ford (1821–93), born in Calais, linked with the German Romantic Nazarene movement and later, in England, the pre-Raphaelite Brotherhood.

Mantegna, Andrea (1431–1506), painter and engraver in Padua and Mantua.

Manton, Rev. Thomas (1620–77), English Nonconformist preacher of repute.

Marcus, David, Hebrew Bible scholar.

Marvell, Andrew (1621–78), English poet, known for *To His Coy Mistress* and political satires.

Masjiahm, Aharon ben (fl. 1692), wrote in Persia a verse version of Judges.

Matheson, Rev. George (1842–1906), Scottish Presbyterian theologian, preacher.

Maurice, Rev. F. D. (1805–72), Anglican advocate of Christian socialism, organized the Working Men's College.

Maurus, Rabanus (776–856), bishop of Mainz.

McCann, J. Clinton, American seminary professor of biblical interpretation.

McFadyen, John Edgar (1870–1933), biblical scholar in Toronto, advocated German critical methods.

McKenzie, John L. (1910–91), American Jesuit biblical scholar.

McKillop, Archibald (1824–1905), Canadian poet.

Mead, Rev. Darius (1807–85), Congregationalist, magazine editor.

Merian, Matthäus (1593–1650), master copperplate engraver, famous for Bible plates and scenes of European people and towns.

Methodius of Olympus (d. c.311), bishop of Lycia, wrote on free will against the Gnostics.

Meyer, Rev. Frederick Brotherton (1847–1929), English Baptist preacher, evangelist in South Africa, the Far East, and North America, wrote devotional works and Scripture biographies.

Miller, Olive Beaupré (1883–1968), Christian Scientist, author and publisher of graded children's stories.

Miller, Rev. Thomas E. (fl. 1900–30), Dunfermline, Scotland, wrote also "portraits" of biblical women (1910).

Milton, John (1608–74), English Nonconformist theologian, politician, poet, famous for *Paradise Lost*, supported Parliament against Charles I and opposed state establishment of the Church of England.

Moore, George Foote (1851–1931), professor at Andover and Harvard, noted for his judicious use of Jewish sources.

More, Sir Thomas (1478–1535), Lord Chancellor under Henry VIII, later executed.

Morell, Thomas (1703–84), librettist of Handel oratorios, a scholar of Greek drama.

Morgan, Thomas (d. 1743), Deist philosopher.

Mortier, Pieter (1661–1711), bookseller and publisher in Amsterdam, turned to engraving and coloring of French, English, and Portuguese maps.

Moser, Barry, illustrator and book designer. His *Pennyroyal Caxton Bible* joins the line of fully illustrated Bibles by Tissot, Doré, and Schnorr.

Motte, Henri (1846–1923), French painter.

Mozley, James Bowling (1813–78), Regius Professor of Divinity at Oxford.

Needler, Benjamin (1600s), English Puritan, scholar at Oxford.

Nel, Philip, South African Hebrew Bible scholar.

Nicholas of Lyra (c.1270–1349), studied the Bible's literal meaning from a vast knowledge of patristic, medieval Latin, and rabbinic texts.

Niditch, Susan, American scholar of Israelite religion and folklore.

Northcote, James (1746–1831), Royal Academy painter, pupil and biographer of Sir Joshua Reynolds.

Northrop, Henry Davenport (1836–1909), writer, editor, on literature and natural history.

Noth, Martin (1902–68), Heidelberg professor, known for *History of Israel* and Pentateuchal studies.

Oesterley, Carl (1805–91), German Romantic painter of the Nazarene circle in Rome, became artist to the court of Hanover.

Officer, Morris (1823–74), Lutheran missionary in Liberia.

O'Neil, Henry (1817–80), Pre-Raphaelite painter of portraiture, landscape, history, and emotional genre scenes.

Opie, John (1761–1807), Cornish saw-pit apprentice turned London society artist at age 21, Royal Academy painter of portraits and historical subjects.

Origen (c.185–c.254), Alexandrian biblical scholar, theologian, Platonic philosopher, and designated a heretic.

Ormerod, Rev. J. C. (fl. 1930–40), taught Bible at a Congregationalist seminary in Bradford, Yorkshire.

Orr, Rev. James (1844–1913), Scottish professor, opposed Darwinism and historical criticism of the Bible.

Ovid (43BCE–17/18CE), Latin poet.

Owen, Rev. John (1616–83), English Puritan.

Patrick, Symon (1626–1707), bishop of Ely, wrote a long-respected Bible commentary.

Pellegrin, Simon-Joseph (1663–1745), abbé, librettist for Pignolet's *Jephté*.

Perkins, William (1558–1602), major English Puritan theologian.

Phillips, Dirk (1504–68), Dutch Anabaptist evangelist.

Pignolet de Monteclair, Michel (1667–1737), dramatist, composed cantatas.

de Pisan, Christine (c.1364–c.1431), French writer, championed the cause of women.

Pink, Arthur W. (1886–1952), influential English Baptist writer in the Calvinist tradition.

Pledger, Rev. Elias (fl. 1660–80), Puritan businessman and divine.

Polzin, Robert, Hebrew Bible scholar in Canada.

Poole, Matthew (1624–79), English Nonconformist theologian, famous for a synopsis of earlier biblical scholars.

Poussin, Nicholas (1594–1665), prominent French artist, mediated classical antiquity.

Pseudo-Philo, name given to the author of a first-century CE history from Adam to Saul's death.

Quarles, Francis (1592–1644), wrote religious poetry beloved of Puritans, but supported politically the Royalists. Had 18 children and was often poor.

Quentel, Heinrich (fl. 1470–80), published in Cologne the first printed Bible with woodcut scenes, influencing numerous subsequent Bibles.

Raleigh, Sir Walter (c.1552–1618), explorer, courtier, poet, threw down his cloak for Queen Elizabeth.

Ramban (Rabbi Moses ben Nahman) (1194–1270), wrote a famous commentary on the Torah and numerous other works on Jewish law.

Ransom, Reverdy C. (1861–1959), African Methodist Episcopal Church bishop.

Rashi (Rabbi Solomon ben Isaac) (1040–1105), brilliant Jewish scholar whose commentaries, which influenced Christian literal interpretation, are still highly valued.

Rembrandt (1606–69), famous Dutch artist.

Robinson, Thomas (1749–1813), Cambridge scholar, vicar in Leicester.

Rogers, Rev. Richard (1550–1618), English Puritan, composed his commentary on Judges from 103 sermons.

Rooke, Thomas (1842–1942), British painter, assistant to Burne-Jones at William Morris's design firm and copyist for Ruskin.

Rubens, Peter Paul (1577–1640), Flemish Baroque painter, influenced by Italian art.

Rupert of Deutz (c.1075–1129), Benedictine scholar.

Ruskin, John (1819–1900), British art critic and social reformer.

von Rute, Hans (d. 1558), Bern playwright.

Saint-Saëns, Camille (1835–1921), virtuoso French organist and composer.

Salomon, Bernard (1510–61), popular artist at the court of Henri II.

Salmasius, Claudius (1588–1653), French Protestant, classical scholar, wrote a defense of Charles I.

Sandys, Edwina, English artist in New York, sculptor of *Christa, Eve's Apple*, and many more.

Schneider, Tammi J., American Hebrew Bible scholar.

Schnorr von Carolsfeld, Julius (1794–1872), German artist of the Nazarene group in Rome, worked for the king of Bavaria, illustrated the complete Bible.

Scott, Rev. Thomas (1747–1821), Anglican, wrote a widely read *Commentary* first issued weekly, 1788–92.

Shakespeare, William (1564–1616), English poet and dramatist.

Sharpe, Dr (fl. 1755), biblical scholar.

Siciolante, Girolamo ["Il Sermoneta"] (c.1521–c.1580), Italian painter.

Simons, Menno (1496–1561), Dutch theologian who shaped Anabaptism.

Simpson, Rev. Bertram F. (1883–1971), became bishop of Southwark in England.

Slater, Rev. Samuel (d. 1704), Anglican, poet.

Smiles, Samuel (1812–1904), Scottish doctor, political reformer, newspaper editor, self-help advocate.

Smith, George Adam (1856–1942), Scottish Free Church professor, widely traveled.

Smith, Gertrude (fl. 1900), wrote *Delight: A Story of a Little Christian Scientist*.

Smith, William (1813–93), edited major dictionaries – of Bible, Christian antiquities, biography.

Smyth, Lindley, Jr. (fl. 1900), American, wrote children's books.

Soggin, J. Alberto, Italian, professor of the Waldensian School of Theology, Rome.

Solomon, Solomon J. (1860–1927), English painter versatile in styles and subjects.

Southwell, Rev. Henry (fl. 1770s), rector of Asterby in Lincolnshire.

Spinoza, Baruch de (1634–77), Dutch Jewish philosopher, a founder of modern biblical criticism.

Spurgeon, Charles (1834–92), English Baptist preacher, popular author.

Stackhouse, Rev. Thomas (1680–1752), biblical historian, vicar of Beenham in Berkshire.

Stanton, Elizabeth Cady (1815–1902), a driving force, with Susan B. Anthony, in the women's rights movement in the USA.

Steele, Rev. Richard (1629–92), English Nonconformist.

Steig, Jeanne, writes amusing verse and prose.

Steinberg, Naomi, American scholar of social life in ancient Israel.

Sterne, Laurence (1713–68), Irish-born Anglican clergyman, preacher, pioneer novelist.

Stowe, Harriet Beecher (1811–96), raised in a Congregationalist minister's family, married a professor of biblical literature, became famous for *Uncle Tom's Cabin* and wrote numerous other works.

Strickland (late Moodie), **Susanna** (1803–85), wrote in England, then Canada, verse, children's books, accounts of colonial life.

Swetman, Joseph (fl. 1615), notorious pamphleteer.

Szyk, Arthur (1894–1951), illustrator, caricaturist, and political cartoonist.

Tallis, John (fl. 1840–60), successful London publisher of illustrated books, maps, and atlases.

Talmage, Rev. T. DeWitt (1832–92), eloquent preacher, edited *Christian Herald*.

Taylor, Isaac, Jr (1787–1865), a trained engraver, became a writer on religion, politics, and biography, with books on enthusiasm, fanaticism, and John Wesley.

Taylor, Jeremy (1613–67), Anglican bishop, wrote two spiritual classics.

Tennyson, Alfred, Lord (1809–92), became Poet Laureate of England in 1850, hugely popular.

Thatcher, G. W. (1863–1950), biblical and Arabic scholar.

Thompson, Rev. William (1806–94), missionary in Sidon, author.

Tissot, J. James [Jacques-Joseph] (1836–1902), French society painter, lived a decade in London, became a recluse painting religious pictures, especially watercolors.

Trible, Phyllis, feminist Biblical scholar, seminary professor.

Trimmer, Mrs [née Sarah Kirby] (1714–1810), famous for *Fabulous Histories* (later *History of the Robins*) which taught children to treat animals kindly. Devoted to properly educating children, later in life she edited *The Guardian of Education*, a forum for discussion and information.

Turretin, Francis (1623–87), Calvinist scholar in Geneva.

van den Vondel, Joost (1587–1679), Dutch Baroque poet and tragic dramatist.

Vermigli, Peter Martyr (1499–1562), Italian Reformer, taught in England.

Visscher, Nicholas (fl. c.1650), Dutch publisher and cartographer.

Voltaire, Francois-Marie Arouet (1694–1778), famous French Deist philosopher, advocated political and religious toleration.

de Vos, Marten (1532–1603), Flemish painter.

Warfield, Benjamin (1851–1921), Princeton theologian, argued for the Bible's verbal inerrancy.

Warren, John Leicester (Lord de Tabley) (1835–95), literary scholar, botanist, poet.

Watson, Richard (1737–1816), Anglican bishop, opponent of Thomas Paine.

Watts, Isaac (1674–1748), English hymn writer (e.g. "O God, our help in ages past").

Webb, Barry, Australian, Hebrew Bible scholar.

Wells, Rev. John (1623–76), Puritan.

White, Ellen G. (1827–1915), Seventh Day Adventist prophet, read and translated writer.

Whyte, Alexander (1836–1921), outstanding Scottish preacher, supported the new biblical criticism.

Wilberforce, Samuel ("Soapy Sam") (1805–73), bishop of Oxford, high churchman.

Wilhoite, Mariel (fl. 1930–50), children's book illustrator.

Williams, Isaac (1802–65), taught in Oxford, wrote for the Oxford Movement.

Williams, Rev. T. Rhondda (c.1860–c.1940), Welsh Congregationalist minister in Brighton, England, Christian socialist and freethinker.

Willis, Nathaniel Parker (1806–67), American editor, journalist, poet.

Wood, J. G. (1827–89), wrote many books on natural history.

Wylie, Jennie (fl. 1900–10), British artist.

Yonge, Charlotte M. (1823–1901), prolific English novelist and children's storywriter.

Younger, K. Lawson, Hebrew Bible scholar and ancient historian.

Name Index

Note: page references for plates are shown in brackets following the plate number.

Subject Index

Note: page references for plates are shown in brackets following the plate number.

DATE DUE

2/4/14			
APR 2 4 2018			
10/25/18			